29.98

HN
90
.V5
C48
2004

Inequality

& Violence

in the United States

D0964907

Inequality & Violence
in the United States

Casualties of Capitalism

second edition

Barbara H. Chasin

Colo. Christian Univ. Library
8787 W. Alameda Ave.
Lakewood, CO 80226

Humanity Books

Published 2004 by Humanity Books, an imprint of Prometheus Books

Inequality and Violence in the United States: Casualties of Capitalism, 2nd ed. Copyright © 2004 by Barbara H. Chasin. All rights reserved. No part of this publication may be reproduced, stored in a retrieval system, or transmitted in any form or by any means, digital, electronic, mechanical, photocopying, recording, or otherwise, or conveyed via the Internet or a Web site without prior written permission of the publisher, except in the case of brief quotations embodied in critical articles and reviews.

Inquiries should be addressed to

Humanity Books

59 John Glenn Drive

Amherst, New York 14228–2119

VOICE: 716–691–0133, ext. 210

FAX: 716–691–0137

WWW.PROMETHEUSBOOKS.COM

14 13 12   5 4

Library of Congress Cataloging-in-Publication Data

Chasin, Barbara H.
    Inequality and violence in the United States : casualties of capitalism / Barbara Chasin.—2nd ed.
        p. cm.
    Includes bibliographical references and index.

    ISBN: 978-1-59102-160-5

    1. Violence—United States. 2. Equality—United States. 3. Capitalism—United States. 4. United States—Economic policy. 5. United States—Social policy. I. Title.

HN90.V5 C48 2004
306/.0973—dc22

                                                              2004004104

Printed in the United States of America on acid-free paper

CONTENTS

PREFACE TO THE
SECOND EDITION

I first started thinking about the nature of violence at the start of my teaching career in the late 1960s. The violence that was on people's minds then was the war in Vietnam and what came to be called "the war at home." The same military forces that were operating in Vietnam were being called to inner cities, college campuses, and Native American reservations. Many questions were raised as people tried to understand these seemingly disparate events.

Amidst heated debates, it became apparent that there were competing conceptions of why there was violence, who was violent, and how violence should be dealt with. There were even different ideas of what violence was. The most conservative point of view blamed violence, whether in Southeast Asia or the United States, on outside agitators of one kind or another who stirred up naive people.

Scholars with a more radical perspective reexamined the history of the United States to better understand what was happening in the 1960s. They discovered that much of the violence of our past was perpetuated by those who were economically and politically more powerful than their victims. This approach drew parallels between the conditions that were producing liberation movements in the Third World and those that fueled protest in the United States. This, in turn, led to an expanded conception of what violence was. Important for my own thinking was the insight that systems can be violent as well as individuals. Violence can be part of the everyday life of a society, with people suffering and sometimes dying because they do not have access to the resources needed for a healthy life.

I wanted to help students understand the events of the time, not just as an academic exercise, but so that they could make more rational choices about their lives. I first developed a course on the sociology of violence in 1970. Since then I have been trying to deepen my understanding of violence in the United States.

When I wrote the first edition of the book in the 1990s, attention was focused on criminal violence in the streets. Since September 11, 2001, the emphasis is on the violence caused by foreign terrorists. Yet our own social system, capitalism, continues to produce violence both at home and abroad that far outweighs what any enemy forces have done. One of the major themes of this book is the damage done to the American people by corporations and the U.S. government. These same institutions have a global reach, and the harm they do is global as well. Although this aspect of U.S. capitalism is beyond the scope of this book, it should be kept in mind.

This edition updates the data presented in the first. I have also added material on the media and firearms and refined my conception of the types of violence. A first step toward reducing violence is to understand what has produced it. I hope this book contributes to that understanding.

ACKNOWLEDGMENTS

I would like to acknowledge the support of Montclair State University in granting me a sabbatical in 1994–1995 to work on the first edition of this book and the librarians at Montclair's Sprague Library who did their best to get me needed materials. I would like to thank the people who gave me advice and encouragement on various parts of the manuscript for either or both editions: David Dodd, Steve Finlay Jr., Peter Freund, Susan Gjenvick, Harold Simon, Gerald Kloby, Jay Livingston, Susan Lowes, Cindy Ness, Maureen Outlaw, and Evelyn Shalom. I am very appreciative of the help of the staff at Humanity Books, in particular Ann O'Hear and Peggy Deemer. I would also like to thank the staff at Humanities Press, who originally published the first edition, especially Melanie Hawley, Sheri Kubasek, and Diane Burke. Most of all, I want to express my thanks to Dick Franke, a (mostly) tireless reader, advisor, computer expert, and all-round support system.

1 PATTERNS OF VIOLENCE
Old and New

W hen I was writing the first edition of this book in the mid-1990s, public officials were identifying violence as a threat to the quality of life in the United States. President Bill Clinton warned in 1993 that the United States faced "an epidemic of violence."[1] David Satcher, director of the Centers for Disease Control and Prevention, claimed, "Violence is the leading cause of lost life in this country today."[2] Researchers found high levels of fear of violence on people's minds.[3]

The violence they were talking about, however, was narrowly conceived. It was violent *crime* that was the focus of attention. More serious threats to the public's well-being were not making headlines. Fear of crime has not gone away, but it has receded and has been superseded by new threats. At the same time, the more serious threats in the recent past have continued into the present and are still not being adequately addressed.

Many of the things we fear fit a commonsense conception of violence. We worry about things that can hurt us or those we care about. But many threats are not readily apparent. We depend on people we trust—experts, authorities, political leaders, and the media—to tell us what they are. Even when a danger seems obvious, it may not be clear how to confront it. Here again, we look for leadership.

The expression 911 used to signify only the phone number for calling emergency services. It is now also recognized by almost everyone as the month and day in 2001 when terrorists hijacked four jumbo jets in the United States. One plane crashed in a Pennsylvania field. One smashed into

11

the fortress of the Pentagon. Each of the other two crashed into one of the towers of New York's World Trade Center, which burned and collapsed. Three thousand people were killed that day. Since 9/11, terrorism from abroad has seemed to be a looming threat, and many aspects of life in the United States have changed in response.

In March 2003 the severe acute respiratory syndrome (SARS) suddenly appeared, with alleged origins in China. Thousands died there, but as of May 2003 the disease had not killed anyone in the United States. The media gave a lot of attention to SARS. People and officials took measures to keep the disease at bay. Some restaurant goers gave up going to local Chinatowns. Vacationers changed travel plans, hospitals built special isolation rooms, and schools disinvited Chinese performers. The University of California at Berkeley banned a number of students from Asian countries from attending summer programs on its campus and prepared special quarantine rooms should any of those admitted become sick. Fear of terrorism and fear of SARS have combined to cause some people to telecommute and teleconference instead of leaving the seeming safety of their own homes and workplaces.[4]

John Graham directs the Harvard Center for Risk Analysis at the Harvard School of Public Health. Not surprisingly, he and other researchers have found that people are most likely to be concerned about hazards that receive lots of media attention, while not paying much attention to far more dangerous features of American society. In his words, "We live in a society that is both paranoid and neglectful about dangers at the same time."[5]

LESS PUBLICIZED THREATS

In order to not neglect dangers, we need to be aware of them. Increasing our awareness requires that we consider threats that do not make headlines, those which are not much discussed by authorities but which cause great suffering and death to people in the United States.

We talk about the weather, but most of us don't fear it. Yet given the right social conditions, the weather can be life threatening. In July 1995 residents of Chicago sweltered when temperatures hit 106 degrees. Sociologist Eric Klinenberg conveys something of the horrors of that hot summer: "Hundreds died alone behind locked doors and sealed windows that entombed them in suffocating private spaces where visitors came infrequently and the air was heavy and still."[6] At least 739 people died from heat-related causes. They were not a random sample of the Windy City's population. How can their deaths be explained? Interacting with the heat, economic status, political power, race, and gender account for these deaths. These combinations of the less publicized factors leading to violence, as defined below, will be the focus of this book.

Community features also contributed to the Chicago death toll. Poor minority neighborhoods have high rates of crime. A number of elderly people were afraid to leave their apartments or even to open their windows. With similar fears, social service providers timed their visits for mornings, thinking the criminals would sleep till early afternoon.[7] There were few stores or gathering spots in the neighborhoods for those willing to venture outside.

The most likely to die were low-income, elderly African American men. Men are more likely than women to be isolated from other people. Others were living in single-room-occupancy hotels. Many of these units had building code violations, poor ventilation, and were not air-conditioned. With malfunctioning elevators, the frail elderly were not able to leave their stifling apartments.

The federal government contributed to the problem. Since the Reagan administration, the federal government has cut back on its low-income energy-assistance supports at the same time that electricity rates have been going up. The elderly poor didn't have the money to pay for air-conditioning. Mayor Richard Daley's city administration had also cut back on services, including subsidies for low-cost housing, which might have allowed low-income tenants to pay for better quality shelter.

There were not enough medical services to provide the necessary care for those who fell sick from the heat, even when their condition was known. In addition, the communication systems necessary to coordinate what services there were experienced "a total breakdown."[8] Given these circumstances, it is apt that a reviewer of Klinenberg's work titled her review "Murder by Public Policy."[9]

Public policies can reduce or increase violence, death, and suffering. With proper measures, probably most of the 739 people who died in the Chicago heat wave could have been saved. "Death by public policy" is far more widespread in the United States than most people realize. The connections between people dying and the political decisions that made them vulnerable are not usually linked by either the media or by public officials.

The Chicago heat wave deaths in 1995 are part of a larger pattern of neglect of the causes of violence that continues in the United States. If babies are murdered, we are horrified and want the killer caught and punished. But each year about twelve thousand infants die because their families are poor.[10] The result in either case is the same: infants who do not survive. People die as a result of shootings connected with the illegal narcotics traffic. But approximately four hundred thousand people die each year from the effects of tobacco, a currently legal commodity.

When snipers shoot people at random, we are outraged. Yet eighteen thousand people die needlessly each year because they lack health insurance. This is six times the number killed in the 9/11 terrorist attacks. These eighteen thousand deaths recur each year and are largely preventable, but the problem is not treated as a national emergency.

The thousands of needless deaths mentioned above result from public policies. These policies reflect deeper processes in the day-to-day workings of American society that make some people more likely to become victims of violence than others. Understanding these processes requires using the knowledge and techniques of social science. In this chapter we shall offer some definitions and concepts that will help us to trace the connection among the factors leading to patterns of violence in this country.

DEFINING VIOLENCE

In this book we will use a definition of physical violence that focuses our attention on the social forces that make our lives less healthy, or more dangerous. Violence refers to acts, intentional or not, that result in physical harm to another person or persons.[11]

There are three major types of violence: interpersonal, organizational, and structural. *Interpersonal violence* is what most of us mean when we think of violence. Identifiable persons injure others and are usually aware that they have done so; in most cases their targets are intentional. In this type of violence usually one or a few individuals attack another. In some instances the perpetrator engages in the violence as part of membership in an informal group, such as a gang or friendship group.

Organizational violence is a result of an explicit decision made as part of individuals' roles in formal institutions such as bureaucracies. Obvious examples are the military and the police. A less apparent example is the corporate executive who decides to let an unsafe product be marketed.

As later chapters will show, decision makers in corporations and government agencies are responsible for organizational violence. In most instances of organizational violence, no particular person is the target of the violence.

Instead, anonymous members of groups, such as consumers of certain products or workers in certain occupational situations, become the victims.

The connection between one's role—expected behavior—and the violent outcome is one of the biggest differences between the organizational and interpersonal forms of violence. In interpersonal violence a person's particular role, for example, husband, usually does not mandate acting in a way that causes harm. In America you can discuss problems with your spouse or you can physically abuse her or, less often, him. Similarly, a parent's role does not require using physical force with a child, but a mother or father may decide to do so. Being a robber doesn't mean you also have to be a murderer. In organizational violence the role connection is the key. Military commanders and police chiefs are expected to order those below them to use violence under certain circumstances. A corporate executive is expected to maintain or increase company profits. Deciding to ignore safety considerations can become part of the job.

Structural violence is the least obvious type. It is an outcome of many years of decision making by those in positions of power. Structural violence occurs when people are harmed because they lack access to resources available to others. If identifiable groups are suffering physically from conditions that could be changed given the existing state of knowledge, while other groups are not suffering, then there is structural violence.

Both structural and organizational violence result from decisions of the most powerful in the society. Structural violence is a consequence of policies that have occurred or accumulated over a long period of time and may involve many decision-making bodies. Organizational violence occurs in a shorter time span and is more clearly an outcome of one or a very few bureaucracies.

Interpersonal violence occurs most often among people of the same economic group and often between members of the same community or household. Organizational violence results from direct or indirect decisions made at the elite level of society, while those suffering are from less privileged groups. Structural violence is an indirect outcome of decisions that have been made by elites as well. The mainstream media and politicians regularly focus attention on interpersonal violence, but they rarely analyze organizational or structural violence nor do they make the connections that would enable us to understand the forces that cause it.

Victims of structural violence, and often organizational violence, do not see and are generally unaware of those responsible for their injuries. Similarly, those responsible rarely see the suffering their actions have caused. No one deliberately killed the Chicago heat wave victims, but why did they not have air-conditioned apartments? Why did they not live in communities with less crime? Why were the elevators broken?

Table 1.1 summarizes the similarities and differences between the three types.

TABLE 1.1. SOME TYPICAL CHARACTERISTICS OF THE THREE TYPES OF VIOLENCE

characteristic	type of violence		
	interpersonal	organizational	structural
number of victims	usually few	many	many
victim(s) can identify perpetrator(s)	usually	rarely	no
perpetrator(s) can identify victim(s)	usually	rarely	very rarely
characteristics of perpetrator(s) and victim(s)	similar or identical social class	different classes	different classes
time between decision and violence	short—often less than one day	at least months	months to years
number of decision makers	one or a very few	a very few	cumulative effect of many decisions
example 1	killer shoots people in fast food restaurant	pharmaceutical company markets known unsafe product	Chicago heat wave victims in 1995
example 2	gang member attacks competitor in drug dispute	U.S. military invades Iraq, March 2003	18,000 die annually from lack of health insurance
main chapters where discussed in this book	10, 11, 12, 13, 15	6, 7, 8, 14	6, 7, 8, 14, 15

There are several reasons to broaden our conception of violence to include organizational and structural violence.

1. These account for more deaths and injuries each year than interpersonal violence.

2. We need to understand these types of violence in order to gain a fuller understanding of the dangers that face many people in our society.

3. We need to analyze these types in order to overcome stereotypes about who the violent people in our society are.

4. We need to understand the nature and causes of structural violence in order to learn what we have to do to create a more humane and less violent society.

THE UNIQUE PATTERNS OF U.S. VIOLENCE

A major theme of this book is that high levels of violence are caused by high levels of inequality within society. Both organizational and structural violence result primarily from patterns of inequality. Even some interpersonal violence derives from inequality, as we will see in later chapters. The United States has higher rates of all three forms of violence and is also more unequal than any other advanced capitalist country.

Income and Inequality

Inequality within a nation can be measured in several different ways. The most straightforward indicators are annual income or total wealth of individuals or households. One frequently used statistic is called the Gini Index. This is a number presented either as a decimal between 0 and 1 or more often as a single whole number between 1 and 100. The lower the number, the greater the equality. The higher the number, the more inequality there is. Table 1.2 presents the per capita gross national incomes (GNI) and the Gini Indexes for the United States and selected wealthy nations with similar economic systems.

The per capita GNI is the GNI divided by the total population. The GNI used to be called the GNP, or gross national product.[12] Table 1.2 shows that in 2001 the U.S. economy generated $34,870 of income for each individual. For a family of four, the economy produced an average income of $139,480. Many families did not receive that amount because the very rich absorbed much of the potential incomes of several thousand households each.

We see from table 1.2 that the U.S. per capita GNI is fourth highest in the world, behind Switzerland, Japan, and Norway. But when we look at the Gini Index of inequality, we find that the United States ranks fifteenth, at the very bottom of the list. This means that Switzerland, Japan, and Norway not only generate more income per person than does the United States, but it also means that average households and individuals get a greater share in the total income. In fact, even some of the countries below the United States in per capita GNI may have more income going to average households and individuals because of the lower levels of inequality as reflected in the Gini Indexes.[13] The U.S. Gini index is 64 percent greater than that of Switzerland, Japan, Denmark, and Sweden. It is 11

TABLE 1.2. ECONOMIC INEQUALITY IN SELECTED ADVANCED CAPITALIST NATIONS

Ranked by Per Capita Gross National Income (GNI)

per capita GNI rank 2001	nation*	per capita GNI 2001	Gini Index of income inequality 1990s	income equality rank 1990s†
1	Switzerland	36,970	25	1
2	Japan	35,590	25	1
3	Norway	35,530	26	5
4	United States	34,870	41	15
5	Denmark	31,090	25	1
6	Sweden	25,400	25	1
7	United Kingdom	24,230	37	14
8	Netherlands	24,040	33	10
9	Austria	23,940	36	12
9	Finland	23,940	26	5
11	Germany	23,700	30	8
12	Belgium	23,340	29	7
13	Ireland	23,060	36	12
14	France	22,290	33	10
15	Canada	21,340	32	9

Notes:

* Iceland, Luxembourg, and Hong Kong have been omitted from the table since their population sizes and social structures are very different from that of the other nations listed.

† Some inequality ranks appear to be missing because of ties. Gini Indexes are for the years 1993 to 1997 depending on the country.

Source: GNI per capita, the World Bank, *World Development Report, 2003: Sustainable Development in a Dynamic World—Transforming Institutions, Growth, and Quality of Life* (New York: Oxford University Press), table 1, p. 234; Gini Indexes, table 2, pp. 236–37. The Gini Index is briefly explained on p. 249 of the source.

percent greater than that of the United Kingdom (England, Scotland, and Wales), the second most unequal nation on table 1.2.[14] In chapter 3 we shall examine the details of the income inequality in the United States that is summarized by our unusually high Gini Index.

The Unique Pattern of U.S. Interpersonal Violence

America's unusually high degree of income inequality is matched by its unusually high rates of interpersonal violence. Table 1.3 compares the United States to these other countries on rates of interpersonal violence. The U.S. homicide rate is 3.1 times that of the next highest country, Finland. The U.S. rape rate is greater than all the other countries on the table for which data are available, except Canada. The U.S. imprisonment rate is more than five times that of the United Kingdom and is more than fifteen times that of Japan, the country on table 1.3 with the lowest rate.

Rape statistics are underreported in the United States and very likely in the other countries as well. It is unlikely that the size of the differences among countries would be substantially altered if all countries had equally complete reporting of rapes. It is possible that Canada's rate is so high partly because women feel freer to report rapes there, but we cannot be sure what accounts for this high figure.

It is important to note that crime itself is not so much the distinguishing feature of the United States. It is the violent forms of crime. Franklin E. Zimring and Gordon Hawkins provide systematic cross-national evidence to show that while other comparable countries' crime rates do not differ that much from our own, the United States is unique in its rates of violent crime.[15] A dramatic example from their study appears in the contrasting patterns between London and New York. Data for 1990 show that London had 67 percent more thefts and 57 percent more burglaries per 100,000 people than New York, but only 9 percent as many murders.[16]

TABLE 1.3 COMPARISONS OF INTERPERSONAL VIOLENCE IN ADVANCED CAPITALIST NATIONS RANKED BY PER CAPITA GNI: RATES PER 100,000

rank in per capita GNI	nation	homicide rate per 100,000, 1995–1999*	rape rate in 1994 per 100,000 women ages 15 and above	imprisonment rate per 100,000 in 1999
1	Switzerland	1.1	9	81
2	Japan	0.6	3	43
3	Norway	0.9	NA	56
4	United States	6.9	97	682
5	Denmark	1.1	22	66
6	Sweden	1.2	50	59
7	United Kingdom	0.8	NA	125†
8	The Netherlands	1.3	NA	84
9	Austria	0.8	16	85
10	Finland	2.2	18	46
11	Germany	0.9	NA	97
12	Belgium	1.6	21	80
13	Ireland	0.8	NA	72
14	France	0.7	27	91
15	Canada	1.4	267	123
U.S. rank of 15		15	9 of 10‡	15

Notes:

NA = Data not available.

*Homicide rate years are between 1995 and 1999 depending on the country.

†Imprisonment rate data are for England and Wales only.

‡U.S. rape rate is 10 of 11 because 4 countries do not have available data on the international tables.

Sources: Homicide rates, World Health Organization (WHO), *World Report on Violence and Health*, table A.8, pp. 308–12; Rape rates, United Nations Development Program (UNDP), *Human Development Report, 2000*, table 226, p. 247; Imprisonment rates, Barclay, Tavares, and Siddique, "International Comparisons of Criminal Justice Statistics, 1999," issue 619, May 2001, http://www.homeoffice.gov.uk/rds/pdfs/hosb601.pdf, p. 7.

The Unique Pattern of U.S. Structural Violence

For technical reasons, it appears impossible at this time to provide direct comparative data on organizational violence by country. In later chapters

TABLE 1.4. INDICATORS OF STRUCTURAL VIOLENCE IN ADVANCED CAPITALIST COUNTRIES, 1999–2001: COUNTRIES RANKED BY PER CAPITA DOMESTIC PRODUCT

				Air Pollution Emissions Per Capita			
rank	country	infant mortality per 1,000 in the year 2000	HIV/AIDS incidence as percent of adults 15–49 for 2001	road accident injuries per 100,000 in 2000	tons of carbon dioxide	kilograms of sulfur oxides	kilograms of nitrogen oxides
1	Switzerland	3	.50	331	6	5	18
2	Japan	4	<.10	734	9	7	11
3	Norway	4	.08	188	8	7	51
4	United States	7	.61	766	20	69	80
5	Denmark	4	.15	138	11	21	47
6	Sweden	3	.08	178	6	10	38
7	United Kingdom	6	.10	405	9	34	35
8	The Netherlands	5	.21	239	11	8	28
9	Austria	5	.24	519	8	7	21
10	Finland	4	<.10	128	12	20	51
11	Germany	6	.10	660	10	16	22
12	Belgium	6	.16	479	12	24	33
13	Ireland	6	.11	205	10	49	34
14	France	4	.33	205	6	16	29
15	Canada	6	.31	504	16	90	68
U.S. rank of 15		15	15	15	15	14	15

Note: < = "less than."

Sources: For infant mortality, United Nations Development Program, Human Development Report, 2002, table 8, p. 174. For HIV/AIDS, table 7, p. 170. For road accident rates, OECD, International Road Traffic and Accident Database, May 2002. For air pollutant emissions per capita, U.S. Census Bureau, Statistical Abstract of the United States, 2001, table 1335, p. 838.

we will present narrative evidence where available. For structural violence, however, statistical evidence can be presented. The data show that the United States has higher rates of structural violence—in the form of pollution, auto accidents, and some illnesses—than the other fourteen richest capitalist nations, as shown in table 1.4.

For the six indicators we have used—chosen because of availability of data—the United States has the worst rates on five and is second from the bottom on the other one. The infant mortality rate (IMR) is the number of infants of every one thousand born alive who die before reaching their first birthday. Most health and development experts consider the IMR one of the most sensitive indicators of a whole package of structural features. The IMR reflects maternal health and access to medical care during pregnancy. It indirectly measures nutrition, sanitation, health care, and the general family security of the infant after birth. The lower the IMR, the more adequate and available are all the services both familial and professional that humans require during their first year of life.

With HIV/AIDS we see a similar relationship. To make the rates comparable to the IMR, the percent of adults age fifteen to forty-nine can be changed to a number per 1,000 by multiplying the table figure by ten. Therefore, the figure for Switzerland is 5 per 1,000, for the United States it is 6.1 per 1,000. For Sweden and Norway it is less than 1 person per 1,000. HIV/AIDS infection rates are reflections of a spectrum of social processes including public policies and personal behavior. It is unlikely that the rates are purely outcomes of sexual license: Sweden is known for its relaxed sexual norms compared to the United States, but Sweden has a far lower rate of HIV infection. Among the possible factors are access to safe sex education and technology, differing rates of intravenous drug use, public regulation of prostitution, and the availability of clean needles for addicts. Some of these factors will be described in more detail in later chapters.

Injuries from road accidents illustrate yet other public policy element of structural violence. The U.S. rate is far higher than all the countries on the table, except for Germany and Japan. Although Japan has an automobile accident rate nearly equal to that of the United States, in Japan the deaths from automobile accidents are 8 per 100,000, whereas in the United States the rate is 15. The U.S. rate is the highest of all the countries listed on table 1.4. Why do so many more people die from the injuries they sustain in road accidents in the United States? The answer is a combination of elements including access to medical care, auto safety regulation, and dangerous sports utility vehicles (SUVs). These are all described in later chapters.

Air pollution emissions per capita provide indirect evidence of environmental harm to humans. Both sulfur oxides and nitrogen dioxide (one of the nitrogen oxides) have been shown to increase spasms in the human breathing apparatus and are among the likely causes of the high and increasing asthma rates in the United States. Between 1982 and 1991, the prevalence of asthma increased 56 percent in Americans under the age of eighteen. High levels of either sulfur or nitrogen oxides also appear to be connected with weakening of the natural immune systems in humans, making them potential elements in a wide range of illnesses.[17]

Why are the U.S. rates of both interpersonal and structural violence so much higher than these other countries? We have said this is because of inequality, but that needs to be more carefully explained. Chapters 3, 4, and 5 will look at how economic inequality, political inequality, and differences in nonpolitical power contribute to violence. Before we do that, however, we will consider some other explanations for the high violence rates in the United States and some problems with these.

NOTES

1. Quoted in "Clinton Cites L.I.R.R. Shootings," *New York Times*, December 12, 1993, p. 57.

2. Quoted in Peter Applebombe, "C.D.C.'s New Chief Worries as Much about Bullets as about Bacteria," *New York Times*, September 26, 1993, sec. 4.

3. See, for example, Albert J. Reiss and Jeffrey A. Roth, *Understanding and Preventing Violence* (Washington, DC: National Academy Press, 1993), p. 1.

4. *Time*'s May 5, 2003, issue cover was about SARS, and the issue contains several articles on the disease; among the many articles in the *New York Times* are Dean E. Murphy, "In U.S. Fear Is Spreading Faster Than SARS," *New York Times* April 17, 2003, pp. A1, A12; Iris Chang, "Fear of SARS, Fear of Strangers," *New York Times*, May 21, 2003, p. A31.

5. Quoted in Kathleen Koman, "Lethal Odds: Life, Death, and the Dice," *Harvard Magazine* (September/October 1996): 19.

6. Eric Klinenberg, *Heat Wave: A Social Autopsy of Disaster in Chicago* (Chicago: University of Chicago Press, 2002), p. 15.

7. Klinenberg, *Heat Wave*, 51, 55, 101–103, 157.

8. Ibid., p. 134.

9. Michaela di Leonardo, "Murder by Public Policy," *Nation*, September 2/9, 2002, pp. 31–35.

10. William S. Nersesian, "Infant Mortality in Socially Vulnerable Populations," *Annual Review of Public Health* 9 (1988): 361, 364.

11. Psychological violence also damages people's lives, but the complexities of defining, measuring, and analyzing that kind of violence are beyond the scope of this book. Psychological violence can lead to "self-directed violence," suicide, or "self-abuse." World Health Organization, *World Report on Violence and Health* (Geneva: World Health Organization, 2002), p. 6.

12. Further definitions and details are available in the World Bank's *World Development Report, 2003: Sustainable Development in a Dynamic World, Transforming Institutions, Growth, and Quality of Life* (New York: World Bank, 2003), p. 246.

13. We cannot say exactly which individuals in what part of the hierarchy are benefiting since the Gini Index does not automatically identify where the inequality is—only how much there is altogether.

14. For further comparisons between the United States and other advanced capitalist economies see Lawrence Mishel, Jared Bernstein, and Heather Boushey, *The State of Working America, 2002/2003* (Ithaca, NY: ILR Press, an imprint of Cornell University Press, 2003), pp. 430–32.

15. Franklin E. Zimring and Gordon Hawkins, *Crime Is Not the Problem: Lethal Violence in America* (New York: Oxford University Press, 1997).

16. Ibid., pp. 6–7, 44–47, 219–21.

17. Ann Misch, "Assessing Environmental Risks," in *State of the World: 1994*, ed. Linda Starke (Washington, DC: Worldwatch Institute, and New York: W. W. Norton and Company, 1994), pp. 131–32.

EXPLAINING AMERICAN VIOLENCE
Four Approaches

T here are several different ways to explain violence. Most of these are explanations only of interpersonal violence. We will look briefly at views that stress our biology. We will then discuss approaches that stress the influence of the media and ones that emphasize guns. Finally, we will summarize the analysis we think is the most useful in helping us understand interpersonal, organizational, and structural violence.

Our explanation stresses the importance of inequality and is employed throughout this book. It uses the conflict perspective in sociology, derived from Karl Marx, which emphasizes the role of economic inequality in understanding social phenomena. Economic inequality is connected to inequalities in the power of different social groups. Traditional conflict theory looked mainly at class differences in society, but modern conflict theory takes account of racial and ethnic inequality as well as gender inequality.

IS IT HUMAN NATURE TO BE VIOLENT? BIOLOGICAL DETERMINISM

The biological approach tries to find some aspect of our physical makeup that can explain why violence occurs. In the words of anthropologists Lionel Tiger and Robin Fox, "We are a naturally aggressive species easily aroused to violence."[1] According to this view, humans have evolved in such a way that violence, for males at least, is a readily available response, not something that is learned. Biological determinists do not discuss female violence. Sociobiology and evolutionary psychology are both examples of biological determinism, stressing the influence of genes on human behavior. This approach would reduce most social science to a branch of biology.[2]

Our biological makeup obviously influences our behavior. We are a particular type of animal and, in a general way, this explains some things about us: our sociability, our capacity for learning, and our ability to have a language that is different from that of any other animal. Biology, however, cannot explain how we will treat each other. The range of human behavior is too wide to be explained by hormones or genes. We are all members of a single species, but some groups are very violent, some very peaceful. A common genetic heritage cannot explain the diversity of behavior found in humans.

Anthropology provides important data with which to critique biological determinism. The most egalitarian societies are bands of hunters and gatherers. Hunters and gatherers generally have low levels of violence both internally and between themselves and other societies. Since we had this kind of society for most of our thousands of years as a species, the cross-cultural data show we are not inherently violent animals, though we are certainly capable of violence. Anthropologist Leslie R. Sponsel explains:

> Human nature may be seen as inherently violent if looked at from a perspective limited mostly to Western societies in recent history. However, this is not necessarily the conclusion if human nature is viewed through the anthropological lens, which brings breadth and diversity of perspective. . . . Cross-cultural studies reveal that relatively nonviolent and peaceful societies exist like the Inuit, Hutterites, Mbuti, San, and Semai among others.[3]

Biological determinism cannot account for these peaceful societies. In more complex ones, such as our own, it cannot explain organizational and structural violence where there is no direct confrontation between the people involved. It cannot even explain why there are varying rates of interpersonal violence.

Some other approaches look not at biology but at aspects of American culture to understand at least certain instances of violence. The media is blamed, especially for youth violence. A number of people and organizations see the existence of a gun culture and the availability of firearms as important to understanding American violence, at least its interpersonal forms.

MAYBE IT'S THE MOVIES, MAYBE THE TV[4]

The United States has a high rate of interpersonal violence, and a number of experts have tried to link exposure to the media to violent behavior. In January 2003, twenty-year-old Jason V. Bautista and his fifteen-year-old half brother were accused of matricide after strangling their mother, decapitating her, and cutting off her hands. After mutilating the body they placed it in the trunk of their car, drove to a ravine, and threw the body there. The head and hands were found in the family's California apartment. The investigating sheriff claimed that Bautista had seen such a dismemberment portrayed on the popular television show *The Sopranos*.[5]

In New York City, in December 1995, eighteen-year-old James Irons and four accomplices seemed to be imitating a scene from the movie *Money Train* when Irons, like a character in the film, sprayed a subway token booth with flammable liquid and set it afire, killing the token seller inside. Eight similar incidents had occurred elsewhere in the city, although these had not led to injuries.[6]

Video games aimed at young consumers are a new way to enjoy violence, whether in one's own home or in video arcades, conveniently located in many shopping malls. One of the most popular of these is Grand Theft Auto, the "best-selling video game" between 2000 and 2002. The goal of the game is to locate the people who stole your cocaine and kill them. According to *New York Times* columnist Bob Herbert, describing the "twisted toys" available for Christmas 2002, in this game:

> all boundaries of civilized behavior have vanished. You get to shoot whomever you want, including cops. You get to beat women to death with baseball bats. You get to have sex with prostitutes and then kill them.

Remarks of players would seem to justify this concern. Colin Smith said, "The drive-by shootings of innocent pedestrians are always fun. It really does bring out the . . . evil in you."[7]

Given the massive amount of television most of us are exposed to, it does seem reasonable to conclude that this activity would have an effect, one that would be compounded by watching movies and listening to violent song lyrics. By some estimates, over the course of a lifetime the average television viewer in the United States "will witness approximately twenty thousand simulated television deaths."[8] Some studies put the figure even higher, claiming that by the time a child reaches the age of sixteen he or she will have watched "50,000 attempted murders as well as approximately 200,000 acts of violence (simulated and real)."[9]

Analysts of media violence see this as having three possible consequences.

- Viewing violence in the media causes real-life violence.
- Media violence desensitizes viewers, making them more accepting of real-life violence.
- Viewing media violence causes an increase in fearfulness and suspicion of others.

Media critics warn that movies, television, music lyrics, and video games are responsible for at least certain kinds of youth violence. Writing in *Harvard Magazine*, screenwriter and journalist David Barry sees an America "in the grip of a violent epidemic that has transformed the country from one of the safest to one of the most dangerous nations on earth." He is certain there is a causal relationship between "the massive and pervasive exposure of American youth to television" and the dramatic rise in homicide rates between 1950 and 1990.[10]

Numerous professional organizations support this view, along with political figures and the public.[11] Medical and social science experts and organizations also firmly assert this alleged causal link. For example, testifying at a 1999 Senate hearing on violence, the then president of the American Academy of Pediatrics, Donald E. Cook, noted that watching violent media leads to an "increased acceptance of violence as an appropriate means of conflict resolution."[12]

In its 1996 booklet *The Social Causes of Violence*, the American Sociological Association summarized some of the many studies done since 1969. In that year, the Surgeon General's Scientific Advisory Committee on Television and Social Behavior began commissioning studies and reviewing existing literature. Three years later the committee concluded there was a strong link between TV and the way young people behaved. A decade later, in 1992, the National Institute of Mental Health stated its agreement, while the American Psychological Association (APA) added its authority to confirming this relationship.[13] The APA was unequivocal in its assertions, stating that "there is absolutely no doubt that higher levels of viewing violence on television are correlated with increased acceptance of aggressive attitudes and increased aggressive behavior."[14]

"Organized Parents of America," a Washington, DC-based organization closely connected to the conservative media organization Accuracy in Media, spent thousands of dollars for a full-page ad in the *New York Times*, asserting their disgust with the seamier side of television and music, stating that these are "teaching children that violence is acceptable." They claimed polls showed that both teens and a broader range of Americans think violence in music and television helped inspire the 1999 Columbine shootings in Littleton, Colorado.[15]

The National Television Violence Study, conducted from 1994 to 1997, warned that not only does "televised violence" lead viewers to be more aggressive but it

> creates emotional desensitization toward real-world violence and the victims of violence. This in turn can result in callous attitudes toward violence directed at others and a decreased likelihood to take action on behalf of the victim when violence occurs.[16]

Jonathan Freedman, a psychology professor at the University of Toronto, reviewed and critiqued studies of the effects of media violence. We shall discuss his findings below. Freedman believes that while fictional violence may have little impact on real-life behavior, depictions of real-life violence

> may affect aggression and crime. Children may imitate violence they observe directly. . . . Moreover, it seems likely that repeated exposure to real violence, either directly or in the media, causes desensitization to subsequent real violence. . . . Perhaps this is what people should be worrying about.[17]

Depictions of suffering can be a way to engage the viewer's mind, leading him or her to reflect upon aspects of social reality or the human condition, depending on the filmmaker's artistic aim. But as film analyst Stephen Prince comments:

> Viewers rarely experience screen violence in this fashion treated in a serious and provocative way that invites reflection and contemplation. . . . Instead, commercial films offer it as spectacle, an easy way get to the viewer emotionally, and to solve narrative issues. And it all becomes ever more unreal, ever more stylized, and disconnected from a viewer's personal experience.[18]

In support of this view, Prince quotes a teenager who killed his mother:

The first stage you see a guy's head being blown off and you feel compassion. The second stage you see it again, you feel compassion, but it's not as strong as the first. . . . The fifth stage you want to do it and you want to do it again.[19]

THE MEDIA AND VIOLENCE: WHAT IS THE EVIDENCE?

How can we know with any accuracy what the effects of media violence on human behavior are? The evidence used in many studies comes from laboratory experiments in which subjects watch a film or video with violence in it. A control group watches a film or video without violence. Then all the subjects are put in a situation where they can act aggressively or not. In such situations an operational definition of aggression is needed. But measuring aggression in a lab is a problem; subjects cannot be given knives or guns. Aggression is thus measured in alternative ways; do the children hit a rubber Bobo doll or puncture a balloon? In nonlaboratory studies teachers are sometimes asked to assess aggressiveness in children, or peers may be asked to do aggressiveness ratings on fellow students.

Jonathan Freedman, mentioned above, has examined about two hundred studies of the relationship between viewing and aggression and viewing and desensitization. He summaries his findings, saying:

In 1999, I began systematically reading and reviewing every single scientific study I could find that dealt with the question whether exposure to film and television violence causes aggression. Having looked at all this research, I concluded that the results do not support the view that exposure to media violence causes children or anyone else to become aggressive or to commit crimes; nor does it support the idea that it causes people to be less sensitive to real violence.[20]

Freedman is willing to grant that some small relationship exists for children under ten.[21] This is not the age group, however, that media critics are usually concerned with.

There were studies that found an association, but Freedman claims that this can be explained in several ways. It could be watching violence that leads to subjects behaving aggressively, or they could be trying to please the experimenter, having guessed what is expected of them.[22] In one experiment, action films, whether or not they had violence in them, elicited higher rates of aggression.[23] What Freedman calls one of the best field studies, conducted over a period of time in residential institutions for boys, found that "those who watched violent television committed *fewer* aggressive acts than those who watched nonviolent television."[24]

When examining relationships between variables, there is another issue that needs to be considered. Correlations do not automatically prove causation. If there is an association between real violence and viewing, how is it to be explained? Do those with a tendency to be violent search out violent shows? What role is an individual's social involvement playing? People who are watching a lot of television are probably not interacting with other people. Children or teenagers who are watching a lot of television are likely to be in lower-income households with little adult supervision. Any of these, alone or in combination, could be the cause of both viewing habits and violent behavior.

Psychologist Leonard Eron's work is often cited to show that there is a link between viewing habits and a propensity toward violence. He followed a group of children over a twenty-two-year period and found that violent individuals were most likely to be heavy watchers of television. In testimony before a congressional committee in 1992, Eron declared, "Heavy exposure of televised violence is one of the causes of aggressive behavior, crime, and violence in society."[25]

Eron also said, however, that "aggressive children prefer violent television, and the violence on television causes them to be more aggressive."[26] In a 2001 report the surgeon general of the United States, David Satcher, explained his reason for not including the media as the cause of youth violence, saying, "It was extremely difficult to distinguish between the relatively small long-term effects of exposure to media violence and those of other influences."[27]

There are some additional things to keep in mind. Legal scholars Frank Zimring and Gordon Hawkins studied the relationship between media and homicide in several advanced capitalist nations. They concluded that no relationship could be found.[28] Homicide rates have gone up and down since the 1970s, but media violence has not followed a parallel pattern, even as violent video games have become popular. In spite of the games' popularity there was actually a decrease in serious violent incidents, including deaths at schools, between 1992 and 1999. However, when killings occurred they were more likely to involve several victims and thus be more dramatic.[29] Zimring and Hawkins even argue that watching violence at home keeps people out of social settings where they might be exposed to or commit violence. In this view, the media are performing a "babysitting function."[30]

We do not have to agree that watching violence helps prevent it. We would contend that it is unlikely that there are positive outcomes from viewing the mayhem that many seem to find entertaining.[31] There is, however, inadequate scientific support for the proposition that the media alone causes violent behavior. Entertainment may encourage a few of those inclined to be violent to actually commit violence. Experiments are very unlikely to find those few individuals who might be driven to imitate a simulated violent act. The more important question is, what has disposed these particular individuals to act violently? Here there are likely to be complex individual psychological factors that should also be considered.

The media may be part of a chain of events that produces a violent act, but they cannot be the only or even the most important cause. Blaming the media for individual or small group acts of interpersonal violence turns attention away from more fundamental causes, including social factors that we shall examine in later chapters.

Politicians who attack the media for causing violence make it appear as though they are concerned with the public's well-being. But their cultural criticisms are very selective. The possible effects of sports violence, country music, or religion are rarely, if ever, mentioned.

In recent years there has been an increase in religious practioners specializing in exorcisms, the driving out of Satan and lesser demons who allegedly produce evil deeds. The Catholic dioceses of both New York and Chicago have official exorcists. Other denominations also encourage the practice. Rev. Bob Larsen, a Denver-based evangelical minister who organizes "exorcism teams," says his aim "is that no one should ever be more than a day's drive from a city where you can find an exorcist." Christians, he explains, were given this right. "It's in the Bible. Christ taught it."[32]

There have been reports of people dying as a result of exorcism rituals. A New York State woman was smothered in 1998 during a ceremony. In Rhode Island, in 1996, a woman died when her son-in-law thrust two steel crosses into her throat. As Reverend Larsen explains, "Dealing with the Devil is ugly work. The Devil is ugly. Evil is ugly. When you get to what I call pure extreme evil, it's not going to be pretty."[33] More recently, in Milwaukee, Ray A. Hemphill performed a ceremony that was supposed to drive the devils from eight-year-old autistic Terrance Cottrell Jr.'s body, transforming Terrance into a normal child. However, following a session with Hemphill in August 2003, Terrance suffocated, and Hemphill was charged with felony child abuse.

Beliefs in supernatural evil-causing forces have also been the justification for deliberate killings. Andrea Yates, a Texas mother who drowned her five children in the summer of 2001, supposedly believed her kids were going to hell unless she saved them by killing them. Claiming she was trying to rid her four-year-old daughter of demons, Sabrina Wright, a New York City mother, drowned her little girl in November of 2001. In 1997 five-year-old Amy Aichelle Burney died after being forced by her mother and grandmother to drink a brew of ammonia, vinegar, oil, and pepper as part of a ritual to rid her of demons. Luke T. Woodham, a Mississippi teenager, was charged in 1998 with murdering two students and shooting at other fellow high school classmates. He was involved in Satanism. In 1996 Heriberto Seda, known as the Zodiac killer because he left astrological signs at the murder scenes, admitted to killing three people and wounding five others in the early 1990s "because they were evil." He was frequently seen carrying his Bible while he reviled drug dealers in his Manhattan neighborhood.[34]

Religious beliefs by themselves do not explain violence any more than does television viewing. These examples illustrate the selective attention given to possible causes. It is politically unwise to attack religion, even though there are clear instances of individuals saying that religion caused them to be violent, but criticizing the media as leading to violence has few costs.

THE CULTURAL APPARATUS: THE MORE YOU WATCH, THE MORE YOU FEAR[35]

Owners of the media have the power to decide the content of what we see. Violence and action are very appealing to producers. Media analyst and critic George Gerbner, former dean of the University of Pennsylvania's Annenberg School for Communication, is convinced that economic motives explain much media content. Violence, he claims, is a "good commodity for the global market." It "travels well, you don't need to translate."[36] In other words, violent entertainment can be more easily exported. Grunts, yells, and moans can be understood in many languages. There is no need to deal with possibly delicate issues of sex or politics, and humor is often culture-bound.

The managers of the media decide how we will be entertained and what information we will have. In chapters 4 and 5 we will be discussing the power of corporate executives, but here we will look at one aspect of that power as part of our discussion of the relationship between the media and violence. Media executives are at the top of what sociologist C. Wright

Mills termed the "cultural apparatus," where information, interpretations of reality, and entertainment are produced and distributed.[37]

The media focuses much more attention on street crime than on the more harmful corporate wrongdoing. A report issued by Arizona State University's School of Justice, "Confronting Violent Crime in Arizona," claims, "Corporate crimes, which are not only prevalent but physically dangerous, even deadly, receive little attention and may not be covered as crime at all, but rather as a business matter." In 1999 media critic Morton Mintz asked the chief of the U.S. Justice Department's Criminal Division, James Robinson, the following question: "How often have you seen or heard of a newspaper editorial or column . . . or talking head criticizing grave corporate crime or misconduct?" Robinson answered, "I can't remember the most recent occasion."[38]

Since the media is both interlocked with major corporations and is also dependent on them for advertising, their reluctance to criticize corporate practices is understandable. Emphasizing street crime over business crime is useful to political figures as well. As George Gerbner points out, "Fear of the mean world is politically exploitable." As we shall see, politicians are not very likely to offer constituents protection from corporate malfeasance, but they do claim they can lessen the harm from other forms of violence.

Journalists engage in self-censorship, a way of protecting their jobs. The Pew Center for the People and the Press polled 287 news personnel in 2000. One-third of those surveyed said they would not report on news that might be harmful to the financial interests of their media outlet or advertisers. Sixty-one percent of investigative reporters believed that corporations influenced what was reported as news. In the same year another study was conducted by the Project on Excellence in Journalism. Here also one-third of TV news directors admitted that they had been asked to either promote positive stories about their advertisers or, at least, stay away from negative ones.[39]

Television news is dominated by crime stories in the belief that this will increase ratings. The motto of television news producers seems to be "if it bleeds, it leads"; "a lurid crime report with a high body count will . . . become the lead story, no matter how insignificant its actual news value." Media commentators sometimes use the phrase "body-bag journalism" to convey how news programming aims toward the sensational.[40]

Television crime coverage does not reflect actual crime rates, according to the media-watch group Fairness and Accuracy in Reporting (FAIR). From January 1989 to January 1992, the three major networks spent an average of "67 minutes a month on crime stories." In the period from October 1993 to January 1994, they were spending over 157 minutes a month on this topic. In the six months between June and November of 1993, media stories of violent crime went up by 400 percent.[41]

If you watched television news in the New York area between 1996 and 1997, you would not know that homicide rates had declined. The director of the city's CBS station, Bill Carey, remarked, "The fact that percentages are down doesn't affect our coverage." Joseph Agnotti, a communications professor at the University of Miami, himself a former executive at NBC news, studied local news programs in eight cities in 1997. His research team discovered that about one-third of local news was devoted to crimes. Agnotti had an explanation: "It's the easiest, cheapest, laziest news to cover because all they do is listen to the police radio, react to it . . . and put it on the air." The team also found that in some of the cities studied the highest ratings were going to stations with the least amount of crime news.[42]

In Los Angeles researchers sampled thirty-five hours of news coverage on local TV, finding that crime stories made up "23 percent to 54 percent of all news coverage." It was news presented as entertainment with little analysis. Much less attention was given to upcoming elections in California. "Of 2,059 minutes of news, just over eight minutes concerned the gubernatorial primary."[43]

Television news has been found by sociologists to have an especially strong impact on viewers' fear of crime. In 1994 Ted Chircos, Sarah Escholz, and Marc Gertz surveyed 2,092 people living in Tallahassee, Florida, at the peak of a media frenzy about violent crime. Listening to television and radio news was significantly related to having a higher level of fear, with white women being the group most likely to be afraid, even though this is a category with a relatively low rate of victimization. The researchers hypothesized that the women were identifying with the victims who were more likely to be white and female than either male or non-white.[44] Nonwhite young males are the most likely, in fact, to be victims of violent street crime.

In January 1994 *U.S. News and World Report* had a cover story on crime, claiming crime has been increasing since 1960, a distortion of the data. Crime rates have gone up and down in that thirty-four-year period.[45] *Time* magazine's August 23, 1994, cover story was "America the Violent," with a subheading noting, "crime is spreading and patience is running out." The bright red cover had a lurid illustration of a sinister-looking young man, with a frightening inhuman face glaring out, not a well-dressed executive with a briefcase. Inside, the reader was told that people are in danger doing the ordinary things of life: going to the hospital, a fast-food restaurant, or the shopping mall.

A *Los Angeles Times* survey reported that 65 percent of respondents got their information about crime from the media.[46] Between June 1993 and February 1994 the percentage of those telling *Washington Post* pollsters that crime was the most important issue facing the country rose from 5 to 31 percent.[47] National survey data also showed a steep rise in the general feeling that crime is the most important problem in the nation. Between January 1993 and January 1994 the percentage of respondents identifying crime as the most important problem in the country rose from 9 percent to 37 percent, a 400 percent increase, but not a reflection of any similar increase in crime rates.[48]

Sociologist Barry Glassner thinks many Americans have excessive fears of things that won't harm most of them while being far less aware of the real dangers confronting many. He calls this a "culture of fear," noting:

> We often fear the wrong things. . . . One of the paradoxes of a culture of fear is that serious problems remain widely ignored even though they give rise to precisely the dangers that the populace most abhors. Poverty, for example, correlates strongly with child abuse, crime, and drug abuse. Income inequality is also associated with adverse outcomes for society as a whole. The larger the gap between rich and poor in a society, the higher its overall death rates from heart disease, cancer, and murder.[49]

These are issues less likely to be attention-grabbing items.

While a careful reading of the media can provide useful information, there is much that is missing or distorted in the analysis we get from newspapers, magazines, radio, and television. For instance, the relationships between corporate goals and resources, political decisions, and the conditions that give rise to interpersonal violence are rarely discussed. The media also do not often report on collective efforts that have helped solve social problems, and they rarely give information on how problems have been alleviated and the quality of life improved in other countries.[50]

When people are aware of a problem, they can help reduce it. We discuss this in the last chapter of this book. But here it is useful to note one example. Drunk driving has become less of a cause of death. Between 1982 and 2001 there was more than a 50 percent decrease in alcohol-related traffic fatalities. These are still high, with 17,448 people killed in alcohol-related accidents in 2001. Nevertheless, years of campaigning against drunk driving and the imposition of safety measures, such as seat belts, have made a difference.[51]

"I'D TAKE AWAY THE GUNS"

Barry Glassner, quoted above, notes "a country out of control with fear shouldn't have [easy access to] guns and ammo."[52] There are many examples of how fear plus guns equals tragedy. In 1995 Sam Walker's wife called him, saying their security company had notified her that their burglar alarm had gone off. He went to their Texas home, found the door unlocked, and got his recently purchased .38-caliber revolver. Checking the house, he went into his daughter's room, saw someone he didn't instantly recognize, and fired, killing sixteen-year-old Sheree who had skipped school.

A similar incident occurred in 1994 in Louisiana. A fourteen-year-old decided to play a prank on her father. She made some noises in her closet, and when he came in the room to see what was happening, she jumped out of her hiding place. Thinking she was an intruder, her startled parent shot and killed her. In Mississippi in December 1995 a three-year-old got up to look at the family's Christmas tree lights while his parents were sleeping. He accidentally tripped a motion detector, setting off an alarm. His frightened stepmother went downstairs with a gun, fired at the moving person she saw, and killed the little boy.[53]

Sixteen-year-old Japanese exchange student Yoshiro Hattori and a friend were on their way to a Halloween party in Baton Rouge, Louisiana, in 1992. Yoshiro wore a costume based on the movie *Saturday Night Fever*. His friend was uncostumed. Looking for the party, they rang the doorbell at the Peairs' family home. Bonnie Peairs answered the door and called to her husband, Rodney, to come with his gun, a .44-caliber magnum. It seems the student did not understand Rodney Peairs's shout of "freeze," and so did not stand still. The homeowner killed him. In 1993 Peairs was acquitted of manslaughter, with the jury apparently finding his actions were based on justifiable fears. In 1994 a judge awarded Yoshihiro's parents $650,000 in damages and for funeral costs. The case became a cause célèbre in Japan, where there were altogether seventy-four shooting deaths in 1991, sixty-seven of which were members of organized crime groups. In the same year the United States, with twice Japan's population, had about thirty-eight thousand firearm deaths.[54]

Fearful of being attacked even in their own homes, and with easy access to firearms, people in the United States are buying weapons. In 2001 survey data showed that 39 percent of respondents had some type of firearm in their home.[55] Philip J. Cook and Jens Ludwig, researchers for the U.S. Department of Justice, found that 20 percent of all gun-owning households had "an unlocked, loaded gun in the house" when they conducted their 1994 survey. The figure was 30 percent for those who owned handguns, which are especially likely to be kept in the owner's bedroom, vehicle, or on their person.[56]

Americans owned 16 million handguns in 1960, but by 1995 this number had risen to 79 million. According to the Bureau of Justice, counting handguns, rifles, shotguns, and the like, there are at least "223 million guns available to the general public." Cook and Ludwig note that "the United States is unique among wealthy nations in its vast private inventory of firearms." Their survey research found that 74 percent of those who owned a weapon owned more than one. Ownership was highest "among middle-aged, college-educated people of rural small-town America." They go on to say, "On any given day, 1.1 million people were carrying guns on their persons outside the workplace, while another 21 million stored guns in their cars or trucks."[57]

The relationship of guns to physical harm is much more obvious than is the relation of the media. To be more accurate, the National Rifle Association's slogan "Guns don't kill people, people kill people" should say, "People with guns kill and injure other people." Of course, firearms themselves do not decide to blast away at someone. There has to be a motivation to use them. Once a decision is made to assault someone, however, having a gun increases the likelihood that such an assault will result in serious injury or death.

There is no lack of examples of angry people with firearms causing great misery. Armed with powerful guns, those intent on suicide are also likely to be successful.

Table 2.1 compares firearms deaths for the advanced capitalist countries used in table 1.2. The year of the data is in parentheses.

The World Health Organization gives data on firearms deaths for forty-five countries. Of these the United States accounts for 68 percent of the total. The countries with similarly high rates are almost all Third World countries, former Soviet states, or countries in eastern Europe. In the United States access to these weapons is easier than in the other countries listed on table 2.1. Firearms are an important contributor to the high rates of death from interpersonal violence in the United States. In addition, in 2000 some type of guns was used in 16,746 suicides.[58]

National data can obscure important differences among particular

TABLE 2.1 FIREARMS DEATHS FOR ADVANCED CAPITALIST COUNTRIES, SELECTED RECENT YEARS

country	total deaths	rates per 100,000 population
United States (2000)	28,663	10
France (1998)	2,964	5
Belgium (1995)	379	4
Austria (1999)	293	4
Canada (1997)	1034	3
Norway (1997)	139	3
Sweden (1996)	183	2
Germany (1999)	1,201	1
Denmark (1996)	101	2
Netherlands (1999)	131	1
Japan (1997)	83	0.1

Source: United States, United States Department of Health and Human Services, *National Vital Statistics Report* 50, no. 15 (September 16, 2002), author's calculation of rate; other countries World Health Organization, *World Report on Violence and Health*, table A.10, pp. 322–23. Numbers have been rounded except for Japan.

Switzerland data are not given.

groups. For the United States in 1999, African American males age fifteen to twenty-four had a rate of thirty-nine firearm deaths per one hundred thousand, Latinos were next with a rate of seventeen per one hundred thousand, while the rate for whites in this age group was three per hundred thousand.[59]

Availability of firearms makes it more likely that attempts at murder or suicide will be successful. Gang-related shootings, deaths of an innocent bystander from a stray bullet, and the use of weapons in domestic disputes do not receive much attention. Shootings that seem less routine, affect the more affluent, or have multiple victims are well-publicized and may give a false sense of danger. This was the case with the shootings in a Littleton, Colorado, high school.

Two Littleton, Colorado, high school seniors were full of anger as they planned the shootings at Columbine High School, on April 20, 1999. On videotapes made before the murders and their own suicides, Eric Harris said, "If you could see all the anger I've stored over the past four years." His friend, Dylan Klebold, confessed, "More rage, more rage, I'm building it up."[60]

In recent years there have been high-profile cases of shootings in which the motivation for the violence was unclear. There was no material gain, there was no argument between identifiable people, the right to kill was not part of the shooter's job. Such a case occurred in October 2002 when John Allen Muhammad and his seventeen-year-old companion, John Lee Malvo, terrified Washington, DC, and its suburbs with their random shootings. By the time they were caught, after a three-week police hunt, ten people had been killed, another three wounded. The dead included a bus driver standing by his vehicle, a man filling his car with gasoline, a woman cleaning her minivan, a man walking, and a woman sitting on a park bench. One man was shot as he worked in his front yard.[61]

In the long run, we want to know what leads individuals to choose to kill others, but in the short run, limiting access to weapons would seem to be one way to reduce the horrific numbers of deaths from firearms.

There is public support for some form of gun control. Surveys in 2000 indicated that 57 percent of respondents thought it more important to control gun ownership than to protect the rights of gun owners. Thirty-eight percent thought it more important to protect the right to own guns, whereas 62 percent thought there was a need for stricter gun-control laws. African Americans are more likely than whites to favor stricter gun control, and women are more likely than men.[62]

On Mother's Day, May 14, 2000, women organized marches in Washington, DC, and other cities, urging that the government support tougher gun-control laws. Hundreds of thousands amassed in the capital. Calling themselves the Million Mom March, mothers told poignant stories of children killed by guns. Some wore T-shirts bearing pictures of relatives who had been killed.[63]

One of the speakers was Patti Nielson, who was teaching her art class at Columbine High School on April 20, 1999. On that day, she said, "My life changed forever." She continued:

> The boys at Columbine were not the first disturbed people to open fire on innocence nor will they be the last. Until we figure out what turns people into killers and prevent it, we cannot make it so easy for them to get guns—especially those for the sole purpose of killing human beings. I believe in our youth, and I know that access to guns alone will not turn them into killers but it is a critical piece of the problem.

Nielson went on to note that it took courage for her to come to the event and then ended by saying, "It's time Congress showed some courage of its own."[64]

Congresspeople have been very reluctant to enact stronger gun-control legislation. One reason is the power of the National Rifle Association (NRA), itself supported by weapons manufacturers. The NRA, with a budget of $135 million in 2000, contributes generously to political campaigns and has to date been successful in preventing stronger legislation from being passed, even after the shootings in Littleton, Colorado.

Republicans more than Democrats are favored by NRA campaign contributions and have close relations with the NRA. Democrats do vie for some of this money. In the 2002 congressional elections, a number of Democratic candidates posed with weapons, showing they were friendly to gun owners. It was, however, the Republican presidential candidate who the NRA was eager to see elected. Kayne Robinson, a vice president in the organization, predicted that if and when George W. Bush won, "We'll have . . . a President where we work out of their office."[65]

Between 1991 and 1999 the NRA gave about $2 million in campaign contributions to the political parties, with 80 percent of that going to Republicans. Sen. Larry Craig of Idaho and his Georgia colleague Bob Barr have both sat on the NRA's board of directors.

In 2000 Wayne La Pierre, the NRA's chief executive officer, was cochair of a major fund-raising event for then governor George W. Bush. Nevertheless, its support is no guarantee that its favored candidates will win. In the 2000 elections six of its seven favored gubernatorial candidates and seven of its nine preferred senatorial candidates lost. One of them, John Ashcroft of Missouri, however, was appointed U.S. attorney general. In this role he has helped prevent stronger controls on these weapons. For example, the U.S. Patriot Act passed in 2001, part of the Bush administration's "War on Terror," discussed in chapter 15, "contains no new provisions for the monitoring or control of firearms" even though these are easily bought in the United States by would-be terrorists.[66] The NRA has also successfully prevented the creation of a national ballistics-fingerprinting base. This would enable law enforcement agencies to identify who had bought the bullets that were used in illegal shootings.[67]

With the aid of political allies, the NRA has been able to prevent the Bureau of Alcohol, Tobacco, and Firearms (BATF), part of the Treasury Department, from becoming a more effective controller of firearms. The BATF does not have sufficient resources to investigate and prosecute suspect gun dealers. In 1999 it had only nine more agents than the 1,631 it had in 1973. In that same period the Drug Enforcement Administration went from 1,370 agents to 4,261.

With relatively limited personnel, the BATF is supposed to investigate gun dealers, suspected arsons, and bombings. It also has responsibility for laws regarding tobacco and alcohol. It operates under a number of restrictions that do not apply to drug-enforcement personnel. For example, BATF agents may not use undercover tactics although drug-enforcement personnel can. According to David Kennedy, who directs a Boston program which has reduced gun availability in that city. "The only fair thing to say is that [BATF agents] have been systematically kept away from doing a vitally important job."[68]

While we are all familiar with Drug-Free School Zone signs, there are far fewer comparable ones reading "Gun-Free School Zone." In a 1995, 5–4 decision, the Supreme Court ruled that the 1990 Gun-Free School Zones Act was unconstitutional. The act passed under Congress's right to regulate interstate commerce had made gun possession within one thousand feet of a school a federal crime. It was the first time since 1937 that the Court had held that Congress had overreached its right to regulate commerce.

Since 1986, when the Firearm Owner's Protection Act was enacted, it has been more difficult to investigate and prosecute weapons dealers. The act also weakened existing laws. For example, if a dealer is found to falsify records, he will be charged with a misdemeanor rather than the more serious felony charge. State laws vary, with some states making it more difficult to acquire firearms, but they can be bought in other states where their purchase is much easier. Licensed gun dealers keep records and require waiting periods before the purchase can be completed. Currently, however, gun shows are exempt from these restrictions. A legal loophole allows weapons from "private collections" to be sold with minimal paperwork. While background checks are usually required of would-be purchasers, these are not necessary if the purchaser buys from an unlicensed dealer at a gun show.

Gun shows attract large crowds, with cumulatively perhaps as many as five million people going to one or more of the thousands of these events each year. Buyers, whether hunters, criminals, white supremacists, mentally disturbed people, terrorists, participants in overseas conflicts, or some combination of these, can browse among vendors offering assault rifles, handguns, bayonets, and ammunition. Those so inclined can also buy weapons that they then sell illegally.[69]

In 1999 the Senate rejected a proposal supported by gun-control advocates that would have created more regulations for these shows. The NRA had lobbied Republican senators for a substitute measure. This measure passed, making it completely voluntary for unlicensed gun dealers to perform background checks on their customers. Commenting on the defeat, California Democratic senator Diane Feinstein lamented, "It's like the NRA lives in here, I find it extraordinarily discouraging." New Jersey Democratic senator Frank Lautenberg wondered, "When will the public's rage finally reach into this place?"[70]

Gun-control advocates argue that one way to lessen the deaths from this source is to treat guns like automobiles, register them, and keep records accessible to any law-enforcement agency. Those favoring weak laws often base their arguments on their interpretation of the Second Amendment, which reads in part, "A well-regulated militia being necessary to the security of a free state, the right of the people to keep and bear arms shall not be infringed."

Since a 1930 Supreme Court decision, this amendment has been interpreted as referring to militia units, not to individuals. Contradicting its claims that it wishes to protect Americans, the Bush administration has given support to opponents of gun control. For example, the president refuses to support legislation that would require background checks at gun shows. As Texas governor, in 1999 Bush signed a bill that made it illegal for any government body in that state to sue gun manufacturers.[71]

Attorney General John Ashcroft claims that the Second Amendment was meant to protect "the right of individuals to keep and bear firearms." He expressed this opinion in a letter to the NRA and then in a letter to all federal prosecutors and a Justice Department brief to the Supreme Court. He has also suggested that the records on firearms purchasers be kept for only twenty-four hours, rather than the now required ninety days. Ashcroft does, however, think that children should be protected from exposure to media violence.[72]

In an effort to reduce firearms deaths, a number of states and localities, using the model of making tobacco companies liable for the health costs of smokers, passed laws seeking damages from arms manufacturers. The industry, however, has been able to influence state legislatures to pass laws granting them immunity from lawsuits. The NRA has made the ban "one of our top priorities," according to its head lobbyist, Jim Baker. As of early 2000 they had succeeded in fifteen states and as of April 2003 were hearing encouraging news from Congress. The *New York Times* reported:

> Beginning a new drive to shield the industry, the House Judiciary Committee . . . approved a bill giving gun manufacturers and dealers immunity against many suits, including ones already in court brought by shooting victims and municipalities. The suits fault the manufacturers for

not adding safety features and for distribution practices that make it easy for criminals to get guns.[73]

Germany provides a contrast to the official U.S. policy. When a young killer entered a German high school in September 2002, killing eighteen people and wounding another ten, the political response was to strengthen that country's already restrictive laws.[74]

Gun control alone will not solve the problem of American violence. It is not relevant to organizational or structural violence. It could, however, reduce death rates from interpersonal violence, accidents, and attempted suicides using firearms. Previously cited violence experts Zimring and Hawkins maintain persuasively that guns should be seen as an important *contributing cause* to physical harm:

> Current evidence suggests that a combination of the ready availability of guns and the willingness to use maximum force in interpersonal conflict is the most important single contribution to the high U.S. death rate from violence. Our rate of assault is not exceptional; our death rate from assault is exceptional. . . . Our considerable propensity for violent conflict would be a serious societal problem even if gun availability and its use were low. . . . When viewed in the light of the concept of contributing causation, the United States has both a violence problem and a gun problem, and each makes the other more deadly.[75]

High levels of inequality in the United States, documented in the next chapter, not biology, the media or guns, are a major reason why we have "a violence problem."

INEQUALITY AND VIOLENCE ARE RELATED

The conflict perspective used throughout this book stresses the ways in which the distribution of wealth and power influences social behavior in the United States. This perspective attempts to explain interpersonal, organizational, and structural violence by looking at the way decisions are made and social resources are used. It considers the impacts these decisions have on individuals and communities. Sometimes these effects are seen quickly, sometimes inequality produces cumulative effects that fit our definition of violence.

In chapters 3, 4, and 5 we shall describe various forms of inequality in the United States; in subsequent chapters we shall show that inequality is associated with violence in a number of ways:

1. Inequality leads to organizational violence and to structural violence when part of the population is denied the needed resources for a healthy life and environment. We shall see that especially in chapters 6, 7, 8, and 9.
2. Interpersonal violence may become a way in which the less privileged react to their situation, for instance, by engaging in street crime; or they may direct their anger at an unjust social order against scapegoats or the weaker and more vulnerable sectors of society. This will be the focus of chapters 10, 11, and 12.
3. Organizational violence in the forms of domestic repression and militarism is used to maintain and even further inequality. This is discussed in chapter 12 and in the chapters on militarism, 13, 14, and 15.

The next chapter will examine the three major types of inequality in the United States: class, race, and gender.

NOTES

1. Lionel Tiger and Robin Fox, *The Imperial Animal* (New York: Delta, 1971), p. 220; Fox's latest formulation is found in *The Challenge of Anthropology: Old Encounters and New Excursions* (New Brunswick, NJ: Transaction Publishers, 1994). Although this quote is from anthropologists, it is not typical of most anthropological thinking on violence.

2. See, for example, Edward O. Wilson, *Sociobiology: The New Synthesis* (Cambridge, MA: Harvard University Press), pp. 547–75.

3. Leslie E. Sponsel, "The Mutual Relevance of Anthropology and Peace Studies," in *The Anthropology of Peace and Nonviolence*, ed. Leslie E. Sponsel and Thomas Gregor (Boulder, CO: Lynne Rienner, 1994), pp. 7–8. The Inuit are more commonly known as the Eskimos, while the Mbuti are central African pygmies, and the San, in southern Africa, are often called Bushmen.

4. This heading and the one "I'd Take Away the Guns" are modified from the lyrics to Cheryl Wheeler's song, "If It Were Up to Me" on her CD *Sylvia Hotel*, Rounder Records, 1999

5. "Son Held in Dismemberment That Is Said to Copy TV Show," *New York Times,* January 28, 2003, p. A12.

6. Clifford Kraus, "Police Arrest 18-Year-Old in Subway Fire," *New York Times*, December 15, 1995, pp. B1, B3.

7. "The Gift of Mayhem," *New York Times*, November 28, 2002, p. A35; John Leland, "Bigger, Bolder, Faster, Weirder," *New York Times*, October 27, 2002, sec. 9, pp. 1, 12; Colin Smith quoted in Warren St. John, "With Games of Havoc, Men Will Be Boys," *New York Times*, May 5, 2002, sec. 9, pp. 1, 4.

8. James Torr, introduction to *Violence in Film and Television: Examining Pop Culture*, ed. James D. Torr (San Diego: Greenhaven Press, 2002), p. 17.

9. Peter Iadiculla and Anson Shupe, *Violence, Inequality, and Human Freedom* (Dix Hills, NY: General Hall, 1998), p. 57.

10. David Barry, "Screen Violence: It's Killing Us," *Harvard Magazine* (November-December 1993): 38. His list of concerned professional organizations is on p. 40.

11. A reference to survey data can be found in Felice J. Levine and Katherine Rosich, *Social Causes of Violence* (Washington, DC: American Sociological Association, 1996), p. 100, n. 38. See also George Comstock and Erica Scharrer, "Public Opinion on Television Violence," in Torr, *Violence in Film and Television*, pp. 71–72. They argue, however, that the public is not particularly concerned with this issue and their alleged worries are a result of media violence being in the news and the ways in which questions are being asked, pp. 72–73.

12. Quoted in Torr, introduction to *Violence in Film and Television*, p. 14.

13. Levine and Rosich, *Social Causes of Violence*, pp. 51–53.

14. American Psychological Association, *Violence and Youth: Psychology's Response* (Washington, DC: American Psychological Association, 1993).

15. *New York Times*, July 18, 2001, p. A21. The text of the ad says it was paid for by Accuracy in Media.

16. National Television Violence Study, "The Effects of Media Violence," in Torr, *Violence in Film and Television*, pp. 108, 210.

17. Ibid., p. 210. At the moment, however, this should be regarded as an untested hypothesis.

18. "A Brief History of Film Violence," in ibid., p. 31.

19. Ibid., p. 32.

20. Jonathon Freedman, *Media Violence and Its Effect on Aggression: Assessing the Scientific Evidence* (Toronto: University of Toronto Press, 2002), pp. x–xi.

21. Ibid., p. 43

22. Ibid., pp. 80–83.

23. Ibid., p. 59.

24. Ibid., p. 90 (emphasis in original).

25. Quoted in Madeline Levine, "Media Violence Harms Children," in *Media Violence: Opposing Viewpoints*, ed. William Dudley (San Diego: Greenhaven Press, 1999), p. 29.

26. Quoted in Brian Siano, "Evidence Connecting Media Violence to Real Violence Is Weak," in *Violence in the Media*, ed. Carol Wekesser (San Diego: Greenhaven Press, 1995), p. 42.

27. Quoted in Torr, introduction to *Violence in Film and Television*, p. 7.

28. Franklin E. Zimring and Gordon Hawkins, *Crime Is Not the Problem: Lethal Violence in America* (New York: Oxford University Press, 1997), app. 5, pp. 237–43.

29. "Multiple Slayings Now More Likely in School Violence," *New York Times,* December 5, 2001, p. A25. Numbers and rates of violent incidents near or in schools for 1993–1998 can be found in Department of Justice, Bureau of Justice Statistics, *Sourcebook of Criminal Statistics—2000* (Washington, DC: Government Printing Office, 2001), table 3.66, p. 241.

30. Ibid., p. 128. They discuss the role of the media in the United States on pages 123–37.

31. For discussions of why people are attracted to vicarious violence see Jeffrey Goldstein, ed., *Why We Watch: The Attractions of Violent Entertainment* (New York: Oxford University Press, 1998).

32. Quoted in John W. Fountain, "Exorcists and Exorcisms Proliferate across U.S.," *New York Times,* November 28, 2000, p. A16.

33. Quoted in ibid. The case of Terrance Cottrell Jr. is reported in Monica Davey, "Faith Healing Gone Wrong Claims Boy's Life," *New York Times,* August 29, 2003, p. A12.

34. "Doctor Says Mother Was 'Driven by Delusions,'" *New York Times,* March 7, 2002, p. A25; Jacob H. Fries, "Mother Drowned Daughter, 4 in Exorcism Rite, Police Say," *New York Times,* November 14, 2001, p. D3; Michael Cooper, "Mother and Grandmother Charged with Fatally Poisoning Girl, 5," *New York Times,* May 19, 1997, p. B3; "Teen-ager Says Satanism Led to Killings," *New York Times,* June 12, 1998, p. A18; N. R. Kleinfeld, "Police Say Zodiac Suspect Admits Attacks That Killed 3 and Hurt 5," *New York Times,* June 20, 1996, pp. A1, B6, B7.

35. The subtitle is a play on the title of Danny Schecter's *The More You Watch, The Less You Know* (New York: Seven Stories Press, 1997). The video *The Killing Screens: Media and the Culture of Violence* has a section titled "The More You Watch, The More Dangerous You Think the World Is." Details are in the bibliography.

36. Gerbner makes this point in the above-mentioned video.

37. C. Wright Mills, "The Cultural Apparatus," in *Power, Politics, and People: The Collected Essays of C. Wright Mills,* ed. Irving L. Horowitz (New York: Ballantine Books, 1963), pp. 405–22. Useful discussions of corporate control of the media can be found in Michael Parenti, *Inventing Reality: The Politics of News Media,* 2nd ed. (New York: St. Martin's Press, 1993); Edward S. Herman and Noam Chomsky, *Manufacturing Consent: The Political Economy of the Mass Media* (New York: Pantheon, 1988); the *Nation* for January 7/14, 2002, and June 3, 1996, devotes much of each issue to this topic.

38. Tom Blazier, "Corporate Crime: At the Bottom of the Press Agenda," *Extra!* May/June 1994, p. 27; Morton Mintz, "No Shame: Corporate Immorality Elicits Little Press Comment," *Extra!* July/August 2000, p. 24.

39. Janine Jackson and Peter Hart, "Fear and Favor 2000: How Power Shapes the News," *Extra!* June 2001, p. 15. The article has numerous examples of this point.

40. Susan Ruel, "Body Bag Journalism: Crime Coverage by the U.S. Media," paper presented at International Conference on Violence in the Media, St. John's University, New York, Oct. 3–4, 1994, p. 6; Walter Goodman, "Crime and Black Images in TV News," *New York Times*, December 23, 1993, p. C14.

41. Janine Jackson and Jim Naureckas, "U.S. News Illustrates Flaws in Crime Coverage," *Extra!* May/June 1994, p. 10; Ted Chiricos, Sarah Escholz, and Marc Gertz, "Crime, News, and Fear of Crime: Toward an Identification of Audience Effects," *Social Problems* 44 (1997): 342.

42. Lawrie Mifflin, "Crime Falls, But Not on TV," *New York Times,* July 6, 1997, sec. 4, pp. 3, 4.

43. Barbara Bliss Osborn, "If It Bleeds It Leads—If it Votes It Don't: A Survey of L.A.'s Local News Shows," *Extra!* September/October 1994, p.15.

44. Chiricos, Escholz, and Gertz, "U.S. News Illustrates Flaws in Crime Coverage," pp. 342, 348, 349, 352, 354. Victimization rates are based on data for 1993 (close to the time the research was done) from Lisa Bastian, *Criminal Victimization, 1993* (Washington DC: Bureau of Justice Statistics, 1995), pp. 4–5. In a more recent study of several Florida communities, these same researchers found that the "perceived racial composition" of viewers' neighborhoods had an effect on levels of fear. If viewers thought their neighborhood was more than 25 percent African American, then the relationship between TV viewing and crime fears held, otherwise it did not. Sarah Escholz, Ted Chiricos, and Marc Gertz, "Television and Fear of Crime: Program Types, Audience Traits, and the Mediating Effect of Perceived Neighborhood Racial Composition," *Social Problems* 50 (2003): 408.

45. Jackson and Naureckas, "U.S. News Illustrates Flaws in Crime Coverage," p. 10.

46. Barry Glassner, *The Culture of Fear: Why Americans Are Afraid of the Wrong Things* (New York: Basic Books, 1999), p. xxi.

47. Jackson and Naureckas, "U.S. News Illustrates Flaws in Crime Coverage," p. 10.

48. U.S. Department of Justice, Bureau of Justice Statistics, *Sourcebook of Criminal Justice Statistics—1994* (Washington, DC: Government Printing Office, 1995), table 2.1, p. 140. An interesting example of the relationship between media coverage of crime and fear comes from Ireland, which has a low crime rate but a rate of concern that compares to that in the United States According to a summary of a study of newspaper coverage of crime, there were "a disproportionate number of stories dealing with extreme and violent offenses." Quoted in Stephen Rosskamm Shalom, *Which Side Are You On? An Introduction to Politics* (New York: Addison Wesley Longman, 2002), pp. 239–40.

49. Glassner, *The Culture of Fear*, p. xviii.

50. For a number of examples of what we can learn from other countries see D. G. Stanley Eitzen and Craig S. Leedham, eds., *Solutions to Social Problems: Lessons from Other Societies* (Boston: Allyn and Bacon, 1998).

51. "Lower Rates of Drunken Driving Deaths," *New York Times*, December 24, 2002, p. A21.

52. Quoted in Johanna Ebner, "Sociologist Takes 'Supporting' Role in Columbine Documentary," *Footnotes*, January 2003, p. 4. *Footnotes* is the newsletter of the American Sociological Association. The documentary is Michael Moore's 2003 Oscar winner *Bowling for Columbine* whose subject is gun culture, fear, and their consequences in the United States.

53. Sam Howe Verhovek, "Unwanted Gun Unimagined Result," *New York Times*, December 13, 1995, p. A18; "A Parent Kills Child Mistaken for a Burglar, *New York Times*, December 12, 1994, p. 18.

54. Adam Nossiter, "Judge Awards Damages in Japanese Youth's Death," *New York Times*, September 16, 1994, p. A12; David E. Sanger, "After Gunman's Acquittal, Japan Struggles to Understand America," *New York Times*, May 25, 1993, pp. A1, A17.

55. *Sourcebook of Criminal Justice Statistics—2000*, table 2.72, p. 150.

56. Philip J. Cook and Jens Ludwig, *Guns in America: National Survey on Private Ownership and Use of Firearms* (Washington, DC: U.S. Department of Justice, Office of Justice Programs, 1997), p. 1.

57. *Sourcebook of Criminal Justice Statistics—2000*, tables 2.68–2.72, pp. 148–50; Cook and Ludwig, *Guns in America*, pp. 1, 2, 8.

58. Zimring and Hawkins, *Crime Is Not the Problem*, p. 122. There has, however, been some decrease in the number of firearms deaths in this country. In 1991 there were 38,317 of these fatalities, "Guns Gaining on Cars as Leading Killer," *New York Times*, January 28, 1994, p. A12. One possible explanation for this is that people who have shot themselves or been shot intentionally or accidentally are getting the medical care that prevents injuries from becoming fatal; Jay Livingston, *Crime and Criminology*, 2nd ed. (Upper Saddle River, NJ: Prentice-Hall, 1996), p. 156; Anthony Ramirez, "One More Reason You're Less Likely to Be Murdered," *New York Times*, August 25, 2002, sec. 4, p. 3.

59. World Health Organization, *World Report on Violence and Health* (Geneva: World Health Organization, 2002), p. 11.

60. Michael Janofsky, "The Columbine Killers' Tapes of Rage," *New York Times*, December 14, 1999, p. A22.

61. Kate Zernike, "Accommodating Fears in a Sniper's Killing Field," *New York Times*, October 12, 2002, pp. A1, A18.

62. *Sourcebook of Criminal Justice Statistics—2000*, tables 2.74–2.79, pp. 151–53.

63. Robin Toner, "Mothers Rally to Assail Gun Violence," *New York Times*, May 15, 2000, pp. A1, A14.

64. "Remarks of Patti Nielson Teacher, Columbine High School to the Million Mom March," http://www.nea.org/speeches/sp000514.html (accessed February 11, 2003).

65. Katherine Q. Seelye, "Democrats Using Finesse, Try to Neutralize the Gun Lobby's Muscle," *New York Times*, September 10, 2002, p. A20; Robinson quoted in Robert Dreyfus, "The NRA Wants You," *Nation*, March 29, 2000, p. 12.

66. James Dao and Don Van Natta Jr., "N.R.A. Is Using Adversity to Its Advantage," *New York Times*, June 12, 1999, p. A10; James Dao, "N.R.A. Tightens Its Embrace of Republicans with Donations," *New York Times*, April 26, 2000, p. A18; Steve Cobble, "Hiding Behind a Curtain," *Tom Paine, Common Sense*, http://www.tompaine.com/feature.cfm/ID/5608 (accessed November 3, 2003).

67. Linda Greenhouse, "High Court Kills Law Banning Guns in a School Zone," *New York Times*, April 27, 1995, pp. A1, D24; "Mike's Message," http://michaelmoore.com/wprds/message/index.php?,essaeDate=2002-10-25.

68. Fox Butterfield, "Limits on Power and Zeal Hamper Firearms Agency," *New York Times*, July 22, 1999, p. A19; Jack Bergman and Julia Reynolds, "The Guns of Opa-Locka: How U.S. Dealers Arm the World," *Nation*, December 2, 2002, p. 21.

69. David G. Anderson, "Assault Rifles Dirt Cheap and Legal!" *New York Times Magazine*, May 24, 1998, pp. 36–38.

70. Frank Bruni, "Senate Narrowly Recrafts Plan to Restrict Gun-Show Sales," *New York Times,* May 13, 1999, pp. A1, A28.

71. Nichols D. Kristof, "Gun Show Fantasies," *New York Times*, June 4, 2002; "Bush Snuffs Bill Banning Anti-Gun Lawsuits," *New York Times*, June 19, 1999.

72. Linda Greenhouse, "U.S., in a Shift, Tells Justices Citizens Have a Right to Guns," *New York Times*, May 8, 2002, p. A1; Bob Herbert, "More Guns for Everyone!" *New York Times*, May 9, 2002, p. A39; Stacy Sullivan, "Shopping for Sniper Rifles," *New York Times*, October 20, 2002, p. 11; "Questions for Ashcroft," *Nation*, July 8, 2001, http://www.thenation.com/doc.mhtml?I=20010716&c=2&s=friedman0129 (accessed February 12, 2003).

73. John Tierney, "A New Push to Grant Gun Industry Immunity From Suits," *New York Times*, April 4, 2003, p. A12.

74. Edmund L. Andrews, "Deep Shock in Germany, Where Guns Are Rare, *New York Times*, April 28, 2002, p. 13; "Mass Killing in Germany Spurs Action to Curb Guns," *New York Times*, May 7, 2002, p. A14. The latter article also mentions how German officials are blaming violent video games for this event.

75. Zimring and Hawkins, *Crime Is Not the Problem*, pp. 122–23.

Chapter 3

INEQUALITY IN THE UNITED STATES

C lass, racial/ethnic, and gender inequality are the three major types of inequality we shall be discussing in relationship to violence. They are intertwined. American ideology emphasizes that individuals are each responsible for their own fate. In reality, however, a person is born into a family that has a given income level, and we do not choose either our gender or our ethnic heritage. Each of these factors has a profound impact on the opportunities available to us, the quality of our lives, our own contribution to violence, and our vulnerability to violence.

CLASS INEQUALITY IN THE UNITED STATES

Economic inequality affects virtually every aspect of Americans' lives.[1] It is probably clear to readers of this book that there are differences in income, material possessions, and in who has the power and the ability to make important decisions. We shall use the term *class* to mean groups of people who have a similar relationship to the economic resources of the society and who, because of that, share a similar lifestyle.

Economic resources come in two forms: income and wealth. Income means payments received regularly, such as wages, social security, welfare, and the like. Wealth refers to assets possessed, what you own that can be bought and sold. Stocks, bonds, and real estate are important forms of wealth in the United States. Wealth produces income in the form of dividends, interest, and rents. The higher your income, the more wealth you can accumulate; the more wealth you have, the higher your income is likely to be. Households differ in their amount of income, but even more dramatically in their wealth.

For most people, their occupation is the principle determinant of their income. Sociologists often use the occupation of the chief earner in the household to assign that household a position in the class structure. Occupations are the sources not only of earners' incomes but also of their position in the economic authority structure, a measure of their power; and occupations are the sources of prestige or social esteem, which is also unequally distributed in class societies. People may have similar incomes, but the conditions under which they work and the esteem they receive may be different. A well-paid factory worker and an assistant professor at a university, for example, might have similar yearly incomes, but the professor will have much more autonomy and control over his or her daily work life, more prestige, and, most likely, greater job satisfaction.

Using the source of income and authority position, we can identify the classes in the United States as shown in table 3.1.

We will consider each of these classes in turn. The capitalist class owns the economic resources in the form of stocks, bonds, and real estate. Many corporate executives are capitalists, but not all capitalists are executives: it is the ownership, not management, of the means of production that puts a family or individual in this class. Over 80 percent of the U.S. population is in the bottom four categories—middle, working, working poor, and underclass. Even the 14 percent in the upper-middle class depends on wages.

Differences in wages and lifestyles can mask the fact that most of us rely on paychecks to support our households and ourselves. The exception is the very small capitalist class that has a large amount of wealth as well as income. While about half of all American households now own stock, the top 10 percent of these owners possess 82 percent of all shares. An example of this lopsidedness comes from looking at the Bass family of oil billionaires. When the stock market took a sharp fall in 2001, they wanted to raise some money. To do this they sold 135 million shares of their Walt Disney stock.[2]

If you have enough assets, you can be rich even without working. On the other hand, if you do work, you may be in any of the other classes, including the poorest. The working poor have the least job security. When they lose their jobs, they often become part of what is now often termed the underclass.[3]

TABLE 3.1
CLASS COMPOSITION OF THE UNITED STATES, 2000

class	typical occupations	percent of households	typical household income, 2000
capitalist	top-level executives	1%	$2 million
upper-middle	upper managers, professionals, medium-sized business owners	14%	$120,000
middle	lower managers, semiprofessionals, nonretail sales workers	30%	$55,000
working	operatives, low-paid craftspeople, clerical and retail sales workers	30%	$35,000
working poor	service workers, laborers, some operatives, clerical workers	13%	$22,000
underclass	unemployed or part-time workers	12%	$12,000

Source: Based on Dennis Gilbert, *The American Class Structure in an Age of Growing Inequality,* 6th edition, (Belmont, CA: Wadsworth/Thompson Learning, 2003), p. 270.

The underclass is made up of those people who have the most tenuous connection to the labor force. The term has become controversial since it is sometimes used to refer mainly to blacks, with the implication that their problems are a result of a unique pathology.[4] If members of the underclass have work, it is sporadic. They may be paid off the books and usually receive no benefits. Government transfer payments, such as welfare, are an important part of their household resources. Used in this way, the term points to our need to understand what puts African Americans dispropor-tionately into this category, while recognizing that whites can also be mem-bers of the underclass. There is no need to assume that personal flaws or community pathologies create the underclass, or that only persons of color can be in this class.[5]

MORE CLASS INEQUALITY

Since the 1970s, those at the top have increased their share of the national income and their ownership of assets, while those at the bottom have found their position worsening. Between 1981 and 1994 there was a 50 percent increase in the percentage of Americans who, in spite of working full-time year round, were making less than a poverty-level wage.[6] This rise in inequality reverses decades of trends toward greater economic equality. In 1929 the richest 15 percent of the population had 17 percent of all income in the United States. This decreased to 12 percent in 1941, and to 10 percent in 1946.[7]

The trend toward greater inequality was accelerated during the 1980s when Ronald Reagan acted like a reverse Robin Hood. As a union tune put it, "Take it from the needy and give it to the greedy. That's what Ronald Reagan says." Of course, no president makes policies on his own; the rest of his administration and Congress were his merry men (mostly), creating and enacting the legislation allowing inequality to increase, a pattern that continued through the 1990s. After analyzing data from the Congressional Budget Office (CBO) priorities, economists Robert Greenstein and Isaac Shapiro concluded that "the [richest] top 1 percent of the population received a larger share of the national after-tax income in 2000 than at any time in the past seventy years." The data reveal "extraordinary" increases for the richest 1 percent whose "after-tax income . . . increased a stunning 201 percent" between 1979 and 2000. No other income group came anywhere near this.[8]

One way to get a picture of this increase in economic inequality is to divide the population into income fifths or quintiles and to examine what percentage of the national income each fifth is receiving. If there were complete equality, each 20 percent of the population would be receiving 20 percent of the national income, and ranking could not occur. There are also data telling us what share the top 5 percent has. Table 3.2 gives us this information.

TABLE 3.2 MONEY INCOME OF FAMILIES, BY QUINTILE AND RICHEST 5 PERCENT: 1973–2000

	1973	1980	1990	2000
Top 5%	16%	15%	17%	21%
highest fifth	41%	42%	44%	47%
fourth fifth	24%	24%	24%	23%
third fifth	18%	18%	17%	16%
second fifth	12%	12%	11%	10%
bottom fifth	5%	5%	5%	4%

Sources: For 1973, Gerald Kloby, "Increasing Class Polarization in the United States: The Growth of Wealth and Income Inequality," in *Critical Perspectives in Sociology,* ed. Berch Berberoglu (Dubuque, IA: Kendell/Hunt Publishing, 1991), pp. 39–53. For 1980, 1990, and 2000, U.S. Bureau of the Census, *Statistical Abstract of the United States, 2002,* table 659, p. 437.

Most working people have seen a decline in their real wages because prices have risen faster than the average paycheck. The wages of those at the top, however, have been increasing, and wages are not their only source of compensation. From 1947 to 1973 many wage earners experienced an increase in their real earnings of about 2 percent each year.[9] This trend has been reversed. Between the early 1970s and the 1990s real wages fell by a total of about 19 percent.[10] The richest 1 percent of all taxpayers received 20 percent of the country's income pie in 1999, an 8 percent increase since 1986, giving them an average income of $914,871.[11]

EXECUTIVES DO BETTER THAN EVER

Corporate executives are one of the very few groups that saw substantial increases between 1970 and 2000. In the ten-year period between 1990 and the end of the century, worker pay rose by 37 percent while CEO pay went up by 571 percent. Inflation during this period increased by 32 percent. CEOs, on the average, now make about 531 times as much as a typical factory worker. In 2000 a typical blue-collar worker made about $24,668. If this person's wages had gone up as much as a typical CEO's, that figure would be $120,491.[12]

Below are compensation figures for some CEOs whose companies or economic areas are mentioned in this book, for example, those in the healthcare and weapons industries. The name of the CEO for 2002 is also

TABLE 3.3. EXECUTIVE COMPENSATION IN 2002: TOTAL OF SALARY, BONUS, STOCK OPTIONS, AND OTHER

company	name	salary	per week	per hour
Aetna	John W. Rowe	$15,575,182	$299,522.73	$7,488.07
Boeing	Philip M. Condit	$3,877,955	$ 74,576.00	$1,864.40
Bristol-Myers Squibb	Peter R. Dolan	$8,491,360	$163,295.38	$4,082.38
Cigna	H. Edward Hanway	$10,493,642	$201,800.00	$5,045.00
General Electric	Jeffrey R. Immelt	$22,678,705	$436,128.94	$10,903.22
Johnson & Johnson	William C. Weldon	$10,067,126	$193,598.57	$4,839.96
Lockheed Martin	Vance D. Coffman	$21,751,248	$418,293.23	$10,457.33
Merck	Raymond V. Gilmartin	$14,008,165	$269,387.00	$6,734.69
Pfizer	Henry A. McKinnell Jr.	$23,562,248	$453,120.00	$11,328.00
United Technologies	George David	$13,618,771	$261,899.44	$6,547.86

Source: New York Times, sec. 3, Money and Business, April 6, 2003, pp. 8–9. Author's calculation of weekly and hourly wages. The average total compensation for the CEOs of the 200 companies that the New York Times published data for was $10,833,076.

identified. In order to highlight how high their remuneration is, we have calculated what it would be if it were given on a weekly or hourly basis, assuming a forty-hour workweek.

By way of comparison, the average compensation for a CEO in Japan is $189,228. In 1999 for every $1 earned by an average worker, a Japanese CEO earned $10. In 2000 this had increased to $12. In 1999 for every $1 earned by an average American worker, an American CEO earned $165. In 2000 this had increased to $180.[13]

Even some high-placed financiers have warned against this trend. The president of the Federal Reserve Bank, William J. McDonough, speaking at an anniversary event of the September 11 attack, warned, "Executive pay is excessive." The big increases over a twenty-year period are "terribly bad social policy and perhaps even bad morals."[14] A very few wealthy individuals and businesspeople have even formed an organization called Responsible Wealth, which agitates for fairer tax laws and critiques executive excess.

UNION MEMBERSHIP DECLINES

The rise in economic inequality reflects another kind of inequality, that of power, the ability to make decisions that affect people's living conditions, actions, and beliefs. In a capitalist society, where employers essentially control the economic resources and decide how these will be used, workers need strong organizations to protect themselves. Part of the explanation for the increase in inequality is the decrease in union membership. With fewer workers in unions, workers are weaker relative to their employers.[15]

On the average the median weekly earnings of unionized workers are higher than for those not in unions. Women, African Americans, and Latinos especially gained from union membership, as table 3.4 shows.

TABLE 3.4. MEDIAN WEEKLY EARNINGS OF FULL-TIME WAGE AND SALARIED WORKERS: JANUARY 2003

men		women		African American		Latinos	
union	nonunion	union	nonunion	union	nonunion	union	nonunion
$740	$587	$667	$510	$615	$477	$623	$408

Source: AFL-CIO (from U.S. Department of Labor), http://www/aflcio.org/aboutunions/joinunions/why join (accessed April 1, 2003).

Benefits were also better for those in unions.

TABLE 3.5 BENEFITS FOR UNION AND NONUNION WORKERS, 1999

Percent Having Selected Benefits		
	union	nonunion
health benefits	73%	51%
pensions	79%	44%
disability	66%	33%

Source: AFL-CIO (from Bureau of Labor Statistics), Web site as above.

By fighting for better working conditions, such as a five-day workweek, occupational health and safety regulations, and so on, unions have benefited even those not in union jobs.

But as we indicated, and table 3.5 shows, the percentage of unionized workers has been steadily shrinking.

TABLE 3.6 THE DECLINE IN UNION MEMBERSHIP

Percent of Labor Force Who Are Union Members

1946	1960	1970	1980	1983	1994	2003
36%	24%	23%	23%	20%	16%	13%

Sources: For 1946, Murray Chass, "As Trade Unions Struggle, Their Sports Cousins Thrive," New York Times, September 5, 1994, p. 1; 1960, 1970, U.S. Census Bureau, Statistical Abstract of the United States, 1980, table 714, p. 429; 1980, Statistical Abstract of the United States, 1987, table 692, p. 408; 1983 and 1994, Statistical Abstract of the United States, 2002, table 695, p. 443; 2003, Steven Greenhouse, "Worried about Labor's Waning Strength, Union Presidents Form Advisory Committee," New York Times, March 9, 2003, p. 22.

Furthermore, public employees are more likely to be unionized than those in the private sector. In 2001, 37 percent of government workers but only 9 percent of those in the private sector belonged to unions.[16]

If unions are so good for workers, then how can this decline be explained? One reason is that many of the jobs held by blue-collar union members have been moved overseas, a result of corporate relocation of manufacturing. One example will illustrate the point, which will be discussed further in chapter 8 when we look at the implications of unemployment for violence. Thousands of jobs in the garment trades have been transferred to low-wage countries such as El Salvador and China. Between 1970 and 1990 this industry lost 335,000 jobs in the United States.[17] Concomitantly, membership in the principle organizations that represented these workers, the International Ladies Garment Workers Union and the American Clothing and Textile Workers Union, went from having 967,000 members in 1972 to 276,000 in 1993, a 71 percent drop.[18]

Employers—with government complicity—have made unionization more difficult. In the United States it was not until the 1930s that workers gained some legal protections for the right to form unions, and to strike. Before this, "trade unions were treated as a criminal conspiracy." There is now a National Labor Relations Act that makes it illegal for employers to interfere with workers exercising their rights to form collective bargaining organizations. Yet the United States lags behind other countries in what rights workers have. For example, employers here have the legal right to replace striking workers, weakening that tactic.[19]

When President Ronald Reagan fired striking air controllers in 1981, he served notice of what his administration's stance toward unions would be. George W. Bush has also shown a hostility toward labor unions. Officials in his administration as well as the president himself have invoked the value of national security in overturning one of the most important protections workers have, the right to collectively bargain with their employer.

Protecting America from terrorism is a new rationale for weakening unions. In early 2002 the president issued an executive order prohibiting unions at several agencies of the Justice Department. He justified the action, affecting about one thousand workers, as necessary to protect national security. The American Federation of State, County, and Municipal Employees (AFSME) had represented the majority of the workers. Steve Kreisberg, an associate director at AFSCME, criticized the action: "We're outraged by this. A lot of these Justice Department workers have been members of unions for twenty years and there's never been an allegation of a problem. It's a very cynical use of the September 11 tragedy by an antiunion administration."[20]

The head of the Transportation Security Administration, Adm. James Loy, denied airport screeners the right to collective bargaining. He justified this by saying, "Fighting terrorism demands a flexible workforce that can rapidly respond to threats."[21] No official has presented evidence showing that unions are a threat to national security. Without collective bargaining, there are few ways workers can protect their families' economic security.

Private companies have their own strategies to discourage workers from unionizing in the first place. Some hold compulsory antiunion meetings and post antiunion literature where workers are sure to see it. A more drastic measure is for an employer to move its facilities if workers unionize. Kate Bronfenbrenner, director of labor education research at Cornell University, has studied the relationship between capital mobility and unionization. She found that in manufacturing and communications 62 percent of employers who were involved in the process to permit workers to vote on whether or not to join a union "threatened to shut down all or part of their operations if workers voted for a union." Fifteen percent actually did carry out this threat after a successful unionization drive.[22]

Wal-Mart provides an example of how a company keeps workers from unionizing. This is a particularly significant example since Wal-Mart is now the world's largest retailer, employing one million workers in its 3,300 stores in the United States. A retail outlet cannot credibly threaten to move its stores overseas, but it can fire active union supporters and impose financial sanctions such as no bonuses if workers unionize. The company also distributes a handbook to managers entitled "The Manager's Toolbox to Remaining Union Free," which, among other advice, tells them to be alert for prounion activities.

Workers do have rights to organize, and sometimes they receive federal protection. In the case of a Las Vegas Wal-Mart, the company was found to have illegally confiscated union literature, intimidated workers, and denied a prounion worker a promotion.[23]

The labor movement also bears some responsibility for the low levels of union membership. Kate Bronfenbrenner has studied union organizing for two decades. She concludes that unions need, for example, to put more resources into organizing campaigns, developing leadership skills among workers, and pressuring employers, especially larger businesses. Unions need, in her words, to "make the cost of fighting the union greater than the cost of recognizing the union." When more aggressive campaigns are waged, she says, the evidence shows that a unionization drive is far more likely to be successful.[24]

TAXATION POLICIES PROMOTE INEQUALITY

The government can use its taxation power to influence the distribution of income. Since the late 1970s, and especially during the Reagan years, the richest 1 percent of the population greatly benefited from changes in the tax laws. Corporations have used their considerable resources to ensure that tax laws favor them and their executives.

While corporate profits rose between 1980 and 1986, taxes on these profits fell at both the federal and state levels.[25] In 1945, corporations provided 50 percent of federal tax revenues; in 1960, 24 percent; in 1970, 18 percent; in 1980, 13 percent; and in 2001, 8 percent.[26] In some years a few corporations have paid no taxes at all. Michael Parenti summarizes the inequities in the tax system by noting that the "working mother with two children, earning $5,000, pays more taxes in a year than any number of giant transnational corporations." The government actually has negotiated treaties that allow corporations to set up headquarters in a country that has no income tax, send their profits there, and greatly reduce their tax burden.[27]

The same pattern of declining corporate tax receipts exists at the state level.[28] Corporations are able to take advantage of what one critic describes as "thousands of loopholes" not available to individual taxpayers. In 1998 General Motors, taking advantage of these, had $4.6 billion in profits but paid less than 1 percent of this in taxes. Some corporations wind up not only paying little or even no taxes but also getting refunds. In 1998 Texaco, Goodyear, and Enron were given rebates.[29]

The wealthiest individuals and households also are able to benefit from the way the tax law is written. In 1999, 2,500 of the very wealthiest individuals, with average incomes of $389,000, paid no federal taxes at all. In May 2003, changes were made in the federal tax code that will further increase income inequality by providing tax breaks that principally benefit corporations and the wealthy.[30] The Bush administration, which championed the new taxation scheme, claimed the changes would spur investment and create jobs. Ten Nobel laureates in economics and hundreds of other economists published a full-page ad in the *New York Times* asserting, these "Tax Cuts Are the Wrong Approach" to dealing with fiscal problems. As the next chapter will discuss, it is not what is best for the country but what is best for Bush's wealthy supporters that drives this policy.[31]

The Internal Revenue Service (IRS) has been more zealous in hunting down cheating by individual taxpayers than by corporate defrauders. *New York Times* reporter David Cay Johnson noted that "the IRS audits the working poor more frequently than the wealthy" and this "is well known." The paper's own study of IRS data concluded that "the agency does not track nonwage income [this goes mainly to higher income individuals] as close as wage income—and in some cases does not verify it at all even as the IRS says that cheating on nonwage income is rising."[32]

The IRS under the Bush administration is going to be making it harder for low-income, working-poor tax filers to receive a tax credit, which in the past has helped diminish the numbers in poverty. To qualify for this, a household must have an income below $34,693. If the tax filers meet certain requirements, they get a check, which in 2001 averaged about $2,000 if there were children in the house. In the future, to receive this money people will have to provide often-difficult-to-obtain documents. In 1999 the IRS lost between $9 billion and $10 billion by paying the low-income tax credits to those who did not actually meet the eligibility requirements. In contrast, corporations were able to conceal billions in profits, reducing their collective tax bill by about $54 billion.[33]

One result of this tax inequity is that less money is available for households to take care of their families' needs. On a wider scale, there is less for social programs, which, in turn, affects the amount of violence in the United States, as we shall show later.

The increase in income inequality has also meant that it is more necessary for many households to have two wage earners. The United States is unique among other industrial nations in having the highest proportion of two-earner households. In the absence of reliable, affordable daycare, this can lead to putting children at risk in makeshift arrangements. In 2001, 63 percent of married women with children under the age of six were working. In 1970, the figure was 30 percent. There are racial differences resulting from the lower incomes of African American households. In 2001, looking at married women with the husband in the house and children under the age of three, 59 percent of white women were working, compared to 72 percent of black women.[34]

Americans also work more hours than their counterparts elsewhere, according to both the International Labor Organization, part of the United Nations, and U.S. government sources. In 1999 the Bureau of Labor Statistics said the average American was working over 350 hours a year more than workers in comparable countries. For example in 1997–1998 the average American worked 1,966 hours a year; his Japanese counterpart worked 1,889, while the typical German employee was at work 1,560 hours. All this means less time for caring for one's family and one's self. This is compounded by American workers having shorter vacations and less paid family leave.[35] Workers in the United States are also working more hours than used to be the case. One study found that between 1980 and 2000 the average U.S. worker added 83 hours to his or her work year.[36]

ETHNIC AND RACIAL INEQUALITY

In the United States people are still treated differently based on their "race" or ethnicity. While their social significance is great, the physical differences used to group people into "races" are superficial. Furthermore, these differences are also so overlapping that clear categorization is impossible. Ethnicity refers to groups with common ancestries and does not carry the same connotations of biological differences. Popular perception and government statistical tables use both the concepts of race and of ethnicity; therefore, we will use both terms here.

Polls conducted to determine people's perceptions of racial inequality show a consistent result: most whites think racial discrimination has been largely overcome, whereas most African Americans believe it persists. Can we tell which answer is more accurate? There have been significant changes since the 1950s and the days of legal segregation. Antidiscrimination laws have been passed and to some extent enforced. African Americans are more visibly present in the media and in certain occupations, such as bank tellers, clerks, and government employees. Occupational inequality, however, persists. By 1983 affirmative action efforts had been in effect for over ten years, and there was emerging talk of "reverse discrimination." Yet African Americans were then, as they are now, under-represented in better-paying positions, as shown in table 3.7

TABLE 3.7 PERCENT OF OCCUPATION AFRICAN AMERICAN—1983 AND 2001

	1983	2001
total percent of labor force	9	11
managerial/professional	6	8
natural scientists	3	5
architects	2	3
engineers	3	6
lawyers/ludges	3	5
doctors	3	5
dentists	2	4
nurses	7	10
college teachers	4	6
elementary school teachers	11	11
social workers	18	25
athletes	9	10
sales occupations	5	9
file clerks	16	14
postal clerks	26	36
craft jobs	7	8
firefighters	7	13
police/detectives	13	17
kitchen work/food preparation	14	11
janitors and building cleaners	23	21

Source: U.S. Bureau of the Census, *Statistical Abstract of the United States, 2002*, table 588, pp. 381–83.

Since occupation and income are closely linked, it is not surprising that there are sharp income differences between whites, blacks, and Latinos, as shown in table 3.8.

TABLE 3.8. MEDIAN INCOME OF FAMILIES AND ETHNICITY

	1980	2000
white	$45,583	$53,256
black	$25,218	$34,192
Hispanic	$29,281	$35,054
black income as % of white income	55%	63%
Hispanic income as % of white income	64%	66%

Source: U.S. Bureau of the Census, *Statistical Abstract of the United States, 2002,* table 657, p. 436. Median income is in constant dollars. Percents are author's calculations.

The above figures do not take educational difference into consideration. Yet even when years of schooling are the same, income inequality persists, as shown in table 3.9.

TABLE 3.9 EDUCATION, RACE/ETHNICITY, AND ANNUAL INCOME: 2002

	not a high school grad	high school	some college	bachelor's degree	doctorate degree
white	$16,623	$25,270	$27,674	$46,894	$87,746
black	$13,569	$20,991	$24,101	$37,422	$75,509
Hispanic	$16,106	$20,704	$23,115	$36,212	NA

Source: U.S. Census Bureau, *Statistical Abstract of the United States, 2002,* table 211, p. 140.

In addition, African Americans have higher unemployment rates than whites and Latinos, even when they share the same educational level. Whites with only a high school education had an unemployment rate of 4 percent in 2001 and so did Latinos. For African American high school graduates the rate was 8 percent.[37]

Education itself is not usually equal. The schooling that African Americans, and often Latinos, receive is of much lower quality than that received by their white counterparts. What Jonathan Kozol calls the "savage inequalities" of the education system put African Americans at a further disadvantage in the labor market.[38] This has implications for who will become a street criminal, discussed in chapters 9 and 10.

GENDER INEQUALITY

Gender is the third important basis of inequality. White women have been the principle beneficiaries of affirmative-action legislation, and as a group have improved their occupational representation more than African Americans, but dramatic gender-based occupational differences still remain, as shown in table 3.10.

TABLE 3.10
PERCENT OF OCCUPATION FEMALE—1983 AND 2001

	1983	2001
total percent of labor force participation	44	47
managerial/professional	41	50
natural scientists	21	34
architects	13	24
engineers	6	10
lawyers/judges	15	29
doctors	16	29
dentists	7	20
nurses	96	93
dental hygienists	99	98
college teachers	36	43
elementary school teachers	83	83
social workers	64	72
secretaries	99	98
bank tellers	81	84
sales occupations	48	49
athletes	18	27
craft jobs	8	9
firefighters	1	3
police/detectives	6	14
kitchen work/food preparation	77	71
private household workers	96	96

Source: U.S. Census Bureau, *Statistical Abstract of the United States, 2002*, table 588, pp. 381–83.

Ethnicity and gender interact to affect a household's income levels. Table 3.11 shows that in each racial/ethnic category, women are earning less than men.

TABLE 3.11 MEDIAN INCOME OF PERSONS WITH INCOME BY RACE/ETHNICITY AND GENDER, 2000

race/gender	earnings	earnings as a percentage of white male earnings
white men	$31,213	100%
black men	$21,659	69%
Hispanic men	$19,829	64%
white women	$16,804	54%
black women	$16,084	51%
Hispanic women	$12,249	39%

Source: U.S. Census Bureau, *Statistical Abstract of the United States, 2002*, table 665, p. 440. Author's calculation of percentages.

Education does not cancel the differences. In 2000 the average earnings of males with a BA or more who were full-time workers was $77,963. For females with the same level of education, the figure was $47,224, or 61 percent of the male earnings.[39]

Because many working women are in lower-paying occupations or find it difficult to work full-time because of childcare responsibilities, households that are dependent on women's wages have lower incomes.

Aging women, especially if they are single, have economic disadvantages that reflect a lifetime of income differences with males. In general, older women have less social security than the average man of the same age because they were less likely to have held jobs that provided pension plans. In 2000, 46 percent of male workers could expect a pension, in itself not a very high percentage, but for women the figure was 43 percent.[40]

People of color, male and female, and white women share disadvantages as we have seen. In the next two chapters we will discuss power in the United States. People of color and women are underrepresented in these levels, whether we are looking at economic or political positions. Subsequent chapters will look at how race/ethnicity and gender are related to vulnerability to violence.

NOTES

1. For very detailed data on the aspects of inequality discussed below see Lawrence Mishel, Jared Bernstein, and Heather Boushey, *The State of Working America, 2002/2003* (Ithaca, NY: ILR Press, an imprint of Cornell University Press, 2003).

2. Stock ownership figures from U.S. Census Bureau, *Statistical Abstract of the United States, 2002*, table, 1185, p. 737; Doug Henwood, "The Nation Indicators," *Nation*, April 9, 2001; Gretchen Morgenson and Riva D. Atlas, "Bass Family in Need of Money, Forced to sell 6.4% of Disney," *New York Times*, September 21, 2001, p. C1.

3. Discussions of this term can be found in James Jennings, *Understanding the Nature of Poverty in America* (Westport, CN: Praeger, 1994), pp. 123–32; Michael B. Katz, ed., *The 'Underclass' Debate: The View from History* (Princeton, NJ: Princeton University Press, 1993); Bill E. Lawson, ed., *The Underclass Question* (Philadelphia: Temple University Press, 1992); William J. Wilson, *The Truly Disadvantaged: The Inner City, the Underclass, and Public Policy* (Chicago: University of Chicago Press, 1987); William J. Wilson, "The Ghetto Underclass: Social Science Perspectives," *Annals of the American Academy of Political and Social Science* 501 (1989).

4. There is a need, however, for a word that refers to the people Karl Marx called the lumpenproletariat, those whose work lives are insecure to a greater extent than other workers. Jacqueline Jones, *The Dispossessed: America's Underclasses from the Civil War to the Present* (New York: Basic Books, 1992), p. 2; Herbert Gans, "Deconstructing the Underclass," in *Race, Class, and Gender in the United States*, ed. Paula Rothenberg, 3rd ed. (New York: St. Martin's Press, 1995), pp. 51–57; Dennis Gilbert, *The American Class Structure in an Age of Growing Inequality*, 5th ed. (Belmont, CA: Wadsworth Publishing Company, 1998), pp. 290–91.

5. For a discussion of how structural and cultural aspects can both be involved in the characteristics of the underclass, see Michael Morris, "Culture, Structure, and the Underclass," in *Myths about the Powerless*, ed. M. Brinton Lykes et al. (Philadelphia: Temple University Press, 1996), pp. 39–42.

6. Jason DeParle, "Sharp Increase along the Borders of Poverty," *New York Times*, March 31, 1994, p. A18.

7. Kevin Phillips, *Wealth and Democracy* (New York: Broadway Books, 2002), p. 71.

8. Center on Budget and Policy Priorities, "The New, Definitive CBO Data on Income and Tax Trends," September 23, 2003, pp. 2, 5.

9. Gary Burtless, "Introduction and Summary," in *A Future of Lousy Jobs: The Changing Structure of U.S. Wages*, ed. Gary Burtless (Washington, DC: Brookings Institution, 1990), pp. 2, 18; Edward N. Wolf, *Top Heavy: A Study of the Increasing Inequality of Wealth in America* (New York: Twentieth Century Fund, 1995), pp. v–vi.

10. "Globalization and the Downsizing of the American Dream," *Global Exchanges* 27, special insert (Summer 1996): 2.

11. "What Did They Do to Deserve All This?" *Too Much* (Summer 2002): 1.

12. "The 1990s: A Stunning Summary," *Too Much* (Fall 2001): 6.

13. Ken Belson, "Learning How to Talk about Salary in Japan," *New York Times*, April 7, 2002, p. 12.

14. Quoted in David Leonhardt and Andrew Ross Sorking, "Reining In the Imperial CEO," *New York Times*, September 15, 2002, sec. 3, p. 10.

15. McKinley L. Blackburn, David E. Bloom, and Richard B. Freeman, "The Declining Economic Position of Less Skilled Men," in Burtless, *A Future of Lousy Jobs*, pp. 60–62.

16. U.S. Census Bureau, *Statistical Abstract of the United States, 2002*, table 628, p. 411.

17. Edna Bonaich and David W. Waller, "Mapping a Global Industry: Apparel Production in the Pacific Rim Triangle," in *Global Production: The Apparel Industry in the Pacific Rim*, ed. Edna Bonaich et al. (Philadelphia: Temple University Press, 1994), p. 23.

18. 1972, U.S. Census Bureau, *Statistical Abstract of the United States, 1980*, table 713, p. 428; 1993, U.S. Census Bureau, *Statistical Abstract of the United States, 1994*, table 682, p. 438. These two unions have merged into the American Clothing and Textile Workers Union.

19. Human Rights Watch, "Unfair Advantage: Worker's Freedom of Association in the United States under International Human Rights Standards," pp. 2–3, http://www.hrw.org/reports/2000uslabor/ (accessed September 2002).

20. Steven Greenhouse, "Bush Citing Security, Bans Some Unions at Justice Dept." *New York Times*, January 16, 2002, p. A14.

21. David Bacon, "Screened Out: How 'Fighting Terrorism' Became a Bludgeon in Bush's Assault on Labor," *Nation*, May 12, 2003, p. 19.

22. Kate Bronfenbrenner, "Uneasy Terrain: The Impact of Capital Mobility on Workers, Wages, and Union Organizing," report submitted to the U.S. Trade Deficit Review Commission, September 6, 2000, p. 8.

23. Steven Greenhouse, "Trying to Overcome Embarrassment, Labor Opens a Drive to Organize Wal-Mart," *New York Times*, November 8, 2002, p. A28.

24. "Declining Unionization, Rising Inequality: An Interview with Kate Bronfenbrenner," *Multinational Monitor* (May 2003): 23.

25. Dan Clawson, Alan Neustadtl, and Denise Scott, *Money Talks: Corporate PACs and Political Influence* (New York: Basic Books, 1992), pp. 91–96; Lawrence Mischel, Jared Bernstein, and Heather Boushey, *The State of Working America, 1992–1993* (Armonk, NY: M. E. Sharp, 1993), p. 117; Kevin Phillips, *The Politics of Rich and Poor: Wealth and the American Electorate in the Reagan Aftermath* (New York: HarperPerennial, 1990), p. 150.

26. Michael Parenti, *Democracy for the Few*, 6th ed. (New York: St. Martin's Press, 1995), p. 81; for 1960, U.S. Census Bureau, *Statistical Abstract of the United States, 1980*, table 446, p. 268; 1980 and 2001, author's calculation based on U.S. Census Bureau, *Statistical Abstract of the United States, 2002*, table 454, p. 308. Phillips, *The Politics of Rich and Poor*, presents somewhat different figures, but the same trend of declining corporate taxes, p. 149.

27. Michael Parenti, *Democracy for the Few*, 7th ed. (New York: Bedford/St. Martin's Press, 2002), p. 73; David Cay Johnston, "Tax Treaties with Small

Nations Turn into a New Shield for Profits," *New York Times*, April 16, 2002, pp. A1, C2.

28. Phillips, *The Politics of Rich and Poor*, p. 150.

29. Greenstein and Shapiro, "The New, Definitive CBO Data on Income and Tax Trends," p. 12.

30. David Soll, "Corporate Taxes," *Z*, June 2002, p. 8.

31. Parenti, *Democracy for the Few*, 7th ed, pp. 72–73; David Cay Johnston, "Living Tax-Free at the Top Rungs," op-ed article, *New York Times*, August 28, 2002, sec. 3, p. 11; ad appeared February 11, 2003, p. A11.

32. David Cay Johnston, "Affluent Avoid Scrutiny on Taxes, Even as I.R.S. Warns of Cheating," *New York Times*, April 7, 2002, pp. 1, 25.

33. Mary Williams Walsh, "I.R.S. Tightening Rules for Low-Income Tax Credits," *New York Times*, April 25, 2003, pp. A1, C4.

34. U.S. Census Bureau, *Statistical Abstract of the United States, 2002*, tables 570 and 571, p. 373.

35. Phillips, *Wealth and Democracy*, pp. 163, 113.

36. Bronfenbrenner, "Uneasy Terrain," p. 3.

37. U.S. Census Bureau, *Statistical Abstract of the United States, 2002*, table 598, p. 390.

38. Jonathan Kozol, *Savage Inequalities: Children in America's Schools* (New York: HarperCollins, 1991).

39. U.S. Census Bureau, *Statistical Abstract of the United States, 2002*, table 666, p. 440 (author's calculation of percentages).

40. Ibid., table 526, p. 350.

4 SOCIAL CLASS AND ORGANIZATIONAL POWER

Capitalists are the most powerful class in our society, and that power is often used to maintain and expand their positions, even at the expense of those others in less privileged classes. Power is the ability to control resources and make decisions that impact many people. We will call those who fill the most powerful positions the elite. Financial capital is an important asset for achieving power. But if money cannot always buy happiness, it can't always buy power, either.

If some lucky reader of this book were to win successive large lotteries, for example, winding up with millions of dollars, that in itself would not make the reader part of the elite. Access to powerful positions is based on being part of the social networks from which elites are recruited, called social capital. Cultural capital, in the form of the right educational credentials and knowing how to speak, look, and behave, is also relevant.

If you are born into the capitalist class, these forms of capital are made available to you. You will be sent to private schools where you will meet people whose families run the major institutions in the United States or have access to those who do. If you are a male and wish to have a powerful position, it is likely you will be able to do so. However, even if you are a member of this class, if you are very liberal or radical, you will not become a part of the inner circle of decision makers. On the other hand, if your origins are working- or middle-class and you are able to further the corporate agenda, with the right opportunities you might become part of this class.[1]

Being a member of a social class means having a particular lifestyle. This extends throughout one's life. Corporate executives live in a "corporate community." As G. William Domhoff describes:

> They band together to develop their own social institutions—gated neighborhoods, private schools, exclusive social clubs, debutante balls, and secluded summer resorts.[2]

Especially important in preparing a small group for powerful positions are the elite boarding schools, "physically remote and socially exclusive," attended by less than 1 percent of all high school students.[3] Following this, future members of the elite are likely to attend prestigious, Ivy League colleges and universities, becoming members of exclusionary clubs, such as Skull and Bones at Yale.

At social clubs, the members, mostly white men, can meet informally, out of the public eye, to discuss economic and political issues and deepen their bonds. One of the most famous of these is the Bohemian Grove, located north of San Francisco. Presidents, cabinet members, CEOs, journalists, academics, and figures from the worlds of art and entertainment can network while enjoying a luxurious break from their work lives.[4]

These institutions help create cohesion and class consciousness, and loyalty to one's classmates, in the social not pedagogical sense. In addition, as discussed in the next chapter, political figures and policymakers may be drawn from or become a part of these social circles. All concerned, then, are more able to act in the interests of the capitalist class, and these actions will seem natural.

There is an organizational aspect to power. Bureaucracies dominate life in the United States. Those who run the bureaucracies have great power, occupying what sociologist C. Wright Mills called the "command posts." While there are over 120 million jobs in the United States, only a tiny fraction of these are "command post" occupations: 5,416 positions or about .005 percent of the total occupations.[5]

The elite are the ones who fill the command post roles. In this book we are concerned with "elite deviance": actions of elites, or their subordinates following their directions, that lead to physical harm (violence) and that are also contrary to generally accepted ideas of what is ethical and moral.[6] Some of the acts may be illegal; others are not. An act is only illegal if it breaks a law, and because of their power, elites can shape what is lawful or not.

Edward Ross, one of the founders of American sociology, described the deviant behavior of the elite in 1907:

Today, the villain most in need of curbing is the respectable, exemplary, trusted personage who strategically placed . . . is able from his office-chair to pick a thousand pockets, poison a thousand sick [*sic*], pollute a thousand minds, or imperil a thousand lives.[7]

Criminologists Marshall B. Clinnard and Peter C. Yeager summarize the similar violence emanating from modern corporate elites:

It includes losses due to sickness and even death resulting from air and water pollution, and the sale of unsafe foods and drugs, defective autos, tires, and appliances, and hazardous clothing and other products. It also includes the numerous disabilities that result from injuries to plant workers, including contamination by chemicals that could have been used with adequate safeguards and the potentially dangerous effects of other work-related exposures.[8]

These are issues that will be discussed in subsequent chapters. Social scientists who study elite deviance agree that these actions by those occupying executive suites actually cost the public more and lead to more physical harm than do the crimes of those in the streets.[9]

For much of its early history, American criminology looked exclusively at the crimes of ordinary people, usually termed street crime. Pioneering work by Edwin Sutherland, starting in the late 1930s, helped focus attention on "white-collar" crime as well. Sutherland pointed out that no one debates the crookedness of the nineteenth century robber barons, the founders of many of today's corporations and banks. In 1890 J. P. Morgan told a gathering of railroad presidents, "I have the utmost respect for you gentlemen individually, but as railroad presidents I wouldn't trust you with my watch out of sight." The gangster Al Capone, Sutherland remarked, referred to businesses as "the legitimate rackets."[10] Folk balladeer Woody Guthrie sang, in a precomputer era, "Some will rob you with a six-gun and some with a fountain pen."

Though there are important studies of corporate crime, it has not been studied with the same detail as have street crimes, or even white-collar crime. Both these types of crime are committed by individuals seeking gain for themselves or a few others. In contrast, as Sally S. Simpson, a sociologist who has done research on this subject, notes, when corporate crimes occur, "illegality is not pursued for individual benefits but rather for *organizational* ends."[11] In addition, the victims of corporate crimes are not individuals or a single firm as with street crime and white-collar crime respectively. Rather, those harmed by corporate lawbreaking are large numbers including workers, communities, and consumers.[12]

Not all company actions that endanger lives, however, are against the law. Corporations are able to use their power, discussed in chapter 5 and below, to prevent the passage of laws that would make certain of their acts illegal. In the words of Russell Mokhiber, editor of the *Corporate Crime Reporter*:

> Corporate lawbreakers double as corporate lawmakers. Corporate America has saturated the legislatures with dollars in order to promote laws making legal or noncriminal what by any common standard of justice would be considered illegal and criminal, and to obstruct legislation that would outlaw the violent activity.[13]

Street criminals are not able to affect the legislative process in this way.

Still, business is not free to do whatever it wishes. Largely due to public pressures, legislation has been passed to protect workers, consumers, and the environment. While these laws do make a difference, companies are often able to weaken or circumvent them or to avoid serious consequences from breaking them. For example, in the 1960s "when Congress passed the auto safety law . . . industry lobbyists defeated an effort to add criminal sanctions to the bill for knowing or willful violations."[14] About thirty years later, when the Justice Department was considering larger fines for corporate lawbreakers, business successfully lobbied to prevent it.[15] The Omnibus Crime Bill passed in 1994 says nothing about corporate crime and allots no money for fighting it.[16]

Federal and state prosecutors have the option of taking a corporate lawbreaker to civil or criminal court, and the former is usually the choice. This means that much of the time there is no jury of ordinary people judging the companies. "Consent decrees" are used—the corporation does not have to admit or deny any wrongdoing but instead agrees to pay a fine and avoids negative publicity and being branded as criminal.[17]

The media, as mentioned in chapter 2, rarely dramatizes tales of corporate misdoing to viewers and readers. Corporate executives may express concern about street crime but not about their own illegal behavior. In October 1994 at the annual meeting of the Business Council, an organization of the country's largest businesses, the CEO of Pepsico observed, "I think most of us feel that violence and crime is a real issue for the country, if not the number 1 issue." The gathering listened to a number of presentations on crime from professors and the police commissioner of New York City. No experts on corporate crime seem to have been invited.[18]

Executives and managers are evaluated and compensated in terms of how well they are helping the corporation to achieve its primary goal, maximizing profits. Thus their own financial worth is tied to the profitability of their companies. Sociologist Michael Useem studied seven of the nation's largest corporations. "More managerial income," he concluded, "was made contingent upon company or division performance in all of the companies," with performance judged by stock value.

Former Harvard president Derek Bok, in his study of executive compensation, confirms Useem's findings. Bok noted, "The ten-, twenty-, and fifty-million-dollar incomes that a few CEOs received in recent years were chiefly the result of stock options designed to motivate them to exert every effort on behalf of their shareholders."[19] Sociologists David James and Michael Soref, in their investigation of firings of top executives, found that "profit criteria appear to be the most important standard by which corporate chiefs are judged and dismissal is the ultimate sanction that conditions their behavior."[20]

CORPORATE POWER, COMMAND POSTS, AND VIOLENCE

Much of the violence in the United States is linked to the decisions of those in the economic and political command posts, with corporations being the most powerful bureaucracies not only in the United States but also in the world. Having control over investment funds and their own profits, corporations make decisions that affect many aspects of our lives. Sociologist Charles Derber aptly describes the corporation as " legal devices for concentrating capital of the many in the hands of the few."[21] Corporations have far greater resources than individuals.

There are corporations whose annual sales are greater than the gross domestic product (GDP) of many countries. In 1997 fifteen U.S.-based corporations were on the list of the one hundred largest economic entities on the planet. For example, the sales figures for General Motors were higher than the GDP of twenty-six countries, including Saudi Arabia, Colombia, Chile, and the Philippines. When Ford and General Motors's sales are combined, the figure for the two automotive giants exceeds "the GDP for all of sub-Saharan Africa."[22]

David Korten, author of *When Corporations Rule the World,* explains the advantages accruing to corporations as compared to individuals:

> The publicly traded, limited liability corporation is capitalism's institutional form of choice because it allows the virtually unlimited concentration of power with minimal public accountability or legal liability. Directors and officers are protected from financial liability for acts of negligence. . . . The same criminal act that would result in a stiff prison sentence, or even execution, if committed by an individual, brings a corporation only a fine—usually inconsequential in relation to corporate assets and likely less than what it gained by committing the infraction.[23]

George Gerbner, quoted in our discussion of the media, describes corporations as a "private government" making the final decisions in many areas of life without being accountable to those whose lives they have affected.[24] There is a history to this power. As industries grew following the Civil War, their owners sought to make themselves as powerful as they could. Among the famous names form this period are John D. Rockefeller, Andrew Carnegie, J. P. Morgan, and Cornelius Vanderbilt.

Although businesspeople from the nineteenth century to the present have opposed government regulation, their ascendancy was only possible because of government action on their behalf. As Derber explains, "Corporations became private governments with quasi-public powers, while government itself became a servant of private interests."[25] This was not always the case. For a time, early in the history of the United States, corporations were limited by state legislatures. But over time corporations became wealthier, aided by federal government actions such as awarding them huge amounts of land, giving them rights over resources, and engaging in military ventures that expanded and protect their power.

Decisions at the federal, state, and local levels favored their wishes over those of workers. Police actions and court decisions often benefited business rather than workers and consumers. The Supreme Court invested corporations with the rights of individual citizens, although the individuals running them were generally exempt from the responsibilities and sanctions that individuals face when they break laws.[26]

The government often used force against workers, not against their employers. There were numerous incidents of workers being physically attacked when they tried to improve horrific working conditions. Looking at labor organizing beginning in 1873, historian Robert J. Goldstein states that in some cases labor itself engaged in violence, but in the form of attacks on property not people, and generally in response to antiorganizing tactics of employers aided by government. He goes on to describes this class conflict:

The great bulk of violence leading to deaths and injuries was initiated by business and government and the great majority of casualties in labor disputes were suffered by workers. . . . Frequently, though not always, there was no apparent relationship between the degree of violence employed and provocations from workers. Another difference between labor violence and government-business violence was that government attempted to seek direct reprisals against workers involved in violence, by arrests, jailings, beatings, and sometimes shootings, while almost invariably those in business or government responsible for violence suffered no legal or other reprisals.[27]

Statistics show the human toll of this government bias. Between 1888 and 1908 seven hundred thousand American workers died as a result of unsafe workplaces.[28]

During this period many workers formed unions. Labor peace was better for business than frequent conflicts and so businesspeople tried to tame the labor movement rather than completely destroy it.[29] They have continued to try to maintain as much power as possible, however.

ORGANIZATIONAL ROLES

Are corporate executives and the politicians who are in command post positions and enact policies leading to violence hard-hearted, evil people? The problem is not as much with the personalities of individuals as it is with a structure of inequality that creates conditions conducive to violence.

Organizations prefer that people with authority not let their own feelings come in conflict with organizational goals. For instance, Robert McNamara, Lyndon Johnson's secretary of defense, was an architect of the Vietnam War and a former president of Ford Motor Company. Describing how he makes decisions, he explains, "I try to separate human emotions from the larger issue of human welfare. . . . I try not to let my human emotions interfere with efforts to resolve conflict."[30]

Capitalist culture encourages materialism and looking out for oneself. Of course, people learn many other values as well. Those who are most accepting of material success as a life goal are likely, if they have the opportunity, to move into the business world. Those with alternative value systems are less likely to seek management positions.[31] The executive editor of *Fortune* magazine describes the typical CEO as being equipped with "a particular set of blinders. Reflection and introspection don't help you pull the trigger on a $20 billion deal or lay off 10,000 employees. You can't waste time on self-doubts."[32] Formal organizations administer various tests to applicants for executive positions to make sure they have not only necessary skills but also the appropriate values and personality traits to meet the needs of the organization.[33]

Government agencies also want personnel who will fit in. The CIA, for example, seeks a person who, in the words of former agent Ralph McGehee, is a doer not a thinker, who is "self-centered and insensitive to others," and is "chameleon-like . . . all things to all people [with] the ability to spot weaknesses in others and use these to his advantage."[34]

Once in a management role, whether at the middle or the top, executives face pressures to accept the means and ends of the company. By the time they reach the top of the hierarchy, most executives have had many years of acting on behalf of an organization, rather than on the basis of their generally accepted morality, should there be any conflict.[35] Reaching goals set by the organization becomes part of their own motivations.

Organizations are sets of interrelated positions. Individuals are socialized to fit into those positions. If they do not, they will probably choose to leave, or they will be fired. Sociologists Ermann and Lundman explain:

> Elites have been socialized by the powerful experiences of working for decades in the world of the large organization. In addition, they are paid to think and act for an organization that can easily replace them should they consistently fail in their efforts to advance its interests.[36]

Social psychology experiments indicate that the role into which one is placed will influence behavior, regardless of one's individual ethics. One of the most famous role-taking experiments is Stanley Milgram's studies of obedience. Disturbed by the Adolph Eichmann trial and the typical Nazi justification of "I was only following orders," Milgram placed subjects in a situation where they were ordered to give shocks to a person—actually a confederate who was not really being shocked—supposedly to see the effect of pain on that person's capacity to memorize lists of paired words. Milgram wanted to know if subjects in a laboratory situation would obey a person whose only real authority came from being presented as a scientist. He was very disheartened to discover that a majority of the subjects, in spite of their own personal discomfort at their acts, did follow orders and gave what they thought were very painful shocks.

Milgram found something else that is relevant to behavior in bureaucracies: the subject's actions were influenced by the behavior of peers. If the peer didn't follow orders, the subject's obedience was much less likely. Alternatively, when there were peers following orders, the obedience rate rose. He concluded:

> When an individual wishes to stand in opposition to authority, he [*sic*] does best to find support for his [*sic*] position from others in his group. The mutual support provided by men [*sic*] for each other is the strongest bulwark we have against the excesses of authority.[37]

In another study students took the roles of drug company board members. They were confronted with a problem a company actually had: their organization had created a drug that was both profitable and dangerous. In this simulation, the students, like their real-life counterparts, tried to prevent the government from banning the product and would not withdraw it from the market.[38]

Diana Vaughn, an expert on the sociology of organizations, points out that "organizations while a great asset that allows us many modern efficiencies have their dark side." Their forms of organization and internal culture have a strong effect on the decisions of individuals who fill the organization's roles. These can lead to "harmful outcomes."[39]

In January 1986 excitement turned to horror as the space shuttle *Challenger* exploded seventy-three seconds after liftoff. Seven astronauts died, including Christa McAulliffe, a grade school teacher.

An investigation later revealed that Morton Thiokol, a major *Challenger* contractor, had allowed defective booster seals to be placed on the shuttle even though company engineers had warned that these might not hold at the low temperatures the craft would encounter. Under strong pressure from a team of senior-level executives and NASA officials to make the shuttle launch—and procure the renewal of the lucrative $400 million solid booster contract at stake—the vice president for engineering at Thiokol testified that he changed his position regarding the safety of the flight after being told "to shed his role as an engineer and take the role of a management person." Morton Thiokol was not the only culprit. Managers at Rockwell International, another shuttle contractor, had falsified reports on defective welding in order "to avoid the costs of rewelding," according to NASA's Inspector General's Office.[40]

Sixteen years later, on February 1, 2003, another space shuttle disaster occurred when the *Columbia* broke apart upon reentering the atmosphere. The seven astronauts on board, representing the United States, Israel, and India, were killed. An investigation by the *Columbia* accident investigation board noted that "cultural traits and organizational practices detrimental to safety and reliability were allowed to develop" at NASA.[41]

Although run by a government agency, the National Aeronautic and Space Agency (NASA), private for-profit contractors build and maintain the shuttle's equipment. Privatization of many aspects of government is a goal for corporations, both in the United States and with U.S. backing in other countries. Following the *Challenger* explosion, 78 percent of NASA's seven hundred technical and scientific personnel agreed with the statement "NASA has turned over too much of the basic engineering and science work to contractors."[42] The General Accounting Office, an agency of Congress, accused NASA of having only "weak" oversight over the contractors.[43]

In the case of the *Columbia*, Lockheed Martin and Boeing formed a consortium called the United Space Alliance to service shuttles. In turn, they subcontracted work to twenty-three other corporations including subsidiaries of Lockheed and Boeing. United Space Alliance would receive a bonus if it could perform under its allotted budget. Reducing the workforce was a way to achieve this goal. One plant managed by Lockheed had 4,800 workers at the beginning of 1986. By 2001 it had 2,040. The dismissed personnel included inspectors and testers of equipment. Many of those who lost their jobs could have provided valuable training to new hires.[44]

THE STRUCTURE AND CULTURE OF ORGANIZATIONS

Bureaucracies have powerful sanctions at their disposal. Keeping one's job, getting promoted, receiving material rewards or punishments, and peer approval or disapproval are all considerations for top and middle management. Self-interest for the decision makers, profit as a goal for the organization, and the structure of the organization all come together to produce the conditions that are associated with violence. In addition, there is an organizational culture discussed below that can promote harmful acts.

It seems harder for people to engage in violence when they identify with those they are harming. The structure of bureaucracies creates "distancing," which makes it easier to engage in actions that injure others. This effect takes several forms.

The Chain of Command

The structure of bureaucracies, corporate or government, means that some people in the organization are carrying out decisions made by those above them, while delegating responsibilities to subordinates. It is easier to deny responsibility for the consequences of decisions one has not made or for actions that one has not personally carried out. Furthermore, the farther down the chain of command a person is, the less responsibility he or she needs to feel for what is happening. Subordinates are just following orders. Many people are each doing a small part of a job that has been organized by others.

Because of the chain of command, employees routinely concentrate narrowly on their own jobs and can avoid thinking about the larger implications of their activities. When a lab technician at B. F. Goodrich confronted his supervisor over covering up faulty airplane brakes, the supervisor responded, "It's none of my business, and it's none of yours. I learned a long time ago not to worry about things over which I have no control. I have no control over this." When the technician pressed the point, the supervisor continued his justification of his own actions, saying, "I just told you I have no control over this thing. Why should my conscience bother me?"[45]

Social Distance

Elites are physically removed from the rest of the population. They lead highly privileged lives; they are unlikely to come face to face with those they may harm. Bureaucratic decision makers do not usually see the consequences of their actions.

Roger Smith, former General Motors chairman, presided over the devastating closing of a number of General Motors plants, including one in Flint, Michigan, and the destruction of a close-knit Polish neighborhood, Poletown, in Detroit to build a factory and a parking lot. Requested to visit these communities to see their pain and possibly reconsider his decisions, he refused, and there was no way to force him.[46] CEOs' private lives, as well as their corporate lives, encapsulate them in a sealed world of shared views. Executives themselves are aware of this. Sociologist Robert Jackall studied decision making by corporate executives. He quotes one on the possibilities of a chemical subsidiary causing cancer:

> Suppose ... you knew that fifty specific people were going to get skin cancer because you produced chloroflurocarbons. You would just stop

production. But suppose that you didn't know the fifty people and it wasn't at all clear that CFCs were . . . entirely at fault? What do you do then?[47]

Workers also understand the consequences of social distance. Donna Miller-Doyle, a New Jersey AT&T employee, feared being fired as the company laid off thousands of workers around the country. Workers at the giant communications corporation had taken job security for granted. Miller-Doyle was laid off but rehired. Reflecting on her future, she said, "I am glad to be back, but I wonder if the ax swings again if I'll be so lucky. I don't think upper management realizes what's happening. They seem too far removed."[48]

An unusual exception to this pattern made the news when the wife of a CEO at Hewlett-Packard died and he took over all her home and child-care responsibilities as well as doing his job. "Here I was a white male, doing really well at H.P. I was suddenly thrust into a different role." Comparing himself to the female employees, he said, "I couldn't cope any better than they did." He subsequently helped the company develop strategies to deal with women's double duties by creating flexible work schedules.[49]

Physical Distance

Even if not from a different social group, the person or persons committing the acts leading to violence may not have to see the effects of what they are doing.

Temporal Distance

There is often a time lag between when decisions are made and their consequences. For example, tobacco products cause cancer but only after many years. This makes it easier to argue that there are other possible causes for the illness than smoking.

Groupthink

Managers in bureaucracies spend their workdays surrounded by people who have a similar worldview, with each person reinforcing the views of everyone else. This mental conformity is sometimes referred to as "group-think," which has been described as "the deterioration of mental efficiency, reality testing, and moral judgment that results from in-group pressures."[50]

When they go home, the decision makers are still surrounded by like-minded people. The editor of *Car and Driver* magazine quotes a former GM executive's description of a life he shared with his peers in the posh Detroit suburb of Bloomfield Hills. "They live together, they play golf together, they *think* together."[51]

NEUTRALIZATION TECHNIQUES

There are a number of ways of talking and thinking about ethical problems that help command post decision makers to feel blameless. One is the use of "doublespeak," a term derived from George Orwell's prophetic novel *1984*. In "doublespeak" language is used which does not have the connotations that the usual vocabulary would have. We have probably all seen the signs at what were once used car lots but are now sites for the selling of "pre-owned cars."

William Lutz is an expert on "doublespeak." A lawyer and English professor, he also was the editor of the *Quarterly Review of Doublespeak*. Lutz points out that

> business is filled with dozens of doublespeak terms for firing or laying off employees, probably because there's so much of that going on these days. ... And as corporations continue to eliminate jobs and get rid of thousands of employees, they continue to invent new ways to avoid saying that they're firing all these people.[52]

When General Motors shut down its assembly plant in Framingham, Massachusetts, in 1987, they called it "a volume-related production schedule adjustment." With equal creativity, Chrysler referred to its laying off of five thousand auto workers in Kenosha, Wisconsin, as "a career alternative enhancement program."[53]

Thirty-five miles from New York City, in Westchester County, is Indian Point, a nuclear power plant that residents fear could be the cause of a lethal accident or become a terrorist target. The name has long had the connotation of potential catastrophe. In an effort to soothe the plant's opponents, the Entergy Corporation has changed the name to the Indian Point Energy Center. In Connecticut the Millstone Nuclear Power Station became just the Millstone Power Station, and the word nuclear has been removed from other nuclear plants around the country.[54]

Some other examples of euphemisms are calling the near meltdown at

Three Mile Island an "abnormal evolution" and a "plant transient," while the Department of Agriculture honored the food industry's request to call "powdered bone" "calcium" on food labels. The military is a good source for manipulative vocabulary. During Ronald Reagan's administration the MX missile, which can deliver ten extremely powerful nuclear weapons a distance of 6,674 miles, was dubbed "the Peacekeeper." Department of Defense critic, retired admiral Eugene J. Carrol, compared this linguistic ploy to "calling the guillotine a headache remedy." When civilians are killed in a war, American officials speak of their deaths as "collateral damage."[55]

Other ways of avoiding feeling pain or guilt for managerial decisions involve the appeal to a higher authority and blaming the victim, also described as condemning the condemner. In the appeal to a higher authority, the decision maker claims to be acting in the interest of a widely accepted moral principle. In blaming the victim, some aspect of that person is alleged to be responsible for his problem. If the person hadn't chosen to smoke, for instance, his health would not have been impaired.

The tobacco company R. J. Reynolds had a page of advertising in the *New York Times* with photos showing the Berlin Wall crumbling, apartheid ending in South Africa, and Russia having a new constitution, while ominously in the United States, freedom is threatened. A photo caption read, "Reins on Smokers' Freedom Tighten." The ad went on to say that the rights of all Americans "could be compromised" if the rights of smokers are violated.[56]

Progress is an oft-cited value. If there are costs to a corporate action, progress justifies it. In a lecture to the Arizona Business Forum, Paul Oreffice, then CEO of Dow Chemical Company, claimed that "environmentalists have now made a profession of standing in the way of any progress." Regarding General Motors' leveling of Poletown, mentioned above, a community of over three thousand people, Roger Smith said, "I'm sorry that people had to get displaced. . . . We have to build freeways; we build power lines. People do get displaced in the name of progress."[57] Of course, people living in affluent Bloomfield Hills are not likely to "get displaced."

The higher authority may be a value, but it can also be scientists who question their colleagues' findings of product danger. Since scientific findings are by their nature tentative, and scientists like other people can be influenced by material rewards, there is always a possibility of finding some alleged experts whose research is supposed to be more valid than that of the corporate critics. A survey compared the views of corporate-employed scientists with academic scientists on what constituted a safe level of exposure to carcinogens. Sixty percent of the academic scientists felt there is no safe level at all, while 80 percent of industry scientists felt there is no health risk at certain exposure levels. In another tobacco industry example, Philip Morris placed a full-page ad in the *New York Times* claiming that "many authoritative sources" question the EPA's conclusions that secondhand smoke is a danger.[58]

PROTECTING THE ORGANIZATION

Organizations engaged in criminal behavior need to keep these actions from being known to the public and to the authorities. This is true of criminal groups, but its also true for corporations, government agencies, and even religious institutions such as the Catholic Church, much in the news because of sexual abuse by priests. Many of these clergy were shielded by their superiors or moved to parishes away from their accusers, whose accusations in any case were denied for long periods of time.[59]

Those who help the organization to meet its goals can expect material rewards that can compromise their personal values. An example comes from an interview conducted with Benton Harlow, an employee of a Midwest pharmaceutical company that distributed an unsafe anticholesterol drug, HE/14. Laboratory animals given the drug developed cataracts and lost their hair. But a lot of money had been invested, and there was a $2 million stock of the drug, making withdrawal from the market unappealing. When the Justice Department investigated this case, Harlow accepted responsibility, was convicted, and given six months probation. He was later interviewed and asked how the company reacted to his conviction. Harlow replied:

> They knew someone had to take responsibility. If I refused then my case as well as a score of others would have gone to trial, which would have been disastrous both for me personally and the company. . . . I was given a substantial raise.[60]

NEUTRALIZING WHISTLE-BLOWERS

Those who question their organizations' actions and follow their conscience may find that life has become very uncomfortable, even dangerous. The term "whistle-blowers" describes employees who call attention to wrongdoing at their workplaces. These individuals are motivated by a sense of personal social responsibility; by concern for their own friends, families, and communities; professional ethics; and/or a desire to see wrongdoing stopped.[61]

Their stories are often very dramatic, and some have been made into movies. Daniel Ellsberg leaked what came to be called the Pentagon Papers during the Vietnam War. This became the subject of the TV docudrama *The Pentagon Papers*. Karen Silkwood, who worked for Kerr-McGhee, and Frank Serpico, a New York City cop, both became subjects of movies bearing their names.

Jeffrey Wigand is depicted in the movie *The Insider*. Wigand worked for the Brown and Williamson tobacco company and revealed the use of addicting ingredients in the company's products. He went from having a very pleasant lifestyle, with country club memberships and a mansion, to running his own foundation and living in an apartment without the accoutrements of wealth. His annual income declined from over $400,000 to about $30,000.

The movie *Erin Brokavitch* details the misdeeds of Pacific Gas and Electric Company (PG&E), whose contamination of a California community's water was responsible for cancers, miscarriages, weakened immune systems, and many other problems. PG& E also operates the California nuclear power facility at the appropriately named Diablo Canyon. Neil J. Aiken, an experienced manager at that plant who publicly criticized the company's safety procedures, was accused of having "paranoid delusions." A Labor Department investigator reported that the psychiatric evaluation

> appears unreasoned considering the fact that the evaluators never considered that other employees had complained about the same problem, there existed a culture where employees were reluctant to voice safety complaints, and the evaluators never checked to see if his thoughts were delusional.

Aiken concluded that even though "the NRC [Nuclear Regulatory Commission] advertises that you don't have to be afraid of retaliation . . . the fact is that no one can stop the corporation from doing what they want to you." He was eventually fired on the grounds that he was a threat to the plant's security even though four of his colleagues petitioned the NRC asking that he be reinstated. The company did grant him early retirement as part of a settlement.[62]

General Electric (GE) dismissed health physicist Frank Bordell in 1988 after he took his worry about radiation exposure and lack of adequate reporting to the Department of Energy (DOE). When the company took no notice of his concerns, he went to the DOE himself and was subsequently fired. Three years earlier GE punished Jack Shannon, manager of industrial safety and hygiene at another site. He was troubled by problems with asbestos and fire. When he reported these problems, the company demoted him, harassed, him and placed him on "permanent disability."[63]

Three engineers who had worked on the *Challenger* testified before a federal commission investigating the disaster, telling of their doubts about the spacecraft's safety. According to a *New York Times* story, they were "stripped of their authority, deprived of their staffs, and prevented from seeing critical data about the investigation."[64]

There are sometimes even more serious repercussions. D. Varnadore worked at a Martin Marietta–operated facility at the federal nuclear facility in Oak Ridge, Tennessee. Varnadore, himself a victim of colon cancer, appeared on a March 1991 CBS news show describing elevated cancer levels among people working at the facility. After this, he was isolated from other workers and given an office filled with radioactive wastes. A spokesperson for the Government Accountability Project, a nongovernmental organization that tries to protect whistle-blowers, said, "What they did borders on attempted murder, knowingly putting a cancer patient with a suppressed immune system in there."[65]

There may even be examples of direct murders of whistle-blowers. Karen Silkwood, fearful of Kerr McGee's mishandling of plutonium at their South Carolina plutonium processing plant, tried to interest the Atomic Energy Commission in the situation but became impatient with their lack of adequate response. She collected documentation of safety problems but was killed in 1974 in a suspicious car accident on her way to meet with a *New York Times* reporter and an official from the Oil, Chemical, and Atomic Workers union. Her collection of documents was never found. A week before she died, she, along with three hundred other workers, was contaminated by plutonium as a result of a plant accident.[66]

In 1985, a shotgun blast killed Judith Penley, a critic of safety at the Commanche Peak nuclear facility, part of the Tennessee Valley Authority energy complex. Her killing, never solved, came "shortly after she had met with interviewers from . . . a private firm hired by the government to investigate complaints at the nuclear facility."[67]

Personal vindictiveness is not the main reason for these punishments. Rather, those ordering them are acting on behalf of their organization. Myron and Penina Glazer, who did an extensive study on whistle-blowing, summarize the reasons for the harsh treatment, list the punishments corporations can use, and give reasons for these retaliatory actions:

> Retaliation is, in fact, part of a rational and planned process initiated by
> an organization to destroy the resister's credibility as a witness. To
> achieve this aim, management often invokes such harsh measures as
> blacklisting, dismissal, transfer, and personal harassment. . . . There are
> several reasons for these excessive punishments. First, management
> insists that employees do not have a right to . . . challenge organizational
> policies publicly. Attempts to overturn decisions made by those at the top
> are defined as acts of insubordination and are considered a threat to the
> orderly procedures required to operate in a businesslike fashion.[68]

In addition, there are fears that the whistle-blowers may become role
models to their fellow employees and examples of moral courage.

Director of the St. Louis University Emerson Electric Center for Business Ethics James E. Fischer describes the David-Goliath relationship between a whistle-blower and his or her target: "The lone whistle-blower is oftenest up against a powerful corporate or government entity with more resources and power. From the get-go you have the likelihood of retaliation."[69] A number of studies of whistle-blowers found that from one-half to two-thirds of them were fired, with this more likely to happen in the private than the public sector. Blacklisting also occurs. However, there is more protection for those with government jobs.

The organization does not want to call attention to itself. It is more rational for those at the command posts, or their subordinates, to make the whistle-blowers' lives miserable so that they leave, rather than firing them outright. C. Fred Alford, in his study of whistle-blowers, found that "a surprising number [of them] have been given closets for offices." A person might be transferred to a job he or she is not able to do well, receive poor performance evaluations, and then be fired.[70] Discrediting the honest individual is another way those loyal to the organization try to minimize potential damage from revelations of the employees. Labeling them as mentally ill is another way to neutralize their activities.

In the movies the whistle-blower is usually vindicated, but in real life justice is not always achieved. There are emotional and financial costs to the whistle-blower, while the organization is usually unscathed. In any case, no executive will personally lose money. Litigation around the issues may drag on for years. The federal government, via the Department of Energy, lessens the costs of its own contractors at nuclear facilities by paying their legal fees when they litigate against whistle-blowers.[71]

This situation led the chair of the House Subcommittee on Oversight and Investigation, Richard M. Burr, to note that the DOE was "providing

Bok, *The Cost of Talent: How Executives and Professionals Are Paid and How It Affects America* (New York: Free Press, 1993), p. 4.

20. David James and Michael Soref, "Managerial Theory: Unmaking of the Corporation President," *American Sociological Review* 46 (1981): 16.

21. Charles Derber, *Corporation Nation: How Corporations Are Taking Over Our Lives and What We Can Do about It* (New York: St. Martin's Griffin, 1998), p. 18.

22. Sara Anderson, John Cavanagh, and Thea Lee, *Field Guide to the Global Economy* (New York: New Press, 2000), p. 68; Joshua Karliner, "Earth Predators," *Dollars and Sense* (July/August 1998): 7.

23. David Korten, *When Corporations Rule the World*, 2nd ed. (Bloomfield, CN: Kumarian Press, 2001), p. 104.

24. In the video *The Killing Screens*, Media Education Foundation, 1994.

25. Derber, *Corporation Nation*, p. 25.

26. Ibid., pp. 128–34.

27. Robert Justin Goldstein, *Political Repression in Modern America* (Cambridge, MA: Schenkman, 1978), p. 3.

28. Korten, *When Corporations Rule the World*, p. 65.

29. For accounts of the violent labor history of the United States, see Philip Taft and Philip Ross, "American Labor Violence: Its Causes, Character, and Outcome," in *The History of Violence in America*, ed. Hugh Davis Graham and Ted Robert Gurr (New York, Bantam Books, 1969), pp. 270–336; Howard Zinn, *A People's History of the United States* (New York: HarperCollins, 1995), pp. 206–46.

30. Quoted in David K. Shipler, "Robert McNamara and the Ghosts of Vietnam," *New York Times Magazine*, August 10, 1997, p. 33.

31. Bok, *The Cost of Talent*, pp. 79, 90.

32. Joseph Nocera, "The Customer Is Usually Right," review of *Jack*, the autobiography of Jack Welch, a former CEO of General Electric, *New York Times Book Review*, October 14, 2001, p. 13.

33. Judith H. Dobrzynski, "Executive Tests Now Plumb New Depths of the Job Seeker," *New York Times*, September 21, 1996, pp. 1, 38.

34. Ralph McGehee, *Deadly Deceits: My 25 Years in the CIA* (New York: Sheridan Square Press, 1983), p. 6.

35. Coleman, *The Criminal Elite*, p. 190.

36. M. David Ermann and Richard J. Lundmann, overview to *Corporate and Governmental Deviance*, 6th ed. (New York: Oxford University Press, 2002), pp. 8–9.

37. Stanley Milgram, *Obedience to Authority* (New York: Harper and Row, 1974), p. 21.

38. Coleman, *The Criminal Elite*, p. 94.

39. "The *Challenger* Space Shuttle Disaster: Conventional Wisdom and a Revisionist Account," in Ermann and Lundmann, *Corporate and Governmental Deviance*, p. 325.

40. Stuart L. Hills, epilogue to *Corporate Violence: Injury and Death for*

Profit, ed. Stuart L. Hills (Totowa, NJ: Rowman & Littlefield, 1987), pp. 192–93; see also Russell Boisjoly, Ellen Foster Curtis, and Eugene Mellican, "Ethical Dimensions of the *Challenger* Disaster," in Ermann and Lundman, *Corporate and Governmental Deviance,* pp. 111–36.

41. "Excerpts from Report of the *Columbia* Accident Investigation Board," *New York Times,* August 27, 2003, p. A18.

42. James Glanz, Edward Wong, and William J. Broad, "Bureaucrats Stifled Spirit of Adventure, NASA's Critics Say," *New York Times,* February 2, 2003, p. A16.

43. R. Jeffrey Smith, John Warwick, and Rob Smith, "Experts Warned of Safety Worries," http://www.msnbc.com/news867623.asp (accessed February 2, 2003). Originally published in the *Washington Post,* February 2, 2002.

44. Glanz, Wong, and Broad, "Bureaucrats Stifled Spirit of Adventure"; David Barstow and Michael Moss, "Amid Quest for a Safer Shuttle, Budget Fights and Policy Shifts," *New York Times,* February 9, 2002, pp. 1, 34.

45. Quoted in Hills, *Corporate Violence,* p. 194.

46. Shown in Michael Moore's film *Roger and Me.* A theme in Moore's documentaries is confronting CEOs with people their decisions have harmed; Ralph Nader and William Taylor, *The Big Boys: Power and Position in American Business* (New York: Pantheon, 1986), pp. 120–28.

47. Quoted in Robert Jackall, *Moral Mazes: The World of Corporate Managers* (New York: Oxford University Press, 1989), p. 127.

48. Quoted in Amalia Duarte, "Workers and AT&T Both Grapple with the Reality of Layoffs," *New York Times,* August 28, 1994, sec. 13.

49. Reed Abelson, "A Push from the Top Shatters a Glass Ceiling," *New York Times,* August 22, 1999, p. 33.

50. Irving L. Janis, *Victims of GroupThink* (Boston: Houghton Mifflin Company, 1972), p. 9.

51. Quoted in Nader and Taylor, *The Big Boys,* p. 77 (emphasis in original).

52. William Lutz, *The New Doublespeak: Why No One Knows What Anyone's Saying Anymore* (New York: HarperPerennial, 1996), p. 115.

53. William Lutz, *Doublespeak: From Revenue Enhancement to Terminal Living: How Government, Business Advertisers, and Others Use Language to Deceive You* (New York: HarperPerennial, 1989), p. 129.

54. Winnie Hu, "What's in a Name? Sometimes It's Fear," *New York Times,* March 23, 2002, p. B4.

55. Jackall, *Moral Mazes,* p. 156; description of MX missile, Ann Markusen and Joel Yudken, *Dismantling the Cold War Economy* (New York: Basic Books, 1992), p. 12: Eugene Carroll quoted in Douglas Martin, "E. J. Carroll, 79, Antinuclear Admiral, Dies," *New York Times,* March 3, 2003, p. B7; Norman Solomon, *The Power of Babble* (New York: Laurel, 1992), p. 49.

56. The ad appeared in the *New York Times,* October 25, 1994, p. A17.

57. Oreffice quoted in Nader and Taylor, *The Big Boys,* pp. 169; Smith quoted p. 127.

58. The ad appeared in the *New York Times*, October 27, 1991, p. A25.

59. For example, see Pam Belluck, Fox Butterfield, and Sara Rimer, "Once Cardinal's Top Aides, Bishops Now Share Shadow," *New York Times*, April 8, 2002, pp. A1, A20.

60. James T. Carey, "Benton Harlow: Distributor of Unsafe Drugs," in Hills, *Corporate Violence*, pp. 164–65.

61. For a social psychological analysis of whistle-blowers, see C. Fred Alford, *Whistleblowers: Broken Lives and Organizational Power* (Ithaca, NY: Cornell University Press, 2001).

62. Matthew L. Wald, "Questioning Whistle-Blower's 'Delusions,'" *New York Times*, April 11, 2000, p. A27.

63. Russell Mokhiber, Julie Gozan, and Holly Knaus, "The Corporate Rap Sheet: The 10 Worst Corporations of 1992," *Multinational Monitor* (December 1992): 12–13.

64. Quoted in Myron Peretz Glazer and Penina Migdal Glazer, *The Whistleblowers: Exposing Corruption in Government and Industry* (New York: Basic Books, 1989), p. 10.

65. Quoted in Matthew L. Wald, "Nuclear Laboratory Whistle-Blower Is Disciplined for Questioning a Test," *New York Times*, February 5, 1992, p. A16; Mokhiber, Gozan, and Knaus, "The Corporate Rap Sheet," p. 14.

66. Deena Weinstein, *Bureaucratic Opposition: Challenging Abuses of the Workplace* (New York: Pergamon Press, 1979), p. 82.

67. Glazer and Glazer, *The Whistleblowers*, p. 146.

68. Ibid., pp. 134–35.

69. Marci A. Nusbaum, "Blowing the Whistle: Not for the Fainthearted," *New York Times*, February 10, 2002, sec. 3, p. 10.

70. Alford, *Whistleblowers*, p. 32.

71. Ibid., pp. 110–12.

72. Matthew L. Wald, "U.S. Still Pays Contractor Bills for Whistle-Blower Lawsuits," *New York Times*, May 24, 2000, p. A22.

73. Alford, *Whistleblowers*, pp. 18–19; "Whistle-Blowers Being Punished, A Survey Shows," *New York Times*, September 3, 2002.

74. For a summary of some of the laws, see Alford, *Whistleblowers*, pp. 107–108.

75. From BBC News, December 22, 2002, http://news.bbc.co.uk/2/hi/business/2599523.stm (accessed March 3, 2003).

76. Rick Lyman, "A Tobacco Whistle-Blower's Life Is Transformed," *New York Times*, October 15, 1999, p. A24. Alford, however, reports that many wish they had not spoken up, *Whistleblowers*, p. 34.

Chapter 5

POLITICAL INEQUALITY
Corporations and Government

I n order to achieve their economic goals, corporations and wealthy shareholders need to have government as their ally. Our economic system may be undemocratic, but we have a democratic political system: we can exercise certain basic freedoms and we can vote. What if the vast majority of us use our rights to vote, to criticize, and to organize to limit the wealth and income of those at the top, to create a more equitable distribution of economic resources, and to make those in the command posts more responsible and accountable for their actions?

In this chapter we shall look at several of the most important ways in which corporations and wealthy individuals use the political system to promote their own interests over the general welfare. The success of these efforts leads to a society in which violence, in all its forms, becomes more likely.

Corporations are generally in agreement on broad government policies and often work in concert, though they may also compete with one another. As G. William Domhoff explains:

> The corporate community is cohesive on the policy issues that affect its general welfare, which is often at stake when political challenges are made by organized workers, liberals, or strong environmentalists.[1]

What would we expect corporations and the wealthy to want from the government?[2]

- Policies that will lower the cost of labor, such as discouragement of union organizing, low minimum wages, no or only unpaid family leave, and welfare policies that force people onto the labor market.
- Weak regulation of their actions, which means few rules, little enforcement of what rules there are, and small penalties for violations. Low funding levels for regulatory agencies and cooperative heads of agencies also help achieve this goal.
- Favorable taxation policies so that the cost of government is paid for by others.
- A foreign policy that allows multinational corporations producing and selling in a global marketplace to make high returns.

As numerous examples in this book will show, this agenda, when successful, contributes to higher levels of violence.

Economic elites are able to influence political decisions so that the general public's exercise of its rights does not unduly hinder profit seeking. The Republican Party is somewhat more congenial to the wishes of business, but corporations also significantly influence the Democratic Party. The Democrats have a more diverse population in their voting base, and party members sometimes reflect this in their political positions.

As will be discussed more below, powerful political figures move in and out of the corporate world, making decisions in each area often with long-lasting consequences for millions of people. They do not have the same relationships with labor unions, health care advocates, environmental organizations, or consumer groups. When leaving office, many former political leaders are offered a great deal of money by corporations and/or go into lucrative businesses themselves. If they angered business firms or cut their ties with the business community during their tenure in office, these financial opportunities would be much more limited. We can assume also that the worldview of most major political figures is consistent with that of the corporate world, with implications for the policies they support.

There are mutual advantages to this relationship. A former commerce secretary in the Nixon White House who became chair of a Wall Street investment company explains what these are:

> When you are in government, you get to meet hundreds if not thousands of people at top levels of business, and government, all over the world. People tend to have seen you in very important government negotiations. You often get access and credibility that may sometimes be difficult to get if you have only been in business.[3]

Henry Kissinger, who was both national security adviser and secretary of state for Richard Nixon and Gerald Ford, founded a consulting company in 1982. He is averse to identifying his clients, but they are believed to include ARCO, ExxonMobil, Coca-Cola, and American Express.[4]

A number of previously highly placed political figures are members of a conglomerate firm created in 1987, the Carlyle Group. One of its three founders, David Rubenstein, was a member of the Carter administration. The Carlyle Group works with energy and health care industries among others and is itself a major military contractor with subsidiaries producing aircraft components and tanks. It has over $13.5 billion in capital. It operates globally, but it is headquartered in Washington, DC.

Among the Americans involved in the company are former President George H. W. Bush; James Baker, who was his secretary of state; and Frank Carlucci, Ronald Reagan's secretary of defense. Carlucci had been a deputy director of the CIA. When he joined the firm, Carlucci also brought a number of colleagues from the Pentagon and the CIA. President George W. Bush also served on the board of a Carlyle-controlled company but left when he ran for the governorship of Texas in 1992. The company had links to the Saudi Arabian bin Laden family, but following the attacks of September 11, 2001, it seemed politic to sever these ties.[5]

When Bill Clinton left the White House in 2001, he was in great demand as a speaker, in his first year out of office giving fifty presentations to banks, advertising agencies, public relations companies, and others. To date he has made nearly $10 million on the corporate lecture circuit. Previous presidents also made a great deal this way, but Clinton was the first to detail publicly to whom he spoke.[6]

William S. Cohen, Clinton's secretary of defense, although a Republican, started the Cohen Group at the end of the Clinton administration, along with three other former members of the Pentagon. He has been using his experience and foreign relationships to advise companies about the political and economic climate in countries they might be interested in. In addition, he travels with business people and uses his contacts to help them make useful connections.

Bruce Babbit, Clinton's secretary of the interior, became chair of a company that is a subsidiary of Cadiz, Inc., and in which Prince Alwaleed bin Talal of Saudi Arabia is also involved. The company develops water resources in the Middle East and California. Cadiz has clashed with environmentalists over the company's plans for using water from the Colorado River.[7]

MECHANISMS FOR INFLUENCING
THE POLITICAL PROCESS

The processes used to ensure government cooperation with corporate agendas are lobbying, financing of parties and candidates, staffing of political positions, and formulating policy.[8] These are used at national, state, and local levels, but we will concentrate on national politics. For discussion purposes, these processes will be considered separately. In the real world, however, all of these are happening at about the same time, with the same organizations and people involved in different activities.

Lobbying

This is how organizations or groups try to influence elected officials to take a particular stand. Of the four processes discussed here, this is the one in which ordinary citizens can have the greatest impact. Anyone can write a letter, send an e-mail or a fax, make a phone call, or visit a congressperson. Since it is votes that determine who gets into office, congresspeople can be made to feel some responsibility to their constituents. Citizens also support organizations that lobby in their behalf, but these often do not have much money compared to business lobbying groups.

There have been many examples of grassroots lobbying around the 2003 war in Iraq. One occurred on February 26, 2003, when an antiwar coalition Win Without War organized a "virtual march" on Washington. The coalition encouraged opponents of the impending war to let their senators and the White House know their feelings. They did, making close to a million calls and sending thousands of faxes. Capitol and White House switchboards and fax machines were tied up for hours.[9] This was an unusual effort at a time of crisis. It is not unusual, however, for citizen groups to visit their congressional representatives to try to persuade them to take a particular position.

Corporate resources for lobbying are much greater than for the rest of the population. They can hire people and firms that specialize in lobbying, and they can offer financial rewards and other perquisites to those they are trying to influence. Furthermore, as investigative journalist William Greider observes, citizens are likely to be

> temporarily aroused by an issue, see reforms enacted and then move on to other concerns. But the corporations do not go away from the legislative debate even in the off-seasons. By their nature, the people and institutions

with large amounts of money at stake are always at the table. It is their business to be there. Their profits depend on the outcomes.

Greider points to a Senate study which found that "on some important matters, industry would invest fifty to one hundred times more resources than the public-interest advocates could muster."[10]

Wall Street Journal reporter Jeffrey H. Birnbaum, who has studied lobbying, writes, "The fact that lobbyists are everywhere all the time, has led official Washington to become increasing sympathetic to the corporate cause. This is true among Democrats as well as among Republicans."[11] As of June 1999 there were 20,512 registered professional lobbyists in Washington, DC. Keep in mind there are only 535 members of the House and Senate. In 1998 the amount spent on lobbying was $1.42 billion.[12]

Spending money on lobbying can bring significant returns. We mentioned corporate desires to impede unionization. Federal Express invested $1,149,150 in lobbying to see to it that there was a phrase inserted into the National Labor Relations Act that would make it more difficult for its employees to unionize. Of FedEx's 110,000 employees in 1996, only its 3,000 pilots were in a union. The measure passed 66–31. Voicing opposition to the company, Sen. Edward Kennedy said, "Federal Express is notorious for its antiunion ideology, but there is no justification for Congress becoming an accomplice in its union-busting tactic."[13]

With their vast resources, corporate lobbyists are able to persuade political figures to become accomplices. In the case of Federal Express, an opponent of the legislation, Wisconsin senator Russ Feingold, reported that his more sympathetic colleagues had flown in Federal Express jets "or gotten other favors." The company regularly makes its planes available to members of Congress. Feingold related that he had gotten "a sense . . . that this company had made a real strong effort to be friendly and helpful to Congress."[14]

Most politicians do not usually socialize with or routinely meet with groups of working people. On the other hand, they wine and dine with and go to parties, resorts, and business gatherings with the corporate elite. In 1989, for example, business lobbyists paid for a $250,000 weekend trip for 142 representatives and their families to the Greenbrier resort in West Virginia. Real estate lobbyist Wayne Thevenot explained that vacations like these

> put you into proximity with some members of Congress—the major players. They get to know who you are. [And you] get to know who they are, something about them personally. Their likes, their dislikes, their family. Getting [*sic*] to develop a personal relationship with them.[15]

A former director of the National Republican Congressional Committee said of the junkets, "We want to provide an informal atmosphere where members of Congress and lobbyists can have meals, play golf or other sports, and have fun."[16] Corporations individually and as part of industry groups are able to hire the services of firms that are in the lobbying business. They also establish lobbying organizations to represent their joint interests.

Lobbyists for insurance companies, the hospital industry, and some medical associations have spent millions of dollars lobbying on health care. The pharmaceutical industry as of 2001 had 625 registered lobbyists and was spending $197 million on lobbying and campaign contributions, more than any other industry. It employs the services of 134 lobbying companies. Its recent goals included being sure that a terrorist attack did not mean they would have to supply free medicines or violate their patent protections.

Following the September 11 terrorist attacks, drug industry representatives met with members of President George W. Bush's administration, seeking to get a quicker timetable for approval of new drugs. Representatives from consumer groups or companies making cheaper generic drugs did not participate in these meetings, which were presented to the public as being part of the country's defense against terrorism.[17]

Professional lobbyists do polling, conduct public relations campaigns, and create phony grassroots organizations. The latter have been dubbed "astro-turf" organizations to highlight their being artificial creations.[18] These organizations try to make it appear as though there is popular support for or against a particular measure. Staged performances for congressional hearings are part of their repertoire. An example comes from the pharmaceutical industry, which is anxious to prevent measures that would bring down costs of prescription drugs. The United States is the only major industrial country that does not regulate the prices of these crucial products. (We will discuss the costs of prescription drugs again in chapter 7.)

The pharmaceutical companies' trade group is called the Pharmaceutical Research and Manufacturers of America. The industry's largest members spent $4 million in 1998 to protect their interests. By 1999 that had risen to $60 million. This is in addition to its advertising budget. Individual companies also have lobbying budgets. These costs are ultimately passed on to the consumer.

With the high costs of prescription drugs an important issue for many, especially older Americans, in the fall of 2000 the Senate was conducting hearings into the price of drugs and considering measures that would allow for cheaper products to be imported. The pharmaceutical industry claimed that government regulations would limit their ability to produce lifesaving products. A woman named Elizabeth Helms claimed to be from a group called Citizens for the Right to Know, but, in fact, she was working full-time for a public relations firm that represents the pharmaceutical industry's interests. Testifying before Congress, Helms claimed that her alleged citizens' group had conducted a survey of eighty pharmacies that showed there was great variation in price, and that if consumers shopped wisely they could cut the cost of their prescriptions by over half. Not only was her organization a phony one, but the survey itself was flawed and did not reveal the variations she stated.[19]

> Other industry-sponsored groups claiming to speak for older Americans are the United Seniors Association, the Seniors Coalition, and the 60 Plus Association. According to the American Association of Retired Persons (AARP) . . . all three organizations have been criticized for years for questionable fundraising practices. . . . All three organizations claim to speak for millions of older Americans although as recently as 2001 none of the three listed any revenue from membership dues on their tax returns.

Most telling, "Virtually all of their largest contributions in recent years have come from the same source—the nation's pharmaceutical industry."[20]

Many lobbyists are former members of Congress or come from other branches of government, giving them valuable access to officials. We previously mentioned that the pharmaceutical industry has 625 registered lobbyists. Over half of these are former congressional staff members, senators or representatives, or other members of government.[21]

As the director of the Center for Public Integrity, Charles Lewis, explained:

> The lawmakers who will be making the biggest killings are those who were the biggest names and who sat on the most powerful committees. Folks like that are potentially worth extraordinary amounts of money, and lobbying firms will shell out for them. [22]

"Shelling out" often means six-figure compensation. A lobbying firm lawyer, Elliot Portnoy, explained why companies are willing to spend so much money:

> It is impossible to calculate the value in helping clients of having a person who is as intimately familiar with the legislative process and who has the depth and breadth of relationships as former members of Congress.[23]

Some examples of this particular revolving door are Thomas Pickering, an undersecretary of state in the Clinton administration who became a lobbyist for the Boeing Company, and former senator and presidential candidate Robert Dole, who went to work for the company whose clients include Brown and Williamson Tobacco. A former chair of the Republican National Committee, Harley Barbour was a lobbyist both before and after he served as chair. His clients included all the major tobacco companies. He provided them with access to key legislators.[24]

In chapter 3 we discussed taxes, an issue of great interest to lobbyists for corporations. In this case, too, former senators, representatives, and treasury officials are in demand to lobby for favorable tax laws. Former senator Robert Dole has also lobbied for tax breaks. Of particular concern to a number of companies was an attempt to repeal tax breaks for companies that are headquartered out of the country in order to avoid taxes.[25]

Financing of Parties and Political Campaigns

To run increasingly expensive media-based campaigns, parties and their candidates need financial backing and will not get this by attacking the interests of potential large contributors. Both the Democratic and Republican Parties receive funds from the same large corporations, although the Democrats also get support from more diverse groups in the population, including labor organizations, who give much more to this party. Table 5.1 shows this for the period 1990–2000.

TABLE 5.1 CONTRIBUTIONS TO MAJOR POLITICAL PARTIES BY SELECTED INDUSTRIES AND ORGANIZED LABOR, 1990–2000

industry or organization group	total contribution 1990–2000	% to Republicans	% to Democrats
health industry	$277,462,518	56%	44%
energy/natural resources	$198,553,941	67%	32%
agribusiness	$212,311,787	67%	33%
labor	$292,162,374	7%	93%

Source: This table is based on tables in Robert Weissman, "The Money Trail, Corporate Investments in U.S. Elections Since 1990," Multinational Monitor (October 2000): 26–29.

Note: The missing 1% in energy/natural resources is due to rounding.

Although labor gives the great bulk of its contributions to the Democrats, the total amount is dwarfed by the cumulative business contributions to both parties. In 2000 business contributed a total of $466 million to Republicans and about $340 million to Democrats.[26]

Table 5.2 indicates the cost of national campaigns. Gerald Lowrie, a senior vice president in AT&T's Federal Government Affairs Office, explained why these contributions are so important, "Government can change the way you live and how you work. If you ignore who is in office it can be at your peril."[27]

TABLE 5.2 THE ESCALATING FUNDING OF CONGRESSIONAL AND PRESIDENTIAL ELECTIONS, 1992–2000

	money raised for congressional elections	money raised for presidential elections
1992	$659 million	$331 million
1996	$791 million	$426 million
2000	$1.05 billion	$529 million

Source: Kevin Phillips, *Wealth and Democracy* (New York: Broadway Books, 2002), p. 324.

Giving money to campaigns is very cost effective. "Billionaires for Bush or Gore" satirized this situation in 2000. Pointing out that there are high returns for relatively small investments, the group explained on their Web site:

> With the help of a professional legislation broker (called a Lobbyist), you place your investment (called a Campaign Contribution) with a carefully selected list of legislation manufacturers (called Members of Congress). These manufacturers then go to work, crafting industry-specific subsidies, inserting tax breaks into the code, extending patents, or giving away public property for free. [28]

As a case in point, they cite Glaxo-Welcomes getting an extension on the patent for the antacid medicine Zantac valued at $1 billion in return for $1.2 million in campaign contributions. They calculated this as a return of 83,333 percent.

From 1991 to June 2001 companies with operations in Puerto Rico gave $14.3 million in contributions. In exchange, they were able to take advantage of a tax break that saved them $627 million.[29]

Although the candidates for both major parties are dependent on corporations, the Republicans receive much more from this source. Table 5.3 indicates contributions from sectors especially relevant for issues discussed in this book.

TABLE 5.3 CAMPAIGN CONTRIBUTIONS
FOR 2000 ELECTIONS

corporate sector	total contributed	% to Republicans	% to Democrats
oil and gas	$25.3 million	79%	19%
pharmaceuticals	$19.3 million	69%	31%

Source: "In the Nation's Capital a Stirring Triumph of Buy-Partisanship," *Too Much* (Winter 2001):1.

Energy companies contributed greatly to George W. Bush from the time he ran unsuccessfully for Congress in 1978, through his successful campaign for the Texas governor's office in 1994, to his 2000 presidential campaign. However, one of the largest, scandal-ridden Enron, also contributed to the Gore campaign, with one of Enron's public relations experts advising that the company should "actively" participate in campaign activities and if Gore became president to "participate in . . . inaugural planning." The goal was to ensure that Enron "become part of the energy and telecom policy of the Gore campaign."[30]

Besides the energy companies, during the campaigns of 2000 the chief contributors to the Republicans included the tobacco and firearms industries. Companies benefiting from contracts for work in Afghanistan and Iraq collectively contributed about half a million dollars to the Bush campaign of 2000. The Democrats also received money from them but only half as much as the Republicans. The companies included Halliburton, Bechtel, and General Electric.[31] (The connection between corporations and military policies will be discussed further in chapter 13.)

For those giving $250,000 or more, there were immediate rewards: accommodations at fine hotels, drinks with Colin Powell, dinners with other important Republicans, and reserved skybox seats at the convention itself. The contributors were hoping for a Bush victory and with it a government that would view their desires favorably. As we have already indicated and will discuss further in following chapters, their wishes were granted.

Campaign contributions intertwine with lobbying. Big business has a much greater impact in both areas than do ordinary citizens. Both branches of Congress enacted rules in 1997 that make it illegal for Congress members to accept gifts from lobbyists, but if the lobbyist wants to make a campaign contribution, that is okay. In exchange for the money, the lobbyist buys access, sometimes in a posh resort setting, to the legislator. In 1997 the mountain resort of Vail, Colorado, was the venue for lobbyists willing to pay $3,000 each to meet with Republican congress members. For the same amount a lobbyist could ski Aspen's slopes with leading Democrats.[32]

Individuals also make campaign contributions. But according to *New York Times* columnist Bob Herbert, this "donor class" is "elite and homogeneous," comprised of "one-quarter of 1 percent of the population." Herbert based his comments on a study conducted by the Joyce Foundation, which used information from the 1996 congressional elections. Of those contributing $200 or more, the figures for which there is information, the breakdown was the following:

- 95 percent were white
- 80 percent were men
- 81 percent had family incomes over $100,000
- 20 percent had incomes over $500,000

The contributors are not necessarily conservative on matters such as abortion or affirmative action, but the researchers concluded, "These major donors on balance oppose national health insurance, additional antipoverty spending, and reductions in defense spending."[33]

Influential politicians have made it clear that there is a quid pro quo. In 1999 the then chair of the Republican Party, Jim Nicholson, in a letter to Bristol-Myers Squib CEO Charles A. Heimbold Jr., requested a $250,000 contribution to the party. He expressed appreciation for Heimbold's "expertise in heath care" and expressed hopes that they would continue to communicate in order to enact "legislation that will benefit your industry." It was not reported whether this particular request was granted. Bristol-Myers Squibb did, however, give over $1.5 million to the Republicans in 1999 and 2000.[34]

Corporations host gala events. For example, prior to the Republican National Convention in 1988, General Motors gave a party for Sen. Robert Dole and his wife, Elizabeth. Among the refreshments was a two-pound tub of caviar worth about $1,000. The automobile company did not slight the Democrats, however, also hosting a reception for Rep. John Dingell of

Michigan, described by the *New York Times* as "one of the auto industry's strongest allies in Congress."[35]

Speaking engagements with large honoraria, an all-expense-paid trip, or simply personal gifts are additional carrots that can be dangled in front of lawmakers. Jack Kemp, for instance, a member of the House of Representatives from 1971 to 1989, secretary of housing and urban development for George H. W. Bush, and Republican vice presidential candidate in 1996, made "$1 million between 1992 and 1995 lecturing to business groups." This was in addition to the $100,000 he earned as a director on six corporate boards.[36]

In 2002 the pharmaceutical company GlaxoSmith Kline, along with Pepsico, Microsoft, and others, arranged a fundraiser for Republican congressional candidates. Appealing for donations, Sen. Bill Frist wrote to potential donors that a Republican-controlled Senate would lead to a relaxing of "the stranglehold of rules, regulations, and restrictions on American business."[37] Many of these rules protect consumers, workers, and other individuals against harm, a point relevant to discussions in this book.

There are some attempts to diminish corporate influence on elected officials. Laws were passed in 1974 stipulating that individuals could give only $1,000 to presidential candidates while political action committees (PACs) could give no more than $5,000. Donations, however, can be made to the parties and not directly to the candidates, which allows circumvention of these laws. These contributions are called "soft money." Charles Lewis, quoted in our discussion of lobbying, explains that the reason the word "soft" is used is because this money is "squishy"; it is difficult to follow its path. He points out that these funds "can grease the skids in Washington for some powerful companies while the average citizen doesn't have access." Democratic fundraiser Alfred C. DeCotis, who has himself raised millions for the party, admits, "If you write a large check, you get to be well known in the party and you get a certain amount of access."[38]

In October 2002 the McCain-Feingold bill was passed, which makes it illegal to give some soft-money donations. In December 2003 the Supreme Court in a 5–4 decision upheld the bill's major provisions.[39] Maine and Arizona have passed campaign-finance reform bills that have had an effect on state and local races. The state provides funds for candidates, and the amount of contributions is limited. This makes it easier to have a more diverse pool of candidates who in turn are compelled to talk to potential constituents in order to raise money, putting them more in touch with ordinary voters.[40]

Staffing of Positions

Capitalists themselves do not usually hold most of the elected offices in this country, but they do hold a significant number, and members of this class are appointed to positions of great influence. As discussed in the previous chapter, they have been socialized at similar institutions and come to their positions as part of social and business networks in which people have developed a similar outlook on how the world should work. Even those who were not born into the elite, such as Lyndon Johnson, Richard Nixon, Jimmy Carter, and Bill Clinton, have moved in elite circles by the time they are ready to hold political office in elected or appointed positions. If not from the capitalist class, politicians are likely to be from the upper-middle class at the time they enter politics; professionally, they are likely to be lawyers.

The House of Representatives is occupationally very unrepresentative of the general population. Domhoff summarized the backgrounds of members of Congress as of 2001. "Taken together business executives, bankers, realtors, and lawyers account for 79 percent of Congress." Of those who were representatives as of 2001, 183 were "business executives, bankers, and realtors." There were 155 lawyers. This is 78 percent of the House. There was one representative from organized labor serving in the House.[41] The Senate is also disproportionately made up of wealthy individuals.

Looking at presidents since the Second World War, John F. Kennedy, George Bush, and George W. Bush were from the corporate class, Jimmy Carter and Ronald Reagan were millionaires who became presidents, as was Lyndon Johnson. Richard Nixon was very wealthy by the time he won election in 1968.[42]

Cabinet officers and heads of federal agencies are also often drawn from the capitalist class. The administration of George W. Bush, selected as president by the Supreme Court in the disputed election of 2000, is a particularly glaring example. Taken together, the "president, vice president, and the secretaries of state, treasury, defense, and commerce" had reported incomes ranging from $91 million to $130 million; their overall wealth ranged from $185 million to $624 million.[43]

Many members of the Bush administration, including the president and vice president, have ties to the energy industry, which has been benefiting from numerous decisions allowing them greater access to public lands and easing regulations governing their operations. This will be discussed further in the next chapter. As summarized by the *New York Times*, "Mr. Bush has named at least 30 former energy industry executives, lobbyists, and lawyers to influential jobs in his administration. Some of them have helped the government carry out major parts of the energy policy without waiting for Congress."[44]

George W. Bush founded his own oil company, which was bought by Harken Energy. As a result of the transaction, he received stocks worth $600,000 and an agreement to pay him $120,000 a year. He owns stock in ExxonMobil, BP, Pennzoil, and General Electric. A former owner of the Texas Rangers baseball team, George W. Bush realized a profit of $15 million when the team was sold in 1998. In May 2003 he reported his financial worth as totaling $8.8 million.[45]

George W. Bush's vice president Richard Cheney was secretary of defense in Bush's father's administration. He reported his net worth in 2003 as about $1.9 million. In 1997 Cheney became CEO of Halliburton, the country's largest provider of services to oil companies, with subsidiaries that include military contractors. In 1999 the company's revenue was $14.9 billion, $675.5 million of that a result of military contacts. (We shall discuss this company again in chapter 13.) Cheney has stock in the company worth $37 million. Halliburton has received billions in federal contracts. It has made large campaign contributions and engages in lobbying as well. In 2001 the income on which Cheney paid taxes was $4.3 million. The previous year he garnered $36 million, much of that from selling his shares in Halliburton.[46]

Secretary of Defense Donald Rumsfeld, in Bush's cabinet, went to Princeton on an ROTC scholarship and became active in Republican politics. He was a congressman, then head of Richard Nixon's Office of Economic Opportunity, ambassador to NATO, and part of Gerald Ford's administration. When Jimmy Carter defeated Ford, Rumsfeld became CEO at G. D. Searle pharmaceutical company, later acquired by Monsanto. At Searle he drastically cut the workforce, raised the company's profits, and when it was acquired by Monsanto, made $12 million. He then became CEO at General Instruments. In addition, he has sat on the boards of directors of Northrop Grumman, Gulfstream Aerospace Corporation, and Amylin Pharmaceuticals, among others. In 1999 the military contractor General Dynamics bought Gulfstream Aerospace.[47]

Bush's secretary of state, Colin Powell, is worth over $28 million. He has also been on the board of Gulfstream Aerospace, which manufactures jets; its customers have included Kuwait and Saudi Arabia. Powell, like Rumsfeld, financially benefited when the company merged with General Dynamics. The former chair of the Joint Chiefs of Staff, as a civilian, was on the board of AOL, which merged with Time-Warner recently, increasing the value of his stock by $4 million. Powell earned nearly $8 million in 2000 for the 108 speeches he made to a variety of corporations, including Kentucky Fried Chicken, Walt Disney, American Express, Arthur Anderson, J. C. Penney, and Coca-Cola.

As of 2004, Powell's son Michael was serving in the Federal Communications Commission (FCC). He was the only FCC member who advocated letting AOL merge with Time-Warner, producing a new communications giant. After the merger President Bush made him chair of this important regulatory body.[48]

Two of George W. Bush's top advisors are Condoleezza Rice and Karl Rove; as with others in this administration, both have close connections to the oil industry. Rice has been a board member of Chevron, which named an oil tanker for her. She has stock holdings in that company worth hundreds of thousands of dollars. Rove has major stockholdings in BP, AMOCO, and Royal Dutch Shell. He also owned stock worth over a million in drug companies. While advisor to Bush, he had meetings with a lobbyist for the pharmaceutical industry, himself a former congressman, and with the president of the Pharmaceutical Research and Manufacturers of America.[49]

Christine Todd Whitman, governor of New Jersey from 1993–2001, was appointed to head the Environmental Protection Agency. As governor she had stressed having corporations voluntarily comply with environmental laws rather than fine them. New Jersey previously had a special environmental prosecutor's office, but Whitman abolished the position. She is a very wealthy woman, owning millions of dollars worth of shares in a number of major companies, including Halliburton, Chevron, ExxonMobil, Phillips Petroleum, Union Carbide, Philip Morris, McDonalds, and Ford.

Elaine Chao, the secretary of labor, has sat on the boards of directors of at least fourteen companies, including Columbia/HCA Healthcare, Dole Food, and Northwest Airlines. She was a banker at Citicorp. In no administration has the secretary of labor come from the ranks of organized labor.

Policy Formation

This aspect of decision making is probably the least well known to the public, and it has received relatively little analysis from social scientists. The policy formation establishment consists of foundations, councils, and commissions that discuss issues and develop strategies. They are sometimes called "think tanks," a term coined during World War II to describe a place where discussions of the war effort could be secretly conducted. Funding for projects frequently comes from government grants but also from corporations, which have been increasing their contributions in recent years.

In these associations, academics, corporate leaders, and government officials meet to develop policies. G. William Domhoff describes the policy formation process as beginning

> in corporate boardrooms and executive suites. It ends in the innermost private offices of the government in Washington, where reporters and sociologists never tread. In between the beginning and the end there are a handful of foundations that provide the experts with money for research ... and influential newspapers and magazines are important in bringing the views of the policy groups to the attention of government personnel.[50]

Some of the most important of the policy-making organizations are the Council on Economic Development, the Business Council, the Council on Foreign Relations, the Ford and Rockefeller Foundations, and the Brookings Institution. The 1970s saw an increase in the number of conservative foundations, which today include the Heritage Foundation, the Hoover Institution, the Manhattan Institute, the Cato Institute, and the American Enterprise Institute.[51] These have played an increasingly important role in influencing public opinion and shaping social life.

The policies that these foundations advocate, often with great success, bring harm to many people. They contribute to maintaining and even increasing inequality. Corporations are very powerful, and without government intervention their actions can damage many lives. The goal of the conservative foundations is to diminish regulation as much as possible. There are also liberal and progressive foundations. These include the Institute for Policy Research and the Economic Policy Institute. They do valuable research and engage in advocacy as well. However, they are less well funded and well connected than the right-wing foundations.

Sara Covington, director of the Democracy and Philanthropy Project, makes clear the significance of the conservative institutes.

> These groups flood the media with hundreds of opinion editorials. Their top staff appear as political pundits and policy experts on dozens of television and radio shows across the country. And their lobbyists work the legislative arenas, distributing policy proposals, briefing papers, and position statements.[52]

Between 1990 and 1993 the progressive publications *Mother Jones,* the *Nation,* the *Progressive,* and *In These Times* were awarded $269,500 from foundations. More conservative magazines, including the *New Criterion,* the *American Spectator,* the *National Interest,* and the *Public Interest,* enjoyed grants worth over ten times as much, $2,743,263.[53]

During the Reagan years the Heritage Foundation, established by the brewer Joseph Coors in 1973, played an especially prominent role. In 1980 the foundation prepared a 1,093-page volume of recommendations for the new president, and more than twenty of its writers became part of the Reagan administration. They worked closely with the Republicans in Congress, seeking cuts in social programs, deregulation of business, and increases in the military budget, all of relevance for issues discussed in this book. Among the well-known names on their board of trustees is Jeb Bush, Florida governor and brother of President George W. Bush.[54]

The conservative foundations are not only interested in promoting what they call "free enterprise." Their agenda includes reducing social supports for the poor, who are seen as moral failures, responsible for their own condition and undeserving of public assistance. The Manhattan Institute helped finance two influential books with this argument: George Gilder's *Wealth and Poverty* and Charles Murray's *Losing Ground: American Social Policy, 1950–1980.* The passage of the tellingly titled Personal Responsibility and Work Opportunity Reconciliation Act of 1996, signed into law by President Clinton, was in part due to the influence of these and similar writings.

These organizations do not advocate policies that would make communities stronger, provide jobs to those needing them, and address the myriad ills facing so many in the United States. Inequality is attributed to genetics and/or a lack of strong personal values. Richard Herrnstein and Charles Murray's *The Bell Curve,* supported by the American Enterprise Institute and published in 1994, claims that genetics accounts for at least 60 percent of a person's IQ score. Since African Americans score lower than those of European descent on tests of mental ability, the conclusion is obvious: unchangeable biology rather than social conditions explains the discrepancy. According to Herrnstein and Murray, people's position in the class structure reflects, not access to opportunities and resources, but their biological inheritance. There is thus no reason to spend money on improving education since "there is reason to think that the job market has been rewarding not just education but intelligence."[55]

The authors ignore the difficulties with defining and testing "intelligence" as well as a number of alternative explanations for the difference in scores.

They claim that lower intelligence is responsible for a plethora of social ills and "may set the stage for a criminal career." They go on to note that those with low IQs cannot understand conventional morality "and are accordingly less inhibited from acting in ways that are hurtful to other people and to the community at large." Although this latter phrase describes a number of corporate actions, they do not include elite deviance in their analysis.[56]

Conservative groups have an interest in influencing students. John Colapinto, a contributing editor to *Rolling Stone*, wrote in the *New York Times Magazine* that

> these groups spend money in various ways to push a right-wing agenda on campuses: some make direct cash "grants" to student groups to start and run conservative campus newspapers; others provide free training in "conservative leadership," often pushing heavily subsidized travel to their "publishing programs"; others provide help with the hefty speaking fees for celebrity right-wing speakers.[57]

Progressive groups do not have the same financial resources to promote student outreach efforts. Right-wing publications receive more than $1 million a year. One right-wing organization alone, the Collegiate Network, donates about $200,000 annually "to 58 student newspapers" and "issues a handbook, *Start the Presses*, to guide students in reaching their classmates."[58] These newspapers are training grounds where the editors and writers are groomed for future positions in academia, public life, and the media.

The prototype for this effort is the *Dartmouth Review*, founded in 1980. The paper became infamous for its racist articles that mocked alleged African American speech patterns, its homophobic stance, and its opposition to affirmative action. Supporters of the publication have included such prominent figures as Patrick Buchanan, Ronald Reagan, and William F. Buckley Jr. After graduation, former editors and writers for these campus publications appear as commentators on talk shows and publish op-ed pieces and books.

Another organization with far-reaching implications is the Federalist Society, which seeks to influence the makeup of the nation's courts, creating a network of federal judges who espouse procorporate, antiaffirmative action positions. In its statement of purpose the society claims that "law schools and the legal profession are currently strongly dominated by a form of orthodox liberal ideology." In contrast, "The Federalist Society for Law and Public Policy Studies [its full name] is a group of conservatives and libertarians interested in the current state of the legal order." It wants the whole legal system to place a high priority on "traditional values."[59]

Members of this society are very wary of government regulations and are generally hostile toward women's rights and civil rights. Court decisions have serious consequences for many aspects of our lives. We need only think of some of the familiar Supreme Court cases, such as the Dred Scott decision, *Plessy v. Ferguson, Brown v. Board of Education of Topeka, Roe v. Wade*, and many others. It was the Supreme Court that decided who would be president of the United States in 2000, choosing George W. Bush by a 5–4 vote. With a different Court, there could have been a different president. Relatively few cases ever reach the highest court, which hears only about seventy-five cases a year. Lower-level appeals courts hear about twenty-eight thousand cases, and the makeup of these courts has far-reaching consequences.[60]

The Federalist Society had its first national meeting in 1982 at Yale Law School, with Robert Bork as the keynote speaker. When Ronald Reagan attempted to appoint Bork to the Supreme Court in 1987, a successful campaign was mounted to oppose him. The campaign included many liberal organizations and individuals but also moderates and even a number of conservative faculty members from the nation's law schools.[61] Other judicial appointments favored by the society have succeeded. Journalist Debra Sontag notes that because judges are appointed for life, what they decide can "reverberate for generations."[62]

A number of members of George W. Bush's administration are members of this society, and one of its most prominent figures, Theodore B. Olson, was appointed solicitor-general, whose job it is to defend the administration's policies before the Supreme Court. Spencer Abraham, one of the founding members, is secretary of energy. Much of the funding for the Federalist Society comes from such conservative foundations as the Sarah Scaife Foundation and the John M. Olin Foundation.[63]

Temporary groups are also formed to arrive at policies that are then presented to the general public. An example of this was the Jackson Hole Group, originally formed in 1990 and named after the Wyoming resort where its members first met. This group rejected the idea of a comprehensive national health care plan. Instead they promoted "managed competition," whereby doctors and hospitals and insurance companies form organizations that will compete for patients on the basis of price and quality. Unfortunately for those with health problems, lower prices can mean not being given more expensive treatments, and it means less choice of physicians as well. Dr. Steffie Woolhandler, a founder of Physicians for a National Health Program, describes this system as an "effort to preserve a role for the insurance industry in health care."[64]

The Jackson Hole Group included Hillary Clinton; representatives from life insurance companies (Prudential, Aetna, Metropolitan, Cigna, and Blue Cross & Blue Shield); pharmaceutical companies and their trade organization, the Pharmaceutical Manufacturers Association; some medical organizations; and Pepsico and General Electric.

The past three chapters have shown some of the major aspects of inequality in the United States. Those who control the corporations influence the political system. This has consequences for the health and well-being of the rest of the population.

NOTES

1. G. William Domhoff, *Who Rules America? Power and Politics*, 4th ed. (New York: McGraw-Hill, 2002), p. xi.

2. Sociologist Val Burris, who has studied the politics of the wealthy, concludes that they differ from other classes in their conservative views. Most end up as "conservative Republicans," although some, not many, will espouse more liberal politics. Burris, "The Myth of Old Money Liberalism," *Social Problems* 47 (2000): 373–75.

3. Leslie Wayne, "Trading on Their Names," *New York Times*, May 2, 2001, p. C2.

4. Ibid.; Katherine Q. Seelye, "Kissinger Promises to Drop Clients If Interests Conflict," *New York Times*, December 2, 2002, p. A12.

5. Sources for this are the Carlyle Group's own Web site, http://www.thecarlylegroup.com/profile.htm; Oliver Burkeman and Julian Borger, "The Ex-President's Club," *Guardian* (London), October 31, 2001, http://www.guardian.co.uk.wtccrash/story/0,1300,583869,00.html; Leslie Wayne, "Elder Bush in Big G.O.P. Cast Toiling for Top Equity Firm," *New York Times*, March 5, 2001, pp. A1, A14; Kurt Eichenwald, "Bin Laden Family Liquidates Holdings with Carlyle Group," *New York Times*, October 26, 2001, p. C4; Greg Palast, *The Best Democracy Money Can Buy: An Investigative Reporter Exposes the Truth about Corporate Cons, Globalization, and High-Finance Fraudsters* (New York: Plume, 2003), p. 104.

6. Richard A. Oppel Jr., "Financial Disclosures Put 3 Candidates and Clintons in Same Realm as Bush," *New York Times*, June 14, 2003, p. A12.

7. James Sterngold, "Ex-Official to Develop Water Plans in Middle East," *New York Times*, March 13, 2002, p. A22.

8. These are modified from G. William Domhoff, *The Powers That Be: Processes of Ruling Class Domination in America* (New York: Vintage, 1979).

9. TrueMajority, one of the members of the coalition, e-mail message to author, March 4, 2003.

10. William Grieder, *Who Will Tell the People: The Betrayal of American Democracy* (New York: Simon and Schuster, 1992), pp. 43, 50.

11. Jeffrey R. Birnbaum, *The Lobbyists: How Influence Peddlers Work Their Way in Washington* (New York: Times Books, 1993), p. 4.

12. David Korten, *When Corporations Rule the World* (San Francisco: Berrett-Koehler Publishers/Kumarian Press, 2001), p. 292.

13. Neil A. Lewis, "Senate Fight over Phrase Demonstrates Word's Effect," *New York Times*, October 11, 1996, p. A16.

14. Neil A. Lewis, "A Lobby Effort That Delivers the Big Votes," *New York Times*, October 12, 1996, pp. 37, 50. Quotes, p. 50. Lewis explains that FedEx was concerned with language in a 1923 railway express law. If the company could get the language changed as it wished, it would be exempt from the National Labor Relations Act and in a better effort to fight union organizing at its company.

15. Quoted in Birnbaum, *The Lobbyists*, p. 25.

16. Leslie Wayne, "A Special Deal for Lobbyists: A Getaway with Law-makers," *New York Times*, January 26, 1997, p. 16.

17. Leslie Wayne and Melody Peterson, "A Muscular Lobby Rolls Up Its Sleeve," *New York Times*, November 4, 2001, sec. 3, pp. 1, 13.

18. Korten, *When Corporations Rule the World*, pp. 292–93; for another health-related example of astro-turf lobbying, see Laura Flanders, "Is It Real . . . Or Is It Astroturf: PR Firm Finds "Grassroots" Support for Breast Implants," *Extra!* July/August 1996, p. 6.

19. Jeff Gerth and Sheryl Gay Stolberg, "With Quiet, Unseen Ties, Drug Makers Sway Debate," *New York Times*, October 5, 2000.

20. Bill Hogan, "Pulling Strings from Afar," *AARP Bulletin* (February 2002): 3.

21. Wayne and Peterson, "A Muscular Lobby Rolls Up Its Sleeve," p. 13.

22. Quoted in Leslie Wayne, "Lucrative Lobbying Jobs Await Many Leaving Government Service," *New York Times*, December 16, 2000, p. A17.

23. Ibid.

24. Leslie Wayne, "With G.O.P. Chief a Lobbyist, Donors Are Clients," *New York Times*, June 8, 1997, p. 30.

25. Alison Mitchell, "Companies Use Ex-Lawmakers in Fight on Offshore Tax Break," *New York Times*, August 10, 2002, pp. A1, A10.

26. Domhoff, *The Powers That Be*, p. 138.

27. Leslie Wayne, "Loopholes Allow Presidential Race to Set a Record," *New York Times*, September 8, 1996, p. 26.

28. Kevin P. Phillips, *Wealth and Democracy: A Political History of the American Rich* (New York: Broadway Books, 2002), p. 326. The Web site is http://www. billionairesforbushorgore.com.

29. This example is from Public Campaign; their document, "Buy Now, Save Later: Campaign Contributions and Corporate Taxation," with many other instances, is available at http://publiccampaign/clean_main.html.

30. Quoted in John M. Broder, "Oil and Gas Fuel Bush Run for President,"

New York Times, June 23, 2000, p. A18; Richard L. Berke, "Enron Pursued Plan to Forge Close Ties to Gore Campaign," *New York Times*, January 18, 2002, pp. 1, 12.

31. John M. Broder and Don Van Natta Jr., "Perks for Biggest Donors, and Pleas for More Cash," *New York Times*, July 30, 2000, pp. 1, 22; Edmund Andrews and Elizabeth Becker, "Bush Got $500,000 from Companies That Got Contracts, Study Finds," *New York Times*, October 31, 2003, p. A1.

32. Wayne, "A Special Deal for Lobbyists," pp. 1, 16.

33. Bob Herbert, "The Donor Class," *New York Times*, July 19, 2000, sec. 4, p. 15.

34. Richard A. Oppel Jr., "Documents Show Parties Often Mixed Fund-Raising and Policy," *New York Times*, December 7, 2002, p. A15.

35. Richard L. Berke, "Companies Supply Parties' Lifeblood," *New York Times*, August 16, 1988.

36. Domhoff, *The Powers That Be*, pp. 140–41.

37. Berke, "Companies Supply Parties Lifeblood"; Richard A. Oppel Jr., "Drug Makers Sponsor Event for G.O.P. as Bill Is Debated," *New York Times*, June 19, 2002, p. A20.

38. Wayne, "Loopholes Allow Presidential Race to Set a Record."

39. Center for Responsible Ethics, "*McConnell v. FEC*: Summary of the Supreme Court's Decision," http://www.feewatch.org/law/court/mcconnelltable.asp, pp. 1–3 (accessed January 2, 2004).

40. Video on Clean Campaigns.

41. Domhoff, *Who Rules America*, p. 143.

42. Ibid.

43. Phillips, *Wealth and Democracy*, pp. xvi–xvii. The Democratic Party's candidate, Al Gore, had five hundred thousand more popular votes than George Bush's son, George W. Bush. There was a dispute over some of the ballots in Florida, where a number of voting irregularities occurred, including turning away many African American voters from the polls. George W. Bush's brother Jeb was governor. At issue was whether the Florida ballots should be recounted. The matter ended up in the Supreme Court, which in a 5–4 decision said they should not be. Florida's electoral votes went to George W. Bush, who then had a majority of electoral college votes. This was the second time in American history that the Republican presidential candidate with fewer popular votes than his opponent became president. The other case was the election of 1876 when the Republican Rutherford B. Hayes went to the White House. He ended Reconstruction, setting the stage for decades of white supremacy in the South. For a detailed account of the disenfranchisement of African Americans, undercounting of votes for Gore, and other aspects of the voting in Florida, see Palast, *The Best Democracy Money Can Buy*, pp. 11–81.

44. Don Van Natta Jr. with Neela Banerjee, "Bush Policies Have Been Good to Energy Industry," *New York Times*, April 21, 2002.

45. "Greasing the Machine," *New Internationalist*, June 2001, http://www.newint.org/issue335/greasing.htm; Richard W. Stevenson, "Bushes' Assets Put at $8.8 Million in Filing, " *New York Times*, May 16, 2003, p. A22.

46. Kenny Bruno and Jim Valette, "Cheney and Halliburton: Go Where the Oil Is," *Multinational Monitor* (May 2001): 22–25; "Cheney's Income Fell Sharply in '01," *New York Times*, April 16, 2002, p. A25; Stevenson, "Bushes' Assets Put at $8.8 Million in Filing."

47. Data from "Bush's Corporate Cabinet," *Multinational Monitor* (May 2001): 17; A&E Biography, *Rumsfeld*, broadcast January 29, 2003; Center for Responsive Politics, "Presidential Profile: George W. Bush's Cabinet," http://www .opensecrets.org/bush/cabinet/cabinet.rumsfeld.asp.

48. "Bush's Corporate Cabinet," p. 21; Center for Responsive Politics, "Presidential Profile: George W. Bush's Cabinet."

49. "Bush Aide at Drug Meeting Held Shares," *New York Times*, July 21, 2001, p. A9.

50. Domhoff, *The Powers That Be*, p. 62.

51. Phillips, *Wealth and Democracy*, pp. 319–20.

52. Sally Covington, "Right Thinking, Big Grants, and Long-Term Strategy: How Conservative Philanthropies and Think Tanks Transform U.S. policy," *CAQ: Covert Action Quarterly* (Winter 1998): 11; for a discussion of how conservative foundations have influenced public debate on global warming, a topic discussed in chapter 6, see Aaron M. McCright and Riley E. Dunlap, "Defeating Kyoto: The Conservative Movement's Impact on U.S. Climate Change Policy," *Social Problems* 50 (2003): 348–73.

53. Ibid.

54. Russ Bellant, *"The Coors Connection": How Coors Family Philanthropy Undermines Democratic Pluralism* (Boston: South End Press, 1991); "What Heritage Foundation Does," *New York Times*, November 18, 1994; Norman Solomon, "The Media's Favorite Think Tank: How the Heritage Foundation Turns Money into Media," *Extra!* July/August, 1996, pp. 9–12. Information on Jeb Bush from Covington, "Right Thinking, Big Grants, and Long-Term Strategy," p. 7.

55. Richard Herrnstein and Charles Murray, *The Bell Curve: Intelligence and Class Structure in American Life* (New York: Free Press, 1994), p. 96.

56. Ibid., pp. 240–41; estimate of genetic component of intelligence, p. 105. Useful critiques of *The Bell Curve* can be found in Russell Jacoby and Naomi Glauberman, eds., *The Bell Curve Debate* (New York: Times Books, 1995).

57. John Colapinto, "Armies of the Right: What Campus Conservatives Learned from the 60's Generation," *New York Times Magazine*, May 25, 2003, p. 32.

58. Emma Ruby-Sachs and Timothy Waligore, "Alternative Voice on Campus," *Nation*, February 17, 2003, pp. 27–29; Colapinto, "Armies of the Right," p. 34.

59. From their Web site, http://www.fed-soc.org/ourpurpose.htm.

60. Debra Sontag, "The Power of the Fourth: How One Appellate Court Is Quietly Moving America Ever Rightward," *New York Times Magazine*, March 2, 2003, p. 40.

61. Domhoff, *Who Rules America?* p. 145.

62. Sontag, "The Power of the Fourth," p. 41.

63. Neil A. Lewis, "A Conservative Legal Group Thrives in Bush's Washington," *New York Times*, April 18, 2001, pp. A1, A20.

64. Quoted in Robin Toner, "Hillary Clinton's Potent Brain Trust on Health Reform," *New York Times*, February 28, 1993, sec. 3, p. 8.

Chapter 6

ORGANIZATIONAL AND STRUCTURAL VIOLENCE AGAINST CONSUMERS AND COMMUNITIES

We want those we care about and ourselves to be as healthy as possible. To this end, we can try to eat sensibly, not smoke, not drink excessively, have periodic check-ups, and so on. There are some things, however, that we cannot do as individuals. Our socioeconomic status has an impact on our health and that is, in turn, dependent on opportunities and resources that are available to us. In addition, corporate decisions based on profit seeking and government regulation or lack thereof will affect our physical well-being.

In this chapter we will look at how the economic and political inequality discussed in the previous three chapters leads to organizational and structural violence in the form of health problems for consumers and communities. The harm described in this chapter results from corporate profit seeking coupled with a lack of stronger government protections; in other words, from the routine workings of the economy and the political system.

CONSUMERS AS VICTIMS OF VIOLENCE

Harm often results as corporate executives and those they employ simply do their jobs. Sometimes their actions are illegal, but if they are prosecuted, the penalties are likely to be relatively small compared to the gains. Corporate lawbreakers rarely go to jail; instead they may have to give a speech or do community service of some sort, options rarely given to street crimi-nals.[1] In 1985 the pharmaceutical company SmithKline pleaded guilty to thirty-four charges resulting from deaths connected to its marketing of a blood pressure drug that could damage a user's kidneys and liver. The com-pany knew of the side effects but did not report them to the Food and Drug Administration (FDA), nor did they label the drug to warn potential users. The company doctors who were involved in this could have gone to jail for fourteen years and/or been fined $14,000 each. Instead the company itself was ordered by a Pennsylvania judge to give $100,000 to a child abuse pro-gram and to perform five hundred hours of community service.[2]

SICKENING "HEALTH" PRODUCTS

Health care companies continue to be a risk to sick people. In 2003 the medical technology firm Guidant Corporation announced it would plead guilty to ten felony charges resulting from deaths and injuries due to one of its products. Guidant sold a device called a "stent-graft" used to strengthen abdominal blood vessels without surgery. Twelve people died when the device malfunctioned, and at least 2,628 patients suffered when the device became stuck in their abdomens. Although doctors reported problems with the stent-graft, company executives willfully hid this knowledge.

Guidant sales representatives, actually there when doctors were implanting the stent-graft, advised doctors to break it in the patient's body and remove the pieces. This procedure had never been subjected to testing. Com-pany whistle-blowers anonymously tipped off the FDA about the extent of the stent-graft failures. In addition to paying the largest fines ever levied against a medical technology manufacture, $92.4 million, Guidant faces thousands of law suits. Guidant executives are not too worried about this, however. One described the litigation as "manageable" since the corporation's liability insur-ance would cover much of the costs. Furthermore, Guidant will be allowed to continue its participation in government programs such as Medicare.[3]

C. R. Bard, Inc., a medical devices manufacturer with over $1 billion a year in sales, pleaded guilty in 1993 to over 390 counts of fraud and human experimentation in the marketing and production of a heart catheter that resulted in at least one death and twenty-two emergency operations. The company had tested the catheters on unknowing patients while they were on the operating table. It also knew that the catheters caused injury to ani-mals, but they concealed this information from the FDA.[4]

It is not unusual for companies to deceive the FDA. Businesses argue that they must protect trade secrets, and the FDA apparently accepts that rationale and so do the courts. Disaster can result. Until 1986, Shiley, Inc., a division of the large pharmaceutical company Pfizer, sold faulty heart valves that resulted in over three hundred deaths. The valves had a tendency to crack when implanted, but company documents showing this information were withheld from the FDA.[5]

The FDA is supposed to check on medical devices, pharmaceuticals, and food products. Yet the agency does not even know how many manufacturers of medical devices they should be inspecting. In past inspections they found problems in at least 16 percent of the cases, but took action in only half of them.[6]

When inspections are carried out, threats to public safety can be discovered. When FDA agents examined the major pharmaceutical company Shering Plough's New Jersey and Puerto Rico plants between 1998 and 2002, the agency "found significant violations of quality control regulations related to facilities, manufacturing, quality assurance, equipment, laboratories, packaging, and labeling." The violations involved about 125 prescription and nonprescription drugs.[7]

Many mothers rely on infant formula and prepared baby foods to nourish their children. Even these have caused problems. For example, Syntex Laboratories in California marketed Neo-Mul-Soy, which had one-fifth of the necessary choline. Since inadequate amounts of choline can result in learning disabilities, the product was eventually recalled, but not before it had been fed to tens of thousands of babies. A positive result was that the FDA, which had not had the authority to regulate infant formula, was given this responsibility in 1980. When the Reagan administration came into office, however, new procedures, mostly suggested by the infant formula industry, were instituted, effectively turning back the clock. Dr. Dennis L. Heuring, who for eight years worked for one of the largest infant formula manufacturers, Mead Johnson, did the analysis justifying the more company-friendly rules. Following this, several more deficient infant formulas went on the market.[8]

WATCH WHAT YOU EAT

Marketing practices, methods of raising animals, and food preparation practices each contribute to our being less healthy than we might be. Ball

Park Franks is the homey sounding name of the hot dogs made by Bil Mar Foods, a subsidiary of the Sara Lee Corporation. Contaminated with the bacteria *Listeria monocutogenes*, however, the meat led to a hundred illnesses and at least twenty-one deaths in 1998 as a result of conditions in one of the plants. It is likely that insufficient testing was responsible for this. The federal government brought charges, and the company pleaded guilty to two misdemeanors and was fined $200,000.[9]

People have been shot in fast-food restaurants, but they have also died or become sick from eating tainted hamburgers. This happened to four children who had eaten their hamburgers at Jack in the Box in 1993.[10] According to Center for Disease Control statistics, food-connected illnesses are responsible for an annual 325,000 hospitalizations and five thousand deaths. *E. coli* bacteria were the contaminant at Jack in the Box. These bacteria alone cause seventy-three illnesses a year and sixty deaths.[11] The Reagan administration had weakened the food inspection process and allowed violators of the law to keep selling their products. George H. W. Bush continued his predecessor's policies.

Under these two Republican presidents, the number of outside inspectors was reduced, and food companies did much of their own checking. With men from the cattle and hog industries heading regulatory agencies, this is not too surprising. One case involved Cattle King, which was selling hamburger meat to school lunch programs in spite of its record of diseased meat and unclean plants. Canada, in contrast, banned its products.[12] Food companies today are still responsible for much of the inspection of their own products.[13] In 2002 eight people died after eating contaminated poultry from a Wampler Foods plant in Pennsylvania. Fifty-four became sick but survived. Pilgrim's Pride, the parent company of Wampler, then recalled 27 million pounds of chicken.[14] *E. coli*-contaminated ground beef from the giant meat packer ConAgra caused one woman's death and made forty-six others sick.[15]

In 1996 federal rules for meat inspection were made somewhat stringent for the first time since 1906. The so-called sniff-and-poke method has been replaced by more scientific procedures. But there are still an inadequate number of inspectors. In 2001 there were 7,500 compared to 12,000 in 1978.[16] In 2002 the number of inspectors increased, but the officials do not have the authority to shut down a plant nor can the Agriculture Department demand that possibly tainted foods be recalled. It can only urge the companies to do this.

The retired former chairman of the government's meat inspectors union, Delmer Jones, declared, "Most any system will work and protect the consumer if you've got two things: teeth and enforcement." Instead of that, he said, there is "smoke and mirrors" at many meat-packing facilities. At the Shapiro Packing plant inspectors found feces and a form of *E. coli*. Shapiro's meat is purchased by fast-food chains, schools, and supermarkets. When Shapiro promised to correct the problems, the department said it could keep on shipping its meat.[17]

Meat from foreign sources is not likely to be safer than domestic meat. Inspections on imported meats declined from 17 percent to only 6 percent, although the amount of meat that crosses U.S. borders has increased since 1997. Defending the policy, Karen Struck at the Department of Agriculture stated, "Yes, the amount of meat inspected is less, but the meat we inspect is inspected more thoroughly."[18]

If the inspectors are too zealous in protecting the public, they can find themselves in trouble. For instance, in New York two meat inspectors were suspended after helping to uncover lax examinations. They brought their case to the agency that is supposed to protect federal employees from unfair treatment, the Merit Systems Protection Board. The board found, according to the *New York Times* account, that they had been "wrongly suspended from their jobs after providing tips that helped investigators uncover abuses among inspectors in New York and New Jersey." Their allegations led to "an intense examination of meat plants" in the two states, "which found unsanitary conditions at nearly two dozen of them." The U.S. Department of Agriculture (USDA) also retaliated against inspectors in California and Arkansas.[19]

It is not family farmers who produce the food for restaurants and supermarkets but large conglomerates raising meat and poultry in factory-like conditions, bad for both animals and the environment. Cattle are raised on feedlots, where the animals' waste is collected into what are picturesquely called "lagoons" but are more accurately described as "huge pools of excrement," which can spread disease and cause water pollution.[20]

Hogs are also raised under industrial farming conditions that can be injurious to the health of people living near the sites. Concentrated in large herds, the animals produce wastes that emit toxic fumes of ammonia and hydrogen sulfide. These mix with dust and get into groundwater. Rural families who live near the hog operations are experiencing neurological damage. Robert Thornell of Paulding, Ohio, lives half a mile from a hog farm cesspool. He suffers from memory loss, moods swings, and other ailments. His wife's health is also impaired. He'd like to move but remarked, "I don't know where to go. I've lived here for forty-four years. This is home to me." Hog owners vigorously deny any connection between their business and people's health problems.[21]

To date, the government has sided with the hog farmers, exempting them from provisions of the Clean Air Act and claiming more scientific evidence is needed to show a connection between their operations and anyone's poor health. An alternative strategy would be to assume that there could be a link and at least temporarily regulate the hog farms. Government regulators who tried to take a more protective approach toward the public's health were discouraged from doing this. Several researchers and inspectors resigned because they were not allowed to do their jobs. One of them, scientist James Zahn, was told that he could not present his research on this issue at a conference. A supervisor suggested to him, "Politically sensitive and controversial issues require discretion."[22]

Meat could be raised in more humane and healthy ways. There could be a more stringent inspection process. In Holland public health officials, not industry-connected personnel, inspect meat, and there are many more regulations affecting how cattle are raised. In the United States the industry has opted for irradiating meat. Although both the World Health Organization and the American Medical Association say that irradiated foods are not harmful, there has been reluctance among consumers to buy foods exposed to radioactivity. There are questions about long-term health risks, and there is evidence that irradiation causes a loss of nutrients.[23] In an attempt to allay potential fears, Sen. Tom Harkin of Iowa added a clause to a farm bill that would allow for calling irradiated meat "pasteurized." An editor of *Food Processing*, a trade journal, explained that supermarket customers are likely to associate the word "irradiation" with "wartime and bombs and bad things."[24]

The way agribusiness grows crops also poses risks to consumers and the environment. About 1.5 billion pounds of pesticides are used in American agriculture on food and industrial crops. Tons of herbicides are sprayed to control weeds and fungi. In 1994 a citizens' organization, the Environmental Working Group, analyzed Midwestern water and found that over 3.5 million people in that region alone were drinking water laced with the same chemicals used to kill weeds. An EPA spokesperson called this study "another in a series of wake-up calls that tells us we can no longer take for granted that our drinking water is safe all the time." But the Clinton administration was unable to defeat pesticide industry efforts against strengthening the Safe Drinking Water Act.[25]

Some of the most dangerous chemicals, such as DDT, are now banned from use in the United States, but American companies still sell them in the

Third World. While harming consumers abroad, these can also come back to the unsuspecting shopper in the United States in what has been called "the circle of poison."[26]

Imported produce poses other dangers than pesticide contamination. Harmful bacteria may cause illness in unsuspecting consumers. Currently only a small amount of imported produce, less than 2 percent, is inspected for this potential problem. Yet between 1999 and 2000 the FDA tested 1,003 samples of imported fresh fruits and vegetables and found that 4.4 percent had dangerous bacteria.

In November 2003 three people died after eating tainted Mexican scallions, and hundreds more became ill. In the 1990s people became sick after eating Mexican cantaloupes and Guatemalan raspberries. Domestic produce can also have disease-causing bacteria though the problem is less common.[27] While consumers can take precautions, such as thoroughly washing produce before eating it, more inspections would reduce the danger.

MORE FAT, LESS HEALTH

The fast-food industry has capitalized on a number of changes in the United States. With more women working and with household incomes stagnant or declining, places that serve inexpensive, familiar food in a dependably clean setting are attractive. Some have their own play areas. The free toys they offer are appealing to children. Tie-in campaigns to popular movies, beneficial to the fast-food chains and to Hollywood, add to the attraction.[28] "Eating out" used to be a relatively rare experience for many working-class families. In 1977 only 16 percent of all meals were eaten elsewhere than one's home. By 1995, 29 percent of meals were being eaten in commercial establishments.[29]

Advertisers work to turn children into consumers who will nag their parents for particular products. People in the business talk about "pester power."[30] This is associated with a new childhood health problem, obesity, which has other causes as well.

Fast food is cheap, and lots of people think it is tasty; you can order it from and eat it in a car. However, it is helping to promote a generation of overweight children whose health problems, including diabetes, will persist into adulthood. Future generations are likely to have the same experience. Since the 1970s the incidence of childhood obesity has doubled, with type 2 diabetes rapidly increasing, especially in Mexican American, American Indian, and African American children. Obese children are more likely to suffer joint problems, asthma, and other respiratory illnesses. When overweight girls become overweight women, they are likely to have problem pregnancies.[31]

About 61 percent of Americans are overweight, with 20 percent fitting the technical definition of being obese. Young people are watching more TV and playing outside less. When parents believe their neighborhoods are unsafe, they may prefer to keep their kids indoors, where they are likely to sit in front of the TV.[32] They are not burning calories, but they are being induced to buy products that will add to their weight. Other industrial countries more strictly regulate children's exposure to ads, making it illegal to have these on TV.[33]

Schools could help to remedy the problem where children are concerned, but instead they contribute to it. Despite a lot of political cant about how important children are, public education finds itself short-changed for revenues. Physical education programs are cut. Corporations come to the rescue, but there is a serious downside to their assistance.

In 1993, in exchange for $12,000, a school district in Colorado agreed to place the first ads for Burger King on school buses and in school hallways. Companies quickly saw the value of creating brand loyalty from an early age. One brochure at the 1997 Kids Power Marketing Conference described "the schoolhouse gates" as the entrance to a "river of revenue." The soft-drink industry provides teaching materials to cash-poor schools; the companies not only gain potential customers but get a tax-deduction as well. Fast-food chains also sell food in schools, while vending machines dispense sodas, cookies, candy, ice cream, and chips. The schools receive money for allowing this.[34]

In 1946 the National School Lunch Program, run by the USDA, was created to provide supposedly healthy food to younger people regardless of income. But the program has evolved into more of a subsidy for agribusiness. The National Cattleman's Beef Association gave $3 million in campaign contributions between 1990 and 2003. The association's lobbyists now serve in the Bush administration, but they have had clout in previous ones as well.

The meat industry is not only concerned with purchases of beef now; they also want kids to develop into adults who think a meal isn't complete unless it has meat in it. When a Clinton appointee was put in charge of the USDA's nutrition programs, she tried to implement healthier school lunches. The cattle industry successfully lobbied against her proposals.[35]

Items that are loaded with saturated fats are common; lots of cheese and beef but very few fresh fruits and vegetables make their way into school lunches. Boston's Children's Hospital has an obesity program. Its director,

David Ludwig, explained that "school districts are under intense budgetary pressure, and often-times nutrition is at the bottom of their priority list."[36]

Diet and exercise are related to income. Those with higher incomes are better able to pay for exercise programs, have parks for free exercise, live in neighborhoods where healthier foods are more available, and receive medical advice regarding their weight. The *Journal of the American Medical Association* noted that:

> the lower rates of counseling among respondents with lower education and income levels . . . are particularly worrisome, because members of lower socioeconomic groups have poorer health outcomes.[37]

There are some interesting community experiences which show that with some effort diet and heath can be improved. In North Karelia, Finland, which had exceptionally high rates of cardiovascular disease, a public health effort has involved the whole community in modifying people's diets, increasing life expectancy and significantly reducing mortality rates. About thirty years ago a local doctor acted on his belief that health is not just an individual matter but reflects the ways a community is organized. Local food producers were persuaded to produce healthier products, ones with less salt content, for example. There were lowering cholesterol contests, special television programs, and antismoking campaigns. The Finnish experiment has become the model for a similar effort in Olmsted County, Minnesota, which since the 1980s has been promoting exercise. Restaurants indicate what are the healthiest items on their menus. Volunteers help to identify these.[38]

THE AUTOMOBILE INDUSTRY IS HAZARDOUS TO OUR HEALTH

The automobile companies and the federal government have made decisions whose cumulative effects have been to create a dependence on privately owned cars. People drive cars because automobiles have been presented as symbols of freedom, happiness, sexual pleasure, and the like, and they are certainly sometimes convenient. However, since alternative means of transportation are not readily available, a result of decades of decisions regarding transportation in the United States, many are very dependent on cars to get to work, to shop, and so on. The automobile companies were actually responsible for the destruction of public transportation in a number of cities, including Los Angeles. This involved breaking antitrust laws, but the penalties were extremely small, about $5,000 for General Motors and the other companies.[39]

From 1956 to 1972 the government spent over $55 billion on the interstate highway system alone. In contrast, only $3.1 billion was allocated from 1970 to 1975 for urban mass transit. This pattern has continued with help (and pressure) from the auto industry. Between 1990 and 1995, for example, the federal treasury provided nearly five times as much to highways as it did to urban mass transit, about $98 billion compared to $22 billion. In 1998 Congress allocated $217 billion for transportation for six years; $37 billion is for mass transit, and $180 billion is for highways and new roads.[40]

The Federal Transit Administration (FTA) is part of the U.S. Department of Transportation. Its mission is to support "high quality public transportation."[41] It is difficult do this on the monies it is allocated. In 2001 per capita spending on highways was $91.40; on the FTA it was $5.60.[42]

The development of highways facilitated the growth of the suburbs. Both of these had a negative impact on racial/ ethnic inequalities, as will be discussed further in chapter 9. Urban sprawl is a concept describing the pattern of people who live in what are technically called "metropolitan areas" but are widely dispersed rather than living in more centralized communities. Sprawl has a number of consequences, but what is relevant here is the effect on commuting patterns. In the United States between 1950 and 1990 the amount of land built upon in fify-eight metropolitan areas rose by 305 percent, much more than the 80 percent rise in population in this time period.[43]

Urban sprawl has increased the use of private vehicles, as workers live farther from their jobs or lack public transportation to get to them. In 2000, 76 percent of workers drove alone to their job, while only 5 percent used public transportation. Adding to the need for private vehicles is the replacement of local businesses by shopping malls.[44]

Transportation decisions are political ones that effectively reinforce inequality. Suburbanites are more likely to be white, to have higher incomes, and to own cars. People in cities are disproportionately of color and more dependent upon public transportation. Jocelyn Elders, surgeon general for a while in the first Clinton administration, described the people at the bus stops and the subway or metro platforms as "the 'have-nots' in our system." Lack of good transportation makes it harder to get to work and to health care facilities.[45]

Dependence on automobiles has negative consequences. In ads, the vehicle moves unimpeded through a scenic setting, often in the majestic wide-open spaces of the West. There is no traffic, the skies are clear, there are no worries about parking, and life seems idyllic. Switch to real-life. Most cars are on roads with vehicles to the left and to the right, in front and behind. More cars, going longer distances, have meant more congestion, which in turn means longer commuting times. Studies done by the Texas Transportation Institute at Texas A&M University in 2001 discovered that while the average driver sat in traffic for eleven hours a year in 1982, by 1999 drivers were enjoying the comfort of their car for thirty-six hours. This is the average just for being in a traffic jam. Some cities are far above the average. For Los Angeles, the figure is fifty-six hours; for Atlanta, fifty-three, up from twenty-six in 1994.[46] The stress this causes is summed up in a new phrase in our vocabulary, "road rage." Traffic jams are not only aggravating; they also add to fuel consumption and pollution.

The automotive companies provide a number of examples of organizational violence. They choose to make more dangerous vehicles. In 1929 General Motors president Alfred Sloane explained why he wasn't having safety glass installed in GM's Chevrolets: "I would very much rather spend the same amount of money in improving our car in other ways because I think from the standpoint of selfish business, it would be a very much better investment. You can say, perhaps, that I am selfish, but business is selfish. We are not a charitable institution—we are trying to make a profit for our stockholders."[47] That attitude has not changed: people are still being killed and injured because companies decide that profits are a higher priority than the well-being of their customers.

The federal government has allowed automobile companies to manufacture vehicles with few serious penalties if they violate safety laws. When the Motor Vehicle Safety Act was passed in 1966, the industry prevented provisions of the act that would have made it a criminal offense to knowingly market a dangerous vehicle. At most, the company could be fined. Few street criminals can influence legislation in this way.

Exposés such as Ralph Nader's 1966 book, *Unsafe at Any Speed*, and an aroused public led to the creation of the Department of Transportation and, within it, the National Highway Traffic Safety Administration. Standards were established for making less harmful cars. The industry fought, of course, as it still fights today against making the safest possible cars. For example, auto manufacturers were able to get the Reagan administration to delay requiring air bags or automatic seat belts. This likely contributed to around nine thousand deaths and sixty-five thousand injuries annually.[48]

The auto industry has also been effective in having speed limits increased, which contributes to deaths on the highways.[49]

The automobile industry uses cost-benefit analyses to decide if it is profitable to cut corners on safety. This is what Ford did in the 1970s with its infamous Pinto. Because of the Pinto's design, in rear-end collisions the gas tank often ruptured, and fire enveloped the vehicle. At least five hundred people burned to death this way. Ford engineers knew of this problem, and Ford actually had a patent on a safer tank. But executives, especially President Lee Iacocca, were eager to come out with a small car that could compete with the then popular Volkswagen Beetle. In such a cutthroat atmosphere, engineers feared bringing up safety issues, one even saying, "With Lee [Iaccoco] it was taboo."[50]

Using the 1972 National Highway Traffic Safety Administration's decision that a life was worth $200,725, Ford concluded that spending $11 a vehicle for a safer fuel system would cost the company more than payments it would have to make from lawsuits.[51]

General Motors manufactured pickup trucks between 1973 and 1987 that were also potential firetraps. Because of the outside placement of the gasoline tanks, the trucks burst into flames if struck from the side. Passengers burned to death or suffered permanently scarring injuries. Company documents showed that GM was aware of the problem as early as 1983 yet continued making the trucks for five more years. In 1993 a Georgia jury awarded millions of dollars to a family whose seventeen-year-old son died of burns in a GM pickup truck.

Douglas Wharton was one of those burned severely. He wondered: "What is America? Is it the corporation GM or am I America? . . . The people that are going to be burned that are kind of faceless, are they America? This decision seems to be saying, 'go ahead and burn . . . Americans can burn.'"[52]

As of 1993, 150 to 300 people had died because of the truck's faulty design. The government gives the low figure, critics the higher one. GM won a victory when the Clinton administration decided not to order a recall of these lethal vehicles. It would have cost GM about a $1 billion to recall and fix the trucks, and a recall would have strengthened lawsuits against the company. In exchange for not having to recall their trucks, GM agreed to contribute $51.3 million to safety programs, including education regarding drunk driving and using seat belts. The amount is equivalent to only 2 percent of the company's profits for 1993.[53] None of the money was earmarked for teaching automakers about the value of human lives.

Automakers are still encouraging consumers to buy life-threatening vehicles, now in the form of sport utility vehicles (SUVs). It is true that customers make a choice to buy these; they are not forced to do so. However, the manufacturers and the government each bear a responsibility for encouraging the use of these in various ways. Manufacturers organize focus groups to find out how to discover the best marketing strategies, while government regulations or lack thereof make it more practical to manufacture a dangerous product.

SPORT UTILITY VEHICLES: THE LATEST AUTOMOTIVE DANGER

SUVs seem to appeal to a desire for power and control.[54] They also appeal to those who are fearful. Market research indicates this; lavish advertising budgets of over a billion dollars in 2000 capitalized on this fear, illustrated by the following examples. A California owner in her Toyota Land Cruiser remarked, "The world is becoming a harder and more violent place to live, so we wrap ourselves with these big vehicles. . . . You have more power."[55]

At a car show, the captain of a Washington State football team looked longingly at a GM Hummer, built to resemble the Humvee used for military transport in the Persian Gulf Wars. Expressing a feeling that SUV manufacturers have cashed in on, Cooper Schwartz explained, "I like something where I can look down into another car and give that knowing smile that 'I'm bigger than you.' It makes me feel powerful."[56] The campaigns to sell SUVs have been successful; over 52 percent of private vehicles sold in 2002 were SUVs.[57]

Some Hummer drivers seemed to feel they were vicariously fighting in the most recent war against Iraq. Sam Bernstein, a fifty-one-year-old Marin County, California, antique dealer, proclaimed, "When I turn on the TV, I see wall-to wall-Humvees and I'm proud. . . . I'm proud of my country and I'm proud to be driving a product that is making a significant contribution." He did not explain what his particular contribution was. There is even an International Hummer Owners Group whose founder, Rick Schmidt, said this vehicle is a symbol of America; to deface it "in word or deed" is to "deface the American flag and what it stands for."[58]

While those sitting high in their SUVs may feel invulnerable, those below them in ordinary cars have their lives threatened. Even those in the SUV are not as safe as they might think.

- SUVs are high; those in lower vehicles cannot always see around them or look through an SUV's windshield when it is in front of them.

- SUVs have longer stopping distances and are difficult to stop on slippery surfaces. Regulations allow them to have brakes that contribute to this.
- SUVs have a tendency to roll over when they hit a guardrail. For every one hundred crashes an SUV will roll over five times, while the rate is 1.7 times for cars. Rollovers are responsible for deaths and spinal and neck injuries leading to paralysis. In the 1990s 12,000 people died in the United States when the SUVs they were in rolled over, often after hitting a guardrail. In the first year of the new century, 2,049 died.[59]

For their passengers, SUVs are not more dangerous than cars. They are more dangerous for those in conventional cars when an SUV-car collision takes place. Below are the death rates for occupants of vehicles that are hit by other vehicles of a particular type.

TABLE 6.1 DEATH RATES FROM COLLISIONS BY TYPES OF VEHICLES INVOLVED, 1995–2000

the vehicle that collides	death rate per 100,000 when struck vehicle is a car
large pickup	293
large SUV	205
small SUV	151
large car	85
compact car	60

Source: Danny Hakim, "Regulators Seek Ways to Make SUVs Safer" New York Times, January 30, 2003, p. C6.

An SUV's construction and greater weight causes its impact on smaller cars to be more deadly. One way to increase the market for SUVs is to stress having one as a form of self-defense when driving.[60] They are also deadly for pedestrians, killing about 11 percent of those they hit, compared to the 7 percent killed by minivans and cars when struck.[61]

More people are killed annually in auto accidents than by firearms, as indicated in table 6.2.

TABLE 6.2 MOTOR VEHICLE DEATHS
AND FIREARMS DEATHS, 2000

Number of motor vehicle deaths	Number of firearms deaths
41,804	28,663

Sources: Motor vehicle deaths, U.S. Census Bureau, *Statistical Abstract of the United States, 2002*, table 103, p. 82; firearms deaths, U.S. Department of Health and Human Services, *National Vital Statistics Report 50*, no. 15 (September 16, 2002).

Automobile accidents cause about two million serious injuries annually and are the leading cause of spinal cord and brain injuries.[62]

An auto-dependent society imposes heavy costs on the environment. These are worsened by SUVs, but they also exist with smaller, more fuel-efficient vehicles. Gasoline emissions cause air pollution. This may cause respiratory ailments, such as asthma. This was demonstrated by an unexpected natural experiment when the 1996 Olympic Games were held in Atlanta, Georgia. During the games private car use was heavily regulated in order to make it easier for tourists to move around the city. A twenty-four-hour mass transit system was put into place; employers staggered work hours, while their employees made more use of telecommuting so people could work from their homes. This went on for seventeen days. Traffic was significantly reduced as the use of public transportation increased.

A team of doctors studied the effects on children between the ages of one and sixteen, comparing their asthma conditions to a period before and after the Games. They found a decrease in asthma incidents among children. There were 42 percent fewer claims for Medicaid asthma-related reimbursements and a 19 percent drop in asthma-related hospitalizations. The physicians concluded that

> by decreasing automobile emissions through citywide changes in transportation and commuting practices, a substantial number of asthma exacerbations requiring medical attention can be prevented.[63]

There are two ways that the government controls fuel economy. One is through congressional legislation. The other is through regulations promulgated by the relevant agency. Regulations are easier to change than laws, and it is easier to get ones favored by the auto industry. One industry victory was having SUVs classified as "light trucks," not automobiles. As such, they were subject to regulations, not the laws that required a fuel efficiency of at least 27.5 miles to the gallon, which were enacted in 1985. If a car exceeds this limit, it is subject to a special tax for "gas-guzzlers." This can add thousands of dollars to the sticker price. Light trucks are exempt from this tax. SUVs have also benefited from favorable tax laws that exempt them from a luxury tax on vehicles costing $30,000 or more.[64]

Cars did become more fuel-efficient, producing less noxious emissions, but that has lessened in recent years. According to the Environmental Protection Agency, if efficiency improved by only three miles per gallon (mpg) for all cars, then carbon dioxide emissions would lessen by 140 million metric tons. In early 2003 the EPA published its ratings on vehicles based on how polluting they were. Of those with the worst records, six were pickup trucks and ten were SUVs. No regular-sized passenger cars were on the list.[65] The average number of miles Americans drive has steadily increased, and this contributes to traffic jams, with noxious substances pouring out of the tailpipes of cars waiting to move.

In 1991 the Natural Resources Council said it considered the car "the worst environmental health threat in many U.S. cities." This statement is too limited since automobiles, SUVs, and trucks are in good part responsible for global warming, a phenomenon threatening the health of individuals and of ecosystems all over the planet. Carbon dioxide, a major component of auto emissions, is one of the most important of these pollutants.[66]

Auto manufacturers spend a lot of money on lobbying and on campaign contributions. Their allies are sometimes appointed to government positions. Spencer Abraham became George W. Bush's secretary of energy. Abraham is a former senator from Michigan who was the single biggest recipient of campaign contributions from the automobile industry in 2000. He received $184,450 but lost nonetheless. As a senator he was a tireless opponent of regulations, including improved fuel-economy standards. Before becoming Bush's chief of staff, Andrew H. Card Jr. had been the head lobbyist for General Motors in 1999 and 2000. In the 2000 election Detroit donated $126,850 to the Bush campaign and $21,765 to that of Al Gore.[67]

With the help of their political allies, auto manufacturers have been successful in keeping down fuel-efficiency standards in general and for SUVs in particular. The United Autoworkers Union (UAW) has played an inconsistent role in acting to lessen the environmental costs. In the 1970s the union supported efforts to make cars more efficient and made a financial contribution to the first Earth Day in 1970.[68] Since then the UAW has generally opposed greater fuel-efficiency, fearing this would lead to job losses.

Legally defined as "light trucks," SUVs are allowed to emit more pollutants than smaller cars. As of 1994 the latter were limited to 0.4 grams of nitrogen oxides per mile, but for SUVs the standard is from 0.7 to 1.1, depending on the model.[69] A recent effort to raise fuel-efficiency was defeated in the Senate, with senators arguing that this would somehow interfere with the freedom of their constituents. On the other side, John Kerry of Massachusetts explained the advantages of fuel-efficiency:

> No American will be forced to drive any different automobile. [But] the U.S. could save a significant amount of oil that we import from the Persian Gulf . . . and simultaneously contribute to the effort to improve global warming problems as well as health in America.[70]

Other countries are doing much better in this regard. In Japan by 2010 cars will have to meet a standard of 35.5 mpg. On the average, cars there now get 30.3 mpg. The European Union is mandating that by 2008 vehicles will have to get 41 mpg, up from 33 mpg in 2000.[71]

DON'T BREATHE THE AIR OR DRINK THE WATER: POLLUTION AS ORGANIZATIONAL AND STRUCTURAL VIOLENCE

Thinking ecologically means taking a long-term view, viewing the earth and its resources as belonging to future generations. Capitalism, on the other hand, generally takes a short-term view: what is profitable now? Corporations make money only when their products are bought, used, and bought again, so there is a vested interest in creating and maintaining markets for materials even (and often) at the expense of the environment.[72] Cost-benefit analysis operates here.

In a 1989 Senate hearing the inspector general of the Environmental Protection Agency was questioned by a senator: "Is it your testimony that EPA's enforcement policies are so weak that it frequently pays polluters to keep polluting and pay EPA's small fines rather than clean up their act?" The inspector general replied: "Absolutely. . . . We have found that over and over again."[73] The costs businesses refuse to pay to engage in cleaner, healthier production then become social costs the public must bear, one way or another.

As a result of a widespread grassroots environmental movement, there is heightened concern about the environment. In recent years, however, business has mounted an often-effective attack on environmentalists, portraying them as enemies of economic growth, as elitists who care more about spotted owls than about working people. Environmental activists are justifiably concerned about the preservation of threatened species, but they are also concerned with the threats to our health that modern corporations have created.

A 1993 study by the American Lung Association estimated that close to twenty-four million people were then breathing dangerously polluted air. Airborne contaminants are believed to be responsible for fifty thousand deaths each year. Emissions from factories, power plants, oil and gas plants, and gasoline-powered vehicles, discussed above, are the major sources of the pollution.

A number of more recent studies have found that emissions of certain pollutants are the likely cause of deaths and medical problems, especially for the elderly. After reviewing more than three thousand studies, the EPA concluded that removing microscopic soot from the air could save thousands of lives.[74]

New York University School of Medicine professor George D. Thurston was part of a research team studying the effect of microscopic soot particles on health, which tracked five hundred thousand people over a sixteen-year period. The study found that soot exposure increased the likelihood of lung cancer and heart disease. This is the case even though the level of soot in city air is less than was the case in 1980 because of clean air rules. Vehicle manufacturers had fought those rules. Thurston commented, "The bad news is that fine-particle air pollution is even more toxic than we had thought before. The good news is we are addressing this problem and there are ways we can further reduce this risk by moving forward with the Clean Air Act and cleaning up these power plants that are a major source."[75]

In the last years of the Clinton administration, Attorney General Janet Reno brought a suit against seven major utility companies, charging they were endangering people's health through their deliberate violation of antipollution regulations. She said, "When children have trouble breathing because of pollution from a utility plant hundreds of miles away, something must be done." The something was to require the plants to install up-to-date equipment, an expense they preferred to avoid.[76]

POLLUTION, CANCER, AND DEATH

"I'm sorry to tell you, you have cancer." This is one of the most dreaded outcomes of a medical examination. As table 6.3 shows, there has been a large increase in deaths from malignancies.

TABLE 6.3 U.S. CANCER DEATHS, 1970 AND 2000

Year	Numbers of Deaths	Death Rate Per 100,000
1970	330,700	163
2000	551,883	202

Source: 1970, U.S. Census Bureau, *Statistical Abstract of the United States, 1995*, table 125, p. 92; 2000, U.S. Census Bureau, *Statistical Abstract of the United States, 2002*, table 103, 104, pp. 82–83.

A number of health experts link this rise to the increased number of manufactured chemicals. These deaths are examples of structural violence. In addition to pesticides, there are about fifty thousand chemicals in industrial use. Chemicals often interact with one another, and the synergistic effects are not completely known. The estimate is that from 60 to 90 percent of cancer is caused by environmental factors, including occupational and consumer exposure to toxins, as well as from smoking. All told there are thousands of preventable cancer deaths a year.[77]

Increased cancer rates have been particularly high in those under age fifteen, with about eight thousand children a year receiving the dreaded diagnosis. The greatest rise has been in two common forms of childhood cancer: lymphoblastic leukemia and brain cancer. Between 1973 and 1990 the former increased by 27 percent, while the latter rose by 40 percent between 1973 and 1994. The director of environmental medicine at New York's Mount Sinai School of Medicine believes that "a strong probability exists that environmental factors are playing a role."[78]

In 2001 two chemical companies in Toms River, New Jersey, agreed to an out-of-court settlement with sixty-nine families in which a child had cancer believed to have been a result of the operations of a number of companies, including Union Carbide and Ciba Specialty Chemicals Corporation. Lauren Kotran developed cancer at the age of six months. The lawyer for the plaintiffs is the subject of the film *A Civil Action*, based on a book of the same name, which depicts the pollution and consequent childhood leukemia that occurred in Woburn, Massachusetts. Studies at the federal and state levels had indicated that chemicals had contaminated water and air in the area.[79]

In spite of the need for federal oversight of companies, during the Reagan administration the EPA's staff was cut by 25 percent, its budget slashed by a third. Cost-benefit analyses were used to determine whether safety standards were economically justifiable. A number of rules were suspended, canceled, or just ignored. The situation was somewhat rectified during the Clinton administration.

During the Clinton administration, the EPA undertook research to further explore the relationship between environmental contamination and cancer. Experts agree that an intensive research effort on this problem is needed.[80] Congress has not acted on this with the same zeal with which they established procedures to locate missing children, a much less prevalent problem, but one that does not involve regulating business.[81]

GEORGE W. BUSH AND THE ENVIRONMENT

The Bush administration's close ties to business, even closer than is usually the case, have exacerbated environmental problems and bode ill for the future. With Christine Todd Whitman as head of the EPA till June 2003, and Gale Norton at the helm of the Department of the Interior, very little has been done to protect the air, the water, and other vital resources. Some existing protections have been rolled back. In 1994, as governor of New Jersey, Whitman abolished the state's position of environmental prosecutor. According to the Newark *Star Ledger*, the creation of this post, the first such office in the country, "had sent a chill through the business community."[82]

Gale Norton's nomination was championed by some of the conservative groups discussed in chapter 5. Under the tutelage of James Watt, Reagan's secretary of the interior, she had worked at the Mountain States Legal Foundation, a fiercely probusiness, antiregulation organization. She also sat on the board of the Defenders of Property Rights, whose title describes their position on regulation.[83]

On entering office, Bush began breaking campaign promises and implementing industries' environmental wish list. One of the broken promises involved lowering emissions of carbon dioxide for the country's power plants. This gas is a major contributor to global warming. The rationale was that the country faces a severe energy shortage, and lowering emissions would make matters worse. The president did not explain why his administration was not seeking alternatives to our fossil fuel dependence. In contrast, Britain and Germany have pledged to cut their carbon emissions by 50 to 80 percent over a fifty-year period.[84]

Bush claims that it is better to allow companies to voluntarily change polluting practices rather than stifle economic growth with undue government regulations. If companies have to choose between what is profitable and what is in the public interest, however, they are not likely to volunteer to cut their profits.

Following the attacks on September 11, 2001, the EPA proposed new rules for regulating security at chemical plants. In another attack on protecting the public, chemical industry trade groups, including the American Petroleum Institute and the American Chemistry Council, successfully disputed the EPA's authority in this regard; industry lobbyists were able to convince administration officials and Republican senators to limit the EPA's ability to oversee their facilities.[85]

Even where regulations would allow prosecution of polluters to protect public health, the EPA is reluctant to act. In November 2003 the agency's legal staff announced they would not prosecute fifty power plants for violating the Clean Air Act. In addition, new rules would allow plants to avoid upgrading their operations, saving them billions of dollars. This decision was made at the recommendation of a task force headed by the vice president. Frank Lautenberg, Democratic senator from New Jersey, said, "Profits are more important than cleaning the air for children who suffer from asthma and seniors who suffer from respiratory diseases.[86]

In March 2002 Eric V. Schaeffer, who had been directing the EPA's regulatory enforcement office since 1997, quit his job, saying, "The White House . . . seems determined to weaken the rules we are trying to enforce." He had been at the EPA since the early 1990s.[87]

TOXIC WASTES THREATEN HEALTH

The EPA estimates that more than seven hundred thousand tons of hazardous wastes are produced each day, about a ton each year per U.S. citizen. Communities are used as sinks, places to dump hazardous waste into the streams, rivers, or the ground. Working-class communities are chosen as sites because politicians and corporate executives expect they will be less likely to resist. In 1984 the government of California went so far as to hire a consulting company, Cerrell Associates, to figure out how they could build garbage incinerators without meeting resistance. Cerrell Associates advised placing them in blue-collar communities: "All socioeconomic groupings . . . resent the nearby siting of major facilities, but the middle and upper socioeconomic strata possess better resources to effectuate their opposition."[88]

A 1983 study by the University of Medicine and Dentistry of New Jersey found that in twenty towns with toxic waste disposal sites, the rate of cancer deaths was at least 50 percent higher than the national average. Besides cancer, industrial toxins are associated with birth defects, miscarriages, lowered fertility, and damage to the immune system. The numbers of pollutants stagger the imagination. Each year, for example, 225 million tons of hazardous wastes are created, 4 million tons of chemicals enter the water, and 160 million tons of pollutants contaminate the air.[89] Some towns, in fact, have been so contaminated they've been closed down and their residents relocated; Times Beach, Missouri, was contaminated with dioxin from a road contractor. Love Canal in New York State was fouled by the Occidental Petroleum subsidiary, Hooker Chemical Company.

Herbicides made with dioxin have been on the market for over thirty years. Dow Chemical Company knew of the potential hazards of this chemical as early as 1965. It successfully opposed an effort by the Carter administration to ban its use. The Reagan administration then curtailed further research efforts.[90]

Lois Gibbs, a former housewife from Love Canal who created and heads the Citizens' Clearinghouse for Hazardous Wastes, spoke of Dow's freedom to poison communities:

> Would you let me shoot into a crowd of one hundred thousand people and kill one of them? . . . It's okay for the corporations to do it, but the little guy with a gun goes to jail. . . . I look at the issue of people being poisoned and it makes me mad.[91]

In 1980, faced with the dramatic catastrophes at Times Beach and Love Canal, and under pressure from angry citizens, Congress passed the Superfund law. Revenues were to be generated from a special tax on oil and chemical companies to clean up hazardous waste sites. Industrial polluters would also pay fines. But, as *Time* magazine journalist Bruce Van Voorst reported, firms often bring their own lawsuits, holding up any settlement that would make them actually clean up the mess they have created: "Companies readily acknowledge that it is worth spending millions of dollars on lawyers to put off spending hundreds of millions of dollars on cleanups." Van Voorst notes that only "180 of the 1,202 sites now on the list have been officially cleaned up." And new toxic waste dumps are being created.[92]

ENVIRONMENTAL RACISM: ORGANIZATIONAL VIOLENCE AGAINST PEOPLE OF COLOR

"Environmental racism" describes an all-too-common phenomenon by which minority communities disproportionately become the destination for toxic wastes. Residents become the victims of unseen assailants. People in positions of power who have no particular desire to harm them find it expedient to use their neighborhoods as sinkholes for toxic, industrial, and military wastes, or as relatively cheap production sites. Housing discrimination, discussed in chapter 9, creates concentrations of minorities in areas that are less politically powerful and therefore more exploitable than white neighborhoods. Some people have less choice about where to settle than others: they can't simply move because they don't want to live next to a dump or a noxious factory.

On Evelina Street in Tucson, Arizona, there are thirty houses. In twenty-nine of them, residents have cancer. In this Chicano neighborhood, the water contains TCE, or trichloroethylene, a carcinogen that came from the operations of Hughes Aircraft, a manufacturer of missiles. Community activists created a map of Tucson, with colored pins showing the location of cases of leukemia, epilepsy, birth defects, and so on. Looking at this map, with the pins concentrated in Latino neighborhoods, Rose Augustine, a local activist, explained, "This is what we mean by environmental racism." Many residents have no health insurance. The federal government had given Hughes contracts and later hired Hughes to clean up the water. The government has the responsibility for protecting the environment. Neither the government nor Hughes, however, did much for the people from Evelina.[93]

The ecological problems of the poor are often a direct result of the greed of the wealthy. Along the U.S.-Mexico border are Chicano communities, *colonias*, that are among the very poorest in the United States. Whereas the 340,000 *colonia* residents are poor, the owners of their shanties are wealthy. Buying parcels of land for a few hundred dollars, the "developers" then sell the land to Mexican immigrants who pay some money down and then make monthly payments of from $50 to $200. With thousands of people making these payments, the profit margins are high. Profits are especially high because the developers do not invest in any infrastructure, such as sewers, water lines, or proper garbage disposal facilities. *Colonia* residents have been forced to build outdoor latrines, which overflow when there are heavy rains. Uncollected garbage attracts disease-spreading rats, and there is a high incidence of tuberculosis, dysentery, and hepatitis. Children have skin rashes and diarrhea. The developers do not pay for dealing with the consequences of their actions, and some have even managed to avoid paying any income tax for many years.[94]

African American communities are also victims of environmental racism. In 1982 the state government of North Carolina made plans to dump more than six thousand truckloads of PCB-contaminated soil into a Warren County landfill. PCBs, or polychlorinated biphenyls, are a carcinogenic hydrocarbon. Now banned, PCBs were a widely used, commercially produced substance containing dioxin and other hazardous substances. There are still tons of PCB-contaminated soil awaiting disposal. One method has been to put the soil into landfills, but the PCBs are likely to leak into the groundwater.

Poor and minority communities are frequently seen as the solution to the problem of where to put industrial wastes. Warren County is the poorest county in North Carolina, and 65 percent of its residents are African American. Concerned citizens mobilized to stop the dumping, with more than five hundred people winding up in jail as a result of their protests. Their efforts failed, the dump was built, but they had provided a model and focused attention on a problem that the environmental movement in general had neglected.[95]

In 1983 the General Accounting Office of the government reported that in the South hazardous landfills were located in predominately black and poor communities. The pattern holds throughout the United States. In 1987 the United Church of Christ issued a report titled *Toxic Waste and Race in the United States*, which concluded that race was the most important factor in the siting of commercial hazardous waste sites, outweighing all other factors, including income, property values, and rate of home ownership. Six years later the EPA also admitted that people of color are more likely to live in polluted communities.[96]

Cleanup at hazardous waste sites in minority communities tends to begin later and is done less effectively than in white communities. Penalties for breaking toxic waste laws are usually less. According to a study done for the *National Law Journal* in 1992, the average fine for violating a hazardous waste law was over $335,000 in white areas and about $55,000.86 in minority communities.[97]

Camden, New Jersey, is one of the poorest cities in the United States, and it is 53 percent African American. The state as a whole is about 14 percent black. According to Olga Pomar, writing in *Shelterforce*, a magazine dealing with housing and community issues:

Camden is home to more than one hundred contaminated sites and hundreds of polluting industries. The city's drinking-water supply has been contaminated for decades and its air pollution levels are among the highest in New Jersey.

One neighborhood, Waterfront South, has fourteen "known contaminated sites," a sewage treatment plant, and one of New Jersey's largest garbage incinerators. Community residents have respiratory problems associated with living in a polluted environment. Twenty-five percent of the students in the local elementary school suffer from asthma.[98]

The town of Emelle, Alabama, is the location of the largest hazardous waste site in the United States, used by forty-five states and several other countries. The town is also 79 percent African American. Farther north, the largest single concentration of hazardous waste dumps is on the South Side of Chicago, where almost all the residents are African American or Latino.[99]

Houston resident and president of the Northeast Community Action Group, Charles Streadit said of a landfill being built in his neighborhood:

A silent war is being waged against black neighborhoods. Slowly, we are being picked off by the industries that don't give a damn about polluting our neighborhood, contaminating our water, fouling our air. . . . It's hard enough for blacks to scrape and save enough to buy a home, then you see your dreams shattered by a garbage dump. That's a dirty trick.[100]

It takes higher incomes to live near the ocean or up on a hill, where breezes blow pollutants away. Poorer people live in congested neighborhoods with fewer trees and little grass but more sources of pollution: traffic, garages, auto repair shops, and small factories.

In Los Angeles 34 percent of whites live in areas with heavily polluted air, which may seem unacceptably high, but 71 percent of African Americans and 50 percent of Latinos are breathing unhealthy air. South Central Los Angeles, for example, has the distinction of being the "dirtiest" zip code in California, 90058. The population there is 59 percent African American and 38 percent Latino. In 1989 over sixteen thousand tons of pollutants, including cleaning and industrial solvents, lead, and ammonia, were discharged into an area measuring less than one square mile.[101]

Scientists at the University of Southern California performed autopsies on one hundred young men aged fifteen to twenty-five who had come from this area. Their deaths had resulted from accidents or acts of violence, not from any disease, but the study concluded, had they reached the age of forty, they all would have had serious respiratory problems. Four-fifths of them had lung abnormalities beyond anything that could be explained by their smoking. The cause was judged to be from breathing the smoggy Los Angeles air. Things are only likely to get worse as budget cuts have led to a lessening of enforcement of air-quality standards, and industry has successfully fought regulations by having clean-air advocates fired from the Air Resources Board, for example.[102]

Businesses clearly cannot be expected to care about the environment, and they use their political power to weaken the protections the government has established. It was through sustained public pressure during the late nineteenth and early twentieth centuries that sewage and garbage disposal, for example, came to be public services. Cities were made healthier and cleaner because of progressive movements.

THERE ARE HEROES

The current struggles for a safer environment date from the 1960s. As awareness of the dangers facing our habitat grew, a movement developed for protecting the planet. Environmentalists achieved victories: the EPA was created in 1970, and clean air and water acts were passed. Membership in environmental organizations grew along with public consciousness.

Corporations feared the consequences of an aroused public opinion and have gone to great lengths to silence environmental activists. Procter and Gamble (P&G), for instance, built a paper mill in Taylor County, Florida, a move initially welcomed for the jobs it provided. The state permitted P&G to use the local river as a dump for the plant's wastes, which included dioxin. Local activists began a campaign against the company they nicknamed "Profit & Greed," but their phones were tapped, they received anonymous threatening phone calls, family pets were poisoned, and one of the female leaders was beaten and raped. The environmental activists were the ones threatened with criminal charges by the sheriff's department: P&G has enjoyed a history of close ties with local officials.[103]

There are numerous incidents of local activists around the country being threatened and injured by antienvironmentalist organizations. Lois Gibbs estimates that "40 percent of people protesting toxic waste sites and incinerators around the country have been intimidated." Oregon Natural Resources Council member Andy Kerr claims, "Death threats come with the territory these days." He was hung in effigy. The home of Pat Costner, research director of Greenpeace's campaign against toxins, was destroyed in an arson attack, and thirty years of research went up in the flames.[104] Antigovernment militias are usually antienvironmentalist as well. Some ranchers, miners, loggers, and farmers claim that public lands should be free of all regulation and that private citizens should be able to do as they please to the nation's natural resources. In southern New Mexico, for instance, local newspapers urged drastic action against environmentalists, with one even suggesting they be drowned in a nearby river.

Environmental organizations have asked that Congress and the Justice Department investigate the harassment of federal environmental officials by paramilitary organizations and antienvironmentalist organizations such as Wise Use.[105] Unable to rely on companies to behave responsibly, or the government to protect the general welfare, people in threatened areas have formed their own groups to deal with environmental threats. Such groups have gathered information about such things as the incidence of cancer and birth defects.

Community health surveys have been undertaken as activists develop skills and knowledge to respond collectively to the power of the corporations and their political allies. They have organized demonstrations and other forms of protest to pressure for the protection of their neighborhoods from incinerators and toxic waste dumps. Organizations such as the Citizens' Clearinghouse for Hazardous Wastes, the National Toxics Campaign, and the Environmental Research Foundation give technical assistance and conduct workshops for local activists.

In spite of formidable obstacles, many local communities are getting together to protect themselves, and there is now a national movement to fight environmental racism. In 1991 the first National People of Color Environmental Leadership Summit was held in Washington, DC. More than 650 participants came from many local and national groups, as well as from Puerto Rico, Mexico, and the Marshall Islands. The conference developed a set of principles calling for environmental protection throughout the world since the same companies that threaten the health of Americans menace communities in the Third World. Those seeking an end to environmental racism want no one, here or abroad, to be victims of the irresponsible practices of multinational corporations and their government allies.

NOTES

1. Russell Mokhiber, *Corporate Crime and Violence: Big Business Power and the Abuse of Public Trust* (San Francisco: Sierra Club Books, 1988), pp. 28–29.

2. "SmithKline Is Fined for Failing to Report Side Effects of Drug," *New York Times*, February 26, 1985, p. A24.

3. Kurt Eichenwald, "Maker Admits It Hid Problems in Artery Device," *New York Times*, June 13, 2003, pp. A1, C2; Melody Peterson, "Medical Concern Will Halt Sales of Artery Device Linked to Deaths," *New York Times*, June 17, 2003, p. C1.

4. Philip J. Hilts, "Manufacturer Admits Selling Untested Devices for Heart," *New York Times*, October 16, 1993, p. 1.

5. Gina Kolata, "Manufacturer of Faulty Heart Valve Barred Data on Dangers, F.D.A. Says," *New York Times*, March 21, 1992, p. 50.

6. "FDA Faulted on Inspection of Medical Devices," *New York Times*, March 26, 1992, p. A17.

7. Russell Mokhiber and Robert Weissman, "Bad Apples in a Rotten System: The 10 Worst Corporations of 2002," *Multinational Monitor* (December 2002): 17.

8. Joan Claybrook, *Retreat from Safety: Reagan's Attack on America's Health* (New York: Pantheon, 1984), pp. 1–8.

9. Russell Mokhiber and Robert Weissman, "Corporations Behaving Badly, The Ten Worst Corporations of 2001," *Multinational Monitor* (December 2001): 17–18.

10. Russell Mokhiber, "The Ten Worst Corporations of 1993," *Multinational Monitor* (December 1993): 12.

11. Melody Petersen and Christopher Drew, "New Safety Rules Fail to Stop Tainted Meat," *New York Times*, October 10, 2003, p. A24; Mark Floegel, "The Dirt on Factory Farms: Environmental and Consumer Impacts of Confined Animal Feeding Operations," *Multinational Monitor* (July/August 2000): 25.

12. Eric Schlosser, *Fast Food Nation: The Dark Side of the All-American Meal* (New York: HarperCollins, 2002), p. 206; Claybrook, *Retreat from Safety*, pp. 22–23.

13. Christopher Drew and Bud Hazelkorn, "Ruling Favors Suspended Meat Inspectors," *New York Times*, April 5, 2003, p. A8.

14. Christopher Drew and Elizabeth Becker, "Plant's Sanitation May Have Link to Deadly Bacteria," *New York Times*, December 11, 2002, p. A32.

15. Petersen and Drew, "New Safety Rules Fail to Stop Tainted Meat," p. A24.

16. Schlosser, *Fast Food Nation*, p. 215.

17. Petersen and Drew, "New Safety Rules Fail to Stop Tainted Meat."

18. Ibid.

19. Drew and Hazelkorn, "Ruling Favors Suspended Meat Inspectors."

20. Schlosser, *Fast Food Nation*, pp. 150, 201–202; Floegel, "The Dirt on Factory Farms," p. 26.

21. Jennifer Lee, "Neighbors of Vast Hog Farms Say Foul Air Endangers Their Health," *New York Times*, May 11, 2003, p. 20.

22. Floegel, "The Dirt on Factory Farms," pp. 26–28.

23. Schlosser, _Fast Food Nation_, pp. 63, 217–18; Floegel, "The Dirt on Factory Farms," pp. 25–26.

24. Elizabeth Becker, "Bill Defines Irradiated Meat as 'Pasteurized,'" _New York Times_, March 5, 2002, p. A18.

25. Quoted in "Weedkillers Imperiling Tap Water," _Newark (NJ) Star-Ledger_, October 19, 1994, p. 14.

26. David Weir and Mark Schapiro, _Circle of Poison: Pesticides and People in a Hungry World_ (San Francisco: Institute for Food and Development Policy, 1981).

27. Marian Burros, "Produce Becoming Increasing Source for Food Illness," _New York Times_, November 23, 2003, pp. 1, 29.

28. Schlosser, _Fast Food Nation_, pp. 4, 47, 48.

29. Greg Critser, _Fat Land: How Americans Became the Fattest People in the World_ (New York: Houghton Mifflin, 2003), p. 32.

30. Schlosser, _Fast Food Nation_, p. 43.

31. Critser, _Fat Land_, pp. 133–46.

32. Ibid., pp. 73–74.

33. Schlosser, _Fast Food Nation_, p. 243.

34. Ibid., pp. 52, 56; Critser, _Fat Land_, p. 81; Elizabeth Becker and Marian Burros, "Eat Your Vegetables? Only at a Few Schools," _New York Times_, January 13, 2003, pp. A1, A14.

35. Barry Yeoman, "Unhappy Meals," _Mother Jones_ (January/February 2003): 44–45.

36. Quoted in ibid., p. 42.

37. Quoted in Critser, _Fat Land_, p. 5.

38. Gautam Naik, "Finns Find a Fix for Heart Disease: Vast Group Effort," _Wall Street Journal_, January 14, 2003, pp. A1, A16.

39. U.S. Senate, Committee on the Judiciary, Hearings before the Subcommittee on Antitrust and Monopoly, Part 4A, "American Ground Transport" (Washington, DC: U.S. Government Printing Office, 1974); Schlosser, _Fast Food Nation_, pp. 16–17. The video _Taken for a Ride_ illustrates how this happened and its consequences.

40. Yale Rabin, "Highways as a Barrier to Equal Access," in _Majority and Minority: The Dynamics of Racial and Ethnic Relations_, ed. Norman R. Yetman and C. Hoy Steele, 2nd ed. (Boston: Allyn and Bacon, 1975), p. 469; 1990–1995 figures from U.S. Census Bureau, _Statistical Abstract of the United States, 1995_, table 479, p. 302; Alison Mitchell, "Public Works at Record Sum in House Vote," _New York Times_, April 2, 1998, p. A1.

41. From the FTA Web site, http:/www.fta.dot.gov/library/intro/misstat.html (accessed November 29, 2003).

42. U.S. Census Bureau, _Statistical Abstract of the United States, 2002_, table 1058, p. 672.

43. Molly O. Sheehan, "Sprawling Cities Have Global Effects," in *Vital Signs, 2002*, ed. Worldwatch Institute (New York: W. W. Norton, 2002), p. 152.

44. U.S. Census Bureau, *Statistical Abstract of the United States, 2002*, table 1388, p. 874. The "public transportation" category includes taxicabs.

45. Jane Holtz Kay, *Asphalt Nation: How the Automobile Took Over America and How We Can Take It Back* (New York: Crown Publishers, 1997), pp. 36, 42. Elders quote p. 36.

46. "Gridlock Eats More Hours, Survey Shows," *New York Times*, May 8, 2001, p. A18.

47. Quoted in David R. Simon and D. Stanley Eitzen, *Elite Deviance*, 4th ed. (Boston: Allyn and Bacon, 1993), p. 122.

48. Claybrook, *Retreat from Safety*, pp. 168–69.

49. Danny Hakim, "Study Links Higher Speed Limits to Deaths," *New York Times*, November 24, 2003, p. A12.

50. Mark Dowie, "Pinto Madness," *The Best of Mother Jones* (San Francisco: Foundation for National Progress, 1985), pp. 62–63.

51. Dowie, "Pinto Madness," p. 65.

52. From WBAI, 99.5 FM, New York City, evening news, December 6, 1994. Tape of broadcast available from Pacifica Radio Archive, 3729 Cahuenga Blvd. West, N. Hollywood, CA 91604.

53. Author's calculation from *Fortune*, April 18, 1993, p. 296.

54. Keith Bradsher, *High and Mighty: SUVs—The World's Most Dangerous Vehicles and How They Got That Way* (New York: PublicAffairs, 2003), p. 112.

55. Quoted in Patricia Leigh Brown, "Among California's SUV Owners, Only a Bit of Guilt in a New 'Anti' Effort," *New York Times*, February 8, 2003, p. A15.

56. Keith Bradsher, "GM Has High Hopes for Vehicle Truly Meant for Road Warrior," *New York Times*, August 6, 2000, p. 14.

57. Danny Hakim, "In the Debate on SUVs There's a New Casualty Count," *New York Times,* March 2, 2002, sec. 4, p. 5.

58. Danny Hakim, "In Their Hummers, Right beside Uncle Sam," *New York Times*, April 5, 2003, pp. C1, C14.

59. Bradsher, *High and Mighty*, pp. 150–51; death statistics, pp. 163–64; for deaths attributed to rollovers for 2002, see Danny Hakim, "Gauging Rollovers on a Track and Not Just on Paper," *New York Times*, October 8, 2003, p. C3.

60. Danny Hakim, "Automakers Agree to Pursue SUV Safety Rules," *New York Times*, February 14, 2003, pp. A1, C2.

61. Bradsher, *High and Mighty*, p. 231.

62. Michael Katz, ed., *The "Underclass" Debate: The View from History* (Princeton, NJ: Princeton University Press, 1993), pp. 102, 104.

63. Michael S. Friedman et al., "Impact of Changes in Transportation and Commuting Behaviors during the 1996 Summer Olympic Games in Atlanta on Air Quality and Childhood Asthma," *JAMA* 285, no. 7 (February 21, 2001): 903.

64. Bradsher, *High and Mighty*, pp. 26, 28, 30.

65. "Gasoline Mileage for New Cars Declines Slightly, EPA Reports," *New York Times*, October 10, 2001, p. A13; Danny Hakim, "A List Some Carmakers Don't Covet," *New York Times*, February 18, 2003, p. C1.

66. Quoted in Kay, *Asphalt Nation*, p. 80.

67. Bradsher, *High and Mighty*, p. 390.

68. Ibid., p. 25.

69. Ibid., pp. 74–75.

70. David E. Rosenbaum, "Senate Deletes Higher Mileage Standard in Energy Bill," *New York Times*, March 14, 2002, p. A28.

71. Bradsher, *High and Mighty*, p. 243.

72. Barry Commoner, *The Closing Circle: Man, Nature, and Technology* (New York: Bantam Books, 1971), has a useful discussion of the relationship between capitalism and pollution.

73. Quoted in William Greider, *Who Will Tell the People? The Betrayal of American Democracy* (New York: Simon and Schuster, 1992), p. 113.

74. Philip J. Hilts, "23 Million People Found Living Where Air Particles Exceed Code," *New York Times*, April 30, 1994, p. 9; "Study Ties Fouled Air to High Urban Death Rates," *New York Times*, February 9, 1993; Matthew L. Wald, "Research Links Deaths with Pollutants," *New York Times*, June 28, 1999, p. A20; Andrew C. Revkin, "Tiny Bits of Soot Tied to Illnesses," *New York Times*, April 21, 2001, pp. A1, A12.

75. Andrew C. Revkin, "Soot Particles Strongly Tied to Lung Cancer, Study Finds," *New York Times*, March 6, 2002, p. A14.

76. David Stout, "7 Utilities Sued by U.S. on Charges of Polluting Air," *New York Times*, November 4, 1999, p. A1.

77. Examples of estimates can be found in Ann Misch, "Assessing Environmental Health Risks," in *State of the World: 1994*, ed. Linda Starke (New York: W. W. Norton, 1994), p. 123; Samuel S. Epstein, *The Politics of Cancer* (San Francisco: Sierra Club Books, 1978), p. 23.

78. John M. Cushman Jr., "U.S. Reshaping Cancer Strategy as Incidence in Children Rises," *New York Times*, September 29, 1997, p. A14.

79. Iver Peterson, "Firms Settle with Parents of Ill Children," *New York Times*, December 14, 2001, p. D5; Iver Peterson, "Study Ties Childhood Cancer in Toms River to Pollution," *New York Times*, December 18, 2001, p. D5; Kristy Sucato, "What's Wrong in Toms River?" *New York Times*, December 16, 2001, sec. 14, pp. 1, 10.

80. Cushman, "U.S. Reshaping Cancer Strategy as Incidence in Children Rises," p. A14.

81. In April 2003 Congress overwhelmingly approved the "Amber Alert Bill," which establishes a nationwide child-kidnapping alert system. At the signing ceremony, the mother and brother of the murdered child for whom the bill was named, along with a surviving kidnapping victim and her parents, joined President Bush. Photo of ceremony, *New York Times*, May 1, 2003, p. 29.

82. Edward A. Gargon, "Cancer Deaths Tied to Wastes in Jersey Study," *New York Times*, July 8, 1982; quoted in Tom Johnson, "Environmental Prosecutor Gets the Axe as Post Created by Florio Is Erased," *Newark (NJ) Star-Ledger*, March 16, 1994, p. 25.

83. James Risen, "Vote Lifts Conservative Land Groups," *New York Times*, January 31, 2001, p. A15.

84. Douglas Jehl with Andrew C. Revkin, "Bush in Reversal, Won't Seek Cuts in Emissions of Carbon Dioxide," *New York Times*, March 14, 2001, pp. A1, A20.

85. Anne-Marie Cusac, "Open to Attack: Bush Gives In to Chemical Companies, Leaving the Nation Vulnerable," http://www/progressive.org/nov03/cusac1103.html (accessed October 22, 2003).

86. Christopher Drew and Richard A. Oppel Jr., "Lawyers at EPA Say It Will Drop Pollution Cases: Looser Rules Will Apply," *New York Times*, November 6, 2003, p. A30.

87. Katherine Q. Seelye, "Top EPA Official Quits, Criticizing Bush's Policies," *New York Times*, March 1, 2002, p. A19.

88. Eula Bingham and William V. Meader, "Governmental Regulation of Environmental Hazards in the 1990s," *Annual Review of Public Health* (1990): 421; quoted in Hawley Truax, "Minorities at Risk," *Environmental Action* (January/February 1990): 21.

89. Claybrook, *Retreat from Safety*, p. 118.

90. David Burnham, "1965 Memos Show Dow's Anxiety on Dioxin," *New York Times*, April 19, 1983, pp. A1, A18.

91. Quoted in Greider, *Who Will Tell the People?* p. 56.

92. Quoted in ibid.

93. Quoted in Marc Cooper, "Sickness on Evelina Street," *Village Voice*, September 7, 1993, pp. 33–37.

94. Allen R. Myerson, "This Is the House That Greed Built," *New York Times*, April 2, 1995, sec. 3, pp. 1, 14; Solomon P. Ortiz, "America's Third World: Colonias," in *Annual Editions: Race and Ethnic Relations 91/92*, ed. John A. Kromkowski (Guilford, CT: Dushkin Publishing Group, 1991), pp. 80–82.

95. Ken Geiser and Gerry Waneck, "PCBs and Warren County," in *Unequal Protection: Environmental Justice and Communities of Color*, ed. Robert D. Bullard (San Francisco: Sierra Club Books, 1994), pp. 43–52; Benjamin F. Chavis Jr., foreword to *Confronting Environmental Racism: Voices from the Grassroots*, ed. Robert D. Bullard (Boston: South End Press, 1993), p. 3.

96. Robert Bullard, "Environmental Justice for All," in Bullard, *Unequal Protection*, p. 17; Peter Marks, "Issues of Race and Pollution Trouble L.I. Town," *New York Times*, November 12, 1994, pp. 23, 27.

97. Bullard, *Unequal Protection*, p. 9.

98. "Fighting for Air," *Shelterforce* (November/December 2002): 9–11, 27.

99. Bullard, *Unequal Protection*, p. 9; Regina Austin and Michael Schill,

"Black, Brown, Red, and Poisoned," in Bullard, *Unequal Protection*, p. 55; Richard Moore and Louis Head, "Building a Net That Works: SWOP," in Bullard, *Unequal Protection*, p. 198.

100. Quoted in Bullard, *Unequal Protection*, p. 5.

101. Jane Kay, "California's Endangered Communities of Color," in ibid., pp. 157–59.

102. Eric Mann, *L.A.'s Lethal Air: New Strategies for Policy, Organizing, and Action* (Los Angeles: Labor/Community Strategy Center, 1991), p. 5; Robert Reinhold, "Hard Times Dilute Enthusiasm for Clean-Air Law," *New York Times*, November 26, 1993, pp. A1, A30.

103. Alecia Swasy, *Soap Opera: The Inside Story of Procter & Gamble* (New York: Times Books, 1993), pp. 206–34. Many dangerous activities of this company are discussed throughout.

104. David Helvarg, "The War on Greens," *Nation*, November 28, 1994, p. 651; Liane Clorfene Casten, "Toxic Burn: Agent Orange's Forgotten Victims," *Nation*, November 4, 1991, p. 551.

105. James Ridgeway, "The Posse Goes to Washington: How the Militias and Far Right Got a Foothold on Capitol Hill," *Village Voice*, May 23, 1995, p. 17; John H. Cushman Jr., "Inquiry Urged into Possible Link between Anti-Government Groups," *New York Times*, May 5, 1995, p. A22; Helvarg, "The War on Greens," p. 651.

Chapter

7

STRUCTURAL VIOLENCE
Class, Race, Ethnicity, and Gender

In chapter 6 we saw how decisions made by corporations and government agencies can cause harm to consumers and to members of communities. This organizational violence resulted from decision makers choosing what is best for the corporate sector over what is healthiest and safest for the public. We also saw how racial inequality leads to communities of color becoming sites for unhealthy hazardous waste. In the next chapter we will discuss the issue of occupational health and safety.

Our individual choices are constrained in many ways by the decisions of the powerful. We are all affected, but those with lower incomes and people of color are more vulnerable. In addition, males and females face differential risks as a result of gender inequality.

THE U.S. HEALTH CARE MODEL

Several aspects of U.S. society impact our health. Is there a strong commitment to public health: to seeing that there is clean air and water, and implementation of other measures that research has shown reduce the possibility of people contracting diseases? For example, nationally mandated inspections of food production and processing reduce the risk of disease from contamination. In chapter 10 we will mention the clean needle exchanges existing in Amsterdam and some other European locales, which reduce the likelihood of intravenous drug users becoming HIV positive.

In the United States the for-profit health care industry has had a major effect on the nature of health practices, with their campaign contributions and lobbying giving them great political influence. Sociologists Peter Freund, Meredith McQuire, and Linda Podhurst summarize this point:

> Attempts to set a broader agenda for the health of the nation are contested by powerful interest groups benefiting from the present pattern of spending for medical care. . . . The power of competing interest groups together with ideology of free-market competition has resulted in an amazingly complex, unwieldy and expensive health care system that is now in crisis.[1]

Prescription medicines are more expensive in the United States than elsewhere. Using the tactics discussed in chapter 5, the pharmaceutical industry is a powerful force in Washington, DC, with six hundred lobbyists protecting its interests. As of 2002, twenty-four of these were former members of Congress. The drug companies spent $30 million to elect friendly legislators to Congress in 2002. Soon after the election, executives of Bristol-Myers Squibb, Eli Lilly, Merck, and others held a conference that one of their lobbyists described as a "strategic planning retreat." The industry plans include preventing passage of legislation that could lower their profits. Their lobbyists won an important victory in November 2003 when new Medicare drug legislation was enacted. The government, which pays for Medicare prescriptions and is thus a major buyer, is prohibited from bargaining for discounts or from demanding lower prices. Prescriptions from overseas, which would be cheaper, continue to be banned. Consumers who have been buying prescription drugs from Canadian providers will find it more difficult to do so.[2]

The companies' high prices take a toll on consumers. Unable to afford to take their prescriptions as directed by their doctors, some elderly people skip doses, share medicines, or make the difficult choice between buying medicine or eating properly. There are about ten million older persons without prescription drug coverage and therefore dependent on government programs. Many elderly patients with heart disease are not receiving the best drugs for their condition, according to a study done by the Harvard Medical School, Boston's Harvard Pilgrim Health Care, and Brigham and Women's Hospital.[3]

Even the nonelderly with jobs that provide prescription plans are cutting back as their co-payments have risen. One study in 2001 indicated that 20 percent of workers interviewed had not filled at least one prescription in order to cut costs. Another 14 percent took a smaller dose than was prescribed, while 16 percent skipped some doses to stretch the medication.[4] A fifty-year old South Carolina waitress, Dolores Stanfield, has not had health insurance for fifteen years, even though she has medical conditions requiring treatment—a spinal ailment and high cholesterol. She goes to a government-subsidized clinic, but it charges $15–$20 a visit, more than she can afford to pay very often, so she keeps her visits to a minimum. Nonetheless she owes the facility $3,000.[5]

Pharmaceutical companies contend that they have to charge high prices in order to pay for the crucial research they do. However, the pharmaceutical industry is the single most profitable industry, and it could have lower prices and still make profits. In chapter 3 we noted the high compensation levels of industry CEOs. The argument is disingenuous in any case because government agencies such as the National Institutes of Health pay for much of the basic research that is later used by Big Pharma, a term connoting the major pharmaceutical companies.

The industry enjoys tax deductions for its huge marketing expenses—$2.5 billion in 2000, while its own research costs (which are less than its advertising costs), are also deductible. In 2000 the after-tax profits of the major pharmaceutical companies were 19 percent of total revenues—more than many Fortune 500 companies. Government-granted patent protection extending up to seventeen years means only the patent-holding company can market a particular drug. It therefore has a lucrative monopoly.[6]

Americans have worse health outcomes than people in a number of countries. For example, life expectancy here is shorter and infant mortality rates are higher. As indicated in chapter 1, other countries do better than the United States on a number of health indicators. There is almost no mention by political figures or the mainstream media of why this is the case, and no discussion of what we might learn from others, including our neighbor Canada. The United States spends 13 percent of its GDP on health care. Canada spends 10 percent; and Germany, 11 percent. U.S. per capita spending on health care in 1999 was $4, 271; Canada's was $1,939. Yet life expectancy here is shorter, and both infant mortality rates and mortality rates for children under five are higher than in Canada.[7]

THE HEALTH INSURANCE MAZE

While other developed industrial nations have some form of comprehensive national health care, the United States does not. Instead, coverage and income are correlated as table 7.1 indicates. However, even a number of those with higher incomes are not covered. These figures do not include dental coverage or insurance for vision services.

TABLE 7.1 HOUSEHOLD INCOME AND LACK OF HEALTH INSURANCE, 2000

household income	percent with no health insurance coverage
less than $25,000	23
$25,000–$49,999	17
$50,000–$74,999	11
$75,000 or more	7

Source: U.S. Census Bureau, *Statistical Abstract of the United States, 2002*, table 137, p. 102.

Marcia Angell, a former editor of the *New England Journal of Medicine* and a lecturer at the Harvard Medical School, contends that a for-profit system of health care is irrational if the goal is to keep people healthy. In a market-based system, she points out, "the pressure is to increase total health-care expenditures not reduce them." While it is in the interest of the nation as a whole to cut down on health-care costs while maintaining quality care, this is not in the interest of the health care and drug industries. Angell argues that this country can "well afford to provide" decent medical care "for everyone if we end the waste and profiteering of our market-based system."[8]

If you cannot obtain private insurance and you are not eligible for government-funded care, then you may do without needed care. In 2003 there were 43.6 million Americans in this predicament, up from 39 million in 2000. Sixty-five percent of those under age sixty-five are dependent on their employers for health insurance. But a growing number of companies are reducing their coverage for employees.[9]

Workers' share of their premium costs are increasing, and their deductibles, the amount paid by the insured before the insurance actually kicks in, are rising. Those who have prescription drug plans are paying more for these. Retirees are less likely to be covered than was previously the case. There is wide variation among employees as to who is insured. Congress members have lifetime comprehensive coverage. Others are not so fortunate. About 10 percent of public employees are uninsured; the figure rises to 34 percent for those working in agriculture, fishing, mining, and construction. These are all occupations with relatively high injury rates.[10]

Thirty-four percent of those working for businesses employing fewer than ten workers are uninsured. Seventy percent of the uninsured are members of households that have a full-time worker. Fourteen percent of white workers are uninsured compared to 25 percent of African American workers and 40 percent of Latino workers.[11] If you lose your job, you are entitled to continue your health insurance, under what is called COBRA. The acronym stands for Consolidated Omnibus Budget Reconciliation Act. However, if your employer had fewer than twenty workers in their business, you don't even have this option.[12]

According to the Institute of Medicine (IOM) there is a false assumption that the uninsured will receive care. In 1999 close to 60 percent of those surveyed believe this. But the uninsured

- are not screened for cancer or are screened later when their disease is more advanced;
- are not adequately treated or diagnosed when they have heart problems or other trauma, and as a consequence are more likely to die even if hospitalized;
- are not given appropriate treatment for HIV and hypertension; and
- do not receive care that meets "professionally recommended standards for the management of chronic disease," and thus are more likely to become blind or have limbs amputated.[13]

As we mentioned in chapter 1, the IOM estimates that eighteen thousand people die each year because they have no form of health insurance.

People with health problems are dependent on private insurance plans or on government-funded Medicaid and Medicare, the latter for those over age sixty-five. Medicaid, however, is only for those meeting certain income requirements, and while Medicare has been a great help to older people, it faces problems. For example, in thousands of instances federal judges have found that the elderly were being denied coverage that they were entitled to. Between 1998 and 2003 there were 98,739 successful appeals. The Bush administration's response to this is to create difficulties for those who would make such appeals. Instead of being able to go before a federal judge, those who think they have a case would go to arbitration or to hearings before officers working for the Department of Health and Human Services. Neither route is advocated by spokespeople for the elderly, who think the present system works well.[14]

Medicare does not provide free medical care; those over sixty-five pay a premium that will rise by 12 percent in 2004. The government reimburses doctors for the costs of caring for Medicare patients, but in 2002 this compensation was cut by 5.4 percent, and further reductions are expected by 2005. Doctors are responding by limiting how many Medicare patients they are willing to treat.

Dr. Mark H. Krotowski, who practices in a Brooklyn working-class community, warned, "The new cuts will force more physicians to turn away Medicare patients. . . . While Medicare reimbursements are going down, our expenses are rising 5 percent to 10 percent a year." He noted, "I love my elderly patients. But they are very sick. They need a lot of attention, a lot of medications and a lot of time. Medicare reimbursement has not kept up with inflation nor the cost of providing care to the elderly." For similar reasons, some doctors turn away those on Medicaid.[15]

POVERTY AND HEALTH

Health care is a problem for many Americans. It is a more acute problem for poor people. Infant mortality has been shown to rise as poverty increases. Summarizing the results of a government study, Dr. John Kiely, chief of the Infant and Child Health Studies Branch of the National Center for Health Statistics, claimed the relationship was "stronger than we expected it to be," with infant mortality rates 60 percent higher for poor women than for those above the poverty line. Because of poverty, as was mentioned in chapter 1, about twelve thousand needless infant deaths occur annually in the United States.[16]

If they survive infancy, poor children face greater threats than their more affluent peers. A study in Boston found low-income children, white and black, to be at greater risk from fire deaths. This is because older, deteriorated buildings in low-income neighborhoods are more likely to experience fires. Adults may be using relatively inexpensive, but dangerous space heaters to cut fuel costs. Life is also more hazardous outside the home for poorer children. They are less likely to have safe places to play and to be supervised by responsible adults.

Inadequate nutrition is another health threat for poorer children. A study done between 1989 and 1992 concluded that in the coldest months of the year, parents could not afford both adequate heat and food. They often chose heat, resulting in a 30 percent increase in underweight children visiting emergency rooms after a cold spell. Homeless families have special difficulties in caring adequately for their children. In New York City shelters for the homeless, for example, children show signs of malnutrition, such as iron deficiency. Without access to kitchens and affordable, nutritious food, their mothers are unable to feed their families properly.[17] With ruthless cutbacks in social services, including food programs, heating assistance, and Aid to Families with Dependent Children (AFDC), the conditions described here are only likely to get worse.

The poor often cannot afford routine dental care, and while no one looks forward to visiting the dentist, it is still preferable to living with the suffering associated with diseased teeth and gums. Speaking to this, the Public Health Service claims, "Millions of Americans have been left behind, resulting in needless pain, increased cost, decreased health, and loss of self-esteem." The report noted that 80 percent of children eligible for Medicaid are not getting dental care. Dental checkups are the best way to detect oral cancer, which strikes about 30,000 victims each year and kills 9,400 in the same period.[18]

Medicaid does not reach over half of those below the official federal poverty line. The officially poor are eligible for Medicaid, but they still must find money for transportation to a health care facility, a place to leave a child, and a doctor willing to accept Medicaid reimbursements. There are also many in the United States whose incomes are too high to qualify for Medicaid but too low for them to afford health insurance.

A person may be forced off Medicaid for a period of time should his or her income rise. New circumstances resulting in a drop in income may mean renewed eligibility. One consequence of this vacillation in income is a lack of guaranteed health insurance. A number of people thus receive medical treatment on an irregular basis. Intermittent access to health care can amount to a death sentence for those with cancer. A provider who knows the patient and can assist him or her not only with drugs but with necessary lifestyle changes can best treat not only cancer but other chronic illnesses such as HIV, diabetes, and hypertension. The same is true of those suffering from mental illness. Without proper and regular treatment, such people may injure themselves and/or others, aside from the psychological anguish they suffer.[19]

Less affluent men and women with colorectal cancer and melanomas, and men with prostate cancer are also more likely to be diagnosed later, and even if they do survive, they do so with a lower quality of life because of the inferior medical care they have received.[20]

Many doctors refuse to practice in areas where they would be dependent on the low Medicaid reimbursements. A 1990 survey in New York City by the Community Service Society found that for a total of 1.7 million people living in low-income, largely minority neighborhoods in Manhattan, Brooklyn, and the Bronx, there were only twenty-eight qualified doctors. Three years later David R. Jones, president of the organization, described this picture as "bleak," pointing out that when the study was done "there was a concentration of older physicians who were nearing retirement, so we have every expectation that the situation has gotten worse." With primary care difficult to obtain, problems that are relatively minor are ignored until they become serious enough to send the sufferer to a hospital.[21]

Lower-income whites have worse health than whites with higher incomes. African Americans have worse health than whites. After comparing groups in sixteen communities in the United States, a research team concluded:

> Typical white Americans who were fifteen years old had higher likelihood of surviving to the age of sixty-five than blacks nationwide or poor fifteen-year-olds. . . . With the exception of white residents of Detroit, the poor whites had higher probabilities of survival than the blacks.[22]

BEING NONWHITE IS DANGEROUS TO YOUR HEALTH

People of color face significant health problems because of overt and covert racial biases in our society. Health differences between whites and people of color illustrate both structural violence and organizational violence. Structural violence is a result of the decades of discrimination that have left African Americans with less choice of jobs and less choice of residential neighborhoods, relegating them to communities that are medically underserved, but more polluted and vermin infested. Organizational violence is exemplified by the government not dealing adequately with these problems. Once the information has become available, how can we explain the continued indifference of policy-making agencies to the facts?

The health department in the South Central section of Los Angeles has had its budget cut at a time when the mostly Latino population has very high levels of heart disease, obesity, lung cancer, and asthma. Seventeen percent of pregnant women receive no prenatal care. This neighborhood has the highest rates of uninsured people in the country, with 47 percent of adults and 28 percent of children lacking insurance as of 1999. Los Angeles County's Director of Health Assessment and Epidemiology summarized the neglect and indifference relevant to explaining this situation:

We've known for a long time that the heath of the community was linked closely to social conditions. . . . Sadly, this is a chronic situation. It goes beyond access to health care or simple issues like that, it goes right to the heart of the community.

Community leaders have been hoping that preventative measures aimed at improving heath would be implemented—such as recreation for children, more prenatal care, and so on.[23] In the present climate of budget cutting, discussed more in chapter 15, this seems unlikely.

As was mentioned previously, the U.S. infant mortality rate is high relative to other developed countries. In 1999 the rate for whites was six per one thousand; for African Americans, the rate was fifteen. Even if the rate for white infants only is used, in 1999 the United States ranked below seventeen other countries. The African American IMR was higher than the IMR of forty-three other countries.[24] Childbirth itself is also more dangerous for black women than for whites. In 1999 maternal mortality rates for whites were seven per one hundred thousand births; for African American women it was twenty-five per one hundred thousand.

Greater rates of poverty mean that more women of color turn to public health services, which are frequently overcrowded and understaffed and may be far from the woman's home. By the time a low-income woman gets to see a doctor, her pregnancy is often more advanced than that of a woman who can afford a private physician. Pregnant African American women are also less likely to be warned by doctors of the dangers of smoking and drinking. In a study of pregnant women, doctors at the National Center for Health Statistics reported that 29 percent of the white women surveyed were not given these warnings compared to about 40 percent of black women.[25] Politicians are not demanding more prenatal care for the poor with the same zeal they have for building prisons.

Minority children are also less likely to be protected against preventable diseases than white children and more likely to be exposed to unhealthy conditions. For example, African American children are less likely than white children to have been vaccinated by age three for diphtheria-tetanus, polio, and measles. Many ghetto children are afflicted with asthma.

Researchers from the Columbia University School of Public Health, Harlem Hospital, and the nonprofit group Harlem Children's Zone conducted screening tests on two thousand children in an area of central Harlem in 2002. They discovered that an unanticipated 25 percent of central Harlem's children had this respiratory disorder; a number had never been diagnosed. Stephen Nichols, a professor at Columbia University Medical School and director of Harlem Hospital Center's pediatrics division, directed the study. He predicted that if there were more thorough diagnostic testing, "the rates might be much higher than suspected in any number of inner-city neighborhoods around the country." He added, "We found that a lot of kids are floating through life without anyone knowing they have asthma."[26]

A number of environmental factors are associated with this disease. These include polluted air and the presence of cockroaches, dust mites, mold, and secondhand smoke. As with all chronic diseases, asthma needs attention early on to keep it from becoming a more severe condition. Asthmatic children are more likely than their classmates to miss school.

African American children are more at risk from lead poisoning than white children. Lead poisoning is a threat to healthy physical and mental development of children and can lessen academic achievement because of its impact on the nervous system. In 1994 the *Journal of the American Medical Association* (*JAMA*) published findings showing that 9 percent of all U.S. children aged one to five have blood-lead levels high enough to cause brain damage. Two years later another *JAMA* article claimed to find a link between elevated levels of lead and aggressive behavior in children, even when other factors, such as having a father in the household, were controlled for. About 22 percent of African American children aged one to two had these dangerous levels. Latino children also have higher levels of lead in their blood than do white children.[27]

Elevated levels of lead can come from toxins leaching through old pipes into water, paint, hazardous waste sites, automobile oil, and oil refineries. Lead is also used in smelting, in battery manufacture, and in some other industries that have higher rates of minority workers; and the workers may carry lead particles home. A major source of this toxic substance is leaded indoor paint, now illegal, but still present in older housing.

Since African Americans are disproportionately poor, they have all the problems of low-income groups as well as some additional ones. In the succinct words of anthropologist Katherine S. Newman, "There is virtually no aspect of the country's health profile that looks encouraging when we consider the inner-city poor."[28]

In Harlem, researchers in 1980 found a lower life expectancy for African American men than for men in Bangladesh, one of the world's poorest countries.[29] A study conducted in 1991 found differences in death rates between African Americans and whites. After comparing groups in a number of communities throughout the United States, the research team wrote, "In Harlem mortality among women relative to that nationwide has not improved since 1980, whereas mortality among men has deteriorated."[30] As table 7.2 shows, recent statistics reveal a continuing discrepancy in life-expectancy rates for males and females depending on their race.

TABLE 7.2 LIFE EXPECTANCY, RACE, AND GENDER, 1999

	African Americans		whites
females	75		80
males	68		75

Source: U.S. Census Bureau, *Statistical Abstract of the United States*, 2002, table 93, p. 73.

A number of factors account for the racial differences in life expectancy, including differences in health care access and the quality of care. In a study of 32,004 black and 189,877 white cancer patients, researchers from New York City's renowned Sloan-Kettering Cancer Center found that five years after an initial cancer diagnosis, 63 percent of whites were alive compared to 52 percent of blacks. They concluded that the reason was not biological but a result of "differences in treatment, stage of disease at presentation, and mortality from other diseases."[31]

Doctors studying colon cancer specifically identified differences in care as responsible for different death rates. When whites and blacks both had chemotherapy and surgery, their survival rates were very similar. But usually they do not have the same care; even after initial treatment, blacks have less follow-up care. Sixty-two percent of whites survive colon cancer compared to 51 percent of African Americans.[32]

African Americans are more at risk from diabetes, associated with diet, although genetics may play some role. Latinos and Native Americans also have higher death rates from diabetes. Diabetes is a more serious disease for African Americans than for whites, even aside from the higher mortality rates. Lack of adequate care in the disease's early stages leads to complications that in turn create an amputation rate double that of whites. The rate of diabetes-related blindness in black women is three times that for white women.[33]

African Americans and Latinos experience higher rates of AIDS than do whites. For the years 1981–2001 African Americans and Latinos together accounted for 57 percent of the 816,149 known cases of AIDS in the United States.[34] However, social policies can impact the incidence of disease in unexpected ways. A study of AIDS and other health problems in poor communities of color in The Bronx, New York, showed not surprisingly that a reduction in fire-protection services increased the number of fires. There were additional consequences. As housing was destroyed, people moved, and social organizations such as churches, youth groups, and block associations lost their members. The remaining buildings became overcrowded. With increased community disorganization came a rise in alcoholism and associated diseases, drug use, and AIDS. Tuberculosis, a disease associated with substandard living conditions, also increased.[35]

There are systemic forces that are producing higher death rates for people of color in greater numbers than any racist murders. Knowledge of these disparities by race and income is not new, yet policymakers do little to remedy this situation.

RACIAL INEQUALITY, STRESS, AND DISEASE

Racial inequality causes stress. Stress is now recognized to be an implicating factor in a number of health conditions. Heart disease is partially a result of stress. While some medical experts claim the higher African American rate is best explained by genetics, this is unlikely. Blacks in Africa do not show any rapid heightening of blood pressure as they get older. Yet in the United States, African Americans start having rapid increases after age twenty-four. A common heart problem among this group is heart enlargement, which is thought to be a consequence of hypertension and high blood pressure.[36]

African American writer James Baldwin once said, "To be a Negro in this country and to be relatively conscious is to be in a rage all the time."[37] One example will show why. Al Tatum, aged twenty-six, seemed fortunate when in 1988, following the closing of the airline maintenance firm he had been working for, he found a blue-collar job paying $12 an hour at Cooper Power, an electrical transformer manufacturer, outside of Milwaukee. This job lasted only four years before he found conditions so bad he had to quit.

Soon after Al Tatum started working for Cooper Power, insulting graffiti about him appeared on the men's room walls. His supervisor told him his fellow workers were just "having fun." Then a fake application form appeared on his desk. Among the items was "Yo Prior Experience: Govt worker. Evangelist. Dope dealer. Postmaster. Pimp." At the bottom was a statement "No photo is necessary since yo all look alike anyway."

He brought charges of discrimination to the Milwaukee Office of the

Equal Employment Opportunity Commission. The case dragged on for two and a half years until a finding in his favor was reached. Eventually there will be a hearing to see if his civil rights were violated. In the meantime, Al Tatum used all the family's savings to open a restaurant that failed. The Tatums then lost the home they had been buying and moved to Kansas City, where he found a job for $5.25 an hour as a baggage handler. He did receive $10,000 in worker's compensation based on his doctor's diagnosis of extreme job-related stress, which impaired his ability to continue working.[38]

Ernest Johnson, a University of Houston psychologist, studied the relationship between anger suppression and blood pressure among one thousand tenth-grade students in Florida. He found "that the black kids were angrier than the whites, but . . . they suppressed their hostility more. The higher the level of suppressed hostility, the higher is their blood pressure."[39]

In a study conducted in the early 1990s, comparing over four thousand African American and white adults, Nancy Krieger and Stephen Sidney found evidence that discrimination and elevated blood pressure were associated. They also found the association to be stronger in people who did not talk about discrimination, who internalized "their experience of discrimination." They concluded that

> the blood pressure differences we observed associated with reported experiences of racial discrimination in conjunction with response to unfair treatment are on par with or exceed those associated with other cardiovascular risk factors targeted for nonpharmacologic interventions (e.g., lack of exercise, smoking, and unhealthy high fat, high-salt diets).[40]

Other studies have also found racism to be associated with stress leading to harmful physiological effects.[41]

Strokes and kidney problems are also sometimes linked to stress. Death rates from strokes for African Americans are twice the rate for whites. While homicide rates add to the mortality rates in places like Harlem, the leading cause of excess deaths there is cardiovascular problems. Hypertension, by damaging blood vessels in the kidneys, exacerbates the rate of kidney failure. In the age group twenty-five to forty-four, black males are twenty times more likely than white men to have kidney failure. African American men, however, are half as likely as white males to receive kidney transplants.[42]

Anger may be transmuted into physical symptoms. It also may be turned into rage loosed on one's fellows, domestic companions, and/or oneself in the form of suicide. Suicide is often clinically analyzed as an inward-directed aggression. Rates among African American males have been rising in the last thirty years, and some analysts attribute this to their enduring problems with racism.

Alcoholism and illegal drug use are ways of coping with anger and stress. Both can become health risks; for example, liver ailments are associated with greater alcohol use. Alcohol is often implicated in cases of interpersonal violence, and while alcoholics, like drug users, can be from any socioeconomic group, experts "see the inner city as a noxious stressful environment that encourages many residents to drink as an escape."[43]

HEALTH ON THE RESERVATION

The economic abandonment of communities, coupled with lack of social support, results in poverty rates in the United States that are higher than anywhere in the developed capitalist world. Native American reservations and inner-city ghettos share a number of characteristics. They are places of low employment, high poverty, and inadequate social services. There are high rates of all types of violence: organizational, structural, and interpersonal. Except for an occasional television documentary or rare film, most people in the United States never see the conditions that the residents of these communities experience daily.

From being 100 percent of the North American population, in control of all the continent's resources, Native Americans are now less than 1 percent of the total U.S. population. Their situation is especially instructive for thinking about the nature of our government. They are the only ethnic group with whom the government has specific treaty obligations, as well as an official agency with responsibility for their well-being, the Bureau of Indian Affairs (BIA). Yet Native Americans are among the poorest of all peoples in the United States and live in some of the worst conditions, reflecting their political powerlessness.

Their condition illustrates both structural and organizational violence. The conquest of the original inhabitants resulted in their displacement from their ancestral lands, loss of their major resources, and attacks on their social and cultural integrity. For generations, the federal government has given major corporations rights to the valuable minerals on Indian lands with relatively little compensation for the Indians themselves.

The problems of Native Americans are well documented and known to government agencies, but the problems remain year after year. In recent years about 200 of the recognized 560 tribes have established casinos on their lands, but less than 1 percent of the total population of this group has benefited from legalized gambling, and the problems associated with poverty and hopelessness persist.[44]

On average, about half of the total Native American population lives on reservations. If you drive through a typical reservation in the Southwest or in South Dakota, you will see landscapes that are often spectacularly beautiful but barren. Men, women, and children lounge idly outside the "trading post" or general store. Inside there is little variety—sacks of flour, cans of lard, hot dogs, components of an unhealthy but inexpensive diet. Broken-down vehicles are in front of shacks. There are few places of employment.

One of the poorest counties in the United States is Shannon County, South Dakota, where Pine Ridge, the Oglala Sioux reservation, is located. A journalist's 1992 description of Pine Ridge conveys the deprivation of its residents: "There is no train, bus, bank, theater, clothing store, drug store, barbershop, restaurant, place to get a car fixed or home delivery of mail."[45]

The Pine Ridge poverty rate was 63 percent, over five times the national rate. In 1999 male life expectancy was fifty-seven years and unemployment was over 70 percent. When then President Clinton toured the reservation in 1999, he met Geraldine Blue Bird, who shares five bedrooms with twenty-seven other people. She showed the president some of the community's dilapidated residences, saying, "See those houses? You notice they don't have no windows. That's because it has to come from the pocket and we don't have that pocket."[46] Because of their poverty people heat their shacks with space heaters, which cause fires, while some freeze because they have no heat.

Like many reservations, Pine Ridge is plagued by hopelessness and an attendant alcoholism that contributes to high rates of domestic and other kinds of interpersonal violence. In 1997 twenty-two-year-old Mr. Kills Right, sitting in a jail cell, arrested because he was drunk, told a journalist of his need to drink. "I drink beer, vodka, whiskey, anything I could get, and when I didn't have any alcohol I used mouthwash and cough syrup to get me drunk. And every day I prayed for death." He had been drinking since he was six years old. His mother died at the age of twenty-eight, pushed through a window. His grandmother was an alcoholic. He joined a treatment program that uses native rituals, and was hoping to cure his problem.[47]

Ellen L. Rothman, a graduate of Harvard Medical School, and her family chose to work on the Navajo reservation in Arizona. She described life there for the readers of *Harvard Magazine*. "Nearly 70 percent of our patients do not have a phone, and 50 percent live without running water or electricity." When an elderly man became unconscious, "the family first had to drive eight miles to reach their nearest neighbor with a phone to alert 911, and then the ambulance had to cover more than 40 miles over unmarked roads to retrieve the patient. The man had already been without a heartbeat for at least one hour by the time the ambulance arrived at the clinic."[48]

The Indian Health Service (IHS), part of the Department of Health and Human Services, provides health service to about 1.5 million members of 560 officially recognized native groups. In 1986 a government report summarizing Indian health status noted, "On almost every health indictor, Indian health remains poorer than that of the U.S. population in general."[49] Fifteen years later, an IHS fact sheet documented the continuing health disparities suffered by native peoples:

- unsafe water and poor sanitation in 8 percent of native homes compared to one percent of the general population
- higher rates of homicide, suicide, and alcoholism than the national average
- a life expectancy that is five years lower than that of other groups, along with higher infant mortality rates
- much higher death rates from several diseases, including tuberculosis and diabetes
- high rates of domestic violence and accidents[50]

Death rates from motor vehicle accidents are higher among Native Americans than for other ethnic groups. This is caused in part by alcohol but also by poor roads and overcrowded vehicles in poor condition, a reflection of low incomes. Services and people are scattered throughout the reservation and the long distances necessary to reach a destination also contribute to the accident rate.[51]

There are about two hundred doctors for every one hundred thousand persons in the general population, but only ninety-six physicians for every one hundred thousand Indians.[52] While in the late 1980s, throughout the United States, per capita spending on health care was $1,800, the IHS was spending half that amount for health care, water, sewer, and sanitation services combined.[53] Funding for the IHS was cut by both the Reagan and Clinton administrations.[54]

The Pima Indians of Arizona are an instructive example of why Indian health is so poor. The Pima have the highest incidence of diabetes in the world, and a rate of the disease that is 8.5 times that of the general U.S. population. As a consequence of this disease, they have an amputation rate of legs and feet that is ten times that of the general population and a dialysis rate twenty-five times higher than for others in this country.

There was no diabetes among the Pima until settlers diverted the Gila River's waters decades ago. The Pima had been dependent on this once quarter-mile-wide river for their farming. It is now dry. When the Pima lost their water, the federal government stepped in, not to protect their resources but to provide an alternative diet.

The diet provided by the government, high in fat, salt, and sugar, is one doctors say is almost certain to produce diabetes. The National Institutes of Health have been studying the Pima for thirty years. According to Dr. James Reed, who helped oversee a federal diabetes program, the research has increased doctors' understanding of diabetes, but the data have not been used to help the Pima.[55]

Environmental racism is a problem for native peoples as well as the communities discussed in the previous chapter. Since reservations are situated in remote areas and their inhabitants have little political power, they seem to the government an excellent solution to the problem of nuclear waste. Some groups are fighting against this use of their land. The Mescaloro Apache's president warned of the "ghost bullets" that would prove fatal to them if they allowed their land to be used as a storage site for tons of radioactive waste.[56]

The government has designated Nevada's Yucca Mountain, a sacred site to the Western Shoshone, to be a repository for seventy-seven thousand tons of nuclear waste. The Shoshone have been protesting the plan not only on religious grounds but because they rightly fear the health threat from what one of their leaders describes as "the most toxic poison."[57] In contrast to the Western Shoshone, however, the Skull Valley Band of the Goshute are deeply divided over building a toxic waste storage site on their land. Some argue that leasing tribal land for the waste provides desperately needed money. Others are afraid of what the site will do to their health.[58]

HEALTH AND GENDER

Women and men face gender-specific health problems caused by gender stereotyping and the corporate search for profits. Gender roles partially account for the fact that men have shorter life expectancies than women;

males are more likely to drive recklessly, to engage in interpersonal violence, to play more dangerous sports, and to do more hazardous work. However, as Diana Laskin Siegal, a member of the Boston Women's Book Collective, summarizes, "Women are treated with less respect and receive poorer medical care than men."[59] The situation is worse for women of color, and aging women have special problems.

In addition to sexist biases in the medical field, women on the average have lower incomes than men, and therefore have health problems associated with this disadvantage. Millions of mothers have no health insurance, although many states now provide at least some health coverage for lower-income children through the State Children's Health Insurance Program. Even so, 12 percent of children in 2000, 8.4 million, had no coverage.[60]

As of 1999 there were 5.9 million mothers without health insurance for themselves, 16 percent of all mothers with young or school-age children. Many of these are working women. In twenty-five states a woman is ineligible for Medicaid if her annual income is above $9,780. A few states are more generous; in Minnesota she is eligible if the family has an income below $40,233. In Colorado the threshold is $6,132; in Alabama it is $3,048. Uninsured women are more likely to do without routine care; if they become seriously ill as a result of this or any other reason, they will confront the problem of who will care for their children.[61]

Summarizing a number of studies, the Institute of Medicine reports that women without insurance or dependent on Medicaid "are more likely to receive a breast cancer diagnosis at a later stage of disease . . . and have [a] 30–50 percent greater risk of dying than women with private coverage." The case was the same with cervical cancer.[62]

WOMEN AND BIRTH CONTROL:
THE DALKON SHIELD

Women have been socialized to believe they are responsible for the consequences of sexual intercourse. Both men and women agreed, according to a 1995 poll, that males "are not responsible enough" to be trusted to provide for birth control.[63] Virtually all the research and marketing of birth control devices, with the exception of condoms, is aimed at women, who consequently bear whatever health risks are associated with contraception.

The emphasis on female birth control devices and the goal of profit have sometimes combined in a lethal way, as in the case of the Dalkon Shield marketed by A. H. Robins Co., beginning in 1971. This intrauterine device had not been adequately tested, but it was very profitable: costing about $.25 to produce, it sold for $4.35. The Dalkon Shield led to pelvic infections, sterility, miscarriages, and birth defects. At least eighteen women died in the United States from using it. The company ignored warnings from its employees, from doctors with infected patients, and from the FDA. When Wayne Crowder, a quality control supervisor at Robins, expressed concern about the Shield's safety, his supervisor responded by saying, "Your conscience doesn't pay your salary" and warned him to be quiet.[64]

With the encouragement of the National Women's Health Network, over ten thousand women sued the company for hundreds of millions of dollars. The company, in turn, defended itself by claiming the women's own sexual practices had caused their problems. A company lawyer even asserted,

> There is not a damn thing wrong with the Dalkon Shield. Ninety percent of these gals, Christ, you ought to read their histories. . . . It's unreal. The number of men they screw would knock you off your feet.[65]

Distribution in the United States stopped in 1975, but the health problems associated with this product continue for those who had used it before this date. The Dalkon Shield was also distributed in at least seventy-eight other countries. Even after marketing ceased here, it continued overseas.

BREAST CANCER

Diseases specific to women, such as breast cancer, have not been studied as thoroughly as male disorders, such as prostrate cancer. Breast cancer is responsible for over forty thousand deaths annually. The incidence of this disease has been increasing, and it is one of the leading causes of death for women. Women are advised to do routine breast examinations, and older women are encouraged to have periodic mammograms in order to find the early signs of potential breast cancer: as with other diseases, prevention is the most effective way of reducing the incidence.

A number of chemicals with carcinogenic properties may be particularly dangerous to women. These chemicals, found in many pesticides, dissolve in fat, making them more potent, and women's breasts contain much fatty tissue. The incidence of breast cancer can be linked to environmental toxins, but a strategy to reduce pollution is resisted by industry.

Although white women experience a greater incidence of breast cancer,

African American women are more at risk of dying from the disease, usually because they see doctors at a later stage of the cancer's development. For the period 1992–1998, the five-year survival rate for white women diagnosed with breast cancer was 88 percent, compared to 73 percent for African American women. The tumors in black women seem to be more aggressive, with tumerous cells dividing and spreading more quickly. Some cancer researchers attribute this to environmental and dietary factors.[66]

Income level is also associated with female cancer patients' five-year survival rates. Uninsured women with breast cancer were found by researchers from Harvard Medical School and Brigham and Women's Hospital in Boston to have more advanced breast cancer "at the time of diagnosis." Even those receiving Medicaid were diagnosed later than higher-income women.[67]

WOMEN AND MEDICAL RESEARCH

For years, studying women's health has been secondary to doing research based on men, although this is beginning to change. Typically white males are the population used to determine medical standards and practices for everyone. Excluding women and minorities from clinical trials of pharmaceutical products has meant that potential adverse reaction in these groups were not known. Conversely, possible benefits from medical practices for women were also studied less. For example, in 1981 a study of the effect of aspirin on heart attacks was begun. All twenty-two thousand people in the study were male doctors because the researchers believed they were the group that could be most trusted to follow the researchers' instructions. "Various medical boards reviewing the design of this and other studies excluding women noticed nothing amiss."[68]

The effect of aspirin on heart attacks experienced by African American women, Latinas, and white women, as well as nonwhite males, was thereby assumed to be exactly the same as that of white men. Other studies have been conducted similarly; AIDS, cardiovascular diseases, and many cancers, which afflict both men and women, have mostly been studied in men. Serious problems may even receive different diagnoses depending on the patient's gender. For example, according to Dr. Joann E. Manson of the Harvard Medical School, who has conducted studies in women's health, heart disease symptoms such as chest pains are more often overlooked in women, who usually receive less thorough treatment for heart disease. A study of thirty-six thousand Medicare patients indicated that men were 18 percent more likely than women to receive the most effective type of pacemaker.[69]

In February 1999, the *New England Journal of Medicine* published a study in which 720 physicians were shown videos in which actors portrayed patients with certain symptoms, including chest pains. Everything about the alleged patients except gender and race were matched. They "found that the race and sex of the patient affected the physicians' decision about whether to refer patients with chest pain for cardiac catheterization. . . . Our findings were most striking for black women."[70]

In 1993 a federal law mandated that when women are included as subjects in studies of drugs and treatments, the results must be reported for each gender. The reason is that males and females sometimes react differently to the same medical treatment. The law, however, has not been enforced, as three separate studies published in 2000 indicated. More recently, in 2001 the Institute of Medicine issued a report stressing the importance of studying sex differences when conducting any health-related research.[71]

The differences we have been describing are at least partly a result of the medical profession's history of being largely a white male profession. As more women enter the medical field, there may be greater concern for their specific health problems. As of 2001 only 5 percent of physicians were African Americans, 5 percent were Latino, and 29 percent were women. White males dominate the medical schools as presidents, deans, and chairs of departments.

Race, ethnicity, and gender clearly play a role in health outcomes. Occupation affects health as well, as will be discussed in the next chapter.

NOTES

1. Peter Freund, Meredith B. McGuire, and Linda Podhurst, *Health, Illness, and the Social Body: A Critical Sociology*, 4th ed. (Upper Saddle River, NJ: Prentice-Hall, 2003), pp. 256, 257.

2. David E. Rosenbaum and Robin Toner, "Medicare Reform: Who Wins and Loses," *New York Times*, November 26, 2003, p. A18.

3. "Inequality in Availability of Heart Drugs Is Found," *New York Times*, October 10, 2001, p. A14.

4. "More Workers Skimp as Drug Costs Rise," *New York Times*, November 25, 2001, sec. 3, p. 10.

5. Robin Toner and Sheryl Gay Stolberg, "Decade after Health Care Crisis, Soaring Costs Bring New Strains," *New York Times*, August 11, 2002, p. 24.

6. "Wanted: Prescription for Easing Drug Prices," *On Campus* (October 2002): 15; Marcia Angell, "The Pharmaceutical Industry to Whom Is It Accountable?" *Public Citizen Health Letter* (August 2000): 1–3. Originally published in the *New England Journal of Medicine.*

7. United Nations Development Program, *Human Development Report, 2002* (New York: Oxford University Press, 2000), table 6, p. 166; table 1, p. 149; table 8, p. 174.

8. "The Forgotten Domestic Crisis," op-ed article, *New York Times*, October 13, 2002, sec. 4, p. 13.

9. Robert Pear, "Big Increase Seen in People Lacking Health Insurance," *New York Times*, September 30, 2003, p. A1; 2000, U.S. Census Bureau, *Statistical Abstract of the United States, 2002*, table 137, p. 102; John M. Broder, "Problem of Lost Health Benefits Is Reaching into the Middle Class," *New York Times*, January 25, 2001, pp. A1, A16; "Keeping Up with Rising Healthcare Costs," *On Campus* (May/June 2002): 16.

10. Milt Freudenheim, "Workers Paying a Larger Share for Drug Plans," *New York Times*, June 12, 2003, pp. A1, C5; Milt Freudenheim, "Employees Are Shouldering More of Health Care Tab," *New York Times*, December 10, 2001, p. C6; Milt Freudenheim, "Small Employers Severely Reduce Health Benefits," *New York Times*, September 6, 2002, pp. C1, C4.

11. Data from Employee Benefits Research Institute Fact Sheet and Kaiser Commission fact sheet on Medicaid and the uninsured, http://www.ebri.org; http://www.kff.org (accessed April 21, 2003).

12. Robin Toner, "Sagging Economy Threatens Health Coverage," *New York Times*, November 12, 2001, p. A12.

13. Institute of Medicine, *Care without Coverage: Too Little, Too Late* (Washington, DC: National Academy Press, 2002), pp. 3–4.

14. Robert Pear, "Bush Pushes Plan to Curb Medicare Appeals," *New York Times*, March 16, 2003, pp. 1, 30.

15. Robert Pear, "Medicare Recipients Face 12.4% Rise in Premiums," *New York Times*, March 26, 2003, p. A12; first Krotowski quote from Robert Pear, "Medicare to Cut Payments to Doctors 44% Next Year," *New York Times*, December 2, 2002, p. A14; Robert Pear, "Many Doctors Shun Patients with Medicare," *New York Times*, March 17, 2002, pp. 1, 34.

16. Quoted in "Infant Deaths Tied to Poverty, Study Confirms," *New York Times*, December 15, 1995, p. A38; William S. Nersesian, "Infant Mortality in Socially Vulnerable Populations," *Annual Review of Public Health* 9 (1988): 361, 364.

17. Matthew L. Wald, "Boston Child Study Finds Death Rate Higher among the Poor and the Black," *New York Times*, August 8, 1985; "Study of Poor Children Shows a Painful Choice: Heat Over Food," *New York Times*, September 9, 1992; Esther B. Fein, "Private Study Finds Many Children in Shelters Have Signs of Malnutrition," *New York Times*, December 14, 1994, p. B3.

18. "Millions Cannot Afford Dental Help, Study Says," *New York Times*,

November 30, 1994, p. C14; Susan T. Reisine, "The Impact of Dental Conditions on Social Functioning and the Quality of Life," *Annual Review of Public Health* 9 (1988): 5.

19. Institute of Medicine, *Care without Coverage*, pp. 58–71.

20. Ibid., pp. 54–56.

21. Elisabeth Rosenthal, "Shortage of Doctors in Poor Areas Is Seen as Barrier to Health Plans," *New York Times*, October 18, 1993, pp. A1, B4.

22. Arline T. Geronimus et al., "Excess Mortality among Blacks and Whites in the United States," *New England Journal of Medicine* (November 21, 1996): 1555. They do not explain why Detroit was an exception to the general pattern.

23. James Sterngold, "Los Angeles Inner City Beset by Chronic Health Problems," *New York Times*, May 3, 2002, p. A19.

24. Infant mortality rates and maternal mortality rates from U.S. Census Bureau, *Statistical Abstract of the United States, 2002*, table 98, p.78. Comparisons based on data from the United Nations, *Human Development Report, 2001*, table 8, pp. 166–67.

25. Bert Burrason, "Infant Mortality in the United States: Racial Differences and Social Stratification," paper presented at the 1994 meetings of the Pacific Sociological Association, pp. 9–10; "Study Finds Racial Disparity in Warnings to the Pregnant," *New York Times*, January 20, 1994, p. A16.

26. Richard Pérez-Peña, "Study Finds Asthma in 25% of Children in Central Harlem," *New York Times*, April 19, 2003, p. D4.

27. Sandra Blakeslee, "Concentrations of Lead in Blood Drop Steeply," *New York Times*, July 27, 1994, p. A18; "The Short Run," *Dollars and Sense* (July/August, 1996): 5; U.S. Census Bureau, *Statistical Abstract of the United States, 1995*, table 210, p. 139.

28. Kathleen Newman, *No Shame in My Game: The Working Poor in the Inner City* (New York: Vintage Books, 1999), p. 54.

29. Colin McCord and Harold P. Freeman, "Excess Mortality in Harlem," in *Crisis in American Institutions*, ed. Jerome Skolnick and Elliot Currie, 9th ed. (New York: HarperCollins, 1991), pp. 426–32.

30. Geronimus et al., "Excess Mortality among Blacks and Whites in the United States."

31. "Racial Gap in Cancer Survival Is Not Biological, Study Finds," *New York Times*, April 24, 2002, p. A18.

32. "Colon Cancer: Care, Not Biology," *New York Times*, August 13, 2002, p. F6.

33. Laurie Kaye Abraham, *Mama Might Be Better Off Dead: The Failure of Health Care in Urban America* (Chicago: University of Chicago Press, 1993), p. 70.

34. Calculated from U.S. Census Bureau, *Statistical Abstract of the United States, 2002*, table 176, p. 120.

35. Deborah Wallace, "Roots of Increased Health Care Inequality in New York," *Social Science and Medicine* 31 (1990): 1219–27; Roderick Wallace, "Urban Desertification, Public Health, and Public Order: 'Planned Shrinkage,' Vio-

lent Death, Substance Abuse, and AIDS in The Bronx," *Social Science and Medicine* 31 (1990): 801–13.

36. Peter E. S. Freund and Meredith B. McGuire, *Health, Illness, and the Social Body: A Critical Sociology* (Englewood Cliffs, NJ: Prentice-Hall, 1991), pp. 29–30; "Deadliest Heart Ailment in Blacks Is Enlargement," *New York Times*, May 24, 1995, p. C13.

37. Quoted in *Time*, August 20, 1965, p. 17.

38. Peter T. Kilborn, "A Family Spirals Downward in Waiting for Agency to Act," *New York Times*, February 11, 1995, pp. 1, 10.

39. Daniel Goleman, "Anger over Racism Is Seen as a Cause of Black's High Blood Pressure," *New York Times*, April 24, 1990, p. A16.

40. "Racial Discrimination and Blood Pressure: The CARDIA Study of Young Black and White Adults," *American Journal of Public Health* 86 (1996): 1376.

41. A summary of these can be found in Rodney Clark et al., "Racism as a Stressor for African-Americans: A Biopsychological Model," *American Psychologist* (October 1999): 805–16.

42. Melvin Konner, *Dear America: A Concerned Doctor Wants You to Know the Truth about Health Reform* (Reading, MA: Addison-Wesley, 1993), p. 35; Abraham, *Mama Might Be Better Off Dead*, pp. 28–29; James E. Blackwell, *The Black Community: Diversity and Unity* (New York: HarperCollins, 1991), pp. 405–406.

43. Margaret S. Boone, *Capital Crime: Black Infant Mortality in America* (Newbury Park, CA: Sage, 1989), p. 131.

44. Richard T. Schaefer, *Racial and Ethnic Groups,* 8th ed. (Upper Saddle River, NJ: Prentice-Hall), p. 190.

45. Peter T. Kilborn, "Sad Distinction for the Sioux: Homeland Is No. 1 in Poverty," *New York Times*, September 20, 1992, pp. 1, 32.

46. Peter T. Kilborn, "Clinton, amid the Squalor on a Reservation, Again Pledges Help," *New York Times*, July 8, 1999, p. 16.

47. Dirk Johnson, "Reversing Reservation's Pattern of Hard Drink and Early Death," *New York Times*, December 23, 1997, p. A16.

48. "Letter from Kayenta," *Harvard Magazine* (September–October 2002): 19.

49. U.S. Congress, Office of Technology Assessment, *Indian Health Care* (Washington, DC: U.S. Government Printing Office, 1986), p. 89.

50. Indian Health Service, "Facts on Indian Health Disparities," Office of the Director of Public Affairs, April 2001. One page.

51. U.S. Congress, *Indian Health Care*, p. 92.

52. Richard T. Schaefer, *Racial and Ethnic Groups,* 5th ed. (New York: HarperCollins, 1993), p. 172.

53. Dr. Joshua Lipsman, "White Man's Medicine," *Nation*, March 26, 1988, p. 401.

54. "Clinton to Hear Indians Upset over Health Cuts," *New York Times*, March 23, 1994, p. A22.

55. "The Pima Plague," segment of CNN, Special Assignment, broadcast March 19, 1995.

56. George Johnson, "Apache Tribe Rejects Move to Store Nuclear Waste on Reservation," *New York Times*, February 2, 1995, p. A16.

57. Evelyn Nieves, "A Land's 'Caretakers,' Oppose Nuclear-Dump Plan," *New York Times,* April 23, 2000, p. 12.

58. Matthew L. Wald, "Tribe in Utah Fights for Nuclear Waste Dump," *New York Times*, April 18, 1999, p. 16.

59. Diana Laskin Siegal, "Problems in the Medical Care System," in *Ourselves Growing Older* (New York: Simon and Schuster, 1987), p. 213.

60. U.S. Census Bureau, *Statistical Abstract of the United States, 2002*, table 134, p. 101; table 138, p. 102.

61. Jocelyn Guyer, Matthew Broaddus, and Annie Dude, "Millions of Mothers Lack Health Insurance Coverage in the United States," *International Journal of Health Services* 32 (2002): 89–106.

62. Institute of Medicine, *Care without Coverage*, pp. 54–55.

63. Jennifer Steinhauer, "Men Avoid Birth Control Responsibility, Poll Finds," *New York Times*, May 23, 1995, p. B10.

64. Susan Perry and Jim Dawson, "Nightmare: Women and the Dalkon Shield," in *Corporate and Governmental Deviance: Problems of Organizational Behavior in Contemporary Society*, ed. M. David Ermann and Richard J. Lundman, 3rd ed. (New York: Oxford University Press, 1987), p. 154. For a discussion of "Corporate Violence against Women," which includes some of the examples given here and additional ones, see Mary White Stewart, *Ordinary Violence: Everyday Assaults against Women* (Westport, CT: Bergin & Garvey, 2002), pp. 209–57.

65. Quoted in Russell Mokhiber, *Corporate Crime and Violence: Big Business and the Abuse of Public Trust* (San Francisco: Sierra Club Books 1988), p. 149.

66. Survival rate figures from U.S. Census Bureau, *Statistical Abstract of the United States, 2002*, table 187, p. 125. There have been increases in survival rates for both groups but the improvement has been greater for white women and the discrepancy remains. "Breast Cancer Twice as Deadly in Blacks," *New York Times*, September 28, 1994, p. C10; Gina Kollata, "Deadliness of Breast Cancer in Blacks Defies Easy Answers," *New York Times*, August 3, 1994, p. C10; Rita Arditti and Tatiana Schreiber, "Breast Cancer: The Environmental Connection," *Resist Newsletter* (May/June 1992): 1–8.

67. Jean V. Hardisty and Ellen Leopold, "Cancer and Poverty: Double Jeopardy for Women," in *Myths about the Powerless*, ed. M. Brinton Lykes et al. (Philadelphia: Temple University Press, 1996), p. 220.

68. Gena Corea, *The Invisible Epidemic: The Story of Women and AIDS* (New York: HarperCollins, 1992), p. 4.

69. Bonnie Liebman, "For Women Only," *Nutrition Action Health Letter* 22 (March 1995): 4; Leonard K. Altman, "Study Finds Sexual Biases in Doctor's Choice of Pacemakers," *New York Times*, February 15, 1995, p. A16.

70. Keving Schulman et al., "The Effect of Race and Sex on Physicians' Recommendations for Cardiac Catheterization," *New England Journal of Medicine* (February 25, 1999): 623.

71. Robert Pear, "Research Neglects Women, Studies Find," *New York Times*, April 30, 2000, p. 16; Robert Pear, "Sex Differences Called Key in Medical Studies," *New York Times*, April 25, 2001, p. A14.

8

VIOLENCE AGAINST WORKERS AND THE UNEMPLOYED

E xecutives' practices for their companies' profit can foster unhealthy working conditions for their employees. Maximizing profits also can be one of the major causes of unemployment, which has negative effects on health as well as implications for interpersonal violence. When employers knowingly permit dangerous and unhealthy workplaces, and avoidable accidents occur, that is organizational violence. The long-term effects of unhealthy workplaces and the effects of unemployment discussed below are examples of structural violence.

ORGANIZATIONAL VIOLENCE

On March 16, 2003, solemn New York City police officers wearing black mourning bands on their chests gathered for a fellow officer's memorial service. Their colleague had been shot while working as an undercover drug dealer. His partner's funeral was scheduled for a few days later. Covering the story, *New York Times* journalist Dan Berry wrote that these deaths were "reminders that heroism and danger are not revealed only on foreign battlefields or in catastrophes like the collapse of the World Trade Center, but also in places as ordinary as Staten Island," where the shootings occurred. Attending the service, New York City mayor Michael Bloomberg called these killings "cold-blooded murder."[1]

TABLE 8.1 OCCUPATIONAL DEATH RATES PER 100,000: SELECTED OCCUPATIONS, 1999

selected occupation	death rate
agriculture, forestry, fishing	23
mining and quarrying	21
construction	14
transportation and utilities	12
police	10

Sources: Nonpolice fatalities from U.S. Census Bureau, *Statistical Abstract, 2002*, table 621, p. 408. Police deaths calculated from tables 320 and 450, *Statistical Abstract, 2001*, pp. 195, 294.

As table 8.1 shows, policing is not the most dangerous occupation. It is a tragedy when people are killed because they were trying to do their jobs. Unfortunately, it happens much more often than need be the case in this country. It is rare, however, for a highly placed government official to refer to the occupational death of ordinary workers as "murder," and the attention death on the job gets is usually scant.

Each year in late April the AFL-CIO has a Workers' Memorial Day commemoration. April 28, 1972, is the founding date of the Occupational Health and Safety Administration (OSHA), discussed further below. This event does not receive much media attention nor do high-ranking politicians make a point of attending. On April 26, 2002, as part of the commemoration, there was a special ceremony in New York to honor the three thousand people, six hundred of them union members, who died during the 2001 attack on the World Trade Center. A banner reading "Mourn for the Dead, Fight for the Living" conveyed the message that continuing the struggle for safer workplaces was an important way to honor the dead.[2]

It isn't rational for an employer to shoot his workers, but it makes economic sense to keep production costs as low as possible. As criminologist Joel Swartz states, in a capitalist society

the general functioning of the system is at the heart of the problem. . . . The tremendous toll in occupational illnesses results from the oppression of one class by another. The people who own corporations try to exact as much wealth as they can from the workers. Improvements in working conditions to eliminate health hazards would eat into the profits that could be exacted.[3]

The weaker workers are in relation to their employer and the more pro-business government is, the more dangerous workplaces are likely to be. It should not be surprising then that, according to the National Safety Workplace Institute, the United States holds the developed world's worst job safety record. U.S. workers are thirty-six times more likely to be killed on the job than workers in Sweden, and nine times more likely to be killed than British laborers.[4]

Working is more dangerous for some people than a chance confrontation with a homicidal street criminal. In 2000, 909 people died because they were assaulted at their workplace, while 5,006 died as a result of an injury connected to their jobs. A minimal estimate of deaths due to illness contracted at work is 50,000. In 2000, then, there were at least a total of 55,006 nonhomicidal workplace deaths. In 2000, the total of all homicides reported in the United States was 13,230.[5]

In addition, in 2000 there were at least 6,331,000 occupationally related illnesses and injuries. A more precise figure is not available, partly because only twenty-nine states and territories collect this data.[6] A 1986 congressional subcommittee noted "the United States is the only large developed country without a national system for reporting occupational disease."[7] In 2003 this was still the case. As experts J. Paul Leigh, Steven Markowitz, Marianne Fahs, and Philip Landrigan point out, where workplace-related health risks are concerned, "little effort has been made to estimate either the extent of these injuries, deaths, and diseases or their cost to the economy."[8]

One of the most dangerous occupations in the United States is meatpacking. Eric Schlosser observed workers in this industry while gathering data for *Fast Food Nation*. A conveyor belt with carcasses moves toward workers with knives at the ready at a rate of four hundred cattle an hour. Trying to keep up, workers cut themselves and develop "cumulative trauma injuries" such as carpal tunnel syndrome at a rate higher than any other American industry.[9] At night the cleanup crews turn on high-powered hoses emitting a mixture of hot water and chlorine on an area where four thousand cattle have been slaughtered. Seeing is difficult, machines are moving, and crew members fall into the machines and into vats. Schlosser's descriptions are reminiscent of those in Upton Sinclair's 1906 novel, *The Jungle*.

WORKERS' VICTORY: OSHA

Business is not omnipotent, and there has been some government attention paid to improving safety in the workplace. Coal miners led the drive for safer workplaces in the 1960s. The folk song "Dark as a Dungeon" describes the mines as places "where the dangers are many, and the pleasures are few." From 1900 to 1945 at least one thousand miners died on the job each year. Faced with horrifying working conditions, with many miners succumbing to black lung disease after years of inhaling coal dust, they engaged in wildcat strikes, marches, and lobbying.[10]

When seventy-eight Virginia miners were killed in a 1968 mine explosion, Congress finally passed a Coal Mine Health and Safety Act. This became the model for a coalition of union, consumer, and environmental activists, health professionals, and members of progressive religious organizations that organized grassroots actions to focus attention on occupational health and safety. In 1970, the Occupational Safety and Health Act (OSH Act) was passed, and a year later the Occupational Safety and Health Administration (OSHA) was created in the Department of Labor.

The act establishing OSHA proclaims that its purpose is "to assure safe and healthful working conditions for working men and women." This legislation recognized the right of workers to know what hazards they face on their jobs, the right to participate in inspections of the plants, and it offered them protection against reprisals for exercising their rights. In 2002 the AFL-CIO estimated that because of OSHA, 254,270 workers' lives had been saved.[11]

This acknowledgement of on-the-job rights opened the doors for further reforms. The act provides financial penalties for violations, timetables to remedy the problems, and an agency within the Health and Welfare Department to engage in research and to develop standards. This is NIOSH, the National Institute for Occupational Safety and Health. Some states have passed their own OSHA bills.

From the beginning, OSHA was kept from being fully effective as a guardian of workers' safety. The penalties were small, and the agency did not have enough inspectors. As a result of corporate America's privileged position vis-à-vis the law, Thomas R. Donahue, secretary-treasurer of the AFL-CIO, noted that "Since 1970 . . . only one person has served time in jail for a willful violation that resulted in the death of a worker. In contrast, seven people have been jailed for violations of a federal statute that protects wild burros and horses."[12] There was no provision for the government, a multibillion-dollar customer for the nation's businesses, to stop doing business with violators of the OSH Act.

In 1996 the General Accounting Office "found that 261 federal contractors, receiving more than $38 billion in government business in fiscal year 1994, received penalties of at least $15,000 each for violating Occupational Safety and Health regulations." In contrast, if a person is found guilty of dealing drugs, including marijuana, that person's family—even if totally ignorant of the crime, including elderly grandparents with no place to go—becomes ineligible to live in federally subsidized public housing and can be evicted. Some have been.[13]

BUSINESS VICTORIES: OSHA WEAKENED

Since 1970, as unions have become weaker and business more powerful, OSHA's potential effectiveness has been undermined. In 2002 OSHA offices at the federal and state levels had a total of 2,238 inspectors, responsible for monitoring about eight million workplaces. If the national OSHA inspectors decided to look at every workplace they were legally allowed to enter, it would take nineteen years to finish the process. In twenty-six states there is no federal or state OSHA protection for about eight million public employees.[14] To date, very few mainstream politicians have called for more policing of the workplace.

Although the OSH Act provides for higher fines, between 1973 and 1985 employers had to pay only $263 on the average. By 2002 that had risen to $910, but with inflation considered that is not much of an increase. When an explosion occurred in a mine owned by the Pittston Coal Company, killing seven miners in 1983, the company was fined $47,000. In contrast, six years later, the United Mine Workers of America was fined over $22 million for strike-related activities that caused no physical harm.[15]

OSHA does not compile all the information necessary to protect workers. The Chemical Safety and Hazard Investigation Board, a federal agency, studied 167 industrial accidents occurring between 1980 and 2002 involving chemical reactions that led to injury or death. It found that over half of the substances were not regulated. The board also found that OSHA, which compiles lists of compounds, does not consider the dangers that can arise from a combination of chemicals. It only considers whether an individual chemical poses a threat.

Sodium hydrosulfite and powdered aluminum interacted to cause an explosion, which killed five Lodi, New Jersey, workers in 1995. Alone each of these substances is harmless. OSHA decided to review its chemical safety regulations. But in May of 2002, the agency decided that stronger regulation was not necessary, denying that lobbying by the chemical industry had anything to do with its decision.[16]

Cancer is an occupational hazard for numerous workers. According to the American Cancer Society there are from eight thousand to twenty-five thousand preventable deaths a year resulting from occupational exposure to toxic chemicals. At least twenty-six thousand toxic substances are used in industry, with about a thousand new ones coming on the market annually. OSHA was supposed to set standards for exposure to hazardous substances, but out of two thousand likely carcinogens used in businesses, OSHA's exposure limits in the 1980s covered fewer than twenty-four.[17]

The Reagan administration was zealous in its attempts to roll back earlier worker gains. In the first two years of Reagan's administration, OSHA's budget was cut by 8 percent, inspections were reduced by 21 percent, and fines by 48 percent. Standards for exposure to noise and lead were reduced. In addition to reducing OSHA funding, the administration limited workers' access to information.

The textile industry provides a useful case. Byssinosis, or "brown lung," is an occupational risk facing these workers in which breathing becomes a torment. As the disease progresses, lung tissue is destroyed. An ex-textile worker described his suffering:

> Since I've had this brown lung, I have come to the point where I can't do much of anything . . . changing clothes, shaving, or taking a bath. Even talking I can't do sometimes. I had to leave the mill at the age of fifty-four. I tried to keep working but I just couldn't.[18]

In 1982 OSHA published a booklet warning workers of the hazards of cotton dust. OSHA head Thorne Auchter found the booklets "offensive." He charged that the cover showing the gaunt face of Louis Harrell "makes a statement that is obviously favorable to one side." He ordered over one hundred thousand copies destroyed. He also ordered that three industrial films and two slide shows dealing with workers' rights and the danger of cotton dust be pulled from distribution.

The Clinton administration claimed to support OSHA's goals, and when he was labor secretary, Robert Reich presented useful data on occupational health and safety to Congress, but OSHA found itself with no more staff or money than before. The Clinton administration did enact strong ergonomics rules, to reduce injuries from repetitive stress. These affect an estimated 1.8 million workers a year and are discussed more below. The Republican-dominated Congress repealed these in 2002. When George W. Bush became president, he advocated voluntary efforts by industry to deal with problems caused by repetitive motion and did not urge strengthening OSHA to protect workers.[19]

According to an AFL-CIO spokesperson, in the first two years of the Bush administration, the average fine for failing to fix a safety violation fell to $2,448. Before Bush took office in 2000 the fine had averaged $7,687. In 2003 Democratic senator from New Jersey Jon Corzine proposed a "Wrongful Death Accountability Act, which would increase to ten years, from six months, the maximum criminal penalty for employers who cause the death of a worker by willfully violating safety laws." An OSHA administrator in the Reagan years, Patrick Tyson considers the current six months maximum "nuts" but also said, "Business would not understand going to a felony."[20]

Business publicly takes the position that laws are not needed, and that voluntary efforts will do the job. A spokesperson for Inland Steel Company told a congressional hearing on expanding OSHA's provisions that employers would use OSHA's educational services, but they should be able to do so "without fear of being penalized. The objective should be to collaborate in pursuit of workplace safety and health and not to catch an employer in a violation."[21] For decades before OSHA's creation, business could have joined with its workers to create safer places of employment. Business's seeming indifference to workers' health and safety, however, is what led to the movement demanding stronger government protections.

In countries where workers have more powerful organizations representing them and a political party that is responsive to their needs, working conditions are safer and healthier. Swedish workers have a number of rights which U.S. workers lack. They can refuse to work in dangerous situations, they supervise the health services that their employers are required to establish in the workplace, and they even have the right to temporarily close a factory if the workers are in immediate danger.[22]

RACE/ETHNICITY AND OCCUPATIONAL JEOPARDY

Many whites do hazardous work. Coal miners, for example, are most likely to be white men. People of color, however, hold a disparate proportion of the most dangerous jobs, a result of the inequality that prevents them from having the same occupational choices as many whites. Robert Davis, a sociologist specializing in health issues, notes: "Historically, blacks have been more likely than whites to be employed in less skilled jobs, where exposures to hazardous substances tend to be greater. This has been the case in the chemical, rubber, and steel industries."[23]

In the South, poultry processors are likely to be African American women. In 1991 a fire swept through an Imperial Food Products chicken processing plant in North Carolina. Twenty-five workers died, and forty were injured by the blaze. The fire had started in a frying machine where chicken parts were prepared for delivery to restaurants. The plant's doors were locked because management feared workers might steal chicken parts.

Sam Breeden, passing by, heard trapped workers screaming, "Let me out." Brenda MacDougal, a survivor, described the plant: "That fryer was dangerous and there were no fire alarms in there . . . those doors in the back stayed shut." Daisy Ratliff, a former employee, described seeing her friends injured and dead: "It was pitiful, it was sad, it was terrible. I used to work on the line breading chickens and it was awfully dangerous in there." Sharing this view, a former worker, David Covington, claimed fires frequently occurred in the plant when "grease or the wasted parts would fall out and hit the flames." Workers had been able to extinguish these fires before a disaster occurred. The plant's manager tried to defend himself, saying, "There were plenty of doors that were open. Certain doors are locked at certain times. I can't tell you which doors were locked, if any were locked." Imperial had not been inspected in its eleven years of operation by either state or federal officials.[24]

Latino factory workers sometimes experience higher rates of occupational hazards than do white or black workers in similar jobs. One explanation could be that their knowledge of English may be poor, with employers often not bothering to instruct them in Spanish. A study in New Jersey found that Latino workers had the highest rates of finger amputations and fatalities at construction sites. A California study found higher concentrations of lead in Latino workers. Of all ethnic groups Latinos are also the most likely to be without health insurance.[25]

Racist attitudes are often part of the indifference to Latino workers' problems. Francisco Calito, from Guatemala, can no longer work because of shoulder injuries sustained while he was assembling golf clubs at the Chicago factory where he'd worked for ten years, making 2,300 golf clubs a day for $5.50 an hour. "I told them about the pain. They said if 'you don't work, you'll be fired.' My supervisor would shake his finger at me. He would kick me. He would tell me, 'I don't like you because you're a Latino.' I worked for two years with the pain."[26]

As we saw in table 8.1, agricultural work is among the most dangerous in the United States. Forty-two percent of farm workers are Latino, although this group is only about 16 percent of the labor force.[27] Agricultural workers are frequently exposed to high levels of pesticides that lead to nerve damage, cancer, sterility, and birth defects.

The United Farm Workers cite a study reported in the *American Journal of Public Health* that claims, "In California agricultural counties where pesticide use is high [there is] almost double the normal risk of having babies with birth defects." Children have been born without arms and legs. Children are exposed to these pesticides. Even if they are not actually working beside their parents, they may be brought into the fields since there is no place to leave them. Home is often not a refuge from the contaminants since pesticide residues cling to the workers' clothes.[28]

It was not until 1987 that agricultural enterprises were required to provide toilets and fresh drinking water for agricultural workers, and the rules are frequently ignored. Dangerous pesticides are used in the fields, and often there are no places for workers to wash. According to the Environmental Protection Agency (EPA), there are three hundred thousand illnesses each year among farm workers from pesticides.[29]

GENDER AND OCCUPATIONAL JEOPARDY

The percentage of women who are part of the paid labor force has increased since the 1950s, with especially large increases since the 1970s. Not only gender but also class and race affect a woman's job opportunities. For example, affluent mothers who can afford child care have more choice of where to work than women who must organize their time around child care.

Primarily female occupations are lower paid and, if not as physically intensive as the manual labor jobs that usually go to men, carry their own physical risks. Working-class and underclass women are less likely to have the credentials for professional or management positions and are therefore more likely than affluent women to accept physically risky jobs. These less advantaged women are also likely to be women of color.

We described the fire at the Imperial Foods plant. Less dramatic health threats are more routine. Poultry processors must keep their hands in almost constant repetitive motion. Betty Harper has had three operations on her hand and can't sleep well because of the pain she feels "the whole time at work and at home."

Journalist Laura Allen, summarizing a report in the *Occupational Health and Safety Journal*, wrote:

> Poultry workers experience the highest risk of debilitating skin diseases of any group of American workers, and there is a whole class of muscular and nervous system disorders endemic to the poultry industry caused by poorly designed tools, the constant rapid, repetitive motion required on the assembly line, and the demanding production pace.[30]

The women at Perdue, for instance, process ninety birds a minute. Janie Knights, who works at a Perdue plant in North Carolina, explains why people continue to stay at these jobs:

> People have to feed their kids; people have to work. Nine of ten of these people are poor, black, uneducated. Many of them are single parents. They're too scared to complain and you can't blame them.[31]

In 1989 OSHA reported two-thirds of the workers in these plants had injuries and were "knowingly and willfully exposed" to health risks by their employers. The plants are cold and noisy, leading to additional health problems. An investigation by Bob Hall, research director of the Institute for Southern Studies, found that Perdue regularly misinformed OSHA about workers' injuries. He quotes an internal memo from a personnel manager who wrote that it is "normal procedure for about 60 percent of our workforce" to get daily doses of "Advil, the vitamin B6, and hand wraps" from the company nurse.[32]

Poultry processing and office work give rise to similar repetitive motion disorders, such as carpal tunnel syndrome, incidences of which are increasing in U.S. workplaces. Blue- and white-collar workers who repeat the same motion for many hours in a day are likely to suffer the tissue damage that comes from this process. In 1987, for every ten thousand full-time workers there were ten cases of repetitive motion ailments; by 1993 the figure had risen to thirty-eight per ten thousand.[33]

Women are much more likely than men to be doing the office jobs requiring repetitive keyboard work. Many companies measure clerical productivity by tracking the speed of the employees' keystrokes. In addition to repetitive motion disorders, clerical workers are susceptible to neck and back pain and cardiovascular and respiratory problems resulting from exposure to toxic substances such as those used in photocopying machines.

The electronics industry, which also employs many women at lower-level jobs, exposes them to toxic chemicals. When used without proper ventilation, these chemicals are suspected of causing cancer, nerve damage, reproductive problems, blood diseases, and so on. There is little regulation of these industries, and, to date, there are few studies of the hazards of the high-tech workplace.

If employment creates hazards, so does unemployment. Below we shall discuss this, looking first at some of the reasons joblessness exists and then at how unemployment is connected to violence.

UNEMPLOYMENT: WHO BENEFITS?

Profits can only be made if workers are paid less than the value of the goods they produce. Inevitably, companies are unable to sell all that has been manufactured, stocks pile up, and people are laid off. This is one cause of unemployment. As unemployment rises, there is increasing competition for jobs, and in the absence of successful collective actions on the part of the working class, a lowering of wages and a worsening of working conditions occurs.

As part of its goal of high profits, capitalism strives to keep down the costs of labor. Unemployment is one of the ways this end is achieved. The creation of what Marx termed the "reserve army of labor" has been a feature of capitalism for hundreds of years.[34] Full employment is very rare in capitalist economies, but there are differences in the support offered for the unemployed, with U.S. workers being in the worst position. Some of the consequences of this unemployment are examples of structural violence.

Government policies can strengthen or mitigate the tendency to unemployment and also affect the impact of joblessness on households. The more social supports there are in the form of unemployment insurance, family allowances, subsidized health care, and so on, the more those in the working class can withstand pressures to take low-paying and unhealthy jobs. Corporations are able to use their political power, discussed in chapter 3, to influence both fiscal and welfare (broadly defined) policies.[35] Foreign policy and militarism, as discussed in chapters 13 and 14, also impact on employment.

When there are "too many" people working, mainstream economists worry. *New York Times* business reporter Louis Uchitelle noted that in early 1994, with the "economy growing strongly and the unemployment rate falling, the Federal Reserve has responded by raising interest rates three times since early February." Raising interest rates makes borrowing more expensive, slowing down economic growth, which would be likely to further increase employment. In November 1994 interest rates climbed to their highest level since 1981, against the expressed wishes of unions.[36]

Unemployment exerts downward pressure on wages by increasing the demand for jobs. In very recent times the problem has become even worse as highly educated workers in the dot-com and telecommunications industries have been laid off. They have been joined by growing numbers of elderly persons whose pensions have been lost or drastically reduced due to the recent drop in stock values, and who are now forced to look for work.

Unemployment is increased not only by federal fiscal policies but also because of the great flexibility that business has in deciding where and how to operate. In 2000 alone, nearly half the workers who lost their jobs did so because of plants or companies shutting down or moving. This figure is comparable to what has happened in other years. Workers of color made up half of those displaced, far more than their representation in the labor force.[37]

Because of advances in communications and transportation, operations can be moved from one region to another within a country or out of the country altogether if this is rational from a profit-making perspective, a phenomenon known as "capital flight." Since the Second World War, U.S. corporations have steadily increased their overseas investments. As a chief financial officer at Colgate-Palmolive said, "There is no mind-set that puts this country first."[38]

Companies can decide to fire workers in order to improve company profitability. Labor costs are one of the biggest expenses for any company. Alan Downs is a management consultant critical of large-scale firings, which he sees as harmful to the larger society. He understands why companies do this, however, pointing out that

> the most attractive aspect of a layoff is that it is an organizational change with clear, predictable consequences: Reducing the payroll lowers expenses. With any other kind of executive action, like process improvement or total quality, the consequences are not nearly as clear or immediate. Months, maybe even years, may pass before those improvements make any noticeable difference in the basic financials. And when they finally have a positive effect, the time and the distance between the actual decision and the result make it very difficult for a specific person to claim the credit for the accomplishment. A layoff, on the other hand, can be decided and announced by a senior executive and within a very short time period that same executive can claim credit for the reduction in expenses.[39]

Though joblessness is bad for workers, the government often sides with business, enacting policies, including international agreements, that increase unemployment. The North American Free Trade Agreement (NAFTA) has been in effect since 1994. It allows for much freer movement of capital and goods between the United States, Canada, and Mexico. Mexico, with its much lower wages and weaker environmental regulation, has been especially attractive to many U.S. companies, who establish *maquiladoras* there. NAFTA has also meant that lower-priced goods can be brought back into the United States free of quota restrictions and tariffs. In the textile industry, factories that had moved south from higher labor cost northern states have left that region in large numbers, taking tens of thousands of jobs, the basis for many a small town's economic well-being. In 1995, of all the jobs lost in the manufacturing sector, 40 percent were in the textile industry, 141,000 jobs.[40]

As a result of NAFTA at least 766,000 jobs have been lost in the manufacturing sector, which provided those with only a high school education or less a chance for a good-paying job. In turn, this has exerted a downward pressure on remaining jobs.[41] There are no estimates for how many service jobs, dependent on the factories, disappeared.

Jobs in the computer and telecommunications sector are also being exported. Writing in *Time*, Jyoti Thottam notes:

> If you've ever called Dell about a sick PC or American Express about an error on you your bill, you have bumped the tip of this "offshore outsourcing" iceberg. The friendly voice that answer your question was probably a customer-service rep in Bangalore or New Delhi.

A computer programmer earning $66,000 in the United States can be replaced by one earning $10,000 in India. Financial analysts predict that half a million of these types of jobs will be lost to skilled American workers who may have thought their training would provide a secure future.[42]

Stock prices often go up after mass layoffs. The military contractor United Technologies laid off 10,500 workers at the end of January 1993; by December its stock had risen by 30 percent. It took IBM only five months to see a comparable rise after firing 60,000 employees. Procter and Gamble, in the same period as IBM, got rid of 13,000 of its workers, but its stock rose by only 13 percent.[43] Salaries rise for the executives doing the firing, who also benefit from the increase in stock values. After reviewing executive compensation, Alan Downs, quoted earlier, concluded, "CEOs who lay off large numbers of employees are paid more than those who don't."[44]

Executives justify their actions by appealing to the higher value, for them, of increasing their competitive edge. When Procter and Gamble decided it would fire at least four thousand workers in the United States between 1993 and 1995, Edwin L. Artz, its CEO, explained, "We have today a healthy, growing business, a strong balance sheet, positive cash flow, state-of-the-art products, and a well-stocked technology pipeline with plenty of opportunities for growth. However, we must slim down to stay competitive."[45]

In 1994 Charles R. Lee, CEO of the telecommunication company GTE, announced that seventeen thousand jobs would be cut. He justified the decision by saying, "This is a defining movement for the company. We intend to be the market leader. . . . But to do that you have got to have competitive costs."[46] When Allied Signal, Inc., announced its plan to fire one thousand workers, about half of its labor force in its Stratford, Connecticut, plant, a company spokesman said,

> While we regret that employment levels in Stratford must be reduced to meet today's demanding market requirements, the result will be a more competitive organization.[47]

Similarly, in 1993 the *New York Times* reported that despite its profitability Xerox was cutting about 10 percent of its work force, ten thousand workers, over the next three years. "Xerox," the article pointed out, "takes its place among financially sound companies seeing higher profits through mass layoffs," and they quoted Xerox CEO Paul A. Allarite, who said, "To compete effectively we must have a lean and flexible organization." Following the announcement, the value of Xerox shares rose.[48]

Corporations do not need permission from anyone to shut down a local operation, in spite of the enormous consequences this will have and even though it may have received tax breaks for locating in a particular place. CEOs decide what to do to increase their organizations' profits. They could decide to reinvest, upgrading their plants and equipment and developing new product lines by paying for research and development. Instead, in many instances, companies have diversified through buying other enterprises. This is usually accompanied by firings. In the 1980s there was an

> avalanche of corporate mergers and acquisitions. More than 4,000 of those unions, worth a record $190 billion, took place [in 1986]. After most of the buyouts, the merged company eliminates staff duplications and unprofitable divisions. In the past six years [1981–1987], for example, General Electric spent $11.1 billion to buy 338 businesses,

including RCA, a $6.3 billion acquisition. During the same period, GE shed 232 businesses worth $5.9 billion and closed 73 plants and offices.[49]

Unlike investors and CEOs, workers and communities pay a high price for corporate downsizing. The companies' suppliers are hurt as well as the fired employees. According to economists Barry Bluestone and Bennett Harrison, the Department of Labor estimates that "for every 100 jobs [lost] in the motor vehicle industry, 105 jobs are wiped out in the direct supplier network."[50]

Local businesses lose customers. On Chicago's South Side in 1950 there were over eight hundred enterprises. In 1996 there were about one hundred. Researcher Loïc Waiquant described the now bleak neighborhood:

> The once-lively streets—residents remember a time, not so long ago, when crowds were so dense at rush hour that one had to elbow one's way to the train station—now have the appearance of an empty, bombed-out war zone. The commercial strip has been reduced to a long tunnel of charred stores, vacant lots littered with broken glass and garbage, and dilapidated buildings left to rot in the shadow of the elevated train line. . . . The only enterprises that seem to be thriving are liquor stores and currency exchanges, those "banks of the poor" where one can cash checks, pay bills, and buy money orders for a fee.[51]

Unemployed workers do not buy coffee or food from the local restaurant, coffee shop, or lunch wagon; they stop having a beer at the local tavern on their way home from work. Their families have less money to go to the movies and to buy clothes and appliances. When the plant shuts down, the lights go out on Main Street. At the very time that there is an increased need for services, the tax base of communities is reduced.

Matters could be mitigated with more generous unemployment benefits, but the federal government has been doing little in this regard, and financially strapped states cannot afford to do so. In any case, not all workers are even eligible for these benefits, and they do not replace a decent salary. If you received unemployment for a year, on the average, your income would be about $12,000.[52]

The real unemployment rate is actually much higher than official figures. The Bureau of Labor Statistics counts as employed even those working as little as an hour a week.[53] If a person has given up looking, is a "discouraged worker," or would work if there were child care available, she or he is not counted as unemployed. Below are some unemployment data for April 2003.[54] There were

- 8.8 million workers officially counted as unemployed, 6 percent of the labor force;
- 4.8 million people working part-time because they could not find a full-time job; and
- 4.4 million discouraged workers.

These numbers come to 12 percent of the labor force either out of work or unable to find full-time jobs, a total of about eighteen million people.

There are racial/ethnic differences in unemployment rates. African Americans usually have an unemployment rate twice as high as that of whites. Teens, aged sixteen to nineteen, in general, currently have high rates of unemployment, with African American teenagers having the highest rates of any group. As of April 2003 the statistics were as follows:

- white unemployment was 5 percent
- African American unemployment was 11 percent
- Latino unemployment was 8 percent
- teen unemployment was 18 percent
- African American teen unemployment was 33 percent

UNEMPLOYMENT CAN BE A KILLER

Unemployment has a number of consequences that are forms of structural violence. It also leads to increases in interpersonal violence as individuals and households experience economic stress. Thomas Cottle, who has done extensive research on the unemployed, summarizes the literature on this topic. He states, "Along with the death or abandonment of a family member, unemployment is the most powerful experience families ever have to sustain. The whole household is affected." He notes many people "actually liken unemployment to an illness. . . ."[55]

Numerous studies have shown a relationship between unemployment, stress, and both physical and mental illness.[56] Thomas Cottle found physical ailments appearing in men within two weeks of losing a job. Other family members also get sick, with flu, headaches, back pains, and digestive-tract problems being among the most common ailments.[57]

In the 1970s social psychologists Ramsey Liam and Paula Rayman matched two groups of forty families: in one set the men had all lost their jobs, in the other they hadn't. During the two-year period of the study, the unemployed husbands were found to have "higher levels of psychiatric symptoms," including depression, anxiety, and hostility. Thomas Cottle discovered, as have other researchers, that a number of people in his sample experienced "psychological disturbances and outright mental illness."[58]

M. Harvey Brenner, professor of health policy and management at Johns Hopkins University, has been studying the relationship between unemployment and physical and mental health since the 1970s. He has found that an approximate 1.3 percent increase in unemployment is correlated with about twenty-one additional deaths a year over what would be the case if the unemployment rate had not risen. Admissions to mental hospitals rise by about 1.8 percent. There are also increases in interpersonal violence.[59]

Suicide rates have also been found to increase as unemployment goes up. Brenner estimates that each 1.3 percent rise in unemployment is matched by the same rise in suicide rates. As one laid-off manager explained, "Working is breathing. It's something you don't think about; you just do it and it keeps you alive. When you stop you die." A year after making this statement he shot himself.[60] Of course, only a small percentage of unemployed people kill themselves: suicide is the most extreme expression of despair. Less dramatic indicators also exist, such as hypertension, higher cholesterol levels, and elevated blood-sugar conditions—all conditions found among unemployed workers after their workplaces closed.

Some laid-off workers increase unhealthy lifestyle practices such as smoking and drinking. These can give rise to cardiovascular diseases, cirrhosis of the liver, and kidney disease. Sickness is exacerbated during unemployment because households are often forced to cut back on medical care for family members. This will especially be a problem for those families with the fewest assets to fall back on. Dr. Lewis Ferman of the University of Michigan's Institute of Labor and Industrial Relations feels that "the relationship between unemployment and physiological or psychological stress is so strong that every pink slip should carry a Surgeon General's warning that it may be hazardous to your health."[61]

In addition to these potential problems, unemployment disrupts accustomed social ties and roles. Studies in Sweden, Finland, and the United States indicate that social isolation, anxiety, and stress, all of which can increase when a job is lost, are associated with deteriorating health.

Unemployment can put pressure on the employed to accept more onerous working conditions, which in turn affect their health. With jobs scarce and unions weak, workers may feel they must choose between a job and a healthy life. In Connecticut, for instance, autoworkers in their late forties and older were getting up before dawn, preparing to drive nearly one hundred miles to jobs at a General Motors assembly plant in New York State. Their former GM plant had closed and, unless they were willing to commute and train for new jobs, they would have no work. Tens of thousands of other GM workers are in similar straits. The auto industry even has a term for workers like this, "GM gypsies." The commuting Connecticut workers, however, did not have much time to travel to their new jobs. The New York plant closed in July of 1996.[62]

With massive downsizing eliminating jobs from blue-collar to managerial and professional jobs, more workers are forced to accept part-time work. This, in turn, means on the average about 60 percent of their full-time pay and no benefits.

In the United States, but not in other industrial countries, when you lose your job, you lose your employer-provided health benefits. Government programs are available, but the eligibility requirements do not guarantee that a person and his family will be able to get affordable care. At the very time when health is threatened, people cannot afford medical care.

How people react to stress depends, to an extent, on what resources are available. Some have more money to start with; some have relatives or friends who can help them.[63] If there were social programs such as national health care, and if unions were stronger, then unemployment would not be such a catastrophe.

High rates of unemployment impact not only on individuals and households but also on whole communities. In the next two chapters we shall look at the relationship between unemployment and street crime, and the violence associated with this. We shall also look at why the communities most affected by unemployment are communities of color.

NOTES

1. "White Glove Farewell to an Officer Who Embraced a Life of Risks," *New York Times,* March 16, 2003, p. 35.

2. From AFL-CIO Web site, http://www.aflcio.org/yourjobeconomy/safety/ns0426a2002.cfm (accessed March 18, 2003).

3. Quoted in David R. Simon, *Elite Deviance,* 5th ed. (Boston: Allyn and Bacon, 1996), pp. 143–44.

4. "U.S. Job Death Rate Still Relatively High," *New York Times*, September 4, 1989.

5. U.S. Bureau of Labor Statistics, *Census of Fatal Occupational Injuries,*

2000, http://usgovinfo.about.com/library/weekly/nfatalitytables.htm (accessed March 18, 2003); homicide data from U.S. Census Bureau, *Statistical Abstract of the United States, 2002,* table 288, p. 186. Table 187, however, gives the figure of 12,943 for murder victims.

6. AFL-CIO Safety and Health Department, *Death on the Job: The Toll of Neglect,* 11th ed., April 2002, http://www.aflcio.org/yourjobeconomy/safety/ns04262002.com (accessed March 18, 2003).

7. Quoted in Jeffrey Reiman, *The Rich Get Richer and the Poor Get Prison,* 3rd ed. (New York: MacMillan, 1990), p. 63. In his 6th edition he has a useful discussion of statistics of occupational hazards versus street crime, pp. 79–88.

8. *Costs of Occupational Injuries and Illnesses,* http://www.pbs.org/wgbh/pages/frontline/shows.workplace/etc/cost.html (accessed January 19, 2003). Book originally published by University of Michigan Press, 2000.

9. Eric Schlosser, *Fast Food Nation: The Dark Side of the All-American Meal* (New York: Harper Perennial, 2002), p. 178.

10. Steven Greenhouse, "Rise in Mining Deaths Prompts Political Sparring," *New York Times,* July 26, 2002, p. A14.

11. AFL–CIO Safety and Health Department, *Death on the Job,* p. 1.

12. U.S. Congress, House Committee on Education and Labor, *Hearings on H.R. 1280, Comprehensive Occupational Safety and Health Reform Act,* 103rd Cong., 1st sess., April 28, July 29, 1993, p. 73.

13. Robert Weissman, "Scofflaw Blacklist," *Nation,* November 8, 1999, pp. 5–6; "In Congress' Hands, the Aftermath of the *Rucker* Decision," *Housing Law Bulletin* 32 (May/June 2002): 122.

14. AFL-CIO Safety and Health Department, *Death on the Job,* p. 5.

15. Editorial, *Nation,* October 16, 1989, p. 409.

16. Andrew C. Revkin, "Data Is Found to Be Lacking on Reactions of Chemicals," *New York Times,* May 30, 2002, p. A18.

17. Charles Noble, *Liberalism at Work: The Rise and Fall of OSHA* (Philadelphia: Temple University Press, 1986), pp. 179–80.

18. Quoted in Joan Claybrook, *Retreat from Safety: Reagan's Attack on America's Health* (New York: Pantheon, 1984), p. 83.

19. Steven Greenhouse, "Bush Plan to Avert Work Injuries Seeks Voluntary Steps by Industry," *New York Times,* April 6, 2002, pp. A1, A12.

20. David Barstow and Lowell Bergman, "OSHA to Address Persistent Safety Violations," *New York Times,* March 11, 2003. pp. A1, A22.

21. U.S. Congress, *Hearings on H.R. 1280,* p. 233.

22. Noble, *Liberalism at Work,* p. 233.

23. "Racial Differences in Mortality: Current Trends and Perspectives," in *Race and Ethnicity in America: Meeting the Challenge in the 21st Century,* ed. Gail Thomas (Washington, DC: Taylor & Francis, 1995), p. 123.

24. Quotes from Ronald Smothers, "25 Die, Many Reported Trapped as Blaze Engulfs Carolina Plant," *New York Times,* September 4, 1991, pp. A1, B7; Peter T.

Kilborn, "Once-Tamed Disease Fells Workers on Pork Packing Plant's Killing Floor," *New York Times*, September 27, 1993, p. A12.

25. Lawrence K. Altman, "Many Hispanic Americans Reported in Ill Health and Lacking Insurance," *New York Times*, January 9, 1991, p. A16.

26. Peter T. Kilborn, "For Hispanic Immigrants, a Higher Job Injury Risk," *New York Times*, February 18, 1992, pp. A1, A15.

27. U.S. Census Bureau, *Statistical Abstract of the United States, 2002*, table 588, p. 383.

28. Marion Moses, "Farmworkers and Pesticides," in *Confronting Environmental Racism*, ed. Robert Bullard (Boston: South End Press, 1994), pp. 161–78; "New Research on Pesticide-Birth Defect Link," *Food and Justice* (December 1988): 8–9.

29. "Federal Laws Found Lacking in Guarding Farm Worker Rights," *New York Times*, February 25, 1992, p. A18; a United Farmworkers' video, *The Wrath of Grapes*, shows what these pesticides do to children and adults.

30. Laura Allen, "Women Workers at Perdue: Chicken in Every Pot, Health Hazards in Every Shop," *Resist Newsletter* (October 1988): 5.

31. Peter Applebome, "Worker Injuries Rise in Poultry Industry as Business Booms," *New York Times*, November 6, 1989, p. A20.

32. Bob Hall, "Perdue Farms: Poultry and Profits," *Multinational Monitor* 10, no. 9 (September 1989): 20.

33. Steve Lohr, "Waving Goodbye to Ergonomics," *New York Times*, April 16, 1995, sec. 3, p.1.

34. Karl Marx, *Capital*, vol. 1 (Moscow: Foreign Languages Publishing House, n.d., originally published 1887), pp. 640–44, has a discussion of the types of surplus labor; useful summaries of Marx's ideas can be found in Paul Sweezy, *Theory of Capitalist Development* (New York: Monthly Review Press, 1942), pp. 87–92, and Harry Braverman, *Labor and Monopoly Capital: The Degradation of Work in the Twentieth Century* (New York: Monthly Review Press, 1974), pp. 386–89. For more discussion of the processes and consequences of creating a surplus labor force, see E. P. Thompson, *The Making of the English Working Class* (New York: Vintage, 1963), and Richard L. Rubenstein, *The Age of Triage: Fear and Hope in an Overcrowded World* (Boston: Beacon Press, 1983), pp. 34–81.

35. Edward S. Herman, "The Natural Rate of Unemployment," *Z* (November 1994): 62–65; Louis Uchitelle, "A Debate on the Greater Evil: Inflation or Chill of Pink Slips" *New York Times*, November 16, 1994, pp. A1, D6; Keith Bradsher, "Federal Reserve Increases Interest Rates by 3/4 Point: Jump Is Largest Since 1981," *New York Times*, November 16, 1994, pp. A1, D6; Theresa Amott, *Caught in the Crisis: Women and the U.S. Economy Today* (New York: Monthly Review Press, 1993), pp. 44–45; Frances Fox Piven and Richard Cloward, *Regulating the Poor: The Functions of Public Welfare*, upd. ed. (New York: Vintage Books, 1993).

36. Louis Uchitelle, "Growth of Jobs May Be Casualty in Inflation Fight," *New York Times*, April 24, 1994, p. 1; Uchitelle, "A Debate on the Greater Evil," pp. A1, D6; Bradsher, "Federal Reserve Increases Interest Rates by 3/4 Point," pp. A1, D6.

37. U.S. Census Bureau, *Statistical Abstract of the United States, 2002*, table 585, p. 380. For 1992 as an example of another year, see *Statistical Abstract of the United States, 1994*, table 645, p. 415.

38. Louis Uchitelle, "U.S. Businesses Loosen Link to Mother Country," *New York Times*, May 21, 1989, pp. 1, 30.

39. Alan Downs, *Corporate Executions: The Ugly Truth about Layoffs—How Corporate Greed Is Shattering Lives, Companies, and Communities* (New York: AMACOM, 1995), p. 16. His criticisms are on pp. ix, 4–5.

40. John Holusha, "Squeezing the Textile Workers," *New York Times*, February 21, 1996, pp. D1, D20.

41. "Ask Dr. Dollar," *Dollars and Sense* (January/February 2003): 38. A higher estimate, 766,000, is given by the Economic Policy Institute, "NAFTA AT SEVEN: Its Impact on Workers in All Three Nations," http://epinet.org (accessed March 17, 2003).

42. Jyoti Thottam, "Where the Good Jobs Are Going," *Time*, August 4, 2003, pp. 36, 39.

43. Downs, *Corporate Executions*, p. 14.

44. Ibid., pp. 27–28.

45. Quoted in Michael Janofsky, "Procter & Gamble in 12% Job Cut as Brand Names Lose Attraction," *New York Times*, July 16, 1993, p. D2.

46. Anthony Ramirez, "GTE Says It Will Cut 17,000 Jobs," *New York Times*, January 14, 1994, p. D1.

47. "Allied Signal Plans to Eliminate 1,000 Jobs at Plant in Stratford," *New York Times*, November 29, 1994, p. B5.

48. John Holusha, "A Profitable Xerox Plans to Cut Staff by 10,000," *New York Times*, December 9, 1993.

49. Quoted in George Russell, "Corporate Restructuring," in *The Reshaping of America: Social Consequences of the Changing Economy*, ed. D. Stanley Eitzen and Maxine Baca Zinn (Englewood Cliffs, NJ: Prentice-Hall, 1989), p. 35.

50. Barry Bluestone and Bennett Harrison, *The Deindustrialization of America: Plant Closings, Community Abandonment, and the Dismantling of Basic Industry* (New York: Basic Books, 1982), p. 71.

51. Quoted in William Julius Wilson, "Work," *New York Times Magazine*, August 18, 1996, p. 28.

52. David Leonhardt, "Georgia Finds Itself in Jobless Benefits Bind," *New York Times*, January 16, 2002, p. A14.

53. Federal government definitions of "employed" and "unemployed" can be found in *Statistical Abstract of the United States, 2002*, pp. 363–64.

54. The data on unemployment are from the National Jobs For All coalition, using U.S. Bureau of Labor statistics, http://www.njfac.org/jobnews.html (accessed May 13, 2003).

55. Thomas Cottle, *Hardest Times: The Trauma of Long-Term Unemployment* (Westport, CT: Praeger, 2001), p. 19.

56. Clifford L. Broman, V. Lee Hamiliton, and William S. Hoffman, *Stress and Distress among the Unemployed: Hard Times and Vulnerable People* (New York: Kluwer Academic/Plenum Publishers, 2001), p. 13.

57. Cottle, *Hardest Times*, p. 19.

58. Ibid., p. 20.

59. Ramsey Liam and Paula Rayman, "Health and Social Costs of Unemployment," *American Psychologist* 37 (October 1982): 1116–23; M. Harvey Brenner, *Economy, Society, and Health* (Washington, DC: Economic Policy Institute, 1992), pp. 4–5.

60. Quoted in Thomas Cottle, "When You Stop, You Die: The Human Toll of Unemployment," in *Crisis in American Institutions*, ed. Jerome Skolnick and Elliot Currie, 9th ed. (New York: HarperCollins, 1994), p. 77.

61. Quoted in Maya Pines, "Recession Is Linked to Far-Reaching Psychological Harm," *New York Times*, June 6, 1982.

62. Kirk Johnson, "Aging Auto Workers Travel Long Roads to Stay in Place," *New York Times*, January 16, 1995, pp. A1, B4; Thomas J. Lueck, "Auto Plant Closes and Developers See Opportunity," *New York Times*, June 27, 1996, pp. B1, B6.

63. Broman, Hamiliton, and Hoffman, *Stress and Distress among the Unemployed*, pp. 2–3.

Chapter 9

INTERPERSONAL VIOLENCE
Street Crime—The Context

A chilling crime occurred at a New York City Wendy's fast-food restaurant on May 24, 2000. Two armed men, John B. Taylor and Craig Godineaux, walked in, rounded up the workers, and forced them to go to the basement, into a walk-in refrigerator. There the intruders covered the employees' heads with garbage bags and their mouths with duct tape. Their hands were tied behind their backs. Then they were shot. Altogether, six people were murdered, two were wounded, and the killers netted $2,400. Several weeks previously "two former Wendy's employees in South Bend, Indiana, received prison terms for murdering a pair of coworkers during a robbery that netted $1,400." Farther west, a grisly scene occurred at a Chuck E. Cheese restaurant in Aurora, Colorado, when a former employee killed four workers, one of them the manager. The police arrived to see not only bodies but also flashing game lights and singing mechanical animals.[1]

Interpersonal violence on the job is an occupational hazard we did not discuss in the previous chapter. Sometimes a worker assaults one of his colleagues. The expression "going postal" describes this, but more often violence is at the hands of a stranger. In 2002 there were 929 assaults in the workplace, of which 73 percent were homicides. The majority of the assaults, 79 percent, were committed with a firearm.[2] The accessibility of guns, discussed in chapter 2, is a factor in these deaths. Workplace violence is especially serious in fast-food restaurants and convenience stores.

201

In the previous chapter we made use of Eric Schlossers's descriptions of the grim working conditions in slaughterhouses. In *Fast Food Nation,* he also describes the physical jeopardy of those employed by fast-food chains, commenting, "The level of violent crime in the industry is surprisingly high. In 1998, more restaurant workers were murdered on the job in the United States than police officers."[3]

What makes these establishments attractive targets for criminals? For one thing, they are likely to have cash on hand. Customers are less apt to use credit cards for their inexpensive purchases. These small bills add up, and the restaurant may have "thousand of dollars in the till." There are no bulletproof barriers shielding employees. There are no guards at the door. In addition, these restaurants are conveniently located "near intersections and high-way off-ramps" facilitating "a speedy getaway." Many are open late at night and early in the morning, times when there are few people around other than the employees. The criminals are sometimes former employees, angry that they have been paid so little for their efforts. One of the Wendy's murderers had worked there.[4]

There are measures that the owners of retail outlets could take that would better protect their workers from this type of violence. In what seemed a rational and humane report, OSHA suggested steps that could be taken in this direction, such as better lighting in the stores and parking lots. The National Restaurant Association did not welcome the suggestions and lobbied against them even though they were to be voluntary. At a conference to discuss the problems of violence, restaurant industry representatives expressed concerns that unfavorable statistics would be gathered and any guidelines could be used in lawsuits.

While workers could be better protected from criminals, this ignores the issue of why some people are making a living by robbing and murdering, whether it be fast-food workers or anyone else. Understanding this aspect of interpersonal violence means looking at the organizational decisions that have resulted in numerous communities being filled with people who find this a tempting alternative because they lack other opportunities.

In affluent, white suburbs, teenagers worry about getting into a good college. In Camden, New Jersey, one of the poorest cities in the United States, the preoccupations are different. At a youth center, a seventeen-year-old writes a poem about being an astronaut. He is not contemplating a future career but imagining a place away from the routine violence of his neighborhood:

Away from guns and ride-by's
    and everyday fights.
Away from gangs and drugs and
    burned out houses and speeding
    cars that run down little kids.

Other Camden youngsters draw pictures of little kids hiding under their beds and pictures of friends who have been shot. Many can recount the details of their friends' funerals.[5]

Crime rates and fear of crime are greatest in minority neighborhoods. When asked in 2000, "Is there any area right around here—that is, within a mile—where you would be afraid to walk alone at night?" 45 percent of black/other, compared to 38 percent of white households, answered yes. One stark statistic helps explain these data. Between 1976 and 1999 the rate for murder and nonnegligent manslaughter for whites was 4 per 100,000; for blacks it was 21. Violence rates for blacks are even more dramatic when age and gender are considered. For both whites and African Americans groups, the rates for males eighteen to twenty-four are highest of all, but in 1999 the rate for white males was 13, while for black males in this age group it was 103.[6]

Why do black communities have the highest rates of criminal violence? Answering this involves looking at how racial inequality interacts with economic and political inequality.

UNSAFE STREETS: NOTHING NEW

Crime and ethnic inequality have coexisted in U.S. cities for over a century. David Dinkins, the former mayor of New York, in his new position teaching political science at Columbia University, read a description of New York to his students:

> Two or three murders take place every day, before breakfast. You risk your life by walking the streets late at night. Homeless people lie in the gutters. Prostitution runs rampant. There are useless expenditures of public money, overtaxation, and improper contracting. The streets are filthy and in disrepair and filled with drivers reckless of human life. There is inadequate health care and TB has reached epidemic proportions and illegal immigrants are entering from ships onto our shores.

This description, sounding like it came from this morning's newspaper, was from 1856.[7] As European immigrants came to the United States from the 1840s to just before WWI, they discovered that jobs were often scarce and discrimination rampant. Those locked out of mainstream opportunities put their feet on alternative ladders: entertainment, sports, and crime, all offering potentially big payoffs. All three, however, have high rates of failure; crime and many sports are physically dangerous, with success often short-lived.

The Irish, the first large immigrant group, were also the first European ethnic group thought of as violent. *Harper's* magazine at the time of the Civil War claimed, "Fully 75 percent of the crimes of violence . . . are the work of Irishmen." In 1890 a prison expert said of the Italians, derogatively called dagos: "The knife with which he cuts his bread he also uses to lop off another 'dago's' finger or ear. . . . He is quite as familiar with the sight of human blood as with the sight of the food he eats."[8]

A 1906 description of Chicago's "Jewtown" claimed that more "murderers, robbers, and thieves of the worst kind" came from this area than any other neighborhood. In turn-of-the-century New York, Jewish women were stereotyped as prostitutes. During Prohibition, 1919–1933, the opportunity to make big money by illegally supplying liquor arose. One judge described bootlegging as a "Jewish crime wave."[9]

THE AFRICAN AMERICAN CRIMINAL STEREOTYPE

African Americans are today's feared ethnic group. In chapter 12 we shall discuss how this image affects relations with the police. Black men get stopped in the streets for being in the "wrong" (i.e., white) neighborhoods, taxis pass them by, and salespeople follow them around stores. In 1994, for example, in my class on the sociology of violence, one of my white students, then employed in a New Jersey men's clothing store, recounted how his manager ordered the sales staff to announce an African American man's entrance. The first one to spot the unwelcome customer was to tell the others, "Mr. Johnson's here." "Mr. Johnson" was then to be watched. Other students working in retailing have described similar incidents, while minority students have described being the victims of unwarranted scrutiny.

Surveys show that whites see African Americans as more prone to committing acts of crime and violence. In his ethnographic study of African Americans in the Chestnut Hill section of a Philadelphia neighborhood, Elijah Anderson found that while blacks realized that street crime "is likely to be perpetrated by young black males . . . many are disturbed by the inability of some whites to make distinctions—particularly between people who are out to commit crime and those who are not."[10]

Many individuals might agree with Boston city councilman James Kelly's statement: "People feel very intimidated by these black males in hooded sweatshirts."[11] Some whites have used this stereotype to their own advantage. For example, in 1988 George H. W. Bush's presidential campaign exploited fears of violent blacks in the Willie Horton ads. In the ads Democratic candidate Michael Dukakis, then governor of Massachusetts, was accused of allowing an African American inmate a prison furlough during which he murdered a white woman. The Bush ads implicitly promised protection from violent black criminals.

In several incidents whites have used the violent stereotype of African American men to try cover up their own crimes. In 1989 a Boston man, Charles Stuart, shot his pregnant wife, then claimed it had been done by an African American man. This touched off a massive manhunt in which many young black men were stopped and questioned by the police; one was charged with the killing and arrested. He was released when Stuart's brother revealed who had actually done the shooting. Stuart subsequently committed suicide. In Milwaukee in 1992 Jesse Anderson falsely claimed two black men had stabbed his wife to death. The evidence indicated he was the killer.

In Yonkers, New York, in 1993, six officers were involved in covering up a fight between two of them. They accused a young black man of the assault to explain one cop's injuries. In 1994 Susan Smith, a South Carolina mother, drowned her two sons then claimed an African American man had taken her car and children. Dr. Alvin Poussaint, a psychiatrist who has written on racism in the United States, described Susan Smith as knowing "what would work best to direct attention away from her: point the finger at a black man." Responding to the South Carolina case, African Americans expressed their feelings about the false accusations. Inez Chappel, a sixty-seven-year-old Baltimore woman, felt the story "just goes to show that racism is alive and well and free in America." In Boston a young hospital orderly, Kevin Pippins, when reminded of the Stuart killing, said, "It was the exact same thing. . . . Why'd she try to blame it on a black man . . . to cover up their hoax they use a black man? That's not good at all." At Northwestern University an African American professor commented on how the Smith case revealed

> once again the stereotypical view of black men in America, . . . they are the other, . . . they are dangerous . . . and they should be imprisoned. It is the same view that causes black men to be stopped, searched, and harassed on a routine basis by the police.[12]

The stereotype has an element of truth: African Americans account for a disproportionate number of those arrested for violent crimes. In 1999, for instance, whites accounted for 69 percent of the total arrests and African Americans for 29 percent, but the latter are only about 12 percent of the population.[13]

The greater likelihood of arrest is partly due to what criminologists call the social ecology of crime. Poorer African Americans generally commit crimes in more public places than whites, making their acts more visible and them more subject to apprehension. They are more likely to live in neighborhoods with lots of geographical mobility. In such areas, with lots of people moving in and out, it is easier for undercover agents to operate than in more stable communities where people have known one another for a period of time.

There is also racial bias in the criminal justice system at every level.[14] Nonetheless, African Americans, who make up about 12 percent of the population, do seem to account for more violent street crime. In 1999 they were 52 percent of those arrested for murder. This last statistic is probably the most reliable, since a large proportion of all murderers are arrested.[15] Despite appearances, it is not race but class that accounts for the overrepresentation of African Americans in violent crime arrests.

When social class is controlled for, there is little difference between whites and blacks in the commission of violent crimes. The dean of Boston's Northeastern University College of Criminal Justice found that when you take income into account, "the discrepancy at which whites and blacks commit crime disappears." Lower-income groups, regardless of ethnicity, commit more street crimes, but as young lower-income white males get older, they are more likely to find legitimate work.[16] Latinos also have lower average incomes and higher unemployment rates than whites, and the discussion below on unemployment and crime is relevant to them.

Some historical background is needed to explain how past economic and political polices have created an underclass that is kept off the opportunity ladder, increasingly put into prisons, and disproportionately comprised of young minority men.

SEPARATE AND UNEQUAL: APARTHEID, U.S. STYLE

During the twentieth century many descendants of European immigrants achieved middle-class lifestyles. We are taught that such success is a result of hard work, family structure, or some other characteristic supposedly lacking among blacks. These explanations, however, overlook the depths and impact of American racism.

The offspring of white immigrants rightly feel that their relatives had a tough time. Many would agree with the sentiments of Catherine Nielsen, who lives in the all-white Chicago neighborhood of Mount Greenwood and thinks discrimination is past history: "It's up to them to paddle their own canoe. They shouldn't always think about the fact that they were slaves."[17]

The racism faced by African Americans extends beyond anything experienced by other ethnic groups and results in the inequalities shown in chapter 3. Political and economic decisions have created a highly racially segregated society. Understanding the scope and tenacity of this segregation is crucial to understanding certain aspects of street crime.

As the United States industrialized following the Civil War, European immigrants provided the cheap labor for an expanding economy. For many of them the economic growth accompanying industrialization eventually provided opportunities that are far less available to African American and Latino urban populations. As immigrants poured into cities in the late nineteenth and early twentieth centuries, they took jobs in factories and participated in the construction of the urban centers in which they were settling.

Italians, for example, were the major ethnic group that built the New York subways. They were three-quarters of the building laborers in New York.[18] Sociologist Stephen Steinberg describes the advantages of Jewish immigrants who already had "industrial experience and concrete occupational skills that would serve them well in America's expanding industrial economy." They were especially concentrated in the garment trade, which was the most rapidly growing of U.S. industries just before the First World War.[19]

Earlier, Irish immigrants had found jobs in municipal government and in police and fire departments, which is why so many police officers and fire fighters march in St. Patrick's Day parades. In New York City a tuition-free city college system between 1847 and 1976 facilitated immigrant children's social mobility. Farther west, German and Scandinavian immigrants benefited from the lands taken from the native population.

While Europeans were finding economic niches, the descendents of African slaves were working as agricultural laborers in the South. As long as their labor was needed, the Southern elite made it difficult for them to leave. African Americans had less freedom of movement than did European immigrants. They were kept tied to the land by the system of sharecropping and denied education and the right the vote that had been promised in the Fifteenth Amendment. Brutality, including gruesome lynchings, was used as a means to intimidate those who might attempt to challenge the racial hierarchy.

Around the time of the First World War, an infestation of boll weevils lessened the need for black labor in the cotton fields. At the same time, the war curtailed the supply of immigrant labor, and blacks could hope to find jobs in manufacturing. The Second World War similarly promised opportunities. Following the war, mechanization in Southern agriculture meant Southern employers again had less need for field workers. These push-pull forces led to waves of African American migration out of the South. Like the Europeans who left their homes to find a better life, millions of African Americans moved north, to a region they called "the promised land."[20]

Over time, the immigrants and their descendents were able to achieve a certain level of comfort. The creation of unions that improved their wages and working conditions was instrumental in this. African Americans, however, were excluded from many of the craft unions established by the immigrants. This exclusion was accompanied by residential segregation.

"CHOCOLATE CITIES, VANILLA SUBURBS"[21]

Immigrants from one European country lived in communities with immigrants from other countries. Their white children moved into even more ethnically mixed, although still white, neighborhoods. But when African Americans moved in, whites moved out of the neighborhood, and increasingly out of the cities. For example, Kathleen Goldsmith and her husband, a Chicago policeman, decided to move from the house they had lived in for thirty-three years after an African American couple moved into their neighborhood. She felt the area was no longer safe.[22]

Organizational as well as more individual decisions have produced a highly segregated society. Douglas S. Massey, director of the University of Chicago's Population Research Center and coauthor, with Nancy Denton, of a major study on contemporary urban segregation, describes how important residential separation is:

> Where you live determines the chances you get in this world. It determines the school your children go to, the crime you're exposed to, the peer influences on your children. If you're isolated from the mainstream, it's not a fair world; it's not a fair contest. Segregation is structural underpinning of the underclass.[23]

Both the government and private business played roles in creating white suburbs and black inner cities. The Federal Housing Administration (FHA) and the Veterans' Administration (VA) were especially important. From its inception, the FHA accepted segregation, stating in its 1939 Underwriting

Manual, "If a neighborhood is to retain stability, it is necessary that properties shall continue to be occupied by the same social and racial classes."[24]

The FHA and the VA made millions of dollars available for housing loans. The FHA lowered risks to banks by providing loan guarantees. The FHA also extended loan repayment periods so that a homebuyer could have lower, more affordable monthly payments. FHA loans were more available for buying a new home than for remodeling an existing city dwelling. Government policy allowed housing conditions to deteriorate, making cities less desirable places to live.

When soldiers returned from World War II, the GI Bill administered by the VA made it financially possible for the veterans to buy their own homes. Whites could more easily obtain VA mortgages.[25] Many moved from the cities. Private lending agencies also helped establish and perpetuate residential segregation. Restrictive covenants were a device used for years to maintain a color barrier. Deeds to property had a clause that the owners would not sell to a group considered "undesirable." The Supreme Court declared these agreements unconstitutional in 1948, but numerous discriminatory practices have continued.

Banks are involved as well, engaging in a practice called "redlining": denying loans to certain areas of the city. This practice was initiated in the 1930s by the federal Home Owners Loan Corporation (HOLC), which had an explicit policy of keeping funds away from black neighborhoods. For years, studies have found continued discrimination by lending agencies. The power of racism is so great that lower-income whites in some localities have found it easier to get bank loans than more affluent African Americans.

New York senator Charles Schumer's staff studied 240,000 home loan applications for 1998. They found that middle-class African Americans, those making over $60,000 a year, were denied loans more often than whites making under $40,000. Denied loans from conventional sources, people of color turn to what have been called "predatory lenders," who charge much higher interest rates, making home buying less affordable.[26]

There are realtors who will not show blacks homes or apartments in certain areas or who say a dwelling is not available when it is. Larger security deposits or down payments have sometimes been required from African Americans. In a blatant, as well as illegal, racist act, a New Jersey landlord placed an Internet ad for an apartment specifying that "whites only" need apply. A state deputy attorney general was shocked, "not because we are so naive as to think that discrimination does not exists but that someone would be so bold as to say something was for 'whites only.'"[27]

Whites who sell to African Americans can be harassed, as happened in Yonkers, New York. Planning to move to Florida, Steven Diamond sold his home to a black family. Unhappy neighbors called him a "traitor" and "blockbuster." Somebody went beyond this, planting an explosive device in his car that shattered the windshield. Others in the area expressed remorse at what had happened, but one woman also expressed fear for herself, "What I'm really worried about," said Martha Cetnarowski, "is, if we become friendly with the new family, what could these people do to us?" In East Rockaway, on New York's Long Island, a building owner who also rented out marina spaces accepted people of color as tenants. Shortly after, the town government refused to give him the necessary permits to run his marina. He sued, and the town was ordered to pay him $750,000.[28]

In 1968, following the urban disorders of the 1960s, Congress passed the Fair Housing Act banning discrimination. Although it is an important statement of national values, the act has not been vigorously enforced. Residential segregation continues, with African Americans and, in recent years, Latinos more concentrated in cities and whites more likely to be suburbanites. The 2000 census revealed that this trend has continued: seventy-one of the largest one hundred American cities had a decrease in white population, with over two million whites leaving. This means a poorer population in urban areas, one that is more likely to be ignored when budget decisions are made. This, in turn, leads to an increase in the social conditions that make street crime more likely to occur.[29]

American cities with large concentrations of deprived populations have a great need for improved social services. As the need is growing, the resources are declining. Some analysts date this trend from the time of Ronald Reagan's administration. During the Reagan and George H. W. Bush presidencies there was a policy of "urban disengagement." From 1981 to 1991 "federal funding of urban programs dropped 68 percent, the first real dollar decline since World War II."[30] The fact that cities are so disproportionately minority partly explains this. This deeply embedded racism "complicates program innovations required to create work, training, housing, and education opportunities."[31]

SEGREGATED CITIES, SEGREGATED JOB MARKETS

Federally subsidized highways made it possible for suburbanites to commute to their city jobs. The suburbs themselves eventually became attrac-

tive to companies; taxes were lower, property cheaper, and suburban house-
wives constituted a pool of educated women available for employment in
the expanding service sector. During the 1970s New York City's suburbs
gained half a million jobs while the city itself lost 95,000. In Chicago's
suburbs 630,000 jobs were created during a period when that city lost
88,000.[32] This movement of jobs into the suburbs put African Americans at
a further disadvantage. Housing discrimination makes it difficult, even for
those African Americans who could afford it, to follow their employer.

If the jobs move and transportation is a problem, then for all practical
purposes, either the jobs are not available or people have less choice of
where to work. Dorothy L. Johnson lives in Detroit and like many of the
Motor City's residents cannot afford a car. With public transportation very
inadequate, she spends two hours in each direction commuting to a
cleaning job outside the city. With a car, the commute would take twenty-
five minutes. She'd like to work closer to home, but, as she says, "there
aren't too many jobs here in Detroit."[33]

Some experts believe that certain bus routes are constructed to make it
more difficult for African Americans to get to the suburbs. A 1995 case in
Buffalo, New York, lends credence to this view. Cynthia Wiggins was a seventeen-year-old African American who was killed as she walked across a
busy highway to an upscale shopping mall. Unable to afford a car, she took
a bus to the mall, but the buses were not allowed to park there. One store
owner said, "You'll never see an inner-city bus on the mall premises."[34]

The effects of suburbanization have been compounded since the 1970s
by a decrease in manufacturing, which has meant the loss of many good-
paying blue-collar jobs. A study of manufacturing plants with one hundred
or more employees for the years 1978–1982 found that in each of those
years an average of nine hundred thousand jobs were lost to plant closings,
translating into more than three million jobs in four years. African American men have been especially hard hit by economic change, since they
were usually the last hired and are the first fired when cutbacks occur.
Throughout the United States between 1979 and 1984, "nearly a third of all
black men working in durable goods manufacturing in the United States
lost their jobs."[35]

New Jersey, my home state, has some of the poorest cities in the United
States due to the economic changes. The New Jersey Council of Churches
reported that "between 1970 and 1985 total employment in the six major
cities decreased by almost 28 percent." In this same period, there was job
growth in the suburban areas.[36] In the decade 1970–1980, close-by

Philadelphia lost 35 percent of its manufacturing jobs. At the end of that period, African Americans had become 40 percent of the city's population as whites continued to move beyond the city limits.[37] A specialist on urban development, John J. Kasarda, summarized the situation for four cities:

> Between 1967 and 1987, Chicago lost 60 percent of its manufacturing jobs, Detroit 51 percent, New York City 58 percent, and Philadelphia 64 percent. During this same period, New York City added over 110,000 manufacturing jobs in suburban rings and Chicago 34,000.[38]

Lawrence Hunter, a forty-eight-year-old Milwaukee, Wisconsin, resident, looks back to the days when "you could go to a foundry and get a job any day." Those days are gone. In Milwaukee, a highly segregated city, between 1979 and 1990 there was a loss of 46,800 manufacturing jobs in the old smokestack industries, with more devastating effects on African Americans than whites. Journalist Isabel Wilkerson described why this was so:

> At factories that laid off only some workers, whites often had seniority and were retained. And even for whites who were laid off, the prosperity of the white parts of the city ensured that new businesses would spring up there, offering jobs suitable for former assembly line workers. Such jobs have generally not appeared in black sections. The result is a city of 628,000 people where black men stand idle on street corners just blocks from the breweries and factories that used to hire them, while well-dressed white-collar workers sell insurance or computers out of some of those same factories now converted into office parks.[39]

A 1986–1987 study of Chicago showed that there are other variables besides job movement that help account for African American male unemployment. The researchers compared a sample of black, white, Mexican, and Puerto Rican males and found that most especially for blacks the problem of job movement was compounded by a lack of transportation alternatives to seek what had become more distant jobs and a lack of relevant skills as a result of lower-quality education. The researchers also found that employers preferred Mexican immigrants to African Americans, even with low levels of education for lower-paying jobs where language skills are not too important. In addition, these jobs are filled through informal networks, with those already holding them, unlikely to be African Americans, bringing in friends or relatives as new openings occur. This is done with the encouragement of the employer.[40]

Living in areas of high unemployment means, among other things, that there are not going to be networks of people who can help each other find jobs. Stanford and Columbia University researchers studied how hiring was done at eighty branches of a western bank. Applicants with a contact had valuable information, not only about the availability of a position but also about how to present themselves in their applications. Some companies pay employees for a referral who is eventually hired.[41] Kathleen Newman's study of jobholders in Harlem found that in short order the employed become "an important resource" for others, and young people know "the value of networking" in order to have "a serious shot at a job." Unfortunately, "the network-poor job seeker doesn't stand much of a chance."[42]

Racist stereotyping still often affects job opportunities. An Urban Institute study of Chicago factory employers summarized their view of African American men. The men were considered "unstable, uncooperative, dishonest, and uneducated."[43]

A white businessman in that city claimed

> Basically, the Oriental is much more aggressive and intelligent and studious than the Hispanic. The Hispanics, except Cubans of course . . . are mañana, mañana, mañana—tomorrow, tomorrow, tomorrow.

But, for him, the least desirable nonwhites were African Americans, whom he described as "the laziest of the bunch."

In a Chicago suburb, the manager of a drugstore was not likely to hire an inner-city job applicant, claiming, "You'd be afraid they're going to steal from you. They grow up that way. They grow up dishonest and I guess you'd feel like, geez, how are they going to be honest here?"[44]

Chicago is not unique. Job audits in other cities, where matched whites and African Americans applied for the same job, have also found stereotyping and discrimination. In her study of Harlem, Katherine Newman found some of her Latino respondents benefiting from some employers beliefs "that Latino immigrants are harder workers than many of the African Americans."[45]

DECREASE JOBS: INCREASE CRIME

Numerous studies show a causal relation between joblessness and crime: first unemployment rises, then violent and nonviolent crime rates. Researchers Mary Merva and Richard Fowles found that from 1976 to 1990 in thirty metropolitan areas each 1 percent rise in unemployment was linked to a 6.7 percent increase in homicides and a 3.4 percent rise in other violent crimes. Putting this into absolute numbers for 1990–1992, they estimate that "increases in the unemployment rate may have been responsible for 1,459 additional homicides; [and] 62,607 additional violent crimes." Boston University School of Medicine researchers were so struck by the relationship between job loss and death rates that they called neighborhoods where this correlation existed "death zones."[46]

The relationship between unemployment and homicide has also been found in a number of international studies. For example, in 1991 about half of English and Welsh prisoners were unemployed at the time of their arrest and were less educated than the general population.[47] Criminologist Elliot Currie summarizes the data on this point:

> The countries that developed humane and effective employment policies had both much lower unemployment and much less crime throughout the postwar period. Between 1959 and 1976 the average unemployment rate in the United States was nearly double that of . . . Italy and the United Kingdom, and between three and four times the average rate in countries like West Germany, Sweden, Norway, Austria, and Japan; while its homicide rate ranged up to more than ten times that of these countries. . . . In a 1976 comparison of twenty-four countries . . . Marvin Krohn of the University of Iowa found that high rates of unemployment were predictably associated with high rates of homicide.[48]

After going up for years, crime rates and attendant rates of violence did drop beginning in the late 1990s. Criminologists have offered a number of reasons, including an improved job market so that crime with its risks became a less attractive occupation.[49] However, unemployment began to increase again in the early years of the new century, and crime rates have also been rising. Washington, DC's, police chief, Charles H. Ramsey, saw a correlation between homicides and an economic downturn, saying, "More pink slips mean more crime. It doesn't take long before you start seeing that impact at street level."[50]

THEY WANT TO WORK

If people really want to work, surely they can find jobs, can't they? In 1982, with African American unemployment officially rising, then president

Reagan was asked what advice he would give the unemployed. He replied that he had seen twenty-four pages of help wanted ads in the newspaper. One reporter decided to check out ads in the *Washington Post*. There were 1,059 jobs listed at a time when there were officially 77,600 people unemployed in Washington, DC. Looking closely, the reporter found some jobs were come-ons for courses, some were far out of town or overseas, and a number paid commissions only. Others required craft skills, a license, or were for managers and professionals. A reporter from *Fortune* conducted a similar study in 1978 in Middletown, New York. Of the 228 jobs advertised, only 142 were full-time positions in the area, covering less than 2 percent of the 7,800 unemployed people in the community at the time. Many of the jobs were for highly skilled persons, such as auto mechanics and nurses.[51]

Journalistic accounts of employment opportunities for disadvantaged youth illustrate how elusive a job can be. Salvatore Martinez lives in the poorest area of Los Angeles and has been looking for work as a laborer. As a high school dropout, ex-gang member, and former jail inmate, he is not likely to be attractive to employers. A futile quest took him to the Vargas Furniture Manufacturing Company where his father once worked. They weren't hiring. The receptionist's comments on Salvatore Martinez contradict the myths about the unemployed as people who just don't want to work:

> If I gave this boy an application, the whole area around would hear about it and people would appear out of nowhere. When we do have jobs, we post them, and we get scores of people, lines and lines of people around the block.[52]

Mike Davis corroborates her belief.

> The scale of pent-up demand for decent manual employment was . . . vividly demonstrated a few years ago when *fifty thousand* predominately black and Chicano youth lined up for miles to apply for a few openings on the unionized longshore in San Pedro [an area of Los Angeles].[53]

Katherine Newman found a strong "work ethic" among the African Americans and Latinos she studied in Harlem. One of the major sources of employment, in an area with relatively few jobs, is in fast-food restaurants. Here, however, she discovered "the ratio of applicants to available jobs is 14:1."[54]

With unemployment rates so high, inner-city employers can hire adults just as easily as they can teenagers, and they do. Newman found that more than half of the recently hired employees at the pseudonymous Burger Barns she studied were over age twenty-three. She concluded that inner-city "employers have choices that suburban mangers in tighter labor markets rarely encounter: they select adults." Older workers are less likely to leave or find that work is competing with school.[55]

In lower-income white neighborhoods, there is more work available than in minority communities. There are more economic enterprises, small businesses, and even some factories. Neighborhoods populated by people of color are more likely to have small groceries than supermarkets, where local teenagers could find part-time jobs. A study in New York City found that in poor neighborhoods there are 17,232 people per supermarket; in more affluent ones, the ratio is 6,580 for each chain market. Movie houses can be rare. The city of Newark, New Jersey, celebrated in 1993 when a multiplex opened after a lapse of twenty-five years. Three years later there was another celebration—this time because a Rite-Aid drugstore had been built. Public housing, a feature of many urban areas, offers fewer job opportunities to local residents than private housing because civil service does hiring.[56]

Oftentimes, applicants outnumber jobs. The unskilled and less-educated stand in line along with unemployed college graduates or experienced blue-collar workers, victims of decisions they had no role in making. Roosevelt Hotel in New York had 700 job openings in 1997, and 4,000 people applied. When Disneyland announced it had openings and accepted applications from the Latino and African American residents in South Central Los Angeles, 6,000 people waited patiently for a chance to apply.[57] When Marriott Hotels announced 296 openings for a new hotel being built on Long Island, New York, 4,508 people showed up. Some stood in line for seven and a half hours waiting for applications. In Cleveland a press account told of 15,000 "unemployed workers, welfare mothers, and teenagers, some standing in the freezing rain for four hours" hoping to be lucky enough to be hired for $4.50-an-hour temporary jobs cleaning up city parks and vacant lots. In Chicago 15,000 competed for 3,800 temporary jobs. In Baltimore, an announcement of 75 openings at the Social Security Administration drew at least 26,200 applicants, mostly African American. With only three interviews per position, the agency was going to use a lottery system to choose applicants. A Social Security Administration spokesman remarked, "This proves what black leaders have been saying for years—people would rather have jobs than be on welfare."[58]

At 7:00 A.M. on March 16, 1995, Jeanne Wright stood in a line already two blocks long. Nine hundred people, mostly African American and Latino, had come to a Labor Department office applying for arduous temporary jobs with no benefits at a New York State General Motors plant. Some even arrived at four in the morning. But as Ms. Wright explained to a reporter, waiting hours for an application was "still better than standing on the welfare line." When a job fair was held in The Bronx, over 5,000 people, many on welfare, competed for the openings. There would not be enough jobs for all the people who wanted them.[59]

On a bitter cold November day in 1993 in Detroit, mostly African American job seekers lined up hoping for work at a gambling casino that was not even approved yet. The 4,000 jobs, which will probably never materialize, would pay less than $20,000 a year. By day's end, over 10,000 had received their applications. Bessie Sibbaluca, on welfare and supporting two children, explained her presence on the line: "There's nothing else happening but crime."[60]

Serious efforts will have to be made if employment opportunities are going to increase in disadvantaged neighborhoods. There are few meaningful steps in this direction, however. Instead of economic investment in the ill-famed South Central Los Angeles in April 2003, the City Council voted for a name change. The neighborhood will be called South Los Angeles on maps and government documents. Marie Mendoza, a seventeen-year-old South Central resident, ridiculed the name change. "This is ridiculous. It's still going to be the neighborhood with the same problems." Instead of meaningless cosmetic changes, she suggested that the council "work harder to reduce crime and create opportunities for poor people."

In the next chapter we will continue our analysis of street crime, saying more about the economic opportunities it offers. We will discuss why drug-related crime is often violent and some of the ways elites benefit from street crime.

NOTES

1. Sarah Kershaw, "Survivor of Wendy's Massacre Offers Gruesome Details," *New York Times*, November 7, 2002, pp. A27, A29; Indiana example, Eric Schlosser, *Fast Food Nation* (New York: HarperPerennial, 2002), pp. 86–87.

2. U.S. Bureau of Labor Statistics, *Census of Fatal Occupational Injuries, 2000*, http://usgovinfo.about.com/library/weekly/nfatalitytables.htm (accessed March 18, 2003).

3. Schlosser, *Fast Food Nation*, p. 83.

4. Ibid., pp. 83–84, 86.

5. Mary Taylor Previte, "What Will They Say at My Funeral?" *New York Times*, August 7, 1994, p. 17.

6. U.S. Department of Justice, *Sourcebook of Criminal Justice Statistics—2000*, table 2.41, p. 129; tables 3.146, 3.147, pp. 314, 315. The ethnic categories are the ones used by the Department of Justice.

7. Maria Newman, "Once His Honor, Now the Professor," *New York Times*, September 14, 1994, p. B9.

8. Quotes from Stephen Steinberg, *The Ethnic Myth: Race, Ethnicity, and Class in America* (Boston: Beacon Press, 1989), p. 116.

9. John Higham, *Strangers in the Land: Patterns of American Nativism, 1860–1925* (New Brunswick, NJ: Rutgers University Press, 1966), p.66; Albert Fried, *The Rise and Fall of the Jewish Gangster in America* (New York: Holt Rinehart and Winston, 1980), pp. 90, 111. Jewish women as prostitutes, William Leach, *Land of Desire: Merchants, Power, and the Rise of a New American Culture* (New York: Vintage Books, 1993), p. 117.

10. Survey data reported in Douglas S. Massey and Nancy A. Denton, *American Apartheid: Segregation and the Making of the Underclass* (Cambridge, MA: Harvard University Press, 1993), p. 95; and Dennis M. Rome, "Murderers, Rapists, and Drug Addicts," in *Images of Color, Images of Crime*, 2nd ed., ed. Coramae Richey Mann and Marjorie S. Zatz (Los Angeles: Roxbury, 2002), p. 72. Quote from Elijah Anderson, *Code of the Street: Decency, Violence, and the Moral Life of the Inner City* (New York: W. W. Norton, 1999), p. 17.

11. Kelly quote from Bob Herbert, "The Soap Opera Machine," *New York Times*, November 9, 1994, p. A27.

12. Rick Bragg, "Mother of 'CarJacked' Boys' Held in Their Death," *New York Times*, November 4, 1994, pp. 1, 30; quotes from Don Terry, "A Woman's False Accusation Pains Many Blacks," *New York Times*, November 6, 1994, pp. 1, 30. Other examples can be found in Rome, "Murderers, Rapists, and Drug Addicts," pp. 71–72.

13. U.S. Department of Justice, *Sourcebook of Criminal Justice Statistics—2000*, table 4.10, p. 366. Data for Latinos is not given.

14. Michael Parenti, *Democracy for the Few*, 7th ed. (New York: Bedford/St. Martins, 2002), p. 132; Marc Mauer, "A Generation Behind Bars: Black Males and the Criminal Justice System," in *The American Black Male: His Present Status and His Future,* ed. Richard G. Majors and Jacob U. Gordon (Chicago: Nelson-Hall, 1994), pp. 88–89; Michael Tonry, "Sentencing Guidelines, Disadvantaged Offenders, and Racial Disparities," report from the Institute for Philosophy and Public Policy (Summer/Fall 1994): 7–13; James E. Blackwell, *The Black Community: Diversity and Unity* (New York: HarperCollins, 1991), pp. 427–28, 456–58.

15. Arrests, U.S. Department of Justice, *Sourcebook of Criminal Justice Statistics—2000*, table 4.10, p. 366.

16. Quoted in Herbert, "The Soap Opera Machine"; Delbert Elliot, "Serious

Violent Offenders: Onset, Developmental Course, and Termination," 1993 Presidential Address to the American Society of Criminology, *Criminology* 3 (1994): 5, 14.

17. Quoted in Isabel Wilkerson, "The Tallest Fence: Feelings on Race in a White Neighborhood," *New York Times,* June 21, 1992, p. 16.

18. Nathan Glazer and Daniel Patrick Moynihan, *Beyond the Melting Pot: The Negroes, Puerto Ricans, Jews, Italians, and Irish of New York City* (Cambridge, MA: MIT Press, 1970), p. 190.

19. Steinberg, *The Ethnic Myth,* pp. 97–99.

20. Nicholas Lemann, *The Promised Land: The Great Black Migration and How It Changed America* (New York: Vintage Books, 1991); Massey and Denton, *American Apartheid,* pp. 29, 43, 45.

21. An unidentified musician's description quoted in Massey and Denton, *American Apartheid,* p. 61.

22. Bill Dedman, "For Black Home Buyers, a Boomerang," *New York Times,* February 13, 1999, p. A15.

23. Quoted in Isabel Wilkerson, "Worse Segregation Than Was Expected Is Found in 10 Cities," *New York Times,* August 5, 1989, pp. 1, 6.

24. Quoted in Massey and Denton, *American Apartheid,* p. 54.

25. Richard T. Schaefer, *Racial and Ethnic Groups,* 8th ed. (Upper Saddle River, NJ: Prentice-Hall, 2000), pp. 258–59.

26. Bruce Lambert, "'Analysis Shows Racial Bias in Lending,' Schumer Says," *New York Times,* April 9, 2000, p. 35; David Leonhardt, "Wide Racial Disparities Found in Costs of Mortgages," *New York Times,* May 11, 2002, p. A23; Jonathan Brown, "Opening the Book on Lending Discrimination," *Multinational Monitor* (November 1992): 8–14.

27. "State Sues Landlord Over 'Whites Only' Web Ad," *New York Times,* August 1, 2000, p. B7.

28. Monte Williams, "Blast Hits Car after Man Sells to Blacks," *New York Times,* July 15, 1997, p. B12; Tina Kelley, "Village Harassed Landlord Who Rented to Blacks, Jury Finds," *New York Times,* October 20, 2000, p. B8.

29. Eric Schmitt, "Whites in Minority in Largest Cities, the Census Shows," *New York Times,* April 30, 2001, pp. A1, A12.

30. Ester R. Fuchs, "The Permanent Urban Fiscal Crisis," in *Big Cities in the Welfare Transition,* ed. Alfred J. Kahn and Shelia B. Kammerman (New York: Columbia University School of Social Work, 1998), pp. 60–61.

31. Kahn and Kammerman, *Big Cities in the Welfare Transition,* pp. 39–40.

32. Elliot Currie, *Reckoning: Drugs, the Cities, and the American Future* (New York: Hill and Wang, 1993), p. 126.

33. Robyn Meredith, "Jobs Out of Reach for Detroiters without Wheels," *New York Times,* May 26, 1998, p. A12.

34. Ibid.; for Wiggins incident, see Richard T. Schaefer, *Racial and Ethnic Groups,* 7th ed. (New York: Longman, 1997), pp. 66–67.

35. Richard Child Hill and Cynthia Negry, "Deindustrialization and Racial Minorities in the Great Lakes Region, USA," in *The Reshaping of America: Social Consequences of the Changing Economy*, ed. D. Stanley Eitzen and Maxine Baca Zinn (Englewood Cliffs, NJ: Prentice-Hall, 1989), p. 174.

36. New Jersey Council of Churches, *The Reshaping of New Jersey: The Growing Separation* (East Orange, NJ: New Jersey Council of Churches, 1988), pp. 18–19.

37. Judith Goode, "'Polishing the Rustbelt,' Immigrants Enter a Restructuring Philadelphia," in *Newcomers in the Workplace*, ed. Louise Lamphere, Alex Stepick, and Guillermo Grenier (Philadelphia: Temple University Press, 1994), p. 206.

38. John D. Kasarda, "The Severely Distressed in Economically Transforming Cities" in *Drugs, Crime, and Social Isolation: Barriers to Urban Opportunity*, ed. Adele V. Harrell and George E. Peterson (Washington, DC: Urban Institute Press, 1992), p. 71.

39. Isabel Wilkerson, "How Milwaukee Has Thrived While Leaving Blacks Behind," *New York Times,* March 19 1991, pp. A1, D22.

40. Robert Aponte, "Urban Employment and the Mismatch Dilemma: Accounting for the Immigration Exception," *Social Problems* 43 (1996): 268–83.

41. Laura Koss-Feder, "In a Job Hunt, It Often *Is* Whom You Know," *New York Times,* January 5, 1997, p. 8.

42. Kathleen Newman, *No Shame in My Game: The Working Poor in the Inner City* (New York: Vintage, 1999), p. 80, 241.

43. Quoted in William W. Goldsmith and Edward J. Blakely, *Separate Societies: Poverty and Inequality in U.S. Cities* (Philadelphia: Temple University Press, 1992), p. 114.

44. Quotes from William J. Wilson, "Work," *New York Times Magazine*, August 18, 1996, pp. 31, 40.

45. Newman, *No Shame in My Game*, p. 179.

46. Mary Merva and Richard Fowles, *Effects of Diminished Economic Opportunities on Social Stress: Heart Attacks, Strokes, and Crime* (Washington, DC: Economic Policy Institute, n.d.), p. 2; Elliot Currie, *Confronting Crime* (New York: Pantheon Books, 1985), p. 119. The term "death zones" is from Thomas Cottle, *Hardest Times: The Trauma of Long-Term Unemployment* (Westport, CT: Praeger, 2001), p. 22.

47. U.S. Department of Justice, Bureau of Justice Statistics, *Profile of Inmates in the United States and in England and Wales, 1991*, p. 1.

48. Currie, *Confronting Crime*, p. 119.

49. Jeff Groger, "An Economic Model of Recent Trends in Crime," in *The Crime Drop in America*, ed. Alfred Blumstein and Joel Wallman (New York: Cambridge University Press, 2000), pp. 281–82.

50. Fox Butterfield, "U.S. Crime Rate Rose 2% in 2001 After 10 Years of Decreases," *New York Times,* October 29, 2002, p. A20; quote from Butterfield, "Killings Increase in Many Big Cities," *New York Times*, December 2, 2001, p. 32.

51. Allan Sheahen, "Poverty in America Is a Serious Problem," in *Poverty: Opposing Viewpoints*, ed. William Dudley (St. Paul: Greenhaven Press, 1988), pp. 21–22; "Help Wanted Ads Don't Add Up," *Dollars and Sense* 93 (January 1984): 13, 17.

52. Quoted in Seth Mydans, "The Young Face of Inner-City Unemployment," *New York Times*, March 22, 1992, p. A24.

53. Mike Davis, *City of Quartz: Excavating the Future in Los Angeles* (New York: Vintage, 1990), pp. 305–306 (emphasis in original).

54. Newman, *No Shame in My Game*, p. 62.

55. Ibid., pp. 231, 232.

56. Alison Mitchell, "Where Supermarkets Are Never Super," *New York Times,* June 6, 1992, p. 25; Shawn G. Kennedy, "Supermarket Invests in Harlem, Long Shunned by Chains," *New York Times*, September 22, 1994, p. B3. The absence of supermarkets causes other problems besides adding to the lack of jobs. People have to shop at more expensive small groceries or travel long distances. Charles Strum, "Six Screens with Melted Butter," *New York Times*, April 4, 1993, p. 40; "Celebrating a Drugstore," *New York Times*, July 10, 1996, p. B1; housing aspect from Mercer Sullivan, *"Getting Paid": Youth Crime and Work in the Inner City* (Ithaca, NY: Cornell University Press, 1989), p. 148.

57. Newman, *No Shame in My Game*, p. 63.

58. William E. Geist, "Waiting in Line and Hoping: 296 Jobs and 4,508 Applicants," *New York Times*, September 28, 1982, pp. A1, B8; "10,000 Stand in Rain for $4.50 Cleveland Jobs," *New York Times*, March 22, 1983; "Officials Say 26,200 Applied for 75 Jobs in Baltimore," *New York Times*, September 21, 1980.

59. Jacques Steinberg, "Jobs with No Future Draw Hundreds," *New York Times*, March 17, 1995, p. A12; Amy Waldman, "Long Line in The Bronx, but for Jobs, Not the Yankees," *New York Times*, October 20, 1999, p. B8.

60. James Bennet, "Mere Hint of Jobs Draws Crowd in Detroit," *New York Times*, December 12, 1993, pp. A1, A29.

10

INTERPERSONAL VIOLENCE
Street Crime—"Getting Paid"

In the previous chapter we discussed the reasons why there are so few legal economic opportunities in African American and Latino communities. Engaging in street crime, which can lead to interpersonal violence, is a way to make money if there are few other options. Economist Richard B. Freeman calculated average earnings from street crime at about $19 an hour in the early 1990s. Others have estimated up to $30 an hour with a monthly income of about $2,000.[1] Crime has other attractions: you set your own hours, you aren't constantly supervised, and there is a certain excitement to engaging in illegal behavior. Much youth crime is done in groups, providing a social network. This helps explain the appeal of gangs.

Several ethnographic studies confirm that the absence of employment opportunities creates a situation where people, including teenagers, choose to become involved in illegal activities. Anthropologist Mercer Sullivan studied employment opportunities and youth crime in three ethnically distinct New York City neighborhoods—white, Latino, and African American. Employment was a problem in all three but mostly so in the African American neighborhood. Youths in each area neighborhood who engaged in crime referred to their behavior as "getting paid," but there were differences. The employed white youths committed some of their crimes at their workplaces and were less observable. If discovered, it was their employers' option whether to report them or not. None of those he studied were ever turned in, and therefore none had criminal records that would later decrease their chances for employment.

In the white and Latino neighborhoods, young men found it easy to break into factories and apartments; but in the African American community there were no factories, and newer project apartments were more secure. Consequently, young criminals personally accosted their victims in undefended public areas such as elevators, stairwells, spaces between buildings, and on the street. After honing their criminal skills in these public spaces close to home, they then applied their abilities farther afield in the subways and downtown area.[2]

SELF-PROTECTION—BEING TOUGH

Violence is associated with the narcotics business, discussed below, but even without this, shootings are much more common in inner-city neighborhoods than elsewhere. Between 1987 and 1994 about 4,900 African Americans and 2,000 Latinos were left paralyzed by shootings. Daniel Appian, who was shot while being robbed of his leather jacket, spoke of himself and his friend, Andrew Aiken, also in a wheelchair as a result of being shot while being robbed of a gold bracelet and $90. Daniel said, "People like Andrew and myself, we are sort of casualties of the ghetto."[3] If you live in a neighborhood where there are high crime rates and you do not want to be a victim yourself, then developing a tough persona can be a form of self-protection.

Katherine Newman, whose research was discussed in chapter 9, found that the Harlem residents she interviewed wanted to keep their children safe. They couldn't move and they couldn't depend on the police; there were no safe spaces for the kids to go. The children had to be taught "defensive strategies to guard their safety" when their parents were not around to protect them. William, one of her teen respondents, explained:

> You gotta have attitude. You gotta have tenacity. In a rough neighborhood, you gotta have balls, simply put. You have a lot of caring people there, as you do in any type of neighborhood that has a bad face to it. But you have to know how to carry yourself.[4]

Elijah Anderson has written of the "code of the street" in order to understand "why it is that so many inner-city young people are inclined to commit aggression and violence toward one another."[5] He sees the high rates of interpersonal violence as arising from the circumstances of life among the ghetto poor—the lack of jobs that pay a living wage and limited basic public services . . . the stigma of race, the fallout from rampant drug use and drug trafficking, and the resulting alienation and absence of hope for the future.[6]

He does not see everyone as behaving in the same way, but circumstances create a situation where a number of young men will become tough and violent. The police, discussed more in chapter 12, are not a protective force for many ghetto residents. Having potential aggressors respect and fear you is a substitute for reliance on formal authority.[7] However, the grim, unsmiling face and swaggering walk that may keep you safe from your peers is likely to make people in other neighborhoods, as well as potential employers, fear and mistrust you.

THE AFRICAN AMERICAN FAMILY AND CRIME: FALSE CONNECTIONS

It is fashionable to blame female-headed households for African American crime. In 2000, 28 percent of black households with children were female headed. For whites the figure was 8 percent.[8] One consequence of female-headed households is that fewer adults are in the household to supervise and control younger people unless there is an extended family member who can help.[9]

Adults in stable two-parent families can watch not only their own children but others as well. In Los Angeles it is estimated that there are over a quarter of a million children between five and fourteen taking care of themselves from the time school ends till a parent returns from work. The city allots few resources for these children, leaving some to find a substitute family in a gang.[10]

Single-parent families, like crime rates, are related to employment opportunities. As the unemployment rate for African American males has risen, so has the percentage of African American female-headed households. Poor employment opportunities, combined with high mortality rates and high rates of imprisonment, mean a sizable proportion of African American males have low potential as good spouses.

There are health reasons why younger black women decide to have children even if a spouse is not a pleasing option. According to Katherine Newman, it is rational to have children at a young age since "poor communities, and especially inner-city neighborhoods, have such high rates of debilitating illness and early death."[11] A younger woman's own mother, who may be needed for child-rearing assistance, is also younger and healthier than she is likely to be later on; the same is true of the would-be mother.

While criticisms of the African American family are common, it is rare to find similar analyses made to explain elite deviance. What kinds of families produce CEOs and government officials who make decisions that cost the lives of hundreds, sometimes thousands of people?

COMMUNITY STRUCTURE AND CRIME

Areas of prolonged high unemployment are going to be poor areas. Not all, however, have high crime rates. Poor rural communities, for example, usually have less crime than urban ones. This is probably because there are fewer opportunities for crime and less anonymity. If people cannot find work, they often move in and out of urban communities. There are more strangers, less concern with what others are doing, and therefore less pressure to conform to accepted norms.

As crime increases in a neighborhood, people become more fearful and retreat as much as they can from the streets. In one study comparing more stable communities in San Francisco with those that were disintegrating due to job loss, researchers concluded:

> Without substantive jobs it is only a matter of time before a community begins to disintegrate as a social unit. . . . On blocks where residents had control and a sense of ownership over public space, there [was] no crack trafficking or "hanging out." Children were able to play outside their homes; older residents kept a watchful eye during the day; and blinds and curtains were open to let sunlight in. In the declining and most depressed areas, children were kept inside their apartments. Despite relatively dense block populations, there were few people on the streets during the day or night. Curtains and blinds were closed twenty-four hours per day.[12]

Fear of crime may even keep people from looking more actively for work. This was the case with 230 mothers, all on welfare for over five years, living in Chicago housing projects. The women moved to the suburbs as part of the settlement of a federal housing segregation lawsuit. Researchers who were studying the African American women found that the women talked about how liberating it was to be able to go out at night and not feel danger. People remarked repeatedly how oppressive it was to live in the projects. They felt they couldn't get a job, because it wasn't safe to be out after dark. And they didn't want to leave their kids alone after school, because they were frightened they would be lured into the gangs.[13]

The women noticed how many more jobs were available in the suburbs than in the city.

WORK-FREE DRUG ZONES

Unemployment is damaging on an individual level, especially for men, as has been discussed in chapter 8. Social movements can combat this feeling by offering social explanations for joblessness. In the absence of such movements, drinking and/or drug use can be a way of alleviating demoralization. Drugs in particular are associated with violent crime.

Unemployment and poverty help widen the market for drug users, and dealing drugs offers alternative economic opportunities just as illegal alcohol trafficking did during Prohibition (1919–1933). In the United States drug use is higher in lower-income white areas than in more affluent minority areas. In some communities, drug trafficking is a major source of money for young people. Studies in Holland and England also show that as unemployment increases so does drug use.[14]

Marietta Powell, a Gary, Indiana, mother of five, is aware of the relation between jobs, drugs, and violence. She told a reporter there are "no jobs in this city for young people, so they're killing each other up over drugs." Gary, Indiana, was once a center of the U.S. steel industry, the flames from the mills visible twenty-four hours a day from the highways skirting the city. In 1996 there were five thousand working at mills, which had thirty thousand workers in the 1960s.[15]

Anthropologist Philippe Bourgois spent five years in Harlem doing research on "the underground economy," which includes drug dealing. He found that youths involved in crime have essentially the same values as the larger population but lack the opportunities to reach socially approved goals of a good material life and respect from others. He describes the dealers he met as "ambitious, energetic," and "attracted to the underground economy precisely because they believe in the rags-to-riches American dream." Some see themselves as entrepreneurs setting up a small business that they hope will grow. With unemployment twice as high in Harlem,

Bourgois concluded, the "economic incentive to participate in the burgeoning crack economy" was "overwhelming."[16]

Mel, a Harlem drug dealer until he was shot seven times when he was eighteen, could be one of the people described by Bourgois. At age twelve he was supporting himself and a younger sister, making $400 a week selling drugs, often to "people from outside the block, outside the city. It was more white people than black people. . . . I figured there was only one way to take care of me and my little sister." As he moved up in the business, he earned $5,000 a week, after expenses, and employed ten others.

Those who control the drug trafficking make the most money and face fewer daily dangers than do the inner-city dealers. Even at the local level, there is a wide range of earnings. Dealers like Mel are making thousands a week. Others are paid less for renting out storage space in their apartments, being lookouts for the police, buying guns, or transporting drugs. Some work eight-hour days and are paid weekly. For a brief while, Mel was making hundreds of thousands of dollars a year, but he's out of business now, spending his days in a wheelchair, paralyzed by a bullet in his spine.[17] There are no statistics on the occupational hazards of drug dealing, but dealers face much greater physical risks than legitimate business people, professionals, or politicians.

THE VIOLENT NARCOTICS BUSINESS

In a New York City courtroom, Nelson Sepulveda testified how his gang killed at least ten people, including a "regular customer" who tried to cheat him with counterfeit money. They also shot members of rival drug-selling gangs, killing several bystanders in the process. During his trial he referred to drugs as "the work" and described the different tasks various "workers" in his gang did, from cutting and weighing to handling payments.[18]

Homicide rates in U.S. cities increased dramatically as drug trafficking increased. When alcohol became illegal during Prohibition, there was also a rise in violent crime. The FBI estimates that minimally in 1993, 1,280 murders were committed during the manufacturing or selling of narcotics. That's about 6 percent of the homicides for that year and does not include murders associated with robbery or intimidation that might be connected with drug dealing. A study of murders in the seventy-five most heavily populated U.S. counties found that in 1988 nearly 20 percent of the arrests involved some aspect of narcotics trafficking.[19]

Criminologist Scott Decker studied gun violence in eleven cities, five of which had the highest violent crime rates in the United States. Decker concluded that it is drug dealers and their associates who are most likely to be using guns, many of them acquired illegally, some traded for narcotics by addicts. Dealers need guns, in Decker's view, to protect themselves from being robbed. New York City's chief narcotics prosecutor concurred with Decker's basic findings, saying, "People have a common misperception, that drug users use guns to support their habits. That is true in some cases. But law enforcement has found it is usually the dealers who have the guns."[20]

In an article published by the National Institute of Justice, the U.S. Department of Justice's research wing, Alfred Blumstein notes that increased youth violence, especially since 1985, can best be explained by the rapid growth of the crack markets in the mid-1980s. To service that growth, juveniles were recruited, they were armed with the guns that are standard tools of the drug trade, and these guns were then diffused into the larger community of juveniles.[21]

Illegal trades are likely to be violent. People who cheat you can't be taken to court for violating contracts. Physical violence is sometimes the only effective way of assuring that debts get paid; it helps maintain hierarchy within criminal organizations and is a common means of fending off competing gangs in the battle for markets. Markets can't be sustained or broadened by ads in magazines or on billboards. Dealers cannot use typical product placement techniques, such as showing their merchandise in a movie or on a television show. Philippe Bourgois found that in East Harlem

> regular displays of violence are necessary for success in the underground economy—especially the street-level drug-dealing world. Violence is essential for maintaining credibility and preventing rip-offs by colleagues, customers, and intruders. Thus behavior that appears irrationally violent and self-destructive to the middle- or working-class outsider can be interpreted, according to the logic of the underground economy, as judicious public relations.[22]

In the Philadelphia inner-city community he studied, Elijah Anderson found that violence was a frequent accompaniment in drug trafficking, with any "business" arguments settled by force and made more deadly by the easy availability of guns.[23]

Crack cocaine seems to be especially associated with violence. Several factors converge to cause this. Crack is relatively cheap and offers possibilities for new markets among those with the lowest incomes. As more dealers try to capitalize on these markets, they use violence to discourage the competition. Some crack dealers were already adept at using violence and transferred these skills to their new trade.[24]

Joan Moore, a sociologist who has studied gangs in East Los Angeles, notes:

> the crack economy has vastly increased the number of drug dealers in several inner-city communities; the technology and availability of cocaine have coincided with a shriveling of decent job opportunities in many of these communities. And, according to recent evidence, crack dealing almost invariably involves violence; dealers threaten both each other and the community.[25]

In the late 1990s there was some decline in the violence that had characterized the early period of the crack trade in the 1980s, but that was at least partly associated with what seems to have been a temporary improvement in employment opportunities.

JUST SAY YES TO DRUGS: GOVERNMENT AND BUSINESS COMPLICITY

In 1989 Sen. John Kerry of Massachusetts chaired hearings of the Foreign Relations Subcommittee on Terrorism, Narcotics, and International Operations. A summary of the committee's findings is an astounding indictment of the U.S. government's involvement in the illegal narcotics business.

> The subcommittee found that the secret Contra war [in Nicaragua, in the early 1980s] provided numerous opportunities for drug traffickers to link up with the Contras, and they did. . . . The subcommittee found cases in which high U.S. officials intervened to stop law enforcement operations aimed at nailing drug kingpins. We found that a United States Ambassador to the Bahamas had shut down a Justice Department drug sting aimed at bringing down corrupt Bahamian Government officials. We learned how high United States officials, including Lt. Col. Oliver North, went to the Justice Department to intercede on behalf of a man convicted of a narco-terrorist assassination plot against a Honduran President. . . . We were told by a former United States Ambassador to Costa Rica that a decision was made by the United States to "put Noriega on the shelf" and take no action against his drug trafficking until the Sandinista government had been overthrown. We also found out that the State Department chose

four companies controlled by drug traffickers to provide assistance to the Contras. As a result, drug traffickers got funds out of the United States public treasury as part of our Contra humanitarian assistance program.[26]

Kerry's list makes it clear that U.S. foreign policy is implicated in narcotics trafficking, and his list can be extended. A CIA-created Haitian intelligence unit was engaged in drug dealing while receiving millions of dollars from our taxes. The United States funded and supplied the rebels against the Soviet-backed government of Afghanistan, even though it was well known they were growing opium for heroin in areas they controlled. During the Vietnam War the government, especially through the CIA, was involved with all phases of the narcotics business, even though one of the by-products of this business was the addiction of thousands of U.S. soldiers.[27]

Investigative journalist Gary Webb, in a series for the *San Jose Mercury News*, compiled evidence that the CIA was instrumental in opening

the first pipeline between Colombia's cocaine cartels and the black neighborhoods of Los Angeles, a city now known as the "crack" capital of the world. The cocaine that flooded in helped spark a crack explosion in urban America . . . and provided the cash and connections needed for L.A.'s gangs to buy automatic weapons.[28]

Contra rebels, supported by the CIA, were selling cocaine in the 1980s and were supposed to be using the profits to buy weapons for overthrowing the Sandinista government in Nicaragua. The CIA provided support and protection for the operation.

A key figure in this endeavor was Oscar Blandon, a Contra leader. In 1986 Congress appropriated about $100 million for the Contra subversion efforts, and the drug money became less important. Blandon was then arrested but served only two and a half years in prison. On his release he became an informant with the Drug Enforcement Agency, which had paid him over $166,000 at the time of Webb's stories.

Cocaine had been used mostly by the affluent, but if the market could be expanded, there was a potential for greatly increasing profits from the drug. Rick Ross, an entrepreneurial drug dealer, became the major disseminator of crack. Webb describes what happened.

[Blandon] and his compatriots arrived in South Central L.A. right when street-level drug users [*sic*] were figuring out how to make the cocaine affordable: by changing the pricey white powder into powerful little nuggets that could be smoked—crack. Cocaine smokers got an explosive

high unmatched by ten times as much snorted power. . . . Anyone with
$20 could get wasted.[29]

Blandon sold the cocaine on consignment to Ross, whose sophisticated
operation turned it into crack that was then sold all over the country.

Ross was unaware of the source of the drug, and it might have made no difference to him had he known. His role, however, does not diminish that of the
government whose responsibility it is to prevent drug trafficking, not abet it.

California congresswoman Maxine Waters, representing South Central
Los Angeles, described her feelings regarding Webb's allegations.

As someone who has seen how the crack cocaine trade has devastated the
South Central Los Angeles community, I cannot exaggerate my feelings
of dismay that my own government may have played a part in the origins
and history of this problem. Portions of this country may have been
exposed, indeed introduced, to the horror of crack cocaine because certain
U.S.-paid government or organized operatives smuggled, transported, and
sold it to American citizens.[30]

California senator Barbara Boxer, in an August 1996 letter to CIA director
John Deutch, wrote, "Even the notion that the U.S. government was
involved in trafficking is sickening." CIA spokesperson Mark Mansfield
called the charges "ludicrous."[31]

In response to Webb's allegations, the CIA issued two volumes based
on an internal investigation of the charges. In 1998 the inspector general of
the agency admitted that the CIA "did not inform Congress of allegations
or information it received indicating that Contra-related organizations or
individuals were involved in drug trafficking." They also failed to provide
information to the Justice Department. The decisions to mislead elected
officials about what was considered a major social problem in this country
were made at the highest levels of the agency. Senator Kerry, after reading
the reports, concluded, "there was a lack of interest in making sure the laws
were being upheld."[32]

The narcotics business is a complex web of relationships in which drug
use and dealing are only a couple of the strands. Social conditions and psychological dispositions may lead some to a desire for narcotics. Other
forces are involved in making narcotics available for illegal marketing. The
notion of "criminal," then, must be broadened beyond street criminals and
organized crime if we are ever to understand the real roots of narcotics violence. Over thirty years ago Malcolm X understood this clearly:

When a person is a drug addict, he's not the criminal; he's a victim of the criminal. The criminal is the man downtown who brings this drug into the country. Negroes can't bring drugs into this country. You don't have any boats. You don't have any airplanes. You don't have any diplomatic immunity. It is not you who is responsible for bringing in drugs. You're just a little tool that is used by the man downtown. . . . Big shots who are respected, who function in high circles—those are the ones who control these things. And you and I will never strike at the root of it until we strike at the man downtown.[33]

The "man downtown" includes elements in the CIA, the military, local police forces, banks, multinational corporations, and organized crime, collaborating and benefiting in various ways from narcotics trafficking. For the military and the armaments industry "narco-terrorism" became a convenient post–Cold War rationale for continuing the arms buildup and padding the defense budget. A congressional staff person told a *Newsweek* journalist, "It's their new meal ticket now that the commies are not their big threat." Gen. Maxwell Thurman confirmed this view, describing the war on drugs as "the only war we've got."[34] Now, of course, there are new rationales for war. However, an alleged "drug-war" is still being fought, mostly in Colombia.

Government officials at all levels are seriously concerned about narcotics. But too many powerful interests benefit from the continuation of this traffic. As will be discussed in chapter 13, U.S. foreign policy is designed to promote the interests of powerful multinational corporations. This sometimes leads to alliances with and protection of high-level drug traffickers.

Banks receive billions of dollars from drug sales by organized crime, money they can then lend or invest. The banks are supposed to report transactions over $10,000 to the Treasury Department and to notify authorities when more than $5,000 is taken out of the United States, but they are lax in doing any of this and the penalties for noncompliance are very weak.

In 1984 the director of the federal Commission on Organized Crime commented, "Banks are part of the problem and . . . I mean brokerage houses, exchange firms, and casinos, too." Financial organizations do not cooperate with law enforcement agencies, making them, in effect, partners in the drug trade in a de facto alliance with organized crime. A spokesperson for the banking industry was indignant about the commission's recommendation that banks be more responsible about reporting questionable transactions, saying, "that leaves this country open to a witch hunt. . . .

Where does it stop?" A lawyer for a prominent brokerage company worried that customers might be scared off by stricter regulations because there would be "an element of Big Brother is watching you."[35]

Major U.S.-based multinational corporations, in the words of a *New York Times* headline, continue to be "Tangled in [a] Web of Drug Dollars." Citibank was accused of having received millions of dollars from drug traffickers, which were deposited in accounts in the Cayman Islands. While street dealers can be highly visible, banks are shielded to some extent by the complex ways in which their business is done. Citibank officials explained "there was a breakdown in our communications internally" and labeled the transactions "an embarrassment." But congressional staff members for a Senate investigating committee thought the situation was more serious. They reported that the banks had "become conduits for dirty money flowing into the American financial system and have, as a result, facilitated illicit enterprises."[36]

In January 2003 Puerto Rico's largest bank, Banco Popular de Puerto Rico, with many branches both on the island and the mainland, agreed to pay $21.6 million to settle a money laundering suit. In exchange, the government will not subject the bank to criminal prosecutions and even praised Banco Popular for "accepting its responsibility."[37] Street-level dealers do not have the option of paying money and then being exempt from prosecution.

Some drug enforcement personnel regret the lenient treatment companies receive. Edward M. Guillen, who heads the DEA's financial investigations division, points out that the "only way we will get results is if we diligently investigate and prosecute not only individuals but the corporations that allow their facilities to be used." Banks are supposed to have procedures to prevent their being used for criminal activities, but a 1999 Senate Permanent Subcommittee on Investigations that looked into money laundering concluded, "a corporate culture of secrecy and lax controls" existed. Furthermore, they noted, "in practice private bank oversight is often absent, weak, or ignored."[38] Given the large amounts of money involved—as much as $1 trillion a year is handled by U.S. financial organizations—it is easy to understand why the banks do this. But why does the government take such a harsh stance toward street-level criminals and have such lenient policies toward the financial sector?

Seventeen states revoke the drivers' licenses of those with drug offenses for at least six months. In chapter 6 we mentioned how families of convicted drug offenders can be evicted from public housing. There are other lasting repercussions for people at the lowest levels of the drug trade. Those convicted on drug charges can be denied food stamps and other welfare benefits for their entire lives. According to a law passed in 1996, if a mother serves more than fifteen months for a drug conviction, she may lose her children. States can choose not to follow this law but most do. According to Herman Schwartz, professor of constitutional law at American University, "92,000 women have been convicted of drug offenses in the states enforcing the law. Of these about two-thirds are mothers with 135,000 children among them."[39]

Russell Selkirk was a student at Ohio State University; Kristopher Sperry was looking forward to attending Arkansas State University. Besides wanting to go to college, both young men have something else in common. They were denied financial aid because they had been convicted of possessing marijuana and, in Sperry's case, drug paraphernalia. No other crime carries this penalty. In 2000 9,200 students were denied assistance under this 1998 law. The 379,000 who ignored the question about drug convictions on the application form received aid. The law does try to be somewhat fair: the length of time you are ineligible for aid depends on the drug offense. For marijuana it's a year, for heroin trafficking it's more. A would-be student who completes a treatment program can become eligible again.[40]

THREE STRIKES AND YOU STILL HAVE VIOLENT CRIME

Millions of people, mainly men but an increasing number of women, are in some way under the supervision of the criminal justice system—in prison, on probation, or on parole. In 1980 there were about 1,840,000 such people; by 2000 it had increased by 351 percent to 6,467,200.[41]

The number of people in American prisons is far greater than that of other industrialized countries, as was shown in chapter 1. With about 5 percent of the world's population, the United States accounts for about 25 percent of the world's total inmate population. This country's prison population has been steadily increasing each year, even when the crime rate falls. As of December 2001, the U.S. prison population was 1,962,220. In 1990 there were 292 prisoners per 100,000 people, but by the end of 2001 that rate had grown to 470 per 100,000. The prison population is disproportionately African American and Latino.

- For every 100,000 African American males, 3,535 are in prison.
- For every 100,000 Latino males, 1,177 are in prison.
- For every 100,000 white males, 462 are in prison.[42]

In 1999, the Justice Department estimated that "11 percent of black males, 4 percent of Hispanic males, and 1.5 percent of white males in their twenties and early thirties were in prison or jail."[43] At current incarceration rates, "an estimated 28 percent of black males will enter state or federal prison during their lifetime, compared to 16 percent of Hispanic males and 4.4 percent of white males."[44] Between 1986 and 1991 "the number of white drug offenders in state prisons increased by 110 percent. The number of black drug offenders grew by 465 percent."[45]

Evidence shows that imprisonment by itself makes little difference to crime rates. Los Angeles County, for example, has a 70 percent recidivism rate. Looking only at drug offenses, the U.S. Department of Justice says "of 27,000 . . . sentenced to probation in thirty-two counties across seventeen states in 1986, 49 percent were rearrested for a felony offense within three years of sentencing."[46]

Criminologist Michael Tonry says, "The clear weight of the evidence in every Western country indicates that tough penalties have little effect on crime rates." Criminologists, the American Bar Association, the Correctional Association of New York, and others agree. In 1993 the National Academy of Sciences, after what Tonry describes as "the most exhaustive and ambitious analysis of the subject ever undertaken," came to the conclusion that "greatly increased use of imprisonment has had little effect on violent crime rates."[47]

Another criminologist, Todd R. Clear, explains why "the police and prisons have virtually no effect on the sources of criminal behavior":

> About 70 percent of prisoners in New York State come from eight neighborhoods in New York City. These neighborhoods suffer profound poverty, exclusion, marginalization, and despair. All these things nourish crime. Isn't it a bit much to believe that removing some men from their streets will change the factors that promote lawbreaking among the many who remain?[48]

Prisons lead to problems. Sooner or later most of those in them are let out, usually with no more marketable skills than when they went in, but with anger and bitterness. Ex-prisoners are not prime candidates for employment. The situation now is even worse than previously, according to journalist Fox Butterfield:

> Because states sharply curtailed education, job training, and other rehabilitation programs inside prisons, the newly released inmates are far less likely than their counterparts two decades ago to find jobs, maintain stable

family lives, or stay out of the kind of trouble that leads to more prison. Many states have unintentionally contributed to these problems by abolishing early release for good behavior, removing the incentive for inmates to improve their conduct, the experts say.[49]

In New Orleans, a dejected ex-convict, twenty-five-year-old Bobby Eubanks, sadly reported, "I've been all over . . . filling out applications. But they don't call. All the applications ask if you have ever been convicted of a crime, and that kills the whole thing right there." He hasn't given up, saying, "I'm trying to do the right thing. I'd like to get married. I just want a chance. That's all I want."[50]

There are legal restrictions on what jobs ex-felons can hold. In New York State, for example, you can learn to be a barber in prison, but you may be turned down for a license to practice this craft because the state body that issues licenses deems you too immoral to cut hair. Depending on the state, if you have done prison time, you may not be licensed to be a teacher, a plumber, or a school bus driver.[51]

It should be noted that several high-ranking officials in the Bush administration were found guilty of various criminal charges stemming from their involvement with the Contras mentioned above. Among those who have not been denied jobs are John Negroponte, Bush's ambassador to the UN, as of 2004, Bush's ambassador to Iraq; Eliot Abrams, who serves on the National Security Council; and John Poindexter, who was named head of the Pentagon's Information Awareness Office. Poindexter is barred from entering Costa Rica, which has designated him as a drug trafficker.[52]

An ex-convict expresses how incarceration increases anger and hostility, "One thing jail does is make you bitter, makes you so you don't care, which is why people beat someone over the head when they are being robbed. They don't care if they hurt them." Imprisonment had not changed this particular young man's intention to make his living by robbery.[53]

American prisons are very harsh, at least the ones for street criminals. There is another tier of prisons for white-collar criminals. A number of people have the attitude "if you do the crime, you do the time." Retribution may be morally satisfying, but it is shortsighted social policy. It is hard to see how the larger society's interest is served by brutalizing both the people locked up and those who deal with them. Amnesty International has documented the human rights abuses that occur in U.S. prisons.

In many facilities, violence is endemic. In some cases, guards fail to stop inmates assaulting each other. In others, the guards themselves are the abusers, subjecting their victims to beatings and sexual abuse. Prisons and jails use mechanical, chemical, and electroshock methods of restraint that are cruel, degrading, and sometimes life threatening. The victims of abuse include pregnant women and the mentally ill.

Health services are inadequate, including for prisoners who are HIV infected or have full-blown AIDS. "Many of these practices violate U.S. laws as well as international human rights standards."[54]

Incarceration is an expensive way to deal with crime. The yearly cost is now close to $440 billion, with each locked-up prisoner costing the taxpayers about $20,000. Some states spend more on prisons than on public higher education.[55] Criminologist Richard Rosenfeld points out that

a fiscal commitment of this scale, even during periods of economic expansion, inevitably reduces the resources available for education, health, child welfare, and other forms of state spending that conceivably have crime reduction effects of their own.[56]

In 2003, with states facing major budget crises, discussed in chapter 14, officials let out offenders, including violent ones, before their sentences were finished. It is unlikely that these offenders had received any serious rehabilitation.

While it may well be necessary to imprison lawbreakers, preventing crime in the first place makes more sense than continuing the lock-'em-up approach. Many crimes are not even reported; most criminals are never caught; many of those who are arrested never go to prison; and, therefore, even if imprisonment worked, crime could continue at high rates.[57]

Some prison policies could help reduce crime and violence. Recidivism rates are drastically reduced when prisoners have access to prison education programs, but these have mostly been ended. The U.S. Department of Education tracked three thousand prisoners in three states for three years and found that 31 percent of those with no class experiences while incarcerated went back to prison, compared to 22 percent of those who had the educational experience. The director of the study, Stephen J. Steurer of the Correctional Educational Association, concluded that "for every dollar you spend on education, you save two dollars by avoiding the cost of incarceration." In addition, rehabilitation of drug users could help them stay out of prison, which would be good for them, their families, and for the taxpayers who would save around $5 billion a year.[58]

James Alan Fox, dean of Northeastern University's College of Criminal Justice, and Sanford Newman, a lawyer who specializes in juvenile justice, prepared a report for Clinton's attorney general, Janet Reno. Their report stressed the importance of "quality after-school programs," describing these as "safe havens from negative influences," providing "constructive recreation, academic enrichment, and community service activities." Such programs "would dramatically reduce crime while helping students develop the values and skills they need to become good neighbors and responsible adults." At least some police chiefs agree. George Sweat of the Winston-Salem, North Carolina, police department lamented the cutting back of after-school sports programs in the 1980s. "It's since then that we've felt the brunt of the juvenile crime." He also felt that programs that put young people into contact with adults would be helpful.[59]

WHO BENEFITS FROM CRIME?

There are those who benefit from this country's high imprisonment rates. With prisons being privatized, there are direct financial gains to the companies that produce the equipment used by the criminal justice system. Prison-related industries made $26 billion in 1995. Why this is the case can be seen by looking at some of the items displayed at the 1996 American Correctional Association convention in Nashville, which featured over eight hundred booths and five thousand visitors.

A security bus with barred windows and interior cells could be bought for $260,000, while a single high-security cell can cost at least $100,000. A temporary cell only costs $40,000, however, while razor wire, should the inmates try to break out, goes for $170 a foot. AT&T's Nashville installation featured phone fraud and call monitoring detection systems and the hopeful statement: "How he got in is your business. How he gets out is ours—AT&T the authorized inmate calling service."[60]

Prisoners are also an ultracheap labor supply for large corporations. In some prisons they may be earning as little as twenty-five cents an hour; in others, they may be paid minimum wage. However, they do not get to keep most of what they earn. While the prisoners may be glad to have something to do and may even gain some useful work experience, they are highly exploitable.[61]

It is not surprising, given the benefits prisons provide to the private sector, that there is an organization to promote this interest, the American Legislative Exchange Council (ALEC). Founded in the early 1970s, its members are conservative state legislators and corporate executives who favor privatization. Its events are funded in part by large corporations, including the Corrections Corporation of America (CCA), the country's largest private prison operator. Between 1994 and 1999 its stock price "increased tenfold."[62] CCA has a representative on ALEC's Criminal Justice Task Force, a task force that has been advocating legislation favoring privatization of prisons. ALEC has been active in promoting "three strikes" laws and other measures that make parole very difficult. These laws add to prison populations.[63]

In a more indirect fashion, capitalists in the United States as a class benefit when the status quo is not challenged, that is, when social protest is at a low level. Those who are oppressed by the system are likely to engage in rebellious activities. Sociologists as well as activists have pointed out that by offering alternative opportunities, crime lessens the anger at high unemployment.

Narcotics especially lessen the possibilities of protest in the most deprived communities. Drug dealers fighting with each other for a piece of the action are not likely to be fighting for a more just society. Those caught up in drug using, trafficking, and the prison system are less likely to be engaged in social protest.

Michael Tabor personally attests to the social-control aspect of narcotics. He began using heroin when he was a thirteen-year-old living in Harlem. He was addicted for five years, stopping when he joined the Black Panther Party in the late 1960s. In an antidrug pamphlet, he wrote of "black youths [who] vent their rage, frustrations, and despair at each other rather than deal with the true enemy." He also wrote of the insidious effects of substances that make the user oblivious to the horrors of daily life in ghettos.[64]

At the National Press Club in December 1994, former surgeon general Joycelyn Elders was asked whether or not legalization of drugs would reduce crime. Her answer is worth a public discussion:

> I do feel that we would markedly reduce our crime rate if drugs were legalized. But I don't know all the ramifications of this. I do feel that we need to do some studies. And some countries that have legalized drugs . . . certainly have shown that there has been a reduction in their crime rate and there has been no increase in their drug use rate.[65]

Her rational approach to the problem of drugs and crime may be one of the reasons she became Clinton's *former* surgeon general. She was only asking for a study. The Clinton administration's response was, "Basically, it's not going to happen."

Several European countries or cities employ a "harm-reduction" strategy for narcotics users. In this approach, drug use is treated as a public health problem much more than a criminal justice one. The aim of the Dutch government, for example, is "to ensure that drug users are not caused more harm by prosecution and imprisonment than by the use of drugs themselves." Needle-exchange programs exist in fifty-two cities. Needles are dispensed in Addict Teller Machines and by health workers in buses; the result has been a decrease in HIV rates among needle users. Some cities in Canada, for example Vancouver, are also adopting harm-reduction tactics. The mayor of the British Columbian city, elected at least partly because of his attitude toward drugs, explained, "The philosophy here is that the drug problem that we have is a medical problem, an addiction no different from gambling."[66]

In Cuba drug trafficking was stopped after the revolution in 1959, and organized crime was kicked out. China also eliminated drug addiction following the revolution. U.S. official policies toward drugs are contradictory. Some that cause great harm such as alcohol and tobacco are legal, and the manufacturers encourage their use. Toward other addicting drugs, there is a "zero-tolerance" policy, even making medical use of marijuana, for example, extremely difficult.

WAR ON CRIME—WAR ON DEMOCRATIC RIGHTS

Current strategies for dealing with crime are not only counterproductive, they also threaten our civil liberties and democratic rights, a trend that has very much increased with the alleged "war on terror" discussed in chapter 15. The "war on drugs" produces its own casualties when the police violently assault innocent people, as discussed in chapter 12. Repressive measures become substitutes for progressive social policies. Metal detectors are a substitute for gun control. Plots on cop shows often imply that ignoring constitutional rights makes the police more effective, and television cops frequently express disdain for constitutional restraints. This reflects real-life attitudes: as a member of the Washington, DC, police's Rapid Deployment Unit said, "This is the jungle. . . . We rewrite the constitution every day down here."[67]

In Florida, when a young black man allegedly killed a British tourist in 1993, sheriff's deputies began rounding up every black male aged fifteen to twenty-two with criminal records involving firearms or stolen cars. The sheriff of Jefferson County, the site of the killing, said, "We have not focused on any one person," but, "we've got some mothers very upset because we're picking up their children."[68] Thousands of young people of color have dossiers compiled on them. In Los Angeles even those not charged with crimes have "their names and addresses entered into the electronic gang roster for future surveillance."[69]

Mass military-like raids occur in African American, Latino, and sometimes poor, white communities in which police kick in doors, push people, and sometimes destroy homes. In New York, Harlem police searching for a drug dealer broke down the door of a woman's apartment, tossing in a concussion grenade. Intended to disorient criminals, they flash and make a loud noise. Alberta Spruill was preparing to go to her job with the city, and the officers were conducting a "no-knock" search based on information from an informant. The Bill of Rights provision against "unreasonable searches and seizures" is not always applicable when the drug war is being fought. The information was wrong, the terrified fifty-seven-year-old woman, who was also briefly handcuffed, had a heart attack and died en route to the hospital.[70]

Terrorized by violent crime, a community may even accept a weakening of their own rights hoping for personal safety in return. At the crimeridden Robert Taylor housing project in Chicago, for example, five thousand residents petitioned a judge to allow warrantless searches of their buildings. One tenant, Daisy Bradford, has come to feel that "sometimes you got to sacrifice your rights to save your life."[71]

Disenfranchising former prisoners is another attack on basic democratic rights that has become part of America's criminal justice system. Marc Mauer, author of "Race to Incarcerate," summarizes these restrictions.

> Forty-six states deny the right to vote to anyone who is imprisoned, thirty-two restrict voting privileges of offenders on probation and/or parole, and in fourteen states anyone ever convicted of a felony loses their right to vote for life.[72]

Because so many African American men have been in prison, as of 1998, 13 percent had lost the right to vote for varying degrees of time. In several states 25 percent of African American men are banned from voting for life. The states are Mississippi, Florida, Alabama, Virginia, Iowa, Wyoming, and New Mexico. This means that "imprisonment itself reduces black . . . ability to influence political life." Altogether, regardless of race, 1.4 million Americans have permanently lost their voting rights; about 3 million are temporarily disenfranchised. Human Rights Watch reports that the United States is the only "democracy" with a policy of disenfranchising ex-prisoners.[73]

PRISONS OR SOCIAL PROGRAMS?

Repressive policies make people think the crime problem is being addressed when it is not. Programs that do show some promise of decreasing crime and violence are not funded adequately, and some have been cut altogether. For example, in East Los Angeles a program where gang members were themselves hired to work with potentially violent gangs was defunded in spite of its apparent success.[74]

Kathleen Newman notes the importance of summer job programs, which give teenagers skills, experience, and contacts they could use as well as knowledge "about what employers are looking for when they make their choices."[75]

Providing funds for prisoners so they can earn college credits has proven to reduce recidivism. The Omnibus Crime Bill passed in 1994, however, prevents such grants, while allotting over $30 billion for repressive measures. The thirty-seven members of the Congressional Black Caucus opposed this bill, calling for social programs instead, but they were not successful.

Those most hurt by changes in the economy can themselves realize there are alternatives to crime. In April 1996 a group of predominately Latino teenagers, some of them gang members, met in Washington to discuss a plan for the government to create alternatives to crime, violence, and incarceration in their communities. Over two decades earlier, in 1972, sixty black gang leaders had presented a similar set of proposals to the Los Angeles city Human Relations Conference that included creating jobs and improving recreation, housing, and schools. The young people, in the words of journalist Mike Davis,

> clearly understood that they were the children of deferred dreams and defeated equality. . . . Black and Chicano gang leaders have always affirmed, in the handful of other instances over the last eighteen years when they have been allowed to speak, decent jobs are the price for negotiating a humane end to drug dealing and gang violence.[76]

However perceptive their insight, these spokesmen lacked the political clout that could have produced social change. Their ideas were not implemented, and conditions in their communities deteriorated further.

Social programs and decent unemployment benefits can help decrease desperation, anger, and violent crime, but business interests consistently oppose these programs. At higher levels of unemployment, and with little public support, workers tend to be more competitive with one another and demand less of employers. Between 1980 and 1990, even as crime was supposed to be our biggest problem, government spending on all employment programs decreased from $10.3 billion to $5.4 billion.[77]

Politicians and the media rarely discuss real alternatives. A scientific approach to the problems discussed in this chapter would be for the government to target a community that has high unemployment and high crime, and to introduce, for a reasonable time period, a massive program of decently paid jobs, recreation, schools, and counseling. This would test whether a support system that helped individuals and families to play a useful role in society would change behavior. It is necessary to punish those who prey on others, but if this is the only approach, the road goes nowhere. As long as social conditions effectively encourage crime, individuals trapped in communities with few alternatives will risk the punishments.

NOTES

1. Richard B. Freeman, "Crime and the Employment of Disadvantaged Youths," in *Urban Labor Markets and Job Opportunity*, ed. George Peterson and Wayne Vroman (Washington, DC: Urban Institute Press, 1992), p. 229; Jeffrey Fagan, "Drug Selling and Licit Income in Distressed Neighborhoods: The Economic Lives of Street-Level Drug Users and Dealers," in *Drugs, Crime, and Social Isolation: Barriers to Urban Opportunity*, ed. Adele V. Harrell and George E. Peterson (Washington, DC: Urban Institute Press, 1992), p. 101.

2. Mercer Sullivan, *"Getting Paid": Youth Crime and Work in the Inner City* (Ithaca, NY: Cornell University Press, 1989).

3. David Rohde, "The Shattered Lives Left by a Street War," *New York Times,* January 16, 2000, pp. 29, 32.

4. Kathleen Newman, *No Shame in My Game: The Working Poor in the Inner City* (New York: Vintage, 1999), p. 217.

5. Elijah Anderson, *Code of the Streets: Decency, Violence, and the Moral Life of the Inner City* (New York: W. W. Norton, 1999), p. 9.

6. Ibid., p. 32.

7. Ibid., pp. 66, 109, 320–21.

8. U.S. Census Bureau, *Statistical Abstract of the United States, 2002*, table 37, p. 42.

9. Newman describes the importance of this in *No Shame in My Game*, pp. 196–98.

10. Mike Davis, *City of Quartz: Excavating the Future in Los Angeles* (New York: Vintage, 1990), pp. 307–308, 315.

11. Newman, *No Shame in My Game*, p. 213.

12. Quoted in Elliot Currie, *Reckoning: Drugs, the Cities, and the American Future* (New York: Hill and Wang, 1993), p. 97. A useful study on neighborhood social controls and crime is Sally Engle Merry, *Urban Danger: Life in a Neighborhood of Strangers* (Philadelphia: Temple University Press, 1981). A large-scale study done in England and Wales also found that crime increased with community disorganization. Robert J. Sampson and W. Byron Groves, "Community Structure and Crime: Testing Social-Disorganization Theory," *American Journal of Sociology* 94 (1989): 774–802.

13. Dirk Johnson, "Move to Suburbs Spurs the Poor to Seek Work," *New York Times*, May 1, 1990.

14. Currie, *Reckoning*, pp. 82–88; Michael Tonry, *Malign Neglect* (New York: Oxford University Press, 1995), p. 4; Clarence Lusane, *Pipe Dream Blues: Racism and the War on Drugs* (Boston: South End Press, 1991), pp. 49, 57.

15. Quote and figures from Don Terry, "Flare-up of Gang Gunfire Vexes Gary, Ind.," *New York Times*, September 14, 1996, p. 6.

16. Philippe Bourgois, "Just Another Night on Crack Street," *New York Times Magazine*, November 12, 1989, pp. 61, 66, 94.

17. Felicia R. Lee, "A Drug Dealer's Rapid Rise and Ugly Fall," *New York Times*, September 10, 1994, pp. 1, 22.

18 Quoted in Dennis Hevesi, "Gang Leader Details Crimes of Drug Ring," *New York Times*, March 1, 1995, pp. B1, B4.

19. Bureau of Justice Statistics, *Drugs and Crime Facts, 1994*, p. 9, and *Drugs and Crime Facts, 1993*, pp. 8–9.

20. Fox Butterfield, "Study Discounts the Role of Drug Users in Gun-Related Crime," *New York Times*, October 8, 1995, p. 36.

21. "Violence by Young People: Why the Deadly Nexus," *National Institute of Justice Journal* (August 1995): 6.

22. Bourgois, "Just Another Night on Crack Street," p. 64.

23. Anderson, *Code of the Streets*, pp. 116–19.

24. Fagan, "Drug Selling and Licit Income in Distressed Neighborhoods," pp. 103–104; Davis, *City of Quartz*, p. 270; Butterfield, "Study Discounts the Role of Drug Users in Gun-Related Crime."

25. Joan Moore, "Gangs, Drugs, and Violence," in *Gangs: The Origins and Impact of Contemporary Youth Gangs in the United States*, ed. Scott Cummings and Daniel J. Monti (Albany: State University of New York Press, 1993), p. 40.

26. *Congressional Record* 135, no. 62 (May16, 1989): 9301.

27. Tim Weiner, "C.I.A. Formed Haitian Unit Later Tied to Narcotics Trade," *New York Times*, November 14, 1993, pp. 1, 12; Elaine Sciolino, "U.S. Urging Afghan Rebels to Limit Opium," *New York Times*, March 26, 1989, p. 4; Alfred W. McCoy, *The Politics of Heroin: CIA Complicity in the Global Drug Trade* (New York: Lawrence Hill Books, 1991).

28. The series called "DarkAlliance" was available on the newspaper's Web

site, http://cgi.sjmercury.com/drugs. This quote is from "Dayone: America's 'Crack' Plague Has Roots in Nicaragua War," *San Jose Mercury*, August 18, 1996, http://cgi.sjmercury.com/drugs/day1main.htm, p. 1 (accessed September 5, 1996). However, the newspaper is no longer making this series available. The articles, along with useful links, are available from Gary Webb's site, which in his words, "has no affiliation with the *Mercury News* and, happily, neither do I." http://home.atbi.com~webb/wsb/html/view/cgi-home.html-.html (accessed March 27, 2003).

29. Gary Webb, "Daytwo: Shadowy Origins of 'Crack' Epidemic," *San Jose Mercury*, August 19, 1996, http://cgi.sjmercury.com/drugs/day2main.htm, p. 5 (accessed September 5, 1996).

30. Quoted in Gary Webb and Pamela Kramer, "Postscript: Waters Calls on Reno, CIA, and Congress for Investigation," *San Jose Mercury* September 4, 1996, http://cgi.sjmercury.com/drugshock/postscript/htm, p. 2 (accessed September 5, 1996).

31. Barbara Boxer's letter to CIA director John Deutch. The letter was printed in the paper on August 29, 1996, http://cgp.sjmerury.com/drugs/boxer829.htm, p. 1. It is interesting to compare the media's coverage of this story with their quick retelling of a tabloid's allegations that presidential advisor Dick Morris had had assignations with a call girl. This story, which appeared at about the same time as Webb's thoroughly researched and documented account, resulted in Morris's quickly resigning from his position. A month after Webb's account in a reputable newspaper, there was still little media coverage of it.

32. James Risen, "C.I.A. Reportedly Ignored Charges of Contra Drug Dealing in '80's," *New York Times*, October 10, 1998, p. A7; and "C.I.A. Says It Used Nicaraguan Rebels Accused of Drug Tie," *New York Times*, July 17, 1998, pp. A1, A2, Kerry quote p. A2.

33. Malcolm X, *By Any Means Necessary* (New York: Pathfinder Press, 1970), pp. 51–52.

34. Quoted in Stephen Rosskamm Shalom, *Imperial Alibis: Rationalizing U.S. Intervention after the Cold War* (Boston: South End Press, 1993), p. 191.

35. Quotes from Leslie Maitland Werner, "U.S. Crime Panel Seeks New Laws to Halt the Laundering of Money," *New York Times*, October 31, 1984, pp. A1, A25.

36. Lowell Bergman, "U.S. Companies Tangled in Web of Drug Dollars," *New York Times*, October 10, 2000, pp. A1, A20; Raymond Bonner, "Citibank Admits to Lapses in Dealings with Offshore Shell Banks," *New York Times*, March 3, 2001, pp. B1, B3.

37. Elizabeth Olson, "Big Puerto Rico Bank Settles U.S. Money Laundering Case," *New York Times*, January 17, 2003, p. C6.

38. Bill Berkeley, "A Glimpse into a Recess of International Finance," *New York Times*, November 12, 2000, p. C10. Many of the stories regarding money laundering are reported as business news, unlike reports of community drug-dealing.

39. Fox Butterfield, "Freed from Prison, but Still Paying a Penalty," *New York Times*, December 19, 2002, p. 18; Herman Schwartz, op-ed article, "Out of Jail and Out of Food," *New York Times*, March 21, 2002, p. A37.

40. Daniel Golden, "Up in Smoke: Tougher Bush Law Hits Students Seeking Aid," *Wall Street Journal*, April 25, 2001, pp. A1, A8; Diana Jean Schemo, "Students Find Drug Law Has Big Price: College Aid," *New York Times*, May 3, 2001, p. A12. For material dealing with many aspects of the continued consequences of imprisonment, see Marc Mauer and Meda Chesney-Lind, eds., *Invisible Punishment: The Collateral Consequences of Mass Imprisonment* (New York: New Press, 2002).

41. U.S. Department of Justice, *Sourcebook of Criminal Justice Statistics—2000*, table 6.1, p. 488.

42. Bureau of Justice Statistics, *Prison Statistics*, http://www.ojp.usdoj.gov/bjs/pripns/htm (accessed March 28, 2003).

43. Allen J. Beck, "Prison and Jail Inmates at Midyear 1999," U.S. Department of Justice, Bureau of Justice Statistics, April 2000, NCJ 181643, p. 1.

44. U.S. Department of Justice, Office of Justice Programs, Bureau of Justice Statistics, *Criminal Offenders Statistics*, http://www.ojp.usdoj.gov/bjs/crimoff.htm (accessed November 4, 2002).

45. Charles A. Shaw, "War on Drugs Unfairly Targets African Americans," *St. Louis Post Dispatch*, April 12, 2000, Common Dreams Web site, http://www.commondreams.org/views/041200-104.htm (accessed November 4, 2002).

46. Seth Mydans, "Racial Tensions in Los Angeles Jails Ignite Inmate Violence," *New York Times*, February 6, 1995, p. A13; Bureau of Justice Statistics, *Drugs and Crime Facts, 1994*, p. 26.

47. Michael Tonry, *Malign Neglect* (New York: Oxford University Press, 1995), pp. 19, 20. On pages 20–24, he critiques officials who argue the contrary, showing the flaws in their analysis; Steve Whitman, "The Crime of Black Imprisonment," *Z*, May/June 1992, p. 69.

48. Todd R. Clear, "'Tougher' Is Dumber," *New York Times*, December 4, 1993, p. 21.

49. "Often, Parole Is One Stop on the Way Back to Prison," *New York Times*, November 29, 2000, p. A1.

50. Peter T. Kilborn, "Flood of Ex-Convicts Finds Job Market Tight," *New York Times*, March 15, 2001, p. A16.

51. Clyde Haberman, "Ex-Inmate Denied Chair (and Clippers)," *New York Times*, February 25, 2003, p. B1.

52. "Bush Appoints Former Criminals to Key Government Roles," in *Censored 2003: The Top 25 Censored Stories*, ed. Peter Philips and Project Censored (New York: Seven Stories Press, 2002), pp. 68–72; Isabel Hilton, "Masters of Deceit," *Guardian*, August 7, 2003, http://www.guardian.co.uk/print/0,3858,4728128-103677,00.html (accessed October 3, 2003).

53. Quoted in Merry, *Urban Danger*, p. 172.

54. Amnesty International, *United States of America: Rights for All* (New York: Amnesty International USA, 1998), p. 55.

55. Fox Butterfield, "Prison: Where the Money Is," *New York Times*, June 2, 1996, sec. 4, p. 16.

56. Richard Rosenfeld, "Patterns in Adult Homicide: 1980–1995," in *The Crime Drop in America*, ed. Alfred Blumstein and Joel Wallman (New York: Cambridge University Press, 2000), p. 151.

57. David C. Anderson, "The Crime Funnel," *New York Times Magazine*, June 12, 1994, pp. 56–58; National Issues Forum, *Crime: What We Fear, What Can Be Done* (Dayton, OH: National Issues Forum, 1987), p. 12.

58. Brent Staples, "Prison Class: What Ma Barker Knew and Congress Didn't," *New York Times*, November 25, 2002, p. A20; Tamar Lein, "Inmate Education Is Found to Lower Risk of New Arrest," *New York Times*, November 16, 2001, p. A22; Timothy Egan, "War on Crack Retreats, Still Taking Prisoners," *New York Times*, February 28, 1999, p. 22.

59. Bob Herbert, "In America: 3:00, Nowhere to Go," *New York Times*, October 26, 1997, p. 15.

60. Jeff Gerth and Stephen Labaton, "Jail Business Shows Its Weaknesses," *New York Times*, November 24, 1995, pp. A1, B18; Donatella Lorch, "The Utmost Restraint and How to Exercise It," *New York Times*, August 23, 1996, pp. B1, B7; Editorial, "A World Leader in Prisons," *New York Times*, March 2, 1991.

61. David Leonhardt, "As Prison Labor Grows, So Does the Debate," *New York Times*, March 19, 2000, pp. 1, 34.

62. Timothy Egan, "Hard Time: Less Crime, More Criminals," *New York Times*, March 7, 1999, sec. 4, p. 1.

63. John Biewen, "Corrections, Inc: Corporate-Sponsored Crime Laws," *American Radio Works*, http://www/americanradioworks.org/features/corrections/lawsl.html (accessed April 14, 2002).

64. Michael Tabor, "The Plague: Capitalism + Dope = Genocide," in *The Triple Revolution Emerging: Social Problems in Depth*, ed. Robert Perrucci and Mark Pilisuk (Boston: Little Brown and Company, 1971), p. 244.

65. Stephan Labaton, "Surgeon General Suggests Study of Legalizing Drugs," *New York Times*, December 8, 1993, p. A23. Useful discussions of the pros and cons of legalization can be found in Currie, *Reckoning*, pp. 148–212; Steve Shalom, "Drug Policy and Program," *Z Papers* (January 1992): 9–17.

66. David Beers, "Just Say Whoa!" in *Solutions to Social Problems, Lessons from Other Societies*, ed. D. Stanley Eitzen and Craig S. Leedham (Boston: Allyn and Bacon, 1998), pp. 228–32; Clifford Kraus, "Canada Parts with U.S. on Drugs," *New York Times*, May 19, 2003, p. A9.

67. Quote from William J. Chambliss, "Policing the Ghetto Underclass: The Politics of Law and Law Enforcement," *Social Problems* 41, no. 2 (May 1994): 179.

68. Quoted in Larry Rohter, "Fearful of Tourism Decline, Florida Offers Assurances on Safety," *New York Times*, September 16, 1993, p. A14.

69. Davis, *City of Quartz*, p. 268.

70. "Big Housing Project Is Raided by Troops," *New York Times*, March 20, 1996, p. A15; William K. Rashbaum, "Woman Dies after Police Mistakenly Raid Her Apartment," *New York Times*, May 17, 2003, pp. B1, B3.

71. Don Terry, "Chicago Project in Furor about Guns and the Law," *New York Times*, April 8, 1994, p. A12. A local judge issued an injunction against warrantless searches. A debate on this proposal can be found on the op-ed page of the *New York Times*, May 7, 1994, p. 23.

72. Marc Mauer, "Race to Incarcerate," in *Understanding Prejudice and Discrimination*, ed. Scott Plous (New York: McGraw-Hill, 2003), p. 180.

73. Mauer, "Race to Incarcerate"; "Sentence: No Vote," *Dollars and Sense* (July/August 1999): 5. See also Rebecca Perl, "The Last Disenfranchised Class," *Nation*, November 24, 2003, pp. 11–14.

74. Moore, "Gangs, Drugs, and Violence," p. 38.

75. Newman, *No Shame in My Game*, p. 73.

76. David Corn, "Ganging Up on Congress," *Nation*, April 29, 1996, pp. 6–7; Davis, *City of Quartz*, pp. 300–301.

77. Currie, *Reckoning*, p. 295.

Chapter 11

INTERPERSONAL GENDER VIOLENCE

On the University of Massachusetts, Amherst, campus, in November 1999 women were offered escort services to protect them from being raped. Four coeds had been sexually assaulted within a few weeks of one another. One student, Sarah Shumaker, lamented, "You expect this kind of a thing being a woman. It's really hard being a woman."[1]

Riding along a country road outside of Laramie, Wyoming, in 1998, a bicyclist saw what seemed to be a scarecrow hanging from a fence. Investigating, he found that it was twenty-two-year-old Mathew Shephard, an openly gay student at the University of Wyoming, who had been severely beaten, burned, and abandoned in bitterly cold weather. He hung on the fence for eighteen hours till the bicyclist discovered him. Shepard was in a coma when found, and he died a few days later in the hospital.[2]

Interpersonal gender violence, the subject of this chapter, like the racial/ethnic violence discussed in the next, cannot be directly linked to capitalism and economic inequality. Instead, the class system creates the conditions that make such violence more explainable. Class, gender, and race also affect access to resources that could help lessen some of this violence.

Interpersonal violence is an expression of inequality: a way to achieve certain ends, including maintaining hierarchy, venting anger and frustration, or asserting one's masculinity. Violence used to maintain inequality may be partly a reaction against attempts by subordinate groups to improve their position. There is obviously still a great deal of inequality, but real gains have been made. Antidiscrimination laws have been expanded, and women now have a legal right to abortions; gays and lesbians have demanded and in some places obtained more rights as well. Many now refuse to pretend that heterosexuality is the only acceptable form of sexuality.

These progressive changes have come at the price of some of the accustomed privileges of white males. A sense of loss can be exacerbated by other stresses—such as an economic crisis, which makes people fearful of their and their children's futures. Right-wing politicians and some religious and media figures help transform this frustration into hostility toward women, people of color, immigrants, gays and lesbians, and, at times, even the government.

Anger is coupled with a socialization process that teaches everyone, but especially males, that physical force is an acceptable way of dealing with problems. Violence becomes the means to try to sustain traditional gender and ethnic roles, and to turn back the clock to a time when, some think, things were better.

Writing on gender violence, Laura O'Toole and Jessica R. Schiffman stress that

> much of the violence in contemporary society serves to preserve asymmetrical gender systems of power. For example, compulsory aggression as a central component of masculinity serves to legitimate male-on-male violence, sexual harassment as a means of controlling the public behavior of women, gay and lesbian bashing and rape as a standard tool in war, in prison, and in too many intimate relationships.[3]

Some social scientists have created terms to emphasize the power dimension of gender relationships. *Hegemonic masculinity* is the way in which being a male is conceptualized in the contemporary United States. Males are supposed "to be powerful, aggressive, rational, and invulnerable," with an ability to control themselves and others. Males vary in how close they come to this ideal: "but the manliness of most will be judged by their ability to measure up to this standard of masculinity."[4]

The term *emphasized femininity* describes expectations for females, with women expected to be "emotional, nurturing, vulnerable, and dependent, sexually desirable and malleable rather than controlling." But while these are expected behaviors, they are not highly valued, with "female" characteristics considered somewhat inferior to "masculine" ones. This "hegemonic masculinity" can become "a breeding ground for gender violence."[5]

DOMESTIC VIOLENCE

In June 1993 a shocked but titillated public learned that Lorena Bobbitt had cut off her husband's penis as he slept in a drunken stupor. Her defense lawyers argued she was temporarily insane, driven to violence by repeated instances of battering and rape by her spouse. A jury accepted this argument and acquitted her. A year later, the ex-football hero turned actor, O. J. Simpson went on trial, accused of murdering his ex-wife, Nicole Brown Simpson, and her friend, Ron Goldman, in a jealous rage.

These high-profile cases focused media attention on spousal abuse and share features with less publicized instances. Lorena Bobbitt, for example, had been abused for several years, her husband feeling he had a right to dominate her life. Simpson also had a history of attacking his wife, who had made at least eight calls to the police for help. When arrested after one of these calls in 1989, Simpson was given lenient treatment: small fines and some community service. Like many batterers, O. J. Simpson felt that what went on between him and his wife was not of concern to the police: he reportedly said after one call, "What are you doing here? This is a family matter."[6]

The terms domestic violence, intimate violence, spouse abuse, child abuse, and elderly abuse are all terms used to describe violence within the same household. Households are miniature power systems, and family values can mean valuing male domination and the right of the more powerful to use violence as a way to control the relationships and maintain household inequality. Family violence experts Richard Gelles and Murray Straus point out the connection between household inequality and domestic violence:

> Our statistical evidence shows that the risk of intimate violence is the greatest when all the decision making in a home is concentrated in the hands of one of the partners. Couples who report the most sharing of decisions report the lowest rates of violence. Our evidence goes beyond the statistics. Over and over again, case after case, interview after interview, we [heard] batterers and victims discuss how power and control were at the core of the events that led up to the use of violence.[7]

Home is not always the warm, cozy sanctuary described by many politicians, and a marriage license, as described by Gelles and Strauss, is for some men "a hitting license."

Sociologist Michael P. Johnson uses the phrase "patriarchal terrorism" to summarize the "systematic male violence" that exists in some families, and includes not only physical attacks but other forms of social control, such as financial dependence, socially isolating the woman, and so on. "Common couple violence," another form of domestic aggression, is more occasional, and females may engage in this as well, though they do so less often.[8]

Familiar men are more dangerous to women than are male strangers. Males, on the other hand, are more at risk from strangers. Between 1993 and 1998, strangers attacked 54 percent of male victims of violence, but for women the figure was 33 percent. Looking just at intimate partner assaults, in 2001, 20 percent of all the violence women experienced was at the hands of an intimate partner, while for males it was 3 percent. In 2001, in 85 percent of intimate partner violence incidents the victim was a woman. An intimate was responsible for one-third of all female murder victims but only 4 percent of male victims.[9]

These figures show why even the generally conservative American Medical Association in 1992 described men as a major health threat to women in this country.[10] When women do attack or murder their partners, it is typically in self-defense after years of abuse. A study of Kentucky women serving time for murder or manslaughter indicated that 40 percent had killed a male abuser. In several cases, the women had tried to get police protection before finally killing their partners in desperation.[11]

Even pregnancy doesn't guarantee immunity. A 1994 study by the Centers for Disease Control and Prevention revealed that male partners batter at least 6 percent of women during their pregnancy, and some of these beatings result in miscarriages or birth defects. Recent studies in Massachusetts and Washington, DC, found that pregnancy increased women's risk of being murdered. The Massachusetts Department of Public Health found that "homicide, most often the result of domestic violence, is the leading cause of death in Massachusetts of women during pregnancy or up to one year following the end of pregnancy." Between 1990 and 1999, 232 women died either while pregnant or in the first year following delivery. Thirty of these were homicides.[12]

Abused women may decide not to call the police for a number of reasons. They may fear reprisals; after all, they live with, and are often economically dependent on, their abuser. Like their male partners, some, too, may feel domestic violence is a personal affair. The police are, in any case, often reluctant to intervene. One badly beaten woman, Tracy Thurman of Torrington, Connecticut, was awarded nearly $2 million from her local police department, who had simply looked on as her husband beat her, inflicting injuries that left her permanently disabled.[13]

There is evidence that police intervention can protect the woman from domestic violence. A study by the National Crime Survey based on data from 1978 to1982 concluded that women who called the police were much less likely to be reassaulted than women who did not make such calls. Research in 1981 in Minneapolis indicated that where men are arrested for spouse abuse, they are less likely to repeat the offense. It is not just fear of punishment that causes the change: there is now public disapproval of his acts as well as a change in the power relationships in the household. By calling the police, the woman has demonstrated some authority and the ability to take some control.[14]

Children are even less powerful in the family hierarchy. Physical punishment for a child's misbehavior is widely accepted and has even been sanctioned in schools by a 1975 Supreme Court decision. In a 1995 poll, 87 percent of the respondents felt spanking was appropriate in some circumstances. However, there is also evidence of changing attitudes: younger parents are more disapproving of corporal punishment than older ones. In many European countries, however, the law forbids spanking.[15] In the United States in 2000 there were 862,455 cases of child abuse and neglect recorded.[16] Children are abused by their mothers as well as fathers or mothers' male companions. Yale University studies suggest that women who are at risk from battering are more likely to be child abusers. Abuse of the elderly is also a problem, but there is little research available. One sociological study estimates that the number of elderly victims is between 700,000 and 1.1 million.[17]

It is widely believed that batterers are most likely to have been physically abused themselves. Children who see their parents engaged in physical violence are more likely to be violent when they establish their own homes. But not all abused children grow up to be violent, and not all violent adults were abused children.[18]

Several other factors help account for domestic violence. Cultural beliefs can play a role. The American emphasis on individualism can lead a troubled person to feel she must take care of her problems rather than seek help from others—help that could, in some cases, possibly prevent violence. In many facets of American life, violence, especially for males, is believed to be an appropriate way to deal with a problem. As we showed in chapter 2, the availability of firearms makes it more likely that any kind of violent encounter will turn deadly.

Stress is an important element for understanding domestic violence. If stress is coupled with social isolation and a lack of emotional and material support, then the likelihood of violence occurring in the household rises. Isolation also means social standards are less of a control on behavior.

Certain variables counteract others, however. Gelles and Straus found no difference between whites and African Americans in rates of child abuse, even though blacks can be expected to have higher rates of stress. The researchers reasoned that African Americans are more likely to be involved in community and church groups and to have relatives to help with child care and financial difficulties.

Domestic violence seems to be higher among lower-income groups, who are likely to have more problems. There are several reasons for this association. Sociologist Mary Stewart points out that "control of economic resources and status resources may be more available to men in the upper class than to men in other classes." The latter therefore are more likely to "use physical violence in order to assert control over their wives." Data from 1987–1994 are illustrative. For every thousand women with incomes below $10,000, there were eleven cases of domestic violence. When the household income was above $30,000, the number of cases dropped to two per thousand.[19]

Less income usually means more problems and fewer possibilities for solving them. There are fewer resources for getting away from the household for a while if the situation there seems overwhelming. Therapy for troubled family members is less of an option in lower-income households.

As we saw in chapter 8, one cause of both stress and lower incomes is unemployment. During the 1979–1982 recession, the American Humane Association, which monitors child abuse, reported a 120 percent national increase in child abuse cases. Thirty-nine states also reported increases in child abuse during this period. For example, in Youngstown, Ohio, as unemployment rose to 21 percent, domestic violence cases increased by over 400 percent.[20]

We expect our homes to make us happy. Major holidays such as Christmas and Easter are times when the family is supposed to be especially joyful and gifts are to be given, however unaffordable. These are also the times when violence is most likely. This helps explain why admissions to hospitals for child abuse rise during the holidays.[21]

Families are private places, and the sanctions against violence are relatively few. Anger that cannot be released elsewhere may often be safely expressed at home. There are serious repercussions if a man beats up his boss, an employee, or an annoying customer, but if he smacks his wife or children, he has an easier time getting away with it. The same holds true if the woman abuses a child. You hear suspicious noises from a neighbor's apartment. What should you do? Ignore it, intervene, or call the police? There are no clear norms or guidelines, but the general sense is that you are not supposed to interfere with other people's households.

If an abusive man won't change his behavior, the woman must choose between accepting the abuse or leaving. Minimally, about 50 percent do leave. The choice is a difficult one: a woman has to find and pay for a new home and arrange care for her dependent children, usually on low earnings. She will have court costs if she files for divorce and if there are custody battles. If her job doesn't provide health care, that will be another economic burden. There are few social supports for an abused woman wanting to make a new life. Even obtaining insurance can be difficult, because a number of companies refuse to provide life, medical, or mortgage insurance to women they think have been physically abused.[22]

Finding a job can be complicated by the male partner's efforts to keep the woman dependent. The Legal and Educational Defense Fund (LEDF) of the National Organization for Women (NOW) conducted a study of abused women who have gone back to school or are in job training programs. The man may promise to provide child care and then renege at the last minute; he may insist on escorting the woman, make harassing phone calls to her, or actually injure her.[23]

An economically needy woman who moves to another state in an attempt to evade her abuser may find she is either ineligible for welfare or able to get only very small payments, because she doesn't meet the new state's residency requirements. The welfare "reforms," currently in effect, will make life harder for women desperate to leave violent homes, imposing restrictions on how long a woman can get benefits, for example.

There is a Family Violence Option (FVO) attached to the 1996 federal welfare bill. This legislation was created by NOW, working with the late Democratic senator from Minnesota, Paul Wellstone, and Washington Senator Patty Murray. As of 2002, thirty-four states and Washington, DC, have adopted the FVO. The FVO's provisions include identifying individuals who have been victims of domestic violence and waiving the time limits for receiving financial assistance. There is, however, variation among the adopting states as to what aspects of the FVO have been accepted.[24]

With affordable housing hard to find, domestic violence becomes one cause of homelessness for women. There are only about 1,400 shelters for abused women in the entire country, and even the best shelters offer only temporary refuge. Pennsylvania, with a relatively good system of shelters, has to turn away eleven thousand women a year. Studies in that state show from one-third to two-fifths of families at homeless shelters were fleeing intimate violence.[25]

When the woman asserts herself and moves out, she becomes especially vulnerable: about three-quarters of the murders of battered women occur when they try to gain control over their lives.[26] Many batterers view their companions' departure as a repudiation of a man's ability to control "his" woman.

The women's movement has helped make domestic violence a public issue, and women's groups have provided services to victims of this violence. Often operating on shoestring budgets, with inadequate or no public funding, women have established shelters, hot lines, and support groups. In the 1970s there were fewer than ten shelters for abused women in the whole country; now there are over a thousand, although—as noted above—this is still inadequate to meet the demand.

Changes in laws and police behavior are a result of the efforts of women's organizations. Nearly half of all police departments now have domestic violence units, and fourteen states and Washington, DC, have mandatory arrest policies. This means the police can arrest a suspected batterer even if the victim does not make a personal complaint. In some areas services are available for men who are trying to change their violent behavior.[27]

RAPE AND SEXUAL ASSAULT

Sexual assault statistics underestimate the prevalence of this type of violence. In the United States in 1999, for every one thousand females, thirty-three were raped. In 2000, according to official statistics, 147,000 females aged twelve or above were raped, while another 114,000 were sexually assaulted.[28]

In a middle-class suburb of Los Angeles, twenty to thirty male high school students in the early 1990s formed a group called the "Spur Posse." Members got "points" for each sexual encounter, consensual or otherwise. Eight of the gang members were arrested, charged with raping and molesting girls, some as young as ten. At least one father proudly exclaimed, "Aren't they virile specimens?" Some community residents excused these attacks with the cliché, "Boys will be boys."[29]

Rape occurs in many societies but is more likely in those where gender inequality is high. In the United States the combination of gender inequality and a wide acceptance of violence in many contexts helps explain why the United States has a high rape rate, as table 1.3 indicated.

Diane Scully, a sociologist who has studied rape, summarizes the cross-cultural findings of anthropologists on this issue:

> Sexual violence is related to cultural attitudes, the power relationship between women and men, the social and economic status of women relative to the men of their group, and the amount of other forms of violence in the society.[30]

Her statement is confirmed for the United States by the findings of Larry Baron and Murray A. Straus, with the University of New Hampshire's Family Violence Research Program. They wanted to explain why rape rates differ dramatically by states. Baron and Straus found that "the more economic inequality, unemployment, and urbanization in a state, the higher the rape rate." They also found that when the general status of women was lower, rape rates were higher.[31]

Male socialization contributes to the occurrence of rape. Males are often taught that a woman wants a male to be dominant, while women learn to be less overt in expressing their sexual desires. Males in all social classes and racial/ethnic groups may feel they are entitled to sex from their wives or if a woman looks "provocative." In 1987, following a "take back the night" march at Princeton University where participants sought to publicize the problem, a group of male students had their own demonstration. Their slogan was "We can rape anyone we want." After a woman was raped and severely beaten in 1989 while jogging in New York's Central Park, a man told a reporter that he didn't understand the beating, "They should've just raped her."[32]

Some people think that males have uncontrollable sexual impulses and that it is a woman's responsibility not to provoke a man sexually. In 1989 a Florida jury acquitted three men accused of raping a woman at knifepoint in a parking lot. The jury focused on the fact that the twenty-two-year-old victim was wearing a tank top with a short lace skirt and no underwear. One male juror defended the decision, explaining, "She asked for it."[33]

One of the most underreported types of rape is marital rape: in some states it is not even a crime unless the couple is separated. This fact caused California state senator Bob Wilson to plaintively ask, "If you can't rape your wife who can you rape?"[34]

Male peer groups sometimes use sexual assault as a way for members to demonstrate their masculinity to one another and to reinforce male bonding. A gang rapist interviewed by Diane Scully reported that "we felt powerful, we were in control. I wanted sex and there was peer pressure. She wasn't like a person, no personality, just domination on my part. Just to show I could do it—you know, macho."[35]

Some gang rapists have been caught when they were overheard bragging about their actions. Interviews by *New York Times* journalists with fifty teenagers in the New York metropolitan area found teenage boys wanting to impress their friends. They feared being thought "soft" and sought "to demonstrate their manhood by abusing or showing disrespect to girls." This attitude was "repeated time and again." These findings were corroborated by a national study of junior high and high school students that found some form of sexual harassment common in junior highs and high schools.[36]

Certain organizational contexts are associated with rape. Members of associations with an emphasis on male bonding, toughness, and, in some instances, violence are especially likely to be involved in rapes. Part of this means loyalty to one's "brothers." This makes it unlikely that even those who disapprove of an act will come forward if a sexual assault has occurred.

Gangs, fraternities, sports teams, and the military are places where males demonstrate their masculinity, which includes having sexual prowess. These are factors that can produce both individual and gang rapes. The other side of this is the members placing a negative value on weakness, on being "effeminate."

In chapter 15 we shall discuss gender violence and militarism. Here we will look at fraternities and athletic teams. Fraternities use a deliberate recruitment process, with many seeking members who fit a macho image. There is a lot of drinking at fraternity parties, which seems to make it more likely that males will engage in sexual assault, but it also means that it is easier to blame the woman for allowing herself to get drunk and therefore more sexually vulnerable. The victim may even have passed out and not realize what is happening.[37]

"Date rape" drugs may be part of an evening's refreshments. GHB, gamma-hydroxybutrate, is one; Rohypnol is another. These produce a stupor in the potential victim. On my own campus, the Department of Campus Safety and Security placed an ad in the student newspaper giving women advice on how to protect themselves against Rohypnol. An article gave similar recommendations with regard to GHB. The company Drink Safe Technologies markets a product that can be used to test a drink for the presence of GHB.[38]

The external environment also plays a role. On many campuses, university authorities have been quite tolerant of the illegal activities of fraternities, some of which have wealthy alumni as past members. It is also damaging to a college or university's image to have publicity about campus rapes.

On campuses, athletes are overrepresented in the ranks of rapists. Jeff

Benedict, a researcher at the Center for the Study of Sport, studied gender violence committed by college athletes at ten schools belonging to the National Collegiate Athletic Association. His research team had access to records that included many incidents never reported to legal authorities. They found that "between 1991 and 1993, male athletes were responsible for nearly 20 percent" of sexual assaults on their campuses "despite the fact that they constituted just 3 percent of the student population."

Benedict's findings were deemed potentially offensive to "the center's [*sic*] most loyal supporters" and were not published by the center, so he published the results himself and continued his research.[39] While he does not believe that being an athlete somehow causes aggression toward women, he does think that this role encourages those who are already disposed to engage in sexual assaults.

Benedict believes one factor explaining his findings is the culture of sports teams, which includes "using sexist locker room dialogue rewarding aggressiveness, [and] legitimizing violence."[40] Both collegiate and professional athletes have high status, and because of this "women who accuse them of rape come under exceptional scrutiny," with their character being the one maligned when they come forth. The victims are discouraged from making accusations at all.[41] Athletes are a source of revenue, and coaches are willing "to maintain scholarships for athletes with a clear disdain for the law."[42]

In Glen Ridge, New Jersey, in 1989, high school athletes Kyle and Kevin Scherzer, Christopher Archer, and Bryant Grober sexually assaulted a retarded girl with a broom handle and a baseball bat while ten other high school football players watched. Bernard Lefkowitz, who wrote *Our Guys: The Glen Ridge Rape and the Secret Life of the Perfect Suburb*, felt that their status as "admired athletes" with traditional ideas about masculinity contributed to their behavior. The defense argued they were just "pranksters," explaining, "Boys will be boys."[43]

Rape can be a way of asserting a sense of power and control. This is illustrated by comments from convicted rapists:

After a rape, I always felt like I had just conquered something.

Rape was a feeling of total dominance. . . . I would degrade women so that I could feel there was a person of less worth than me.

I decided to rape her to prove I had guts. She was just there.[44]

Rapists may feel temporarily empowered by sexual assaults, but rape victims suffer for a long time. Some rape victims still experience fear and anxiety years after the attack. Victims often feel humiliated, fearful, depressed, and their own sexual relationships are affected. Some even blame themselves for being attacked.

The women's movement has helped victims by creating rape crisis centers and hot lines and by changing the way law enforcement deals with rapes. Policewomen are now more available to question rape victims. Interrogating a victim about her sexual history, which used to be a common practice in courts, is usually not permitted. Some states have adopted laws providing that victims need not show bruises proving they resisted the attack. Corroborating witnesses are also not as imperative as they once were to establish a woman's credibility.

FORCED MOTHERHOOD OR ACCESS TO SAFE, LEGAL ABORTIONS

One of the great victories of the women's movement was the 1973 Supreme Court decision, *Roe v. Wade*, legalizing the right to an abortion. Without this right, women were in effect forced to be mothers if they were raped, if their contraceptive methods failed, or if they didn't use contraception.

The right to terminate an unwanted pregnancy is not so much a point of contention for the capitalists as for conservative Christian groups. It makes political sense for the Republican Party to be more antichoice since fundamentalist Christians, valuing a patriarchal family, provide a large number of Republican votes. Robert J. Billings, who founded the Moral Majority in 1979 and served in Reagan's Department of Education, successfully persuaded the Republicans to use the abortion issue as a way to win traditionally Democratic Catholics over to the Republicans.[45]

When abortions were illegal, some women sought them anyway, with dangerous consequences. No one is sure exactly how many deaths resulted from illegal abortions. In 1961 there were 320 recorded deaths as a result of complications from illegal procedures. Since 1974, or subsequent to *Roe v. Wade*, there have been fewer than five a year.[46] Some doctors willing to perform abortions are motivated by the horrors they witnessed when abortion was illegal. Dr. David McDowell remembers "seeing vaginal lacerations from hangers, and wards full of women with infections from criminal abortions. I remember a gal who had a piece of a wood packing crate in her."[47]

New horror stories are appearing of anguished women like twenty-three-year-old West Virginian Mary Jiveden, who became pregnant as a result of date rape. Unemployed, divorced, and with a two-year-old, she felt she could not afford another child. Each clinic she went to said her pregnancy was too advanced for them to give her an abortion, and as she continued her search, her pregnancy kept advancing. When finally she discovered she could have an abortion in Wichita, Kansas, for a whopping $2,500, she just gave up, saying, "I don't know how I'm going to make a life for myself and these kids."[48] How many other women are effectively coerced into becoming mothers? How many are making major financial sacrifices that may damage their own and their families' health in the long run? How many women are staying in unhappy, possibly abusive, relationships because they are trapped by an unwanted pregnancy? How many unwanted babies have become abandoned, abused, or even killed?

There is no medical procedure that men are entitled to that is so restricted. Since 1976, the Hyde Amendment has prohibited the use of Medicaid funds for abortions unless a woman's life is in danger, or, since 1993, if the pregnancy results from rape or incest. Women in the armed forces cannot obtain abortions at military hospitals. After being selected president, George W. Bush appointed antichoice supporter John Ashcroft to be attorney general and has nominated antichoice judges to federal benches.

Medicaid does not pay for abortions. Women who are eligible for Medicaid are also not entitled to have government coverage for the abortion pill RU-486. The administration also encouraged the National Cancer Institute to produce material for its Web site linking abortions to breast cancer. After further investigation, the posting was withdrawn. The Bush administration is also hostile toward teaching young people about contraception, insisting that abstinence is the only correct way to limit pregnancies. In addition, the administration has cut funding for international family-planning organizations.[49]

Claiming that "at last, the American people and our government have confronted the violence and come to the defense of the innocent child," President Bush, in November 2003, signed the Partial Birth Abortion Ban Act, restricting late-term abortions for women. Among those attending the signing ceremony was Cardinal Edward M. Egan. There is no medical term "partial-birth abortions"; physicians refer to the outlawed procedure as "intact dilation and extraction." This abortion method is exceedingly rare. There are no exceptions in the bill signed by the president to protect the health of the mother. The legislation was opposed by the American Medical Association and the American College of Obstetricians and Gynecologists, the latter stating that it is a woman and her doctor who "are the appropriate parties to determine the best method of treatment." This bill threatens doctors with up to two years in prisons and fines if they perform an intact dilation and extraction. Both pro- and antichoice groups agree that this bill is a way to undermine *Roe v. Wade*. A similar law, however, enacted in Nebraska in 2000, was overturned by the Supreme Court, and it remains to be seen if this law will survive legal challenges.[50]

Teenagers in many states have to get parental consent for abortions. Sometimes both parents' consent is needed even if the person lives with only one. This places at least some teens at risk of punishment from an angry mother, father, or both.

The right to an abortion is limited by income, age of the potential mother, geographical locality, and by the number of abortion providers. In 84 percent of all counties, containing 31 percent of the country's women of childbearing age, there are no doctors willing to perform the procedure. Fewer hospitals are providing abortions, and less than 15 percent of medical schools mandate abortion training.[51] Twenty-five states have mandatory waiting periods; in thirty-two, a minor needs parental consent; and in thirteen, insurance coverage for abortions is restricted.[52] Many of the doctors who do abortions are getting older, and many will be retiring soon.[53]

Why are doctors so reluctant to provide a legal medical procedure? One answer may be that it has become life threatening for doctors to perform abortions. In fact, it is dangerous for anyone to work at an abortion-providing facility. In 1998, as Dr. Barnett A. Slepain stood by his kitchen window chatting with his family, James C. Kopp shot a bullet from an assault rifle, killing the doctor. Also in 1998, a bomb exploded at an Alabama clinic, killing a guard and wounding a nurse. A Pensacola, Florida, provider, Dr. David Gunn, was killed in March 1993. A year later in the same town, Dr. John Bayard Britton and clinic escort James H. Barrett were murdered. Mr. Barrett's wife was also wounded while providing escort services. Two clinic workers, Shannon Lowney and Leanne Nichols, were shot to death in a Boston suburb in 1995. In 1994 there were at least four hundred death threats to choice advocates. In 1993 Wichita, Kansas, abortion provider Dr. George Tiller was wounded outside the clinic where he worked, and antichoice demonstrators who held weekly rallies in Southern California assaulted a doctor outside his home.[54]

Some of the most zealous antichoice forces have formed alliances with racist and paramilitary organizations and are engaging in terrorism against abortion facilities. Fanatical forced-motherhood groups have published manuals that give advice to would-be assassins, bombers, and arsonists, and their manuals have been put to use. Tom Burghardt, a researcher and reproductive rights activist, compiled the following grim tally using 1982–1994 data from the Bureau of Alcohol, Tobacco, and Firearms: "37 bombings in 33 states; 123 cases of arson; 1,500 cases of assault, stalking, sabotage, and burglary; and some $13 million in property damage."[55]

Antichoice groups defend their actions, physically violent or otherwise, by claiming they are saving "babies'" lives. In 1995 a supporter of John Salvi, who murdered Lowney and Nichols, the Boston suburb clinic workers, said, "When people are involved in killing babies, then it's justified to save the babies. Babies deserve to be defended at any cost."[56] The argument that abortion is murder is based on the assumption that human life begins at conception and that the developing fetus is already a baby. To accept such arguments is to accept that the religious beliefs of some should be the basis for preventing all women from having access to safe, legal means of ending unwanted pregnancies.

SOCIALIZATION FOR MASCULINITY AND HOMOPHOBIC VIOLENCE

A militant heterosexuality can be part of some men's self-conception. Steven Mullins and Charles Monroe Butler killed Billy Jack Gaither Jr. in 1999, asserting that Billy Jack had made unwanted advances. In reprisal, they beat Billy Jack with an ax handle and cut his throat.[57]

Television talk show host Jenny Jones promised twenty-four-year-old Jonathan Schmitz that she would present him with a secret admirer if he would appear on a March 1995 show. She didn't tell him his admirer was a man, Scott Amedure. Three days after the taping, Schmitz shot and killed Amedure. He told the police that the humiliation he had experienced had "eaten away" at him.[58]

Men are more likely to be attacked than women; their behavior is more violating of acceptable norms of maleness. Of the 1,317 incidents of homophobic crimes reported to the police in 1999, 915 were directed against males.[59] Several studies of homophobic violence show a minimum of 20 percent of gay respondents experiencing at least one physical assault at some time. Even larger numbers have been threatened. In some cases the attackers accused their victims of being responsible for AIDS.[60] A study of homicides, sponsored by the New York City Gay and Lesbian Anti-Violence Project and covering the period between 1992 and 1994, labeled the violence "gruesome," a description fitting the cases we have described.[61]

Violence has been found to be heightened for gay victims who are people of color. In Fairmont, West Virginia, for example, Arthur Warren Jr., a gay black man, was beaten and kicked by two seventeen-year-olds who also drove a car over his body, hoping to make the killing look like an auto accident. Antigay picketers attended the funeral carrying signs indicating that the victim, a sinner, deserved to die and was now in hell.[62]

Like victims of rape, victims of homophobic attacks experience symptoms for a long time afterward. They may change their behavior, become surreptitious about expressing their feelings, and avoid locations they think are dangerous.

Homophobia partly stems from gender inequality as a way males can distance themselves from "feminine" qualities within themselves. A man insults another by comparing him to a woman; a nondominant husband is "hen-pecked," or, more crudely, "pussy-whipped." There are no comparable terms that females use toward one another. It is not an insult, for example, for a young girl to be called a "tomboy." It is acceptable for girls and women to wear clothing associated with males, but the reverse would most likely subject a man to ridicule or worse. The epithets "fag" and "fairy" connote weakness: "real men" are strong and tough and show their maleness by sexual prowess with women. "Real women" are sexually attracted to men and should not be "tough" or "butch."

For decades in the United States, homosexuality was widely considered to be a shameful perversion. To be identified as such was to jeopardize one's physical safety, one's livelihood, and social ties. Many gay men and women internalized the stigma that they were unhealthy, damaged people. There have been important changes, however, many dating from the 1969 "Stonewall Rebellion" in New York's Greenwich Village, when gays and lesbians fought the police during a raid on the Stonewall bar.

Gays and lesbians have struggled for the right to be open about who they are and to have equal access to jobs and a family life. They have challenged the stereotypes that label them as dangerous and "perverted." Many have refused to be ashamed and have created organizations to fight for their rights. But there is still prejudice, discrimination, and violence against homosexuals.

Influential figures who oppose gay and lesbian rights help legitimate homophobic feelings. Dr. Laura Schlessinger of radio and TV, for example, proclaimed on her broadcast of June 9, 1999, "The debate over gay rights—Rights. Rights! Rights? . . . Why does deviant sexual behavior get rights?"[63]

Conservative politicians strengthen homophobic attitudes. In September 1996 Congress passed a "Defense of Marriage Act," which denies federal recognition to same-sex marriages. Arguing against passage of the bill, Democratic senator Edward Kennedy from Massachusetts pointed out that "this bill is designed to divide Americans, to drive a wedge between one group of citizens and the rest of the country solely for partisan advantage." Defending the bill, West Virginia Democrat Robert Byrd alleged, "The drive for same-sex marriage is, in effect, an effort to make a sneak attack on society by encoding this aberrant behavior in legal form."[64]

More recently, in 2003, Republican senator from Pennsylvania Rick Santorum attacked legal moves to overturn a Texas sodomy law. These laws have been used sometimes to prosecute homosexuals. He denounced the decisions, saying, if you can have whatever kind of sex you want, then "you have the right to bigamy, you have the right to polygamy, you have the right to incest, you have the right to adultery. . . . All those things are antithetical to a healthy, stable, traditional family."

Tom DeLay and the House Republicans praised Santorum for "standing on principle." The president of the Gay and Lesbian Medical Association, in a letter to the *New York Times*, had a more critical view. Dr. Kenneth Haller pointed out that the Republicans "have done much to make the lives of lesbian and gay kids harder and have given fresh ammunition to those who would torment them."[65]

The Supreme Court ruled 5–4 in 2000 that it is legal for the Boy Scouts to exclude gays. There was not universal approval of this decision, and the organization lost some of its financial support. Some communities removed their support for the Boy Scouts; Los Angeles was one of these.[66] The Court's decision did validate antigay feelings among those having them. It also produced heartache for those boys who will not be allowed to be part of the scouting tradition.[67]

Some lower-court judges also validate homophobia: some lesbian mothers have lost their rights to their own (biological) children, not because they were deemed bad caretakers, but simply because of their sexual orientation.

In some states and counties where gay rights laws have been passed, right-wing organizations have organized to overturn them. They have also campaigned against textbooks and library books that present homosexuality as a legitimate lifestyle. One argument right-wingers use against federal funding for public television has been that it shows homosexuality in a positive light.

In West Virginia in 2003 a school program to encourage tolerance on many levels, including for homosexuality, came under fire from the Family Foundation, a fundamentalist Christian organization. Two hundred members of the Foundation, wearing "God Made Adam and Eve, Not Adam and Steve" T-shirts, went to a state Board of Education meeting and attacked the tolerance program, which was suspended.[68]

These types of actions and the statements and actions of powerful people and institutions help maintain a climate in which, for some, only heterosexuality is acceptable. If gays and lesbians are such a threat, it makes sense to use violence against them. In the same way, there are individuals, encouraged by powerful voices, who feel they have a right to use violence against racial and ethnic minorities, as discussed in the next chapter.

NOTES

1. "Massachusetts Campus Tense after Attacks on Women," *New York Times*, November 21, 1999, p. 32.

2. James Brooke, "Gay Man Beaten and Left for Dead; 2 Are Charged," *New York Times,* October 10, 1998, p. A9. The case became the basis for the critically acclaimed play *The Laramie Project.*

3. Preface to *Gender Violence: Interdisciplinary Perspectives*, ed. Laura O'Toole and Jessica Schiffman (New York: New York University Press, 1997), p. xii.

4. "The Roots of Male Violence," in O'Toole and Schiffman, *Gender Violence*, p. 8. This is their discussion of terms originally developed by R. W. Connell.

5. Ibid.

6. Quoted in Tamar Lewin, "Case Might Fit Pattern of Abuse, Experts Say," *New York Times*, June 19, 1994, p. 21.

7. Richard J. Gelles and Murray A. Straus, *Intimate Violence: The Causes and Consequences of Abuse in the American Family* (New York: Simon and Schuster, 1988), p. 92.

8. Michael P. Johnson, "Patriarchal Terrorism and Common Couple Violence: Two Forms of Violence against Women," *Journal of Marriage and the Family* 57 (1995): 283–94.

9. U.S. Department of Justice, Bureau of Justice Statistics, *Sourcebook of Criminal Justice Statistics—2000*, table 3.17, p. 196. These rates are about the same for whites, African Americans, and American Indians, but data for Latinos is not given; Callie Marie Rennison, "Intimate Partner Violence 1993–2001," U.S. Department of Justice, Bureau of Justice Statistics, February 2003, p.1; table 3.18, p. 197. Homicide rates, table 3.152, p. 317.

10. Nancy Gibbs, "Till Death Do Us Part," in *Crisis in American Institutions*,

9th ed., ed. Jerome H. Skolnick and Elliott Currie (New York: HarperCollins, 1994), p. 233.

11. Ronald M. Holmes and Stephen T. Holmes, *Murder in America* (Thousand Oaks, CA: Sage Publications, 1994), p. 20.

12. Philip J. Hilts, "6% of Women Admit Beatings While Pregnant," *New York Times*, March 4, 1994, p. 20; A. G. Riozzo et al., "Pregnancy a Risk Factor for Homicide," http://www.aast.org/01abstracts/01absPoster_105.html (accessed March 30, 2003); "MDPH Releases New Report on Pregnancy-Associated Deaths, May 28, 2002," http:/'www.stte.ma.us/dph/media/2002/pr0528.htm (accessed March 30, 2003).

13. Kathleen J. Ferraro, "Cops, Courts, and Woman Battering," in *Violence against Women: The Bloody Footprints*, ed. Pauline B. Bart and Eileen Geil Morgan (Newbury Park, CA: Sage, 1993), p. 167.

14. Lisa G. Lerman, "Prosecution of Wife Beaters: Institutional Obstacles and Innovations," in *Violence in the Home: Interdisciplinary Perspectives*, ed. Mary Lystad (New York: Brunner/Mazel, 1986), pp. 262–65; Demie Kurz, "Battering and the Criminal Justice System: A Feminist View," in *Domestic Violence: The Changing Criminal Justice Response*, ed. Eve S. Buzawa and Carl G. Buzawa (Westport, CT: Auburn House, 1992), p. 30; Lawrence W. Sherman and Richard A. Berk, "The Specific Deterrent Effects of Arrest for Domestic Assault," *American Sociological Review* 49 (1984): 261–72.

15. Clare Collins, "Spanking Is Becoming the New Don't," *New York Times*, May 11, 1995, p. C8. On European laws, see Sarah Lyall, "European Rights Court to Hear Case of British Boy's Caning," *New York Times*, October 10, 1996, p. A11.

16. U.S. Census Bureau, *Statistical Abstract of the United States, 2002*, table 320, p. 201.

17. American Public Health Association, position paper 9211, "Domestic Violence," pp. 3–4; Evan Stark and Anne H. Flitcraft, "Women and Children at Risk: A Feminist Perspective on Child Abuse," in *Women's Health, Politics, and Power: Essays on Sex/Gender, Medicine, and Public Health*, ed. Elizabeth Fee and Nancy Krieger (Amityville, NY: Baywood Publishing Co., 1994), pp. 313–19; Gelles and Straus, *Intimate Violence*, p. 63.

18. For a critique of the idea that a battered child necessarily becomes a battering adult, see Stark and Flitcraft, "Women and Children at Risk," p. 132. There is some evidence that children who have been abused are more likely to become violent criminals; Cathy Spatz Widon, *The Cycle of Violence* (Washington, DC: U.S. Department of Justice, 1992).

19. Mary Stewart, *Ordinary Violence: Assaults against Women* (Westport, CT: Bergin & Garvey, 2002), p. 100; Bureau of Justice Statistics, *Violence between Intimates*, November 1994, p. 2.

20. Child abuse data, Anne Crittendon, "Recession vs. Babies," *New York Times*, May 23, 1984; Youngstown data, "Private Violence," *Time*, September 5, 1983, p. 24.

21. Gelles and Straus, *Intimate Violence*, pp. 94–96.

22. "State Officials Move to Aid Abused Women on Insurance," *New York Times*, March 19, 1995, p. 30.

23. Catherine T. Kenney and Karen R. Brown, *Report from the Front Lines: The Impact of Violence on Poor Women* (New York: NOW Legal Defense and Education Fund, 1996).

24. Information from NOW'S Legal and Education Defense Fund, "Family Violence Option" State-by-State Summary, http://www.now.org/issues/economic/welfare/071102alert.html (accessed May 16, 2003).

25. Patricia Horn, "Beating Back the Revolution," *Dollars and Sense* (December 1992): 13, 22.

26. Ibid., p. 13.

27. Ibid., pp. 13, 22.

28. U.S. Department of Justice, Bureau of Justice Statistics, *Sourcebook of Criminal Justice Statistics—2000*, table 3.120, p. 27; table 3.1, p. 186. For difficulties in knowing rates of sexual assault, see Terri Spahr Nelson, *For Love of Country: Confronting Rape and Sexual Harassment in the U.S. Military* (New York: Haworth Maltreatment & Trauma Center, 2002), p. 66.

29. Quoted in Jane Gross, "Where 'Boys Will Be Boys' and Adults Are Befuddled," *New York Times*, March 29, 1993, p. A13; Seth Mydans, "High School Gang Accused of Raping for 'Points,'" *New York Times*, March 20, 1993, p. 6.

30. Diane Scully, *Understanding Sexual Violence: A Study of Convicted Rapists* (Boston: Unwin Hyman, 1992), p. 48.

31. Larry Baron and Murray A. Straus, *Four Theories of Rape in American Society: A State-Level Analysis* (New Haven, CT: Yale University Press, 1989), p. 185. Availability of pornography was also related to higher rape rates, although they downplay this association and are very concerned about the censorship issue. The evidence on pornography is controversial, with no clear nonlaboratory relationship proven. However, minimally, we can say that pornography illustrates the objectification of women and helps strengthen myths regarding women's sexual desires.

32. Quotes from an editorial in the *Nation*, May 29, 1989, cover. The Central Park Jogger case, as it was known, made headlines again in 2002. Five Harlem youths had confessed to the crime after long interrogations, which they later claimed were coerced. They spent from nine to thirteen years in prison, until a man confessed to the attack and DNA evidence corroborated his statements. In prison, three of them had insisted they were innocent. Because they refused to be penitent, they had no chance of parole. Their alleged actions gave rise to a new term, "wilding," meant to convey their depravity. Susan Salney, "Convictions and Charges Voided in '89 Central Park Jogger Attack," *New York Times,* December 20, 2002, pp. A1, B5; Jim Dwyer and Susan Salny, "Youths' Denials in '89 Rape Case Cost Them Parole Chances," *New York Times,* October 16, 2002, pp. B1, B8.

33. "Defendant Acquitted of Rape," *New York Times*, October 7, 1989.

34. Jay Livingstone, *Crime and Criminology*, 2nd ed. (Englewood Cliffs, NJ: Prentice-Hall, 1994), p. 185.

35. Ibid., p. 156.

36. Melinda Henneberger and Michel Marriot, "For Some, Rituals of Abuse Replace Youthful Courtship," *New York Times*, July 11, 1993, pp. 1, 33.

37. Peggy Reeves Sanday, *Fraternity Gang Rape: Sex Brotherhood and Privilege on Campus* (New York: New York University Press, 1990); Patricia Yancey Martin and Robert A. Hummer, "Fraternities and Rape on Campus," in *Rape and Society: Readings on the Problem of Sexual Assault*, ed. Patricia Searles and Ronald J. Berger (Boulder, CO: Westview Press, 1995).

38. "Here's One Way to Turn Off a Date," *New York Times*, January 12, 2003, Education Life sec., p. 7

39. Jeff Benedict, *Public Heroes, Private Felons: Athletes and Crimes against Women* (Boston: Northeastern University Press, 1997), p. x.

40. Ibid., p. 26.

41. Ibid., pp. 110–23.

42. Ibid., p. 147.

43. Bernard Lefkowitz, *Our Guys: The Glen Ridge Rape and the Secret Life of the Perfect Suburb* (New York: Vintage, 1997), p. 9; quote in Robert Lipsyte, "Must Boys Always Be Boys," *New York Times*, March 12, 1993, p. B7.

44. Quotes from Craig Wolf, "5 Youths Arrested in Rape of Coney Island Jogger," *New York Times*, April 14, 1994, p. B1; Ian Fisher, "Court Asked to Reinstate Rape Counts," *New York Times*, April 16, 1994, p. 27; Henneberger and Marriot, "For Some, Rituals of Abuse Replace Youthful Courtship," pp. 1, 33; Scully, *Understanding Sexual Violence*, pp. 158, 141, 142.

45. "Robert J. Billings Is Dead at 68, Helped Form the Moral Majority," *New York Times*, June 1, 1995, p. D21.

46. Frederick S. Jaffe, Barbara L. Lindheim, and Philip R. Lee, "Legal Abortion Improves Public Health," in *Abortion: Opposing Viewpoints*, ed. Bonnie Szumski (St. Paul, MN: Greenhaven Press, 1986), p. 148.

47. Quoted in Tamar Lewin, "Hurdles Increase for Many Women Seeking Abortions," *New York Times*, March 15, 1992, p. 18.

48. Ibid.

49. Lawrence K. Altman, "Panel Finds No Connection between Cancer and Abortion," *New York Times*, March 7, 2003, p. A22. For a list of Bush's antichoice actions, see editorial "The War against Women," *New York Times*, January 12, 2003, sec. 4, p. 14; "Government Limits Abortion Pill Coverage," *New York Times*, April 1, 2001, p. 22.

50. "President Bush Signs Partial Birth Abortion Ban Act of 2003," http://www.whitehouse.gov/news/releases/2003/11/20031105-1.html (accessed December 6, 2003); Robin Toner, "Measure Banning Abortion Method Wins House Vote," *New York Times*, June 5, 2003, pp. A1, A33; Sheryl Gay Stolberg, "Senate Approves Bill to Prohibit Type of Abortion," *New York Times*, October 22, 2003, pp. A1, A20; Robin Toner, "For G.O.P., It's a Moment," *New York Times*, November 6, 2003, pp. A1, A18.

51. Marlene Gerber Fried, "Reproductive Wrongs," *Women's Review of Books* 11 (July 1994): 7; "Shrinking Choice," *Nation*, May 29, 1995, pp. 743–44; Lewin, "Hurdles Increase for Many Women Seeking Abortions."

52. Kate Zernike, "Thirty Years after Abortion Ruling New Trends but the Old Debate," *New York Times*, January 20, 2003, p. A16.

53. Linda Villarosa, "Newest Skill for Future Ob-Gyns: Abortion Training," *New York Times,* June 11, 2002.

54. Lisa A. Foderaro, "Defense Intends to Make Trial of Doctor's Killer a Forum on Abortion," *New York Times*, March 3, 2003, p. B5; Rick Bragg, "Bomb Kills Guard at an Alabama Abortion Clinic," *New York Times*, January 30, 1998, pp. A1, A11; Ronald Smothers, "Abortion Doctor and Bodyguard Slain in Florida," *New York Times*, July 30, 1994, pp. 1, 26; Sara Rimer, "Gunmen Kills 2 at Abortion Clinics in Boston Suburb"; and John Kifner, "5 Are Wounded in 2 Shootings in Minutes," *New York Times*, December 31, 1995, pp. 1, 8, 9.

55. Tom Burghardt, "Neo-Nazis Salute the Anti-Abortion Zealots," *CAQ: CovertAction Quarterly* (Spring 1995): 26.

56. Quoted in Robert Pear, "Authorities Trying to Find the Reason for Clinic Attacks," *New York Times*, January 2, 1995, p. 10.

57. Kevin Sack, "2 Confess to Killing Man Saying He Made a Sexual Advance," *New York Times*, March 5, 1999, p. A10.

58. Quoted in Janice Kaplan, "Are Talk Shows Out of Control?" *TV Guide*, April 1, 1995, p. 10.

59. U.S. Department of Justice, Bureau of Justice Statistics, *Sourcebook of Criminal Justice Statistics—2000*, table 3.134, p. 305.

60. Kevin T. Berrill, "Anti-Gay Violence and Victimization in the United States: An Overview," in *Hate Crimes: Confronting Violence against Lesbians and Gay Men*, ed. Gregory M. Herek and Kevin T. Berrill (Newbury Park, CA: Sage Publications, 1992), pp. 19–45.

61. U.S. Department of Justice, Bureau of Justice Statistics, *Sourcebook of Criminal Justice Statistics—1993*, table 3.118, p. 375, and *Sourcebook of Criminal Justice Statistics—1994*, table, 3.105, p. 330; quote from David W. Dunlap, "Survey Details Gay Slayings around U.S.," *New York Times*, December 21, 1994, p. D21.

62. Francis X. Clines, "Slaying of a Gay Black Spurs Call for Justice," *New York Times*, July 13, 2000, p. A16.

63. Kristi Robles, "Dr. Laura Schlessinger: How Dangerous Is She?" *National Now Times* (Summer 2000): 17.

64. Eric Schmitt, "Senators Reject Both Job-Bias Ban and Gay Marriage," *New York Times*, September 11, 1996, p. A16. The Senate vote was 85–14. Another bill banning workplace discrimination against gays and lesbians was also defeated but by only one vote.

65. Santorum quoted in Adam Nagourney and Sheryl Gay Stolberg, "Impolitic, Maybe but in Character," *New York Times*, April 25, 2003, p. A22; edi-

torial, "Rally Round Intolerance," *New York Times*, May 4, 2003, sec. 4, p. 12; Tom DeLay quoted in Carl Hulse, "Republican Lawmakers Back Senator in Gay Dispute," *New York Times*, April 30, 2003, p. A22; letter, "Senator Santorum and His Critics," *New York Times*, May 2, 2003, p. A32.

66. Sarah Tippit, "If Boy Scouts Can Bar Gays, L.A. City Council Can Dump Scouts," *Newark (NJ) Star-Ledger*, November 29, 2000, p. 11.

67. Kate Zernike, "Scouts' Successful Ban on Gays Is Followed by Loss in Support," *New York Times*, August 29, 2000, pp. A1, A16.

68. Michael Winerup, "Promoting Tolerance, Not Paying Heed," *New York Times*, February 5, 2003, p. B9.

RACIAL AND ETHNIC INTERPERSONAL VIOLENCE

M any acts of violence can be interpreted as mechanisms for the maintenance of accustomed hierarchies. Some interpersonal violence can also be an outlet for the stress caused by corporate and political decisions that lead to such problems as unemployment. Many of the most serious problems in people's lives cannot be solved by their own efforts and seem overwhelming.

Using violence against others weaker than oneself is a low-risk way of feeling a sense of control and a reminder to both assailant and victim of who is more powerful. Some of this interpersonal violence can take the form of bias crimes. The homophobic attacks we discussed in the previous chapter fall into this category, as does much racial and ethnic violence.

BIAS CRIMES

Three white men—Shawn Allen Berry, Lawrence R. Brewer, and John Allen King—offered James Byrd Jr., a forty-nine-year-old African American man, a ride in a pickup truck. Somewhere along the way they chained their passenger to the rear bumper of their vehicle and dragged him along the road, dismembering his body. Two of the men were members of a white supremacist group called the Confederate Knights of America, which they had joined while in a Texas prison.[1]

Bias crimes, also called hate crimes or ethnoviolence, occur against a person who is identified as a member of a group toward which there is some degree of socially approved hostility. These despised targets are seen as violating the attackers' self-conception, their property, and/or their values. The ideas that justify such violent crimes are legitimated by prominent figures in our society. In addition, popular culture, films, television, and advertising help perpetuate stereotypes with slanted portrayals.

Hate crimes have three characteristics that distinguish them from other crimes. First, the attacks are often astonishingly vicious, especially considering the victims did nothing to their attackers. In street assaults, only about 7 percent of the victims have injuries that warrant hospital treatment, whereas 30 percent of hate crime attacks send the person to the hospital.[2] Second, hate crimes are often committed by groups of four or more assailants. This fact helps explain the brutality of the assaults. The larger the group, the less any single individual need feel responsible for his or (less often) her actions. The members of the group effectively give each other support for their behavior and create an atmosphere in which people are allowed to suspend their normal moral judgments. Finally, those committing hate crimes are generally young males. In racially motivated bias crimes, young men feel they are protecting their neighborhoods and families. White teenagers interviewed in Brooklyn express unequivocally why they attack African Americans:

> You go on missions to impress your friends. You get a name as a tough guy who is down with the neighborhood and down with his people.

> I have a reputation as a tough guy who defends the neighborhood and I want to keep it. People know when you've taken care of people who don't belong in the neighborhood. You get respect. Especially if it is some of the blacks.[3]

FINDING SCAPEGOATS

In 1989 sixteen-year-old African American Yusuf Hawkins was thought to be dating a white girl in Bensonhurst, Brooklyn. He was actually in that section with some friends looking for a used car. About twenty neighborhood white teenagers formed a mob. Hawkins was shot and killed, and his companions were injured. In anguish, Yusuf Hawkins's father lamented, "To see my son's life wasted because of some . . . fool with a gun in his hands who saw nothing but a black man is a very, very vile thing to me. Who will pay for this? Who will pay?" White residents, however, expressed no sense of remorse. A white teenage girl asserted, "The black people don't belong here. This is our neighborhood."

Howard Beach in Queens, New York, is a largely Italian American enclave. One sixteen-year-old bragged, "We own the turf of this neighborhood. If Whoopi Goldberg came into this neighborhood she'd be killed." The actress never came to Howard Beach, but on December 10, 1986, three black men did. Their car had broken down, and they went into a local pizza parlor to eat. On leaving, they were chased down by youths armed with bats, golf clubs, and tree limbs. One escaped with minor injuries, another was badly beaten, while the third, Michael Griffith, twenty-three, ran into traffic and was killed by an oncoming car.[4] Four people were indicted, three were convicted of manslaughter, and the fourth was acquitted on all counts. The community, however, supported the attackers, denying charges of racism and jeering the interracial march two thousand people held to protest this killing and other racial violence. A similar response greeted marchers protesting Yusuf Hawkins' death in Bensonhurst, also a mostly white, working-class community.

Having relatively little in a society that prizes material possessions, these white youth lay claim to their neighborhood; it is theirs. In another area of Brooklyn, in 1997 seventeen-year-old Larry Jackson showed a *New York Times* reporter a scar, the result of a beating from over a dozen white teenagers who struck him with a hockey stick when he walked onto a basketball court in a nearby Italian American community, Carroll Gardens. A white youth on that basketball court explained why such a violent attack would occur, "It's boundaries. You pass the line, you get chased out." Kevin Teague, an African American United Parcel Service worker working in this neighborhood, was chased, hit by a car, kicked, and beaten with a steering wheel lock and a baseball bat. A disapproving white resident of Carroll Gardens predicted that the young men who attacked Kevin Teague would not "shed a tear. They're going to wear this as a badge of honor. That's the scariest thing of all."[5]

Economic downturns have hurt many in the United States. When unemployment rises, even those with jobs can become anxious and fearful. A job today is no guarantee of a job tomorrow. People seek to understand these problems. Why doesn't the system they believe in work for them? Feeling unjustly treated, they turn their anger against scapegoats, especially African Americans, who they think are getting special treatment through affirmative action.

A study of attitudes in white, working-class areas with histories of racial conflict illustrates the anger white teenagers have about unemployment. Many felt that they were losing jobs to African Americans. One said, "You know I been lookin' for work for awhile but I can't get a job 'cause they're givin' them all to the black people." They described blacks as dangerous criminals who get away with their crimes. A black comes to your neighborhood for one thing, to "look for trouble," and the violence against African Americans was justified as a form of community defense.[6]

Scapegoats are not chosen at random. They are groups who are (1) socially approved targets of hostility; (2) vulnerable, less protected against physical attacks; and (3) visibly different from the majority, with some characteristic such as skin color or accent that allows them to be singled out.

It is almost a reflex for some to blame people of color for their problems. When there was an 11 percent increase in hate crimes between 1991 and 1992, the director of Los Angeles County's Human Relations Commission explained: "People are more angry, more hostile, there's more bitterness. . . . There are many people out there who are threatened by the changes in their personal economic circumstances, and they use this occasion to stereotype and scapegoat others."[7]

An instructive example of scapegoating comes from northern New Jersey. In the early 1980s towns with overbuilding and inadequate drainage experienced damage following heavy rains and subsequent floods. One woman pondered her losses, including "two cars, my son's motorcycle, the French provincial in the living room . . . my husband's worked all his life for this. Everyone talks about the poor people. What about the middle class? We're paying for those people in Newark to sit around so they don't have to work." She is blaming the largely black and Latino population of Newark for her plight. She then finds another group to accuse:

> I used to work nights. Right now I have to get a job to put my house in order, but I'm not qualified to do anything. I tell you it's not right. How long are you going to be able to hold a job when they're letting in people from other places?

She understands the government isn't always on her side: "I got five kids living at home. Four of them are older and work. The government lets me claim only one on my income tax. Is that fair? No one is giving us the answers."[8] She has answers, however. Immigrants, blacks on welfare, they are all somehow implicated in her lack of qualifications, her inability to find work, and her high taxes. Some politicians encourage this kind of thinking, a substitute for rational analysis of social conditions. Over and over one hears that "they" are responsible for the problems of the good, hard-working (white implicitly understood) people, and the media very rarely correct the misrepresentations.

As with the Willie Horton ads mentioned earlier, politicians take advantage of white fears. When three white students claimed they were denied admission to the University of Michigan because they were white, George W. Bush attacked the university's admissions policies, which do take race and ethnicity into consideration when evaluating applicants. In a nationally televised speech in January 2003, the president attacked the university for using "a quota system."

Many whites mistakenly think that in several areas there are "quotas" for minorities regardless of any qualifications a person might have. This is false. Quotas are exceedingly rare and are usually illegal. Quotas are not used at the University of Michigan as was pointed out by Lee C. Bollinger, the university's former president who is now president of Columbia University.[9] There was no legal need for Bush to have said anything at all regarding this case. The Supreme Court in October 2003 upheld the right of the university to consider race when making decisions.

A month before Bush's comments, Republican Senate majority leader Trent Lott of Mississippi infuriated supporters of racial equality when he said if Strom Thurmond had been elected president in 1948, "we wouldn't have had all these problems over these years." He also mentioned that his state had gone for the South Carolina governor and that "we're proud of it." The remark offended so many because of Thurmond's unrelenting opposition to civil rights. This was not the first time Senator Lott had shown support for racist policies and positions.[10] As a result of the controversy, President Bush felt compelled to distance himself from the remarks, and Lott resigned as Senate majority leader but not from the Senate.

In his 1992 North Carolina senatorial campaign, Jesse Helms used an ad depicting the white hands of a job seeker crushing and flinging away a letter of rejection. The commentary blamed affirmative action for having cost the white man his chance. Ex-Klansman David Duke, changing his sheets for a respectable dark suit, was elected to the Louisiana state legislature in 1989 and almost became Republican governor of that state in 1991. He changed his clothes but not his basic message. In his campaign, Duke, founder of the National Association for the Advancement of White People, attacked an allegedly growing welfare system, asking, "Why should your tax dollars go to people to buy lottery tickets?" In April 2003

Duke, who had swindled his followers out of hundreds of thousands of dollars, began a fifteen-month prison sentence in a Texas federal prison. He had been found guilty of tax and mail fraud.[11]

Former Republican senator and 1996 Republican presidential nominee Robert Dole encouraged whites to feel they are the victims of affirmative action, alleging:

> The people in America are paying a price for things that were done before they were born. We did discriminate. We did suppress people. It was wrong. Slavery was wrong. But should future generations have to pay for that?[12]

Sen. John McCain used the anti-Asian ethnic slur "gook, referring to his North Vietnamese army captors," several times in his bid to win the California Republican primary vote in 2000. The press mostly ignored these comments.[13]

The FBI issues national hate crime statistics. According to their figures, in 2001 there were a total of 9,730 "offenses," a 21 percent increase from the 8,063 record in 2000. Much of that increase was a result of attacks on those believed to be "Arab," discussed more below. African Americans are consistently the most frequent victims of racially motivated attacks. In 2001 they were 31 percent of the 12,020 hate crime victims.[14]

In Jersey City, New Jersey, in 1987, Dr. Karushal Sharan, an Indian doctor, was severely beaten with an iron pipe by three men in their early twenties, one of them an off-duty police officer. In the same year, in the nearby city of Hoboken, four teenagers were involved in killing Navroze Mody, also an Indian. They assaulted Mody with bricks and repeatedly kicked him but left his white companion alone. The feelings expressed by some of the white residents reveal deep-seated racial resentment; Jersey City and Hoboken were once thriving blue-collar communities, but the factories are gone, and the future for working-class white kids without college educations is bleak.

One Jersey City youth complained, "They're not clean, they smell, they take our jobs." His father was a construction worker, but the son can't find decent-paying work and is trying to become a boxer. His mother is bitter. "I have no future here," she lamented. "My kids have no future here, we're lost." She resents the fact that she's lived in Jersey City all her life but can barely afford her rent, much less buy a house, while Indians come and buy property.[15]

Sometimes the economic anxieties behind bias crimes are very clear. Vincent Chin, a twenty-seven-year-old Chinese American, was celebrating his upcoming marriage in a Detroit bar when he was confronted by two laid-off autoworkers, Ronald Ebens and Michael Nitz. They mistook him for a Japanese and yelled, "It's because of you we're out of work." Later they followed him out of the bar and beat him to death with a baseball bat. A judge fined the two men $3,780 and gave them three years on probation. Following protests by outraged Asian Americans, the U.S. Department of Justice filed civil rights charges against the assailants. Nitz was acquitted, Ebens sentenced to twenty-five years. On appeal this sentence was overturned, and in a subsequent retrial in 1987, Nitz was again acquitted. Ten years later, in California, a Japanese real estate consultant was killed after being harassed by two men who also blamed the Japanese for their unemployment.[16]

Twenty years after the death of Vincent Chin, mainly Asian American college students held a commemorative meeting, which included a march to Vincent Chin's grave. They carried a banner that had been used at the protest march at the time of the killing, white with Vincent Chin's last words in bright red, "It's not fair." He had said that before lapsing into a coma.[17] In 1999 the FBI reported 363 bias offenses against people with Asian backgrounds.

Each hate crime attack is a statement to all people of color that their freedom is restricted. They cannot freely live where they want, go where they want, or conduct the ordinary business of life: buying a car, eating a slice of pizza, going to a bar, walking down the street. In 1996 one of my students of Indian descent described the impact of anti-Indian acts on his family and himself. Years after the killing of Navroze Mody, he wrote about how they no longer shopped for Indian groceries in Jersey City.

> My dad felt it was too risky to go there and buy groceries because he was afraid of us getting hurt. I myself felt a little scared inside even though I lived very far from Jersey City. I was in eighth grade then and couldn't think of any reason why someone would want to hurt me just because of my race.

African American anger and resentment can also lead to bias crimes, although African Americans are still much more likely to be victims than assailants. Some of these incidents are well publicized. On December 7, 1993, evening rush hour passengers on the Long Island Railroad—reading, daydreaming, dozing—suddenly heard gunshots from Colin Ferguson's 9 mm handgun. Seventeen people were injured and six died. He reportedly wanted to get even with whites who he felt had mistreated him. In 1992 there occurred the severe beating of Reginald Denny, a white truck driver pulled from his van during the uprising that followed the verdict in the police beating of Rodney King, discussed below.

Jews and Koreans have been targets of black rage. In Crown Heights, Brooklyn, African Americans and Jews live in close proximity. Some blacks believe Jews have been given preferential treatment in housing and seem to be more affluent than they are. In the summer of 1991 a car driven by a member of a Jewish sect, the Hasidim, struck and killed a seven-year-old-black boy. Many African Americans believed that a Hasidic ambulance driver had callously ignored the boy. There was rioting, and some days later, a twenty-nine-year-old Australian rabbinical student was stabbed to death by a black assailant.[18]

Koreans, who have economic advantages and educational backgrounds that many U.S blacks lack, frequently set up stores in African American neighborhoods where rents are lower and there are few large supermarkets. In 1991 in Los Angeles, Soon Ja Du, a Korean American grocer, got into a fight with fifteen-year-old Latasha Harlins, accusing her of shoplifting a $1.79 bottle of orange juice. Although she gave him the money, he killed her anyway with a shot to the back of her head as she was leaving. The African American community was outraged when a court sentenced Du to a fine of only $500 and some community service. During the next year's uprisings, nearly two thousand Korean businesses were looted and burned.[19]

Since September 11, 2001, people who are assumed to be from the Middle East and/or believed to be Muslims have become victims of hate crimes. From being among the least common bias crimes, in the words of the FBI, "anti-Islamic religion incidents . . . in 2001 became the second highest reported among religious-bias incidents . . . growing by more than 1,600 percent." There were "554 victims of crimes motivated by bias toward the Islamic religion."[20]

Sometimes people of other ethnicities are mistaken for "Arabs" and targeted. In Queens, New York, a man killed four storeowners, convinced they were Middle Easterners, though only one actually was. The government's singling out of people from the Middle East and Pakistan for special repressive measures sends the message that these people are not to be trusted.

Some clergy have vilified Islam, as have several prominent conservative figures. Billy Graham's son, the evangelist Franklin Graham, described Islam as "a very evil and wicked religion." Graham delivered the invocation at George W. Bush's inauguration. Jerry Vines, past president of the Southern Baptist Convention, the largest Protestant denomination in the United States, described Muhammad as a "demon-possessed pedophile."

Pat Robertson, who operates the Christian Broadcasting Network, and the Reverend Jerry Falwell have attacked Islam as a violent religion. Paul Weyrich and William Lind wrote a booklet called "Why Islam Is a Threat to America and the West." Ann Coulter, a prominent right-winger often on TV talk shows, said of this group, "We should invade their countries, kill their leaders, and convert them to Christianity."[21]

Robert E. Pierre, writing in the *Washington Post* about Arab Americans in Dearborn, Michigan, describes their reaction to having "their relatives called in for random interviews. Their brethren . . . being held in U.S. jails on suspicion of terrorism, some without a hint from the government about their alleged crimes." He quotes Rita Zawideah, founder of the Arab American Community Coalition.

> Women are being followed in their cars for wearing a *hijab* [head covering]. One woman had her health insurance dropped by a company that told her, "We don't sell to immigrants." We don't know what rules, what rights we have as U.S. citizens.[22]

Reflecting on the World War II internment of Japanese Americans, a Dearborn resident said, "Arabs who live in this country are Americans, too. Haven't we learned anything since World War II? I don't think so." As the war with Iraq began in March 2003, more Arab Americans became disquieted. Zeinab Abba, nineteen, worried, "As soon as something happens like this, I am not looked at as an American." Her sister was afraid to wear her *hijab* to school.[23]

Some disturbed individuals commit murderous hate crimes. One of the significant things about these acts is that a person feeling great rage chooses as targets people he has learned are undesirable human beings, members of despised ethnic groups. In the Pittsburgh suburb of Mount Lebanon, Richard Baumhammers shot his Jewish neighbor, an Indian grocery store employee, an African American student, and two Asian restaurant workers. Baumhammers, who was undergoing psychiatric treatment, also sprayed two synagogues with bullets. A congregant at one of the synagogues said, "We're strongly opposed to all this gun action in America. With guns, people with mental problems and hate in their hearts have the opportunity to devastate the community."[24]

In Bloomington, Indiana, August Smith, who had changed his first name from Benjamin because it sounded like a Jewish name, fired a handgun at those he considered the "mud people"—Asians. The former Indiana University student also killed one Korean and one African American and wounded a total of nine others—Jews, Asians, and African Americans. He ended his spree by killing himself. Previously, he had shot Asians and African Americans at the University of Illinois and Jews, Asians, and African Americans in Chicago suburbs.[25]

While attending the University of Illinois at Urbana-Champaign, August Smith had met a campus recruiter for the World Church of the Creator, a racist, anti-Semitic organization. Smith was also associated with the White Nationalist Party, distributing leaflets of both groups.

ORGANIZED HATE GROUPS

Following the April 1995 bombing of an Oklahoma City federal building, the media spotlight turned to organized armed hate groups. The attention was overdue: groups with explicitly racist agendas have long been a feature of American society. They are indicative of the anger and suspicion that exist among some whites, and their readiness for violence makes them very dangerous.

There have been no reports of organized racist groups among non-whites, and there is not much analysis of why this is the case. One reason could be that such groups are unlikely to be tolerated by the authorities and would be quickly detected and repressed at an early stage. In the past, even nonviolent expressions of black pride have been viewed in the larger community with hostility and fear. This was the case with the "black power" movement in the 1960s and 1970s. Black power was a call for African American communities to run their own economic and political institutions and an affirmation of the worth of their African heritage. Whites, however, felt it was a racist attack on them.

Hate groups are sometimes collectively referred to as neo-Nazis because of the similarity between their agendas and that of the German fascists, whom they openly admire. Such groups offer support, advice, companionship, excitement, and hope to lonely, bored, and pessimistic white people. Their activist program seems an alternative to the empty promises of traditional politicians.

The organizations are antiliberal, antiblack, anti-immigrant, antigovernment, prowhite Christian supremacists, and they are often heavily armed. White opponents of their ideas are labeled "race traitors" and become potential victims of violence.

Prisons are a fertile recruiting ground for racist organizations, which seem to be tolerated, and perhaps even encouraged, by prison authorities. Recently, members of racist prison gangs, on their release, have been moving into northern Utah. They can be identified by their tattoos, often acquired while they were incarcerated. They have engaged in armed robberies, auto thefts, burglaries, and drug trafficking. The chief of intelligence for the Utah Department of Corrections noted, "White Supremacy has absolutely exploded within our prison system since the mid-1990s. And it's growing all over the nation." The World Church of the Creator is among the largest of these. As a "church" its members can hold meetings in prisons.[26]

There are no firm figures on how large these organizations are. Their active membership is estimated at from ten thousand to twenty thousand with at least two hundred thousand supporters.[27] It is believed that they are directly responsible for about 15 percent of violent racial incidents. However, their messages may incite actions by others not directly involved in their organizations. They have rock bands, computer networks, and cable TV shows. Ex-Klanner and founder of the White Aryan Resistance (WAR) Tom Metzger has a cable show based in San Diego called *Race and Reason*. Among other things, the show tells interested viewers how to contact the "Aryan Update" hot line.

WAR racism wasn't limited to American blacks. The organization was held responsible for the beating death of an Ethiopian student in Portland, Oregon. In 1988 skinheads armed with baseball bats and steel-plated shoes attacked Mulugeta Seraw and two friends. Mulugeta Seraw died of a fractured skull, and his friends had lesser injuries. One assailant was eventually sentenced to life imprisonment and the two others to twenty-year sentences. The attackers were found to be closely connected to Metzger's group.

Alan Berg was a talk show radio host at station KOA in Denver, Colorado, and unusually liberal for his profession. He often got into arguments with white supremacist listeners, challenging their claims that the Holocaust never happened and that Jews run the government and the banks. One evening in June 1984, he drove into his driveway and was killed as he left his car. Thirteen shots were fired at him from a submachine gun. The murder weapon was eventually found in Idaho, where a number of white supremacist groups were headquartered, and two men, members of the Order, were found guilty of violating his civil rights. This may seem a strange charge given that Berg was murdered. However, this is the way in which the federal government is able to prosecute racially motivated murderers. There are federal civil rights laws, but only a very few types of homicide are federal crimes, and bias killings are not among them.

REPRESSIVE POLICE VIOLENCE: KEEPING A LID ON

Police violence can be an example of both organizational violence and interpersonal violence, which is the major focus here. Even when the police engage in interpersonal violence, there are elements in the structure and culture of police departments that help account for the "above the call of duty" violence committed by some police officers.

In March 1991 George Holliday awoke a little after midnight, disturbed by noises from the street below. Looking out of his window, he saw a helicopter and six police cars. On the ground, an African American man, Rodney King, was trying to evade police blows and kicks. Holliday used his new video camera to record one of the most famous incidents of police brutality in recent history. His ninety-second video showed four cops hitting King fifty-six times as he lay on the ground while fourteen others, ten from the LAPD, the rest from other agencies, watched.

Holliday's videotape of the incident seemed clear enough evidence that the police engaged in excessive force. Nonetheless, there were whites who claimed that only reasonable force had been used. The police were tried and acquitted in Simi Valley, a virtually all-white community. Their acquittal was followed by what has been repeatedly described as the costliest riot in U.S. history: at least thirty-eight people died, and there was over $1 billion worth of property damage. The protests resulted in federal charges against several officers. Two were found guilty by a Los Angeles jury, yet the judge sentenced them to two-and-a-half-year prison terms out of the possible ten years they could have received. These were the two who, after beating King, deprecated the seriousness of their attack. One radio conversation went: "I haven't beaten anyone this bad in a long time." The response from a second caller was: "Oh not again. . . . Thought you agreed to chill out for a while."[28]

The King case was a dramatic example of a pattern of racism in the LAPD. Three years after this incident, veteran LAPD officer Mark Fuhrman's racism was exposed during the O. J. Simpson trial. During his years on the force, Fuhrman had openly expressed contempt for people of color as well as for women, including his own colleagues. He had used racial epithets, planted evidence, and may even have tortured suspects. Yet in an example of denying responsibility for the behavior of individual officers, LAPD chief Williams claimed that Fuhrman's behavior was atypical of his police force, saying, "The few bad apples that came out in the trial such as Mark Fuhrman are not reflective of the LAPD."[29] Although the department knew his beliefs and behavior, Fuhrman remained on the force until he voluntarily retired.

Fuhrman was not just one "bad apple" in a nonracist barrel. In 1990 alone, Los Angeles paid over $11 million in suits against the department. African Americans filed 41 percent of the 4,400 misconduct charges made against the LAPD between 1987 and 1990. In 1982, ten years prior to King's beating, LA's longtime police chief Darryl Gates offered this defense of the chokehold, a method of restraint favored by the LAPD that had resulted in numerous fatalities: "In some blacks when it is applied the veins or arteries do not open up as fast as they do in normal people."[30]

In brief, the higher levels of the police force, responsible for the conduct of those they supervised, explicitly encouraged racist attitudes. Those in the city government responsible for the running of police agencies apparently did not have a problem with these biases, either.

African Americans throughout the country frequently experience beatings, shovings, and humiliating searches from the police. Some are killed even though they have committed no offense. In 1996 Amnesty International issued a report on police brutality in New York City, which has the nation's largest urban police department. Amnesty documented the disproportionate number of people of color physically abused and sometimes killed, often by shots in the back, in situations that, according to Amnesty, "did not warrant the use of lethal force" and were "in violation of police guidelines and international standards."[31]

Internationally agreed-upon UN documents specify when force can be used by the police. The criteria are set forth in the UN Basic Principles on the Use of Force and Firearms by Law Enforcement Officials and in the UN Code of Conduct for Law Enforcement Officials. Police departments in the United States have their own similar guidelines. Amnesty International summarizes the intention of these guidelines. Force is to be used "as a last resort; when used," it must be in proportion "to the threat encountered and designed to minimize damage or injury." However, "in many instances these guidelines are disregarded and police officers have used levels of force entirely disproportionate to the threat faced."[32]

In 1998 Amnesty documented the physical and financial costs of police brutality:

> Thousands of individual complaints about police abuse are reported each year and local authorities pay out millions of dollars to victims in damages after lawsuits. Police officers have beaten and shot unresisting suspects; they have misused batons, chemical sprays, and electroshock

weapons; they have injured or killed people by placing them in dangerous restraint holds. The overwhelming majority of victims in many areas are members of racial or ethnic minorities.[33]

On July 4, 1996, a twenty-five-year-old unarmed African American man, Nathaniel Levi Gaines Jr., was shot in the back by New York City police officer Paolo Colecchia, who already had several complaints against him. In 1994 he had been briefly suspended for giving false information during an investigation of some of these. Nathaniel Gaines Sr. expressed his feelings about his son's death: "We are not oblivious to the history of the criminal justice system. We didn't want to say that his life was taken because he was born with his skin dark. But there is no other explanation."[34]

An example of nonfatal brutality comes from the case of Abner Louima. The thirty-three-year-old Haitian immigrant who lived in Brooklyn was working as a security guard trying to earn money for an American college education. After attending a nightclub, he along with several others intervened in a fight outside the club. The police came on the scene; Louima was arrested and taken to the station house, where police lieutenant Justin Volpe sodomized him with a broom handle. Howard Safir, then police commissioner, described the incident as "a rare event."[35]

The fatal shooting of Amadou Diallo in February of 1999 was memorialized in Bruce Springsteen's "41 Shots." The title refers to the number of bullets fired at Diallo by four members of the NYPD's Street Crime Unit (SCU). Nineteen of the bullets struck him. The unit's motto was "We Own the Night."

What happened in this case illustrates several points made here about racism and the police, including the stereotyping of African American men and support for racist behavior from their own organizational hierarchy. The four cops were by their account looking for a rapist. They spotted Diallo and thought his behavior suspicious. Recounting the events, Officer Sean Carroll said, "He stepped backward, back into the vestibule . . . like he didn't want to be seen. . . . I am getting a little leery, from the training, of my past experience of arrests." Then while the wary officers watched, Diallo reached for the right side of his jacket and removed something Carroll assumed was a gun. Carroll shot at Diallo, and then the others started firing as well. Carroll described what happened after the shooting stopped: "When I removed the object from his hand, which I believed to be a gun, I grabbed it, and it felt soft. I looked down at it . . . and I seen it was a wallet."[36]

One of the officers in the Diallo case had five unsubstantiated civilian complaints against him; another had one that involved a fatal shooting.

After protest marches the police were indicted on several different charges, including murder, manslaughter, and reckless endangerment. Their trial was held in Albany, New York, on the grounds that an unbiased jury could not be found in New York City itself. The four were acquitted of all charges. Amadou's disappointed mother, Kadiatou Diallo, lamented, "No human being deserves to die like that. Standing in front of your doorway where you live. Is that a crime? All he was doing was going home."[37]

Between 1997 and 1998 the Street Crime Unit, described in numerous accounts as "elite," had conducted searches of forty-five thousand men, almost all of color, and had made nine thousand arrests. This means that 80 percent of these "stop and frisks" showed no wrongdoing. In turn, it indicates that the SCU, and very likely the regular police as well, are singling out people for police attention on the basis of what sociologists call "ascribed characteristics," those aspects of yourself you can't change, in this case race, gender, and age.

Yvette Walton was one of the very few African American women assigned to the Street Crime Unit. Following the Diallo shooting, she was fired after she publicly accused the unit of racist behavior. She took her case to federal court where she was defended by the New York Civil Liberties Union. The judge found that her First Amendment rights had been violated, stating, "She would not have been dismissed had she not spoken out publicly on behalf of 100 Blacks in Law Enforcement on an issue of immediate and substantial concern to the Department." He also described the police department's own witnesses against her as "incredible."[38]

Four years after Amadou Diallos's death, Salimanto Sanfo left her home in Burkina Faso and came to New York City. She made her first long trip to attend ceremonies in memory of her husband, Ousmane Zongo, who had been fatally shot by plainclothes police officer Bryan Conroy. Conroy was searching a Manhattan warehouse looking for people who were bootlegging CDs. The unarmed Zongo, who had an art repair workshop in the building and had nothing to do with the bootlegging, was shot four times. Conroy defended himself by asserting that Zongo kept approaching him.[39]

Most killings receive less attention than Diallo's. In order to put a face on what would otherwise be anonymous statistics, families of victims, the National Lawyers Guild, the October 22nd Coalition to Stop Police Brutality, Repression and the Criminalization of a Generation, and the Anthony Baez Foundation created the Stolen Lives Project. The project documents unjustified killings, mostly of people of color, by law enforcement agents and the U.S. border patrol. For the period 1990 to 1999 they documented over two thousand cases covering forty-eight states and Washington, DC. Seventy-five percent of the cases described in the book are African American or Latino.[40]

The Anthony Baez Foundation was started by the family of a young Latino man living in the Bronx who was killed in 1994 by officer Frances Livotti. Baez, who suffered from asthma, was playing touch football with his three brothers outside their home. The ball hit Livotti's car. He got out and began beating the youngest brother, David. When Anthony tried to mediate, Livotti put him in a fatal chokehold. Community protests resulted in Livotti being brought to trial. He was acquitted even though the presiding judge maintained there was a "nest of perjury" among Livotti's colleagues. He was, however, found guilty of violating Anthony Baez's civil rights.[41]

The violent tactics of the war on drugs combine with racial stereotypes to lead to some police brutality. Around the country there are thirty thousand SWAT teams who target alleged gang members and drug dealers, using loose criteria as to who belongs in these categories. In 2000 one of the teams, the Los Angeles Police Department's CRASH unit, was itself investigated. CRASH stands for Community Resources Against Street Hoodlums. A hoodlum could be identified if he was a young person wearing "gang" clothes, having tattoos, or associating with gang members. The violent assaults of CRASH members against inner-city young men were revealed when an officer was found to be dealing in cocaine himself, stealing the drug from the police evidence room. In hopes of a lighter sentence for his own crimes, he revealed incidents of planting guns on suspects, beating people, and turning immigrants over to the Immigration and Naturalization Service.[42]

In March 2000 three undercover officers who claimed they wanted to buy drugs from him stopped Patrick Dorismond, like Diallo, a New York City security guard. He became indignant at being taken for a dealer. A fight ensued, and Det. Anthony Vasquez shot him to death. In an example of victim blaming, then mayor Rudolph Giuliani said that Dorismond was no "altar boy" and had a "pretty bad record." He also released sealed arrest records from Dorismond's youth. Patrick Dorismond's family sued the city, which settled with them for $2.25 million. This, like other financial settlements, is done at taxpayers' expense. A month earlier the mayor had claimed that blacks were overly fearful of the police, whose behavior he described as "a model of restraint."[43]

Pulitzer prize–winning writer David K. Shipler, who has done research on police racism throughout the United States, said about two years of data collection, "I have encountered very few black men who have not been has-sled by white cops."[44] In recent years this hassling has been given a name, *racial profiling*.[45] Many African Americans tell, for example, how they were stopped by the police for "driving while black." Often this is a very unpleasant experience without direct physical consequences, but some-times police suspicion of people of color leads to injuries.

Profiling on the New Jersey Turnpike became an issue in the late 1990s when, then governor and former EPA head, Christine Todd Whitman, ap-pointed her embattled attorney general, Peter G. Verniero, to the New Jersey Supreme Court even though his legal experience was relatively lim-ited. Verniero had presided over a state police agency that engaged in racial profiling.[46]

A training manual for troopers titled "Occupant Identifiers for Possible Drug Couriers" identified particular ethnic groups that should be viewed with suspicion. The list included African Americans and Latinos who were driving together. Apparently acting on this advice, in 1998 two troopers stopped a van and shot at the four men in it, three black and one Latino. Three of the vehicle's occupants were injured. A study of stops for 1997 conducted by New Jersey's major newspaper, the *Star Ledger*, revealed that 73 percent of those arrested on the New Jersey Turnpike were people of color. Racism among the state troopers affects the troopers themselves. African American and Latino troopers testified that on the job they had been subjected to racial slurs and discrimination.[47]

On the West Coast as well as the East, African Americans and Latinos are more likely to be stopped by the police than are other groups. In San Diego blacks are 8 percent of the driving-age population but account for 12 percent of all traffic stops and 20 percent of those who are searched. Latinos make up 20 percent of the driving-age population but account for 29 percent of traffic stops and 50 percent of searches. As of 2000 five states had passed laws making it illegal to stop people just because of their race, and a number of departments have mandated collecting data on traffic stops. In New Jersey state troopers' cars are now supposed to be equipped with video cameras.[48]

Racial profiling of New Jersey drivers is partly an outgrowth of the way the war on drugs is conducted. The Drug Enforcement Agency in 1989 enlisted the New Jersey State Police into their "Operation Pipeline" meant to curtail the movement of drugs from Florida to various U.S. cities. Even though black and Latino troopers revealed that they were supposed to use ethnicity and race as criteria for who to stop and statistical evidence mounted of disproportionate stopping of people of color, no investigation of possible abuses took place.[49]

Racism puts African American officers in danger from their own colleagues. Don Jackson, a Long Beach, California, cop, was investigating police racism for a local TV station. He was stopped, and his head was shoved through a window. In Philadelphia a black female officer was beaten with fists and flashlights by fellow police who mistook her for a suspect. She identified herself as a police officer, but they kept hitting her. She said, "It was like Rodney King—only I'm a cop. Even if I wasn't a cop, they had no right to beat somebody like that. Not in the head. You hit in places you're taught to hit."

Minority cops attest to the extra dangers they face when out of uniform. The chairwoman of the National Black Police Association claims, "Police who are not in uniform and who are black are subject to being attacked much quicker than white officers who are not in uniform."[50] In New York City at least, African American officers don't shoot white ones. William R. Bracey, former head of the black police organization, the Guardians Association, notes that no African American "cop has . . . shot another officer while on duty or in civilian clothes or killed him. Black officers know that there's another side."[51]

Not all white cops are racists, but, as we have seen, police departments in many parts of the United States tolerate the attacks described above. A professor who beats up nonwhite students or a bank teller who makes racist remarks to her or his customers would unlikely be able to keep her or his job, but police officers with racist assault records often stay on the force.

Institutional racism has resulted in appalling social conditions for many minorities and is largely responsible for high rates of street crime, as we saw in chapters 9 and 10. Into this situation come the police, with an impossible and frustrating job. They are supposed to prevent crime, yet they are unable to remedy the conditions that cause crime. There is pressure to make arrests, to show the public that city government is fighting crime, which many whites—including police—view as a natural product of communities of color. The police are as likely as anyone else to hold the stereotype that sees African American and Latino males as violent criminals. These factors help explain police violence toward blacks and Latinos.

The structure of police forces heighten the likelihood of acts of violence committed by the police against the very people they are supposed to be protecting. Police departments are organized in a quasi-militaristic way, with the police trained to go out to fight "wars."[52] A sense of "us" against

"them" heightens the solidarity of the police and their willingness to protect each other, which sometimes includes concealing acts of brutality. The
Amnesty report mentioned above refers to "the 'code of silence' in which
police officers refuse to testify against their colleagues."[53]

The bureaucratic tactics discussed in chapter 4 come into play in police
departments. In New York a committee that was supposed to review police
shootings of colleagues was disbanded without issuing any recommendations. Former chief of patrol William R. Bracey, quoted above, sat on the
short-lived committee. He explained:

> The Police Department just didn't want to touch the race issue because it
> was too politically explosive. So they just stopped having meetings, and
> if they ever issued a final report they never told us committee members
> about it.

Bureaucratic doublespeak veils the violence. In New York the police department refers to reacting on the basis of stereotypes as the "symbolic
opponent syndrome."[54]

African American writer James Baldwin graphically described ghettos as
"occupied territory" where police keep an eye on the inhabitants, making sure
they stay in their place, in effect, playing the role of a colonial army.[55] The
term occupying army is still used by those in the ghettos, and the police themselves see this as a valid description. A police station in The Bronx called itself
"Fort Apache" after the Western fort used to control that group of Indians.

Under these circumstances, minority communities don't see the police
protecting them from their real victimizers—exploitative landlords and
indifferent politicians. In fact, the only representatives of city government
who are consistently in their neighborhoods are the armed police acting as
judge, jury, and sometimes executioner.

Some police officials and officers themselves understand the forces
that lead to excessive use of force. A former New York City official, John
S. Pritchard III, explains:

> The underlying causes of brutality for a lot of cops in New York and other
> big cities are fear, racism, and misunderstanding of other cultures. They
> fear that new immigrants and new arrivals in the city are unwashed hordes
> about to take over the streets.[56]

Philip Boniface, a consulting psychologist for police departments, describes
how attitudes that lead to brutality develop. He notes that many recruits

come on the job full of idealism that they are heroes going to help people. They soon get frustrated about many conditions that they are powerless to stop. After a year or two, some of them begin to view the neighborhood as populated with adversaries, people without virtue who don't deserve respect.

He explains how peer pressure and the inequality between the police and neighborhood residents exacerbate the problem.

You have young armed men who have never had power before beginning to believe that the streets they patrol are their streets and they have the power and mastery over people they encounter. Many of them quickly assume a tough-guy attitude. Otherwise they fear their peers will look on them unfavorably.[57]

In *New York Times* op-ed pieces two police veterans expressed eloquently the untenable situation existing between police and ghetto residents. Edmund Stubbing had worked six years in Harlem when in 1980 he wrote of his experiences on one block there.

I am a police officer. To me the block is a graveyard in a sea of the drowned and the drowning. . . . The whole scene is disturbing and frustrating. I believe that the problem of West 127th Street has its root in international and domestic economic and political policies. I also believe that what I do does absolutely no good. . . . My frustration ironically spills onto the other victim in this absurdity—the "enemy."

He goes on to describe how his job causes him to becomes more callous, "I don't really like what I do, what I am. I resist it somewhat but as time goes on, as the condition grows stronger, I resist less."[58] Twelve years later, Ira Socol, a former New York City cop wrote:

We send our police out to fight a . . . war on crime . . . trained for "combat" and with no political support for efforts to win the hearts and minds of the inner-city population. . . . Do the police become racist? Certainly. Do they become violent? It happens.[59]

In Paterson, New Jersey, in February 1995 an officer shot an unarmed sixteen-year-old who was allegedly dealing drugs. The youth died several days later, and young people rampaged through the streets in rage. One twenty-five-year-old, who refused to give his name, said, "You can't put a lid on boiling water."[60] Yet that is what the police are expected to do.

THE POT BOILS OVER: URBAN REBELLIONS

Police violence has been the spark igniting the anger that has set off urban upheavals since at least 1935, the year of the famous Harlem uprising. The investigating commission at that time wrote: "The insecurity of the individual in Harlem against police aggression is one of the most potent causes for the existing hostility to authority." In 1968, a year after 164 urban disturbances, the National Advisory Commission on Civil Disorders reported, "Negroes firmly believe that police brutality and harassment occur repeatedly in Negro neighborhoods."[61]

The rebellions resulted from the conditions described previously: unemployment, bad schools, and poor housing. Police violence, however, seems to be an especially provocative indicator of the callousness of the larger society toward people of color. It is somewhat ironic then that the immediate response to disorders is usually large amounts of force.

In May 1993 then president George H. W. Bush, visiting Los Angeles to speak "about our course as a nation," attacked federally funded social programs and welfare, which, he claimed, robbed people of "their sense of responsibility." On the programmatic side, he said the police needed more money and that government policies toward the poor must "foster personal responsibility." Vice President Dan Quayle explained that the LA disorders resulted from a "poverty of values."

Two onlookers at the 1992 LA rebellion offer deeper insights. As he stood watching the burning buildings, Ervin Mitchell Jr., a thirty-one-year-old African American engineer, reflected:

> Almost everybody I know has been harassed and much worse by the police. Young blacks and Hispanics have been persecuted, beaten, and pulled out of our cars because of stereotypes. We're tired of being treated like garbage. We're tired of living in a society that denies us the right to be considered as a human being.

His companion, Michael Ming, a twenty-three-year-old student, agreed, adding: "The way the whole entire system is structured, the rich get richer, the poor get poorer. It provides almost no hope for most folks, especially black folks."[62]

NOTES

1. Rick Bragg, "Unfathomable Crime, Unlikely Figure," *New York Times,* June 17, 1998, p. A12.

2. Daniel Goleman, "As Bias Crime Seems to Rise, Scientists Study Roots of Racism," *New York Times,* May 29, 1990, p. C5. For descriptions of a number of hate crimes that illustrate the savagery of these attacks, see Mike Davis, *Ecology of Fear: Los Angeles and the Imagination of Disaster* (New York: Vintage Books, 1998), pp. 405–10.

3. Quoted in Howard Pinderhughes, "The Anatomy of Racially Motivated Violence in New York City: A Case Study of Youth in Southern Brooklyn," *Social Problems* 40 (1993): 488.

4. Quote from "Mean Streets in Howard Beach," *Newsweek,* January 5, 1987, p. 24.

5. Douglas Martin, "In Brooklyn, 2 Worlds on an Edge," *New York Times,* September 28, 1997, p. 35.

6. Quotes from Pinderhughes, "The Anatomy of Racially Motivated Violence in New York City," pp. 478–91; see also Pinderhughes, "'Down with the Program': Racial Attitude and Group Violence among Youth in Bensonhurst and Gravesend," in *Gangs: The Origin and Impact of Contemporary Youth Gangs,* ed. Scott Cummings and Daniel J. Monti (Albany: State University of New York Press, 1993), pp. 82, 87.

7. Quoted in Somini Sengupta, "Hate Crimes Hit Record High in 1992," *Los Angeles Times,* March 23, 1993, pp. B1, B8.

8. Quoted in Michael Norman, "Flood Victims, Perplexed, Angry, and Plucky," *New York Times,* April 19, 1984, p. B2.

9. Neil A. Lewis, "President Faults Race Preferences as Admission Tool," *New York Times,* January 16, 2003, pp. A1, A26. In contrast to the administration's attack on affirmative action at the University of Michigan, over three hundred organizations, including major corporations and unions, along with some military and political figures defended affirmative action as an important tool that helps businesses and provides important experiences for students. Diana Jean Schemo, "300 Groups File Briefs to Support the University of Michigan in an Affirmative Action Case," *New York Times,* February 18, 2003, p. A14.

10. Adam Nagourney and Carl Hulse, "Bush Rebukes Lott over Remarks on Thurmond," *New York Times,* December 13, 2002, p. A1.

11. Helms quoted in Jack Levin and Jack McDevitt, *Hate Crimes: The Rising Tide of Bigotry and Backlash* (New York: Plenum Press, 1993), p. 38; Duke quoted in Don Terry, "In Louisiana, Duke Divides Old Loyalties," *New York Times,* October 31, 1991, pp. A1, B9; "Duke Going to Prison," *New York Times,* April 16, 2003, p. A13.

12. Dole quoted in Steven A. Holmes, "Backlash against Affirmative Action Troubles Advocates," *New York Times,* February 7, 1995, p. B9.

13. "Word for Word/Asian-Americans," *New York Times*, March 5, 2000, sec. 4, p. 7.

14. FBI, "Hate Crime Statistics, 2001," http://www.fbi.gov/ucr/hatecm.htm. (accessed April 16, 2003), table 1. The FBI's statistics are gathered from data submitted by law enforcement agencies around the country. Since not all incidents are reported, not all police departments submit data, and classification can be erroneous, these statistics underestimate the incidence of hate crimes.

15. Quotes from the video *Pockets of Hate* (Princeton, NJ: Films for the Humanities, 1988).

16. Quotes from Levin and McDevitt, *Hate Crimes*, p. 58; U.S. Commission on Civil Rights, *Civil Rights Issues Facing Asian Americans in the 1990s*, February 1992, pp. 25–26; Seth Mydans, "Killing Alarms Japanese-Americans," *New York Times*, February 26, 1992.

17. Lynette Clemetson, "A Slaying in 1982 Maintains Its Grip on Asian-Americans," *New York Times*, June 8, 2002, pp. A1, A19.

18. This and several other anti-Semitic incidents involving African Americans are discussed by Richard Goldstein, "The New Anti-Semitism: A *Geshrei*," in *Blacks and Jews: Alliances and Arguments*, ed. Paul Berman (New York: Delta, 1994), pp. 204–16.

19. A discussion of minority bias crimes can be found in Levin and McDevitt, *Hate Crimes*, pp. 137–48; the Latasha Harlins incident is discussed by Wanda Coleman, "Remembering Latasha: Blacks, Immigrants, and America," *Nation*, February 15, 1993, pp. 187–91.

20. FBI, "Hate Crime Statistics, 2001."

21. Nicholas D. Kristoff, "Bigotry in Islam and Here," *New York Times*, July 9, 2002, p. A21; Susan Sachs, "Baptist Pastor Attacks Islam, Inciting Cries of Intolerance," *New York Times*, June 15, 2002, p. A10.

22. Robert E. Pierre, "Fear and Anxiety Permeate Arab Enclave Near Detroit," in *Annual Editions: Race and Ethnic Relations, 03/04*, ed. John Kromkowski (Guilford, CN: McGraw-Hill/Dushkin, 2003), pp. 180–81.

23. Ibid., p. 181; Zeinab Abbas quoted in Jodi Wilgoren and David Leonhardt, "A Mundane Thursday, Shadowed by Foreboding," *New York Times*, March 21, 2003, p. B11.

24. Francis X. Clines, "Shootings Leave Pittsburgh Suburbs Stunned," *New York Times*, April 30, 2000, p. 14.

25. Bill Dedman, "Midwest Gunman Had Engaged in Racist Acts at 2 Universities," *New York Times*, July 6, 1999, pp. A1, A14.

26. Nick Madigan, "North Utah Faces Influx of Racists," *New York Times*, April 4, 2003, p. A12.

27. Elinor Langer, "The American Neo-Nazi Movement Today," *Nation*, July 16/23, 1990, p. 85.

28. Quotes from Seth Mydans, "In Messages, Officers Banter after Beating in Los Angeles," *New York Times*, March 19, 1991, pp. A1, A18.

29. Kenneth B. Noble, "Police Department Reeling after Verdict," *New York Times*, October 15, 1995, p. B8.

30. Jerome H. Skolnick and James J. Fyfe, *Above the Law: Police and the Excessive Use of Force* (New York: Free Press, 1993), p. 3; Gates quote from "Coast Police Chief Accused of Racism," *New York Times*, May 13, 1982, p. A24.

31. Amnesty International, *United States of America: Police Brutality and Excessive Force in the New York City Police Department* (New York: Amnesty International, June 1996), p. 11.

32. Amnesty International, *United States of America: Rights for All* (New York: Amnesty International, October 1998), pp. 18–19.

33. Ibid., p. 17.

34. Bob Herbert, "Grief and Justice," *New York Times,* July 19, 1996, p. A27.

35. Dan Barry, "Officer Charged in Man's Torture at Station House," *New York Times*, August 14, 1997, pp. A1, B3. Sapir quoted from Joseph P. Fried, "U.S. Takes Over the Louima Case: 5th Suspect, a Sergeant, Is Indicted," *New York Times*, February 27, 1998, p. B5.

36. Quotes in Howard Chua-Eoan, "Black and Blue," *Time*, March 6, 2000, pp. 26–27.

37. Quoted in ibid., p. 25.

38. Benjamin Weuser, "Officer Fired for Criticisms, Judge Finds," *New York Times*, October 28, 2000, pp. B1, B4.

39. Shaila K. Dewan, "Far from Africa, a Young Wife Mourns," *New York Times*, August 8, 2003, pp. B1, B2; "Family of West African Immigrant Mistakenly Killed by Police to Sue New York City," http://www.bet.com/articles/1,,c1gb7037-7849,00.html (accessed December 6, 2003).

40. Stolen Lives Project, *Stolen Lives: Killed by Law Enforcement, 1999*. The Web site for the project is http://www.october22.org. Their phone number is 888-nobrutality. North and South Dakota are the two missing states.

41. Ibid., p. 13.

42. Tom Hayden, "LAPD: Law and Disorder," *Nation*, April 10, 2000, pp. 6–7.

43. Quotes from Eric Lipton, "Giuliani Cites Criminal Past of Slain Man," *New York Times*, March 20, 2000, pp. B1, B4; William Glabers, "City Settles Suit in Guard's Death by Police Bullet," *New York Times*, March 13, 2003, pp. B1, B2; Elisabeth Bumiller, "Mayor Says Criticism of Him over Diallo Verdict Is Political," *New York Times*, February 29, 2000, p. B5.

44. David K. Shipler, "Khaki, Blue, and Blacks," *New York Times*, May 26, 1992, p. A17.

45. For a useful discussion of racial profiling, see David A. Harris, *Profiles in Injustice: Why Racial Profiling Cannot Work* (New York: New Press, 2002).

46. David Kocieniewski, "Whitman Narrowly Wins Fight to Put Verniero on the Top Court," *New York Times*, May 11, 1999, pp. B1, B5.

47. Michael Raphael and Joe Donohue, "Turnpike Arrests: 73% Minority," *Newark (NJ) Star-Ledger*, April 8, 1999, pp. 1, 21; David Kocieniewski, "New

Jersey Troopers Say They Are Afraid to Testify," *New York Times,* August 31, 1999, p. B5.

48. Barbara Whitaker, "San Diego Police Found to Stop Black and Latino Drivers Most," *New York Times,* October 1, 2000, p. 31; David M. Herszenshorn, "Turnpike Shooting Leads to Cameras in Patrol Cars," *New York Times,* June 16, 1998, pp. B1, B5.

49. David Kocieniewski and Robert Hanley, "An Inside Story of Racial Bias and Denial," *New York Times,* December 3, 2000, pp. 5, 56.

50. Quotes from "Black Plainclothes Officer Says the Police Beat Her," *New York Times,* January 13, 1995, p. A14.

51. Quoted in David Kocieniewski, "Officers Confronting Officers: Old Rules Still in Place," *New York Times,* March 28, 1996, p. B3.

52. Skolnick and Fyfe, *Above the Law,* pp. 113–33.

53. Amnesty International, *United States of America Police Brutality and Excessive Force,* p. 2.

54. Quoted in Kocieniewski, "Officers Confronting Officers."

55. James Baldwin, "A Report from Occupied Territory," *Nation,* July 11, 1996, p. A27.

56. Quoted in Selwyn Raab, "City's Police Brutality Report Card: Complaints Down, Needs Improving," *New York Times,* August 17, 1997, p. 41.

57. Quoted in ibid.

58. Edmund Stubbing, "The Performance Becomes the Reality," *New York Times,* August 4, 1980.

59. Ira Socol, "Trained to Do Our Dirty Work for Us," *New York Times,* May 2, 1992, p. 23.

60. Robert Hanley, "Unrest Follows a Police Shooting in Paterson," *New York Times,* February 25, 1994, p. B5.

61. Quotes in Skolnick and Fyfe, *Above the Law,* p. 78; and U.S. Riot Commission, *Report of the National Advisory Commission on Civil Disorders* (New York: Bantam Books, 1968), p. 302.

62. "Excerpts from Speech by Bush in Los Angeles," *New York Times,* May 9, 1992, p. 10; Quayle quoted in Andrew Rosenthal, "Quayle Says Riots Sprang from Lack of Family Values," *New York Times,* May 20, 1992, p. A1; onlookers quoted in Don Terry, "Decades of Rage Created Crucible of Violence," *New York Times,* May 31, 1992, p. 24.

Chapter 13

MILITARISM AND VIOLENCE
Who Benefits?

Many Americans think of the country's military as defenders of freedom. U.S. soldiers are said to fight for democracy, for the "free world," to protect our homes and families. Military personnel themselves may also believe this to be their fundamental purpose. But the U.S. military establishment produces far-reaching consequences, many of them poorly understood by large sections of the public. In this and the following two chapters we will use the term *militarism* to refer to the maintenance of a large military establishment that goes far beyond the needs of national defense, the ideas that justify military actions, and the actions themselves.

U.S. militarism is associated with all three types of violence, as we shall analyze in this and the following two chapters.

- Organizational violence occurs when the bureaucracy plans and produces weapons systems and when the government executes a military action.
- Structural violence is a consequence of the spending priorities for maintaining the world's largest military establishment, effectively robbing the public of health, education, or other spending needs that facilitate the conditions leading to physical harm.
- Interpersonal violence at home is connected with militarism. When the United States is at war in other countries, it happens when soldiers go beyond their battlefield orders and engage in additional vio-

lence, sometimes against civilian populations.

We will also discuss how militarism contributes to the erosion of democracy, making it harder to create a more egalitarian, less violent country.

An important aspect of militarism is its connection to the overall patterns of inequality in the United States and the world, including its many connections to the drive for corporate profits that is associated with so much violence within the United States. In this chapter we shall examine how corporations and the rich benefit from an overextended and excessive military whose needs go far beyond defense of the majority of the American people. In the next two chapters we shall consider the costs of militarism to the American people.

The eminent British historian Arnold Toynbee in 1961 saw the United States as similar to imperial Rome. Unfortunately the comparison is still relevant:

> America . . . now stands for what Rome stood for. Rome consistently supported the rich against the poor in all foreign communities that fell under her sway; and, since the poor, so far, have always and everywhere been far more numerous than the rich, Rome's policy made for inequality, for injustice, and for the least happiness of the greatest number.[1]

The U.S. government uses several methods to try to guarantee that the leaders of other countries have polices favorable to U.S. business interests. Progressive governments are to be toppled lest they become models for other countries as well as obstacles to corporate expansion. The strategies listed below are not mutually exclusive. Among the most important techniques are:

- Interference in foreign elections. Funds are channeled, often through the CIA to conservative parties so they, rather than more radical parties, will win at the polls. There are many examples of this, including western European countries following the Second World War, in 1970 in Chile, in 1987 in Haiti, and in 1989 in Nicaragua.
- Exerting economic pressures. If an elected government engages in progressive social change, U.S. policymakers will attempt to destabilize it. This is done through measures, such as economic sanctions, that lower the quality of life for many in the population in the hopes the people will overthrow their government. This tactic has been used against Cuba since 1960, and Iraq between 1991 and 2003. It

was also used in Chile in the early 1970s.
- A U.S. military invasion. U.S. troops may be used to install and then protect an unpopular but probusiness regime. Vietnam is a major example.
- Creating and maintaining surrogate armies. The U.S. public is not always supportive of direct U.S military invasions. This is an alternative when force is deemed necessary. Surrogate armies have the task of either overthrowing a popular government, or, when there is an unpopular government in power, of strengthening its military forces. Central America in the 1980s provides examples here, but there are many other cases where this tactic has been used.[2]

Many of the consequences of these strategies have been harmful for the rest of the world, but they are beyond the scope of this book.

Probusiness policies abroad promote inequality and violence at home. While the United States lags behind other developed capitalist countries in expenditures for social spending that can lessen violence, the military is one area where this country has been and continues to be the biggest spender. With about 5 percent of the world's population, the United States accounted in 1980 for 24 percent of the total military spending in the world. In 2001 this had doubled to 48 percent.[3]

Our taxes pay the costs of war and preparation for war, with the average family contributing over $3,000 annually to the military budget between 1975 and 1992.[4] The major victims of this spending are the people whose countries have been invaded by U.S. military forces. Their enormous pain and suffering can only be alluded to here, but there have been many victims of U.S. militarism in this country as well. This will be discussed in the following chapter; here we will look at who benefits from military spending, preparations for war, and foreign interventions.

The sums that have been spent on wars, invasions, weapons, and so on are hard to conceive, with the lowest estimate at over $4 trillion between the end of World War II and 1994. In 2001 the military received $396.6 billion. This is the publicly acknowledged budget, but there is also a classified military budget adding up to about $36 billion a year—most of that accounted for by the CIA's classified appropriation of about $28 billion a year.[5] Military spending data do not include the military-related expenditures of NASA and the Department of Energy, whose work on nuclear energy has many military implications and which runs nuclear weapons installations.

One way to try to get a perspective on these vast sums is to suppose that you, the reader, have won a stupendous lottery. First, imagine you have won a million dollars to be given to you in $1,000 checks, fifty weeks out of each year, until the money is all gone. If this were the case, you would receive your weekly check for the next twenty years. That would be nice, but what if you had won a billion dollars? You, and your heirs, would get a $1,000 a week for the next twenty thousand years. And if you won a trillion dollars, the checks would be in the mail, assuming there was one, for the next twenty million years. Journalist and author William Blum presents another way to conceptualize the amount spent on militarism by pointing out that "in one year the United States spends on the military more than $17,000 per hour, for every hour, since Jesus Christ was born."[6]

FROM WAR TO "DEFENSE"

Until September 11, 2001, there was no obvious threat to Americans from outside forces, and fear had to be created to justify high military spending. When hijackers flew two jets into the twin towers of the World Trade Center, another into the Pentagon, while a fourth hijacked plane crashed in a Pennsylvania field, war no longer seemed something that happened in faraway places to other people. These terrorist attacks have been used to manipulate public opinion and to legitimate measures that are highly questionable. We will look at this after discussing pre–September 11 propaganda efforts.

Powerful individuals began creating the illusion that we were a nation under siege from hostile forces very soon after World War II. The United States alone among the warring nations was unbombed except for the single attack on Pearl Harbor. The United States thus emerged as the world's economically and militarily strongest country. Yet the people of this country were soon led to believe they were in great danger and were told it was necessary to support an unprecedented peacetime military establishment.

The language manipulation discussed in chapter 4 was used to this end. For over one hundred and fifty years the United States had a Department of War. Then, in 1947, in what euphemisms expert and professor of English William Lutz describes as "the doublespeak coup of the century," the War Department was transformed into the Department of Defense.[7] Two years after the war officially ended, the general public may have felt financial resources could be used for peacetime purposes, but how can you argue against spending money to "defend" your country? The Union of Soviet

Socialist Republics (USSR), or the Soviet Union, was portrayed as the major threat to the United States.

If there had been a critical examination of this alleged threat by the media and public figures, its hollowness would have been evident. The Soviet Union, the world's first socialist state, had suffered immense destruction during World War II. Twenty million people were killed, 15 cities, 1,710 towns, 70,000 villages, 32,000 industrial enterprises, and the infrastructure of railroads, highways, and bridges, were in ruins. Yet only a year after the war was over, the Cold War had begun.

Government, schools, Hollywood, and the media taught the U.S. public to fear the Soviet Union, our former wartime ally, a main force in the defeat of German fascism. These agencies could have used their influence to build support for a peaceful world. Instead the public was told that the Soviets were engaged in a fearsome military buildup. We had to close the gap or become Soviet slaves. The only genuine gap was between the propaganda and the actuality of the arms race. The United States had a head start in this contest that it maintained until the collapse of the Soviet Union in 1990.

For its part, the Soviet Union had good reason to fear U.S intentions. The United States stationed troops in more than seventy countries, including Guam, Panama, Germany, Greece, the United Kingdom, Turkey, the Philippines, South Korea, and Cuba. As of 1980, Soviet troops were in about six foreign countries, none bordering the United States.[8] These circumstances are at least a partial explanation of the Soviet's own arms program, which was then used to further justify the U.S. buildup. Even though the Cold War is now over, the U.S. military still has over 350 bases worldwide.[9] We can truthfully say, "The sun never sets on the United States flag."

If one looks at the sequence of events, almost all major arms buildups in the Soviet Union were in response to U.S. initiatives. In 1949 NATO was created as a military alliance of the United States, western European countries, and Turkey. Particularly disquieting to the Soviets was the inclusion of Germany, which had invaded Russia twice in the twentieth century. The Warsaw Pact, a Soviet-led military alliance of the eastern European countries, was formed two years later. The Soviet Union developed an atomic bomb in 1949, four years after the United States, and a hydrogen bomb in 1955, three years after this country. Robert C. Aldridge, an expert in the arms race, pointed out in 1983:

> During almost four decades of the nuclear age it has been the United States which has led virtually every escalation in weapons production while the Soviet Union has, for the most part, tried to catch up. At only two points in

the arms race did the Soviets have leading breakthroughs—when they launched the first intercontinental ballistic missile (ICBM) and when they put the first satellite into orbit; both in 1957. But their early accomplishments in those fields were shallow. The USSR had neither the resources nor the momentum to press ahead and the U.S. soon surpassed them.[10]

The argument that the U.S. military buildup was a response to a Soviet threat does not hold up. This menace was knowingly exaggerated by government agencies and spokespeople to justify new weapons systems or greater military appropriations. Thus, during the Kennedy administration, U.S. citizens were warned there was a dangerous "missile gap"; they were not told it was the Soviets on the minus side.

In chapter 4 we quoted Robert McNamara, secretary of defense from 1961 to 1968. Before heading the Defense Department, he was president of Ford Motors and later became head of the World Bank. In 1982 he admitted that he had lied about the military power of the USSR; acknowledging that the alleged weapons gap under his watch "was a function of forces within the Defense Department that . . . were trying to support their particular program—in that case, an expansion of U.S. missile production—by overstating the Soviet force."[11]

In 1995 this member of the power elite also admitted that the administrations in which he served consistently misled the U.S. public about the war in Vietnam. These lies were a way to try to win support for an increasingly unpopular war. Lyndon Johnson, who presided over the huge troop buildup in Southeast Asia, secretly acknowledged that the Gulf of Tonkin incident, the rationale for the U.S. escalation, had never happened, saying to McNamara, "When we got through with all the firing, we concluded maybe they [the North Vietnamese] hadn't fired at all." [12] These lies prolonged the war. With each additional year came additional thousands of deaths, maimings, and all the other horrors attendant upon that invasion.

Exaggerations, distortions, and falsehoods continued up until the collapse of our supposed enemy. The Reagan administration warned that the Soviets would be capable of a nuclear first strike that could destroy this country's defense system. Later, administration officials admitted there was no real threat.

A study of military spending in 1980 by the congressional investigating agency, the General Accounting Office (GAO), found a pattern of lies by the Pentagon to justify building very expensive weapons systems. While parts of the report are classified, an unclassified summary claimed there had been

dubious support for claims of . . . high performance, insufficient and often
unrealistic testing, understated cost, incomplete or unrepresentative reporting, lack of systematic comparisons against the weapons they were to replace, and unconvincing rationales for their development in the first place.[13]

Soviet efforts to reduce tensions were rejected without a public discussion
of whether these should not at least be seriously explored as an alternative
to an arms buildup.[14]

WHO BENEFITS? THE MULTINATIONALS

The key to explaining the military buildup since 1945 is the desire of those
at the command posts to protect and increase the profits of the multinational
corporations and the armaments industry. To do this, they need compliant
governments. By1945 the United States was the strongest capitalist country
and had replaced Great Britain as the dominant imperialist power. The figures below show the growth of U.S. investments abroad.[15]

1970	$75 billion
1980	$215 billion
2000	$1 trillion

Overseas investments are an important source of corporate profits. In
1950 profits from non-U.S.-based operations accounted for 3 percent of the
gross profits of all U.S. companies; by 1997 the figure was 13 percent.[16] To
ensure these profits, companies want the lowest possible labor costs, the
largest possible markets, and the cheapest possible raw materials.

The multinationals use a "global assembly line" to produce products or
components where wages are low. This contributes to the unemployment in
the United States discussed in chapter 8. For example, in 1970, 214,000
workers were making shoes in this country; in 1990 that number had
shrunk to 74,000, and by 2001 there were only 26,000 employees in this
line of work. Nike's line of athletic shoes used to be produced in Maine by
workers earning about $7.00 an hour. Now Nikes are all made in Asia. In
Indonesia a typical Nike worker is getting $1.03 a day, or $.14 an hour, putting her below the Indonesian government's own poverty line. There is no
benefit to U.S. consumers. The price of the shoes does not reflect the very
low labor costs.[17]

For many years, when fans rose as the Star Spangled Banner was played at the beginning of a baseball game, they were unaware that the baseballs were manufactured in Haiti by women earning about $.09 for each baseball they stitched, or about $3.00 a day. Their employer, Rawlings Sporting Goods, sold the balls for $3.50–$4.00 each in the United States. The United States supported a series of dictators in Haiti and only reluctantly came to give tepid support to Haiti's first democratically elected president, Jean Baptiste Aristide. In 1986, fearing unrest in Haiti, Rawlings moved to a free-trade zone in Costa Rica. It pays no taxes or import duties on its raw materials. The workers currently make $.30 a day, but the retail price of a ball is now about $15.00.[18]

With friendly governments in power, U.S. corporations also have access to less unionized and less regulated marketplaces. Goods that are banned here or face declining demand can be profitably sold overseas. Tobacco products, pesticides, infant formula, and pharmaceutical products are among these dangerous exports. In chapter 7 we gave the example of the Dalkon Shield.

Increasingly at our local supermarkets, we can find flowers, fruits, vegetables, and seafood imported from Third World countries. There is no need to wait for spring and summer for asparagus, peas, strawberries, peaches, and plums. These products, imported by multinationals, are grown on land that used to be used mainly for subsistence agriculture. As agribusiness gains access to this land, poor peasants find themselves forced to leave, moving to the increasingly overcrowded cities in their own country or crossing the unfriendly borders of the United States where they are then blamed for the unemployment that has been caused by the multinational corporations.

MAKING THE WORLD SAFE FOR CORPORATE INVESTMENT

A basic assumption of U.S. foreign policy has been that corporate-friendly governments are to be encouraged, supported, and, if necessary, put into power even against the resistance of their own populations.[19] Vietnam, Chile, and Nicaragua are a few relevant examples here. This leads to the overthrow of progressive governments. The military is also used to overthrow heads of state who may not be progressive but show too much independence, standing in the way of corporate goals. The invasions of Panama in 1989 and of Iraq in 2003 illustrate this.

Intervention in support of business interests is not new. Early in U.S.

history this interest centered on the Caribbean and Latin America. Since the 1823 proclaiming of the Monroe Doctrine, warning European powers to keep out of the Western Hemisphere, the United States has intervened militarily in this region alone over sixty times.

In 1935 Gen. Smedley Butler, twice awarded the Medal of Honor, reflected on his Marine career, comparing it to that of a gangster.

> I spent thirty-three years and four months in active service. . . . And during that period I spent most of my time being a high-class muscle man for Big Business, for Wall Street, and for the bankers. . . . I was a gangster for capitalism. . . . Thus I helped make Mexico . . . safe for American oil interests in 1914. I helped make Haiti and Cuba a decent place for the National City Bank boys to collect revenues in. I helped purify Nicaragua for the international banking house of Brown Brothers in 1909–1912. I brought light to the Dominican Republic for American sugar interests in 1916. . . . In China in 1927 I helped see to it that Standard Oil went its way unmolested. During those years, I had, as the boys in the back room would say, a swell racket. Looking back on it, I feel that I could have given Al Capone a few hints. The best he could do was to operate his racket in three districts. I operated on three continents.[20]

Faced with intolerable conditions resulting from national and international inequalities, people in the Third World form movements for social change. Socialist or strongly nationalist governments will want to use resources for creating services for the general population, not for increasing stockholder dividends in the developed capitalist countries.

The United States has opposed progressive change and revolutions since 1917 when, along with the other capitalist countries, it invaded Russia to try to prevent the Soviet revolution from succeeding. In the 1930s and 1940s the United States supported the anti-Communist forces of Chiang Kai Shek against the Communist forces led by Mao Tse-tung in China. For over forty years the United States has been trying to overthrow the socialist government in Cuba.

Following the success of the Soviet and Chinese revolutions, subsequent movements for progressive change were portrayed as examples of expanding Communism. From the 1950s to 1975 the United States tried to prevent a Communist-led revolution from succeeding in Vietnam. As early as 1954 Secretary of State John Foster Dulles was declaring that in Southeast Asia, Communist Russia and its Chinese Communist ally were seeking to impose their totalitarian system, posing "a grave threat to the whole free community." He asserted that the United State must meet these threats resolutely and with "action."[21]

While the Soviet Union existed, it was held responsible for revolutionary movements around the world. U.S. policy toward El Salvador in the 1980s is an example of this. Documents "proving" the Soviets were behind nationally based efforts at social change were fabricated. The State Department in early 1981 issued a "White Paper" that was supposed to show the Salvadoran rebels were agents of a Communist plot emanating from the USSR. According to the document, although there were real problems in El Salvador, they were being exploited by "hostile outside forces," in particular, "Cuba, backed by the Soviet Union . . . operating through Nicaragua." The aim of these "outside forces" was to transform any indigenous movement "into a totalitarian state, threatening the region and robbing the people of their hopes for liberty." Should they prove successful, this would be "a serious threat to the United States. . . ." The White Paper's principle author later admitted that portions of this document were exaggerated and "misleading." [22]

These arguments were fig leaves for violence and repression. In Latin America, as in Southeast Asia, U.S.-backed forces have engaged in some of the most horrible atrocities against populations recorded in recent years. Following Vietnam, there was widespread opposition to large-scale intervention using U.S. troops. Surrogate armies are one response to this. Another response is the use of highly destructive, very technologically sophisticated weapons that replace the need for thousands of combat forces.

Many of those directing terror operations against local civilian populations in Latin America received their training at what used to be called the School of the Americas (SOA). Nicknamed the "School for Assassins" by critics, the SOA changed its name to the Western Hemisphere Institute for Security Cooperation (WHISC) in 2001.

About sixty thousand Latin American military officers have been trained at SOA/WHISC. Many are accused of gross human rights violations. Each November since 1990 the school, housed at Fort Benning, Georgia, has been the scene of an annual protest. In 1990 ten people led by a Maryknoll priest, Fr. Roy Bourgeois, demonstrated. In 2001 there were ten thousand protesters. Their goal is the closing of the school, and they have been lobbying Congress to stop appropriating money for it. The vote in recent years has been close, but to date the school continues to receive funding. Its annual budget of $4.2 million comes from U.S. taxpayers, most of whom do not even know it exists. Jack Nelson-Pallmeyer explains SOA/WHISC's purpose:

The school trains Latin American soldiers on behalf of elite clients in the United States and throughout Latin America to defend and promote economic and strategic interests in a hemisphere marked by massive injustice. U.S. foreign policy generally and the SOA specifically support policies and systems that enrich a powerful minority while leading to widespread poverty, gross inequalities, a strained environment, and constricted or nonexistent democracy. As U.S. Army General Maxwell Taylor once said succinctly. "As the leading 'have' power, we may expect to have to fight to protect our national valuables against envious 'have-nots.'"[23]

Training manuals used by the school have advised beating and torturing prisoners, threatening their families, and blackmail.[24]

Chile is an instructive example of the procorporate nature of U.S. foreign policy and how it leads to violence. In 1970 a progressive candidate, Salvador Allende, was elected president. His early reforms included nationalizing some industries and redistributing some land. Greater workplace democracy was established, with workers electing the managers of some factories. A full spectrum of political parties continued to exist. In the United States those at the command posts went to work to undo these changes. Henry Kissinger, discussed in chapter 3, was Nixon's secretary of state at the time. He stated his conviction that the Chilean people had no right to elect Allende as their president, commenting, "I don't see why we need to stand by and watch a country go Communist due to the irresponsibility for its own people."[25]

The CIA, aided by U.S. companies and working with the Chilean military, was instrumental in the 1973 overthrow of Allende's government. General Augustus Pinochet became the head of a new, highly repressive government. International Telephone and Telegraph (ITT) was one of the corporations involved in the coup. The United States also used its influence in international lending agencies such as the World Bank to ensure that economic assistance to the Allende government did not occur. Nixon assured the corporate world that the United States would cause the Chilean economy to "scream." Edward Korrey, the U.S. ambassador to Chile promised, "Not a nut or a bolt will reach Chile under Allende. We will do everything in our power to condemn the Chilean people to the utmost poverty and deprivation."[26]

A look at *New York Times* headlines regarding Chile graphically illustrates the pattern.

3/21/73   "C.I.A-I.T.T. Plans on Chile Reported"
9/22/73   "Military Junta in Chile Prohibits Marxist Parties"
9/25/73   "Ousted Bosses Back at Chile's Plants"
9/26/73   "Chile's Military Chiefs Abolish Nation's Largest Labor Group"
10/20/73 "Chile to Return Seized Companies"
11/12/73 "Private U.S. Loans in Chile Up Sharply"
9/20/74   "C.I.A Is Linked to Strikes in Chile That Beset Allende"
5/30/75   "Chile Accused of Killing Labor Leaders"
10/19/75 "Evidence Growing on Torture in Chile"
12/22/76 "World Bank Votes Loans to Chile of $60 Million with U.S. in Favor"
10/4/79   "Chile Attracts U.S. Business"

In November 2000 the Clinton White House's Chile Declassification Project made public twenty-four thousand documents that had been secret up to that point. These give further detailed information of the U.S. government's actions to topple Allende, create disorder in Chile, and bring about a more procorporate government.[27]

A minimal estimate of those killed by the Pinochet regime is 3,172, including several Americans working with the Allende government. One, thirty-one-year-old Charles Horman, was the subject of the film *Missing*. The torture, repression, and murder of tens of thousands of people did not deter investment. Referring to Goodyear's decision to invest in postcoup Chile, Jack Carter, the manager of the company's Chilean plant, commented, "I don't think we spent five minutes talking about human rights."[28]

Although the U.S. government publicly claims to be a champion of human rights, there is a strong correlation between human rights abuses in a country that is receiving U.S. aid and high levels of corporate investment. State Department approval is necessary for arms sales. A country's respect for human rights issues is not the criterion that determines if this approval will be made. According to the anti–weapons proliferation organization, Council for a Livable World, "In 1999 alone . . . governments with some of the worst human rights records received American weapons and training."[29]

THE MILITARY-INDUSTRIAL COMPLEX

The relationship between the military and big business has come to be called the *military-industrial complex*. Dwight D. Eisenhower used the phrase to describe the symbiotic alliance between the two in his farewell address on January 13, 1961. He warned:

> Now this conjunction of an immense military establishment and a large arms industry is new in the American experience. The total influence— economic, political, even spiritual—is felt in every city, every state house, every office of the federal government. In the councils of government, we must guard against the acquisition of unwarranted influence, whether sought or unsought, by the military-industrial complex. The potential for the disastrous rise of misplaced power exists and will persist.[30]

The alliance persists more than fifty years after Eisenhower's warning.

Weapons industries spend millions on lobbying and campaign contributions. It's a good investment since they receive billions in contracts. Lockheed Martin spent $5.7 million on these activities from 2001 to 2002. It received $22.9 billion in government contracts in 2002. Boeing also did well, spending in these years $5.5 million and receiving contracts worth $19.6 billion.[31]

There are close connections between highly placed political figures, military officers, and the arms industry. Several Boeing executives became members of the Reagan administration, including Assistant Secretary of the Navy Melvyn R. Paisley, Deputy Assistant Secretary of the Navy Harold Kitson Jr., and Thomas K. Jones, Deputy Undersecretary of Defense. Secretary of the Navy John F. Lehman had an economic interest in a military-oriented consulting firm.

Henry Kissinger served on President Reagan's Foreign Intelligence Advisory Board, described by the *New York Times* as "a hush-hush group with access to the nation's most sensitive intelligence." His position there was a valuable resource for the consulting firm he established in 1982 that had weapons manufacturers as major clients.[32]

Reagan's chairman of the Joint Chiefs of Staff, General David Jones, joined General Electric's board of directors. GE not only makes light bulbs and dishwashers but also engines for fighter planes and military helicopters. It has made missiles in the past. Physicist Edward Teller, a longtime advocate of a strong military, encouraged Reagan's support for a laser-based defense system, the Strategic Defense Initiative or "Star Wars." He received stock in a laser company that would benefit from such a program, as did other Reagan advisors and associates.[33]

John Tower, who as a Texas senator was chair of the Armed Services Committee, became a consultant for Rockwell International, Textron,

Martin Marietta, and LTV Aerospace and Defense. George H. Bush appointed him to the Foreign Intelligence Advisory Board.[34]

In the Clinton administration, William Perry, secretary of defense, was an advisor on Strategic Defense Initiative programs while serving on the boards of directors of several military suppliers. Perry participated in other military budget discussions involving his interests. He is also a stockholder in United Technologies, which manufactures the Blackhawk helicopter.

Very influential members of George W. Bush's administration have strong ties to military contractors. They are among the people who decided if there would be a war with Iraq, how the war would be conducted, and how a post–Saddam Hussein country would be restructured.

The Defense Policy Board is little known to the American public. The undersecretary of defense appoints its members with approval from the defense secretary, and its deliberations are classified. As of 2003, nine of its thirty members are "linked to companies that have won more than $76 billion in defense contracts in 2001 and 2002."[35]

Vice president under George W. Bush, Richard W. Cheney, who was George H. W. Bush's secretary of defense, was president of Halliburton during the eight years between his cabinet positions. In September 2003 Cheney stated that he had "no financial interest" in the company but a Congressional Research Service report shows he received $4,160,000 from them in 2002 and owns $433,333 in stock options. The company made campaign contributions of $709,320 during the 2000 elections, 95 percent of that going to Republicans.[36]

In 2003 Halliburton and its subsidiary Kellogg Brown and Root received contracts for reconstruction in postwar Iraq worth billions of dollars. There was no competitive bidding. Kellogg Brown and Root also has contracts to supply the army and navy services "like cooking, construction, power generation, and fuel transportation." They also were chosen to build a prison camp in Guantánamo Bay, Cuba, following the war in Afghanistan.[37]

In December 2003 Halliburton was hard-pressed to explain why it was charging the American government $2.64 a gallon for oil it bought in Kuwait that would be resold in Iraq. In October 2003 the company was criticized for charging the U.S. government $1.59 a gallon for gasoline available from Turkey at $.98 a gallon. The company's fees for these transactions are described by oil business analysts as unusually high. Economist and owner of an oil industry consulting firm Phil Verlager said, "that's a monopoly premium." Other companies, he added, "would salivate to have this sort of contract."[38]

Kellogg Brown and Root was originally Brown and Root when it started as a small construction company in Texas. In the 1930s the company's founders enjoyed close ties with rising politician Lyndon Johnson. *New York Times* journalist Richard Oppel, recalling the company's history, reported, "With Johnson looking out for Brown and Root—and the company funneling huge sums to his campaigns, money that brought an Internal Revenue Service investigation—the company soon landed contracts worth hundreds of millions of dollars to build military bases and warships" during the Vietnam war.[39]

Another big winner of the contest for postwar contracts paid for by tax dollars has been the Bechtel Corporation, well connected to the Reagan and Bush administrations. Casper Weinberger, Reagan's secretary of defense, was on its board of directors and George Schultz, Reagan's secretary of state, is a director. One of the vice presidents is Jack Sheehan, formerly a Marine general and now on the Defense Policy Board.[40]

In 1983 Donald Rumsfeld, presently secretary of defense, was a Middle East peace envoy. He met with Saddam Hussein, hoping to convince him to allow Bechtel to build an oil pipeline in Iraq. The meeting occurred after there was knowledge that Iraq had used chemical weapons in Iran.[41] His efforts failed, but critics of the second war against Iraq used a photo of him shaking hands with Hussein to show the secretary's contradictory attitude toward the dictator.

Beginning in 2003 Bechtel was building roads, irrigation systems, power plants, schools, hospitals, and port facilities in Iraq, awarded contracts worth minimally $680 million.[42] In the past, Bechtel engaged in illegal financial transactions when it was one of the companies running the Department of Energy's nuclear reactor at Savannah River.[43]

The corporation, aware of accusations that it is unfairly benefiting from its political ties, issued a press statement denying this is the case. The statement points out that they "engage in the political process as do most companies in the United States." They admit they express "support for elected officials who support [our] positions," adding, "This is legal, ethical, and common." Furthermore, their rebuttal notes, "We do not expect or receive political favors or government contracts as a result of these contributions." In any case, Bechtel "does not rank among the top corporate political contributors and is relatively even-handed toward the two major political parties." Their campaign contributions in 2002 totaled $1,297,465, of which 59 percent went to Republicans.[44]

High-ranking military personnel after retirement are offered lucrative positions by military contactors. Thousands have moved into these jobs.[45] While still in uniform, they obtain weapons adding to their status. These same military personnel will later advise on the purchases of weapons systems.

The connections just described do not in themselves prove that particular weapons systems or strategies are not useful for defense. They do suggest the possibility, however, that self-interest rather than genuine national security needs could be involved in military spending decisions. Members of an elite group that benefits very directly when interventions occur are part of the process that decides if there will be war or peace. There is a strong possibility of a conflict of interest between what is good for the country and what is good for the military-industrial complex. This being the case, a high degree of scrutiny of military actions is warranted. Unfortunately, the mainstream media rarely provide such scrutiny.

The Pentagon does not encourage corporations to be patriotic by cutting their costs or contributing more to the national budget through taxes. While politicians extol the magic of the marketplace and the wonders of competition, the Pentagon and the private sector have a different way of conducting business. There is little competitive bidding and enormous opportunities to pad costs. Typically a cost-plus pricing system is used. The contractor gets back its stated costs of production plus a percentage, so the higher the costs, the greater the profits. Profits are higher on military goods than civilian ones.

The Pentagon has paid ludicrously high prices for goods. Lockheed produced a toilet seat made of plastic and fiberglass for use in fighter planes. The seats cost $640.09 each. Pratt and Whitney charged the Air Force $17.59 for a bolt. If the Air Force purchasing officer had gone to a local hardware store instead, he could have bought this item for less than $.25. Boeing originally charged the Air Force $748.00 for pliers but reduced the price to $90.00 when the higher price became a minor scandal.[46]

Subsidized by the taxpayers, profitable military industries take advantage of tax loopholes and sometimes do not even pay taxes. Between 1981 and 1983 this was the case with Grumann, Lockheed, General Electric, General Dynamics, and Boeing. Collectively these companies had $10.5 billion in profits. For these same years, the top twelve contractors who did pay taxes paid only an average rate of 1.5 percent on their reported profits.[47]

There are costly problems of mismanagement and outright fraud. The *New York Times* reported in 1990 that "twenty-five of the one hundred largest Pentagon contractors have been found guilty of government fraud in the last seven years, some more than once. Yet not one has been barred from government contracting." The illegal acts included bribery, kickbacks, overcharging, and lying about weapons tests results.[48]

Nonmilitary ways to achieve a more peaceful world are rarely publicly discussed. One way to protect the world against aggression would be to sharply reduce the international arms trade in which U.S. companies play a leading role. The Congressional Research Service, part of the Library of Congress, reported that in 2001 the United States was the largest seller of weapons to developing countries. This has been the case for many years. In 1996 the United States accounted for over 50 percent of the weapons sold in the world.[49]

The government subsidizes the arms export sector through a number of agencies, including the Foreign Military Sales Program and the Defense Security Assistance Agency. In 1995 the Clinton administration was spending $7 billion for that purpose. The environmental technology industry is seeking to increase its exports, but received only about $605 million, less than 10 percent of the weapons industry. According to the Congressional Budget Office, the arms industry would do fine even without government support.[50]

STILL LOOKING FOR AN ENEMY

Although the socialist countries of eastern Europe, including the former Soviet Union, became capitalist in the 1990s, we are apparently still not safe. The forces that benefit from intervention and from military spending have found new "threats" to the well-being of the American people, new ways to justify keeping military spending at high levels. In no part of the world does any nation or even combination of nations come close to this country's spending. With the mightiest arsenal that has ever existed on the planet, with no nation coming close to this military force, we are still allegedly never safe enough to sharply reduce the billions spent on weapons, many of them weapons of mass destruction.

The Pentagon has continued to use terms that imply or state directly the idea that U.S. military might is used for defending all of us or for the good of those being attacked. The 1989 invasion of Panama was "Operation Just Cause." The 1991 war against Iraq was first termed "Operation Desert Shield." The intervention in Afghanistan that began in 2001 was named "Enduring Freedom," while the 2003 war on Iraq was dubbed "Operation Iraqi Freedom," a phrase ubiquitously displayed on TV's extensive programming on the war.

There are several new "imperial alibis" for intervention and for keeping military spending high. The "drug war" discussed earlier is an excuse justifying intervention in Colombia where there is an ongoing civil war. Another rationale for high levels of military spending is the "rogue state" perspective, which claims that countries such as North Korea, Iran, Libya, and Syria are our enemies, armed with sophisticated weapons and led by moral renegades. In 1994 the most allegedly dangerous nations together spent about $9 billion. This was less than 4 percent of the U.S. figure of $258 billion for that year.[51]

A brief look at each of last two wars on Iraq shows the speciousness of some recent arguments for intervention. In 1991 Iraq was portrayed as an aggressor nation, armed with weapons of mass destruction. There was little mention that these weapons had been sold by Western companies with the approval of their governments. There was not much discussion either of the circumstances of Iraq's invasion of Kuwait, which was siphoning off Iraqi oil.[52] It is possible that diplomacy and/or economic pressures could have achieved an Iraqi withdrawal without the carnage of the war. Neither strategy was given much chance.

Aggression itself is clearly not the reason why the first war with Iraq occurred. Punishing another country for its aggression is a very selective process. If the United States based its foreign and military policy on deterring aggression, we would, for example, have intervened in Indonesia in 1975 to stop the invasion and occupation of East Timor, where Indonesian forces, which occupied that country until 1999 in defiance of international law, killed two hundred thousand people, a third of the population.

The second Bush administration's invasion of Iraq in 2003 was justified in several different ways. Each of the official reasons needs to be examined. Saddam Hussein, the head of the Iraqi government, was frequently described as another Hitler: not toppling him was tantamount to the appeasement policies of the late 1930s. There were, however, significant differences between the two dictators: Hitler commanded the forces of a major industrial power, while Saddam Hussein headed a poor country whose infrastructure had largely been destroyed by attacks since 1991 and by the continuing effects of U.S. sanctions. Hitler made clear his intent to conquer the world; Hussein invaded Kuwait in 1991, thinking he had the approval of the United States for this. In 1979 he invaded Iran but the U.S. government showed no disapproval of this. There is no evidence that he had expansionist desires toward the rest of the globe.

Another supposed reason for the invasion was that Iraq possessed "weapons of mass destruction." Other nuclear powers—Israel, India, Pakistan, Russia, the United States—face no such restraints. Repeated inspections by UN teams could find no evidence that these weapons existed, and as of February 2004 none had yet been discovered. If Iraq had a fearsome arsenal, why wasn't it used against the invading U.S. forces? Why should Iraq have been the only country in the world forced to give up such weapons?

Repeatedly, the Bush administration and British prime minister Tony Blair, one of the few foreign supporters of the American position, claimed that Iraq had violated UN resolutions to destroy its weapons, and in defiance of these resolutions was developing its nuclear arsenal. Documents that turned out to be forged were presented to the British and American public. The documents alleged that Iraq was buying uranium from Niger. Israel, on the other hand, has violated numerous resolutions regarding its occupation of Palestinian territory and has refused to allow an independent Palestinian homeland.[53] No major political figure has advocated sanctions against Israel, the largest single recipient of U.S. aid. Why is this the case?

Saddam Hussein became the personification of evil for killing and torturing his own people. The accusations of political repression were true but could hardly explain an invasion. Why had Hussein received U.S. support in the past when Iraq was engaging in these very same acts? There are many countries in the world where torture is used and human rights are routinely violated. These include Egypt and Pakistan, major recipients of U.S. assistance.

Amnesty International accuses the U.S. government of supplying "arms and security equipment to governments and armed groups that have committed torture, political killings, and other human rights abuses in countries around the world. It has trained military officers who have committed human rights violations."[54] Earlier we discussed the School of the Americas, whose graduates include notorious human rights violators. Why was Iraq singled out for punishment?

Another ploy to win support for the war was to link Saddam Hussein to the World Trade Center and Pentagon attacks of September 11, 2001. This seems to have been a successful propaganda move. From about a third to a half of those polled believed this falsehood.[55] In fact, of the nineteen hijackers, *none* was from Iraq, and no link between any of them and that country has been found. Several were Saudi Arabian and Egyptian nationals. Al Qaeda, the terrorist group they were connected to, enjoys support in several countries, including Pakistan, where some of its operatives have been arrested. No al Qaeda members were ever identified in Iraq. CIA analysts complained that they were pressured to write reports showing a connection, but they couldn't find one. One employee reported, "A lot of analysts have been upset about the way the Iraq–al Qaeda case has been handled."[56] Yet in several speeches in March, Bush repeated the accusation. For instance, in a press conference on March 7, he said:

> Iraq is part of the war on terror. Iraq is a country with terrorist ties. . . . It's a country that trains terrorists, a country that could arm terrorists. . . . My job is to protect the American people.[57]

At war's end on April 30, 2003, President Bush, in military regalia, copiloted a plane onto the deck of the aircraft carrier *Abraham Lincoln*, where he once again emphasized the antiterrorism rationale for the war:

> The battle of Iraq is one victory in a war on terror that began on September 11, 2001 and still goes on. . . . The liberation of Iraq is a crucial advance in the campaign against terror. We have removed an ally of al Qaeda and cut off a source of terrorist funding. . . . No terrorist network will gain weapons of mass destruction from the Iraqi regime, because that regime is no more.[58]

Where is the evidence that shows the Iraqi government bore any responsibility for the events of September 11, 2001?

If none of these rationales hold, then why did the invasion occur? Antiwar critics and protests around the world seemed convinced that the administration's goal was control of Iraq's oil and domination of the region. Saudi Arabia has the largest oil reserves in the world, and Iraq is second with about 112 billion barrels. Government spokespeople denied oil had anything to do with hostility to Saddam Hussein's government. Former press secretary Ari Fleisher insisted, "It is not a factor. This is about preserving the peace and saving the lives of Americans." Donald Rumsfeld, on the television show *60 Minutes*, also denied that oil had anything to do with the war. Calling allegations that the resource was a motive "myth," he vehemently declared, "It has nothing to do with oil, literally nothing do with oil."[59]

On the other hand, Grant Aldonas, an undersecretary of commerce, assured a business gathering that the war "would open up this spigot on Iraqi oil."[60] Before the spigot can be opened, Iraq's oil infrastructure, damaged by a curtailing of the industry due to sanctions imposed in 1991, will need to be rebuilt. The contracts for this rebuilding are worth billions. Oil analyst for Credit Suisse First Boston Bank Mark Flannery noted, if its "your tanks that dislodged the regime and you have fifty thousand troops in the country . . . then you're going to get the best deals."[61] In previous chapters we discussed the close ties between the Bush administration and the oil companies. When Saddam Hussein was in power, his government decided which foreign companies would share in the profits from oil. Now it is highly likely that a new Iraqi regime with officials selected by the Bush administration will be making those decisions. The administration chose Ahmed Chalabi to head an interim government. He predicted, "American companies will have a big shot at Iraqi oil."[62]

Although it causes violence and great suffering, war has advantages for the power elite. In addition to reconstruction contracts and oil deals, war can distract the public from problems such as the ones we discussed earlier, unemployment, unaffordable health care, crime, and a failing social infrastructure.

The war on Iraq provided an opportunity to further frighten the American people, to convince them that the world is full of "evil" that must be eliminated. This has become a new rationale for military spending and actions. A militaristic stance toward the rest of the world has caused great harm in the past to the American people. We will discuss that harm in the next two chapters.

NOTES

1. Quoted in Felix Greene, *The Enemy: What Every American Should Know about Imperialism* (New York: Random House, 1970), p. 190.

2. For many examples of the uses of these tactics, see William Blum, *Rogue State: A Guide to the World's Only Superpower* (Monroe, ME: Common Courage Press, 2000); and his *Killing Hope: U.S. Military and CIA Interventions Since World War II* (Monroe, ME: Common Courage Press, 1995). An excellent account of a number of U.S. interventions can also be found in Jerry Kloby, *Inequality, Power, and Development: Issues in Political Sociology*, 2nd ed. (Amherst, NY: Humanity Books, 2004), pp. 246–340.

3. 1980, U.S. Census Bureau, *Statistical Abstract of the United States, 1992*, table 532, p. 339; 2001, calculated from *Statistical Abstract of the United States, 2002*, table 1370, p. 860.

4. Military percentage from U.S. Census Bureau, *Statistical Abstract of the United States, 2002*, table 1370, p. 860; tax figure from Anne Markuson and Joel Yudken, *Dismantling the Cold War Economy* (New York: Basic Books, 1992), p. 10.

5. Tim Weiner, "The Pentagon's Post–Cold War Black Budget Is Alive and Prospering," in *Censored: The News That Didn't Make the News—and Why*, ed. Carl Jensen (Chapel Hill, NC: Shelburne Press, 1993), pp. 52–53; Tim Weiner, "The Worst-Kept Secret in the Capital," *New York Times*, July 21, 1994, p. B10. Weiner won a Pulitzer Prize in 1988 for his reporting on the secret military budget.

6. Blum, *Killing Hope*, p. 13.

7. William Lutz, *DoubleSpeak* (New York: HarperCollins, 1989), p. 170.

8. Common Agenda Coalition and the National Priorities Project, *Creating a Common Agenda* (Northampton, MA: National Priorities Project, n.d.), p. 58; David R. Simon and D. Stanley Eitzen, *Elite Deviance*, 4th ed. (Boston: Allyn and Bacon, 1993), p. 166; Albert Szymanski, *The Logic of Imperialism* (New York: Praeger, 1981), p. 195.

9. Michael Parenti, *Democracy for the Few*, 7th ed. (Boston: Bedford/St. Martins, 2002), p. 80.

10. Robert C. Aldridge, *First Strike: The Pentagon's Strategy for Nuclear War* (Boston: South End Press, 1983), p. 256.

11. Quoted in Stephen Rosskamm Shalom, *Imperial Alibis: Rationalizing U.S. Intervention after the Cold War* (Boston: South End Press, 1993), p. 28; discussions of distortions of Soviet military power can be found also in David Gold and Stephen Rose, *A Primer on the Arms Race* (Baltimore, MD: Social Graphics Co., 1983); Simon and Eitzen, *Elite Deviance*, pp. 180–82.

12. For an example of McNamara's revised thinking, see R. W. Apple Jr., "McNamara Recalls, and Regrets Vietnam," *New York Times*, April 9, 1995, pp. 1, 12. His thoughts are elaborated in his memoirs, *In Retrospect: The Tragedy and Lessons of Vietnam* (New York: Times Books, 1995); Johnson quoted in David E. Sanger, "New Tapes Indicate Johnson Doubted Attack in Tonkin Gulf," *New York Times*, November 6, 2001, p. A18.

13. Quoted in Tim Weiner, "Military Accused of Lies over Arms," *New York Times*, June 28 1993, p. A10.

14. Shalom, *Imperial Alibis*, p. 26.

15. 1970 figure from U.S. Census Bureau, *Statistical Abstract of the United States, 1978*, table 1502, p. 865; 1980, *Statistical Abstract of the United States, 1996*, table 1293, p. 79; 2000, *Statistical Abstract of the United States, 2002*, table 1272, p. 788.

16. James Heintz, Nancy Folbre, and the Center for Popular Economics, *The Ultimate Field Guide to the U.S. Economy* (New York: New Press, 2000), p. 179.

17. Number of workers, 1970, from U.S. Census Bureau, *Statistical Abstract of the United States, 1978*, table 676, p. 416; for 1990, 2001, *Statistical Abstract of the United States, 2002*, table 603, p. 395; Nike material from Jeffrey Ballinger, "The New Free-Trade Heel," in *Annual Editions: Global Issues 93/94*, ed. Robert M. Jackson (Guilford, CT: Dushkin Publishing Group, 1993), pp. 130–31.

18. Tim Weiner, "Low-Wage Costa Ricans Make Baseballs for Millionaires," *New York Times*, January 25, 3003, p. 3; Allan Ebert, "Un-sporting Multinationals:

Baseball Manufacturers Taking a Walk on Workers Rights," *Multinational Monitor* (December 1985): 11–12.

19. For a useful categorization of the types of governments that the United States has attempted to overthrow, see Michael Parenti, *The Terrorism Trap: September 11 and Beyond* (San Francisco: City Lights Books, 2002), p. 82.

20. A full list of U.S. military actions from 1798–1945 can be found in appendix 2 of Blum, *Killing Hope*, pp. 444–52; Butler quoted in Tariq Ali, *The Clash of Fundamentalisms: Crusades, Jihads, and Modernity* (New York: Verso, 2002), p. 260.

21. Quoted in *Vietnam and America: A Documented History*, ed Marvin E. Gettleman et al. (New York: Grove Press, 1985), p. 53.

22. *The Report of the President's National Bipartisan Commission on Central America* (New York: Macmillan Publishing, 1983), p. 5; Shalom, *Imperial Alibis*, p. 31.

23. Jack Nelson-Pallmeyer, *School of Assassins: Guns, Greed, and Globalization* (Maryknoll, NY: Orbis Books, 2001), p. 14.

24. Steven Lee Myers, "Old U.S. Army Manuals for Latin Officers Urged Rights Abuses," *New York Times*, September 22, 1996, p. 13; Eric Schmitt, "School for Assassins, or Aid to Latin Democracy," *New York Times*, April 3, 1995; Roy Bourgeois, "Human Rights Watch: School of Assassins," Z , September 1993, pp. 14–16. School of Americas Watch is an organization dedicated to exposing and eventually closing down SOA/WHISC. Its Web site is http://www.soaw.org. Useful videos on this subject include *School of Assassins*, *The New Patriots*, and *Hidden in Plain Sight*.

25. Quoted in Jerry Kloby, *Inequality, Power, and Development: The Task of Political Sociology* (Atlantic Highlands, NJ: Humanities Press, 1997), p. 190. Now published by Humanity Books, Amherst, NY.

26. Ibid., p. 190.

27. Peter Kornbluh, "Accountability on Chile," *Nation*, December 11, 2000, p. 8.

28. Number of deaths is from Chile's National Commission for Truth and Reconciliation, 1991 document, reported in "Chile under Pinochet—a Chronology," *Guardian*, January 15, 1999, p. 2, http://www.guardian.co.uk/Pinochet_on _trial/Story/0,2763,20922. Quote from Juan de Onis, "Chile Attracts U.S. Business," *New York Times,* October 4, 1979.

29. Noam Chomsky and Edward S. Herman, *The Political Economy of Human Rights, Volume I* (Boston: South End Press, 1979), pp. 42–46; see also Edward S. Herman, *The Real Terror Network* (Boston: South End Press, 1982), pp. 128–30. Council for a Livable World, http://www.clw.org/atop/hrreport01/ index.html (accessed May 17, 2003). The council correlates the State Department's own data on human rights abuses and on the arms trade.

30. Quoted in Victor Perlo, *Militarism and Industry: Arms Profiteering in the Missile Age* (New York: International Publishers, 1963), p. 23.

31. Douglas Jehl, "Air Force Pursued Boeing Deal Despite Concerns of Rumsfeld," *New York Times*, December 6, 2003, p. C2.

32. "Chronicle," *New York Times,* February 16, 1990.

33. Linda Greenhouse, "Boeing Wins Plea on Severance Pay," *New York Times*, February 28, 1990; Judith Miller, "Navy Secretary Said to Keep Ties to Company Aiding Arms Makers," *New York Times*, December 27, 1982, pp. A1, B11; Jeff Gerth, "Reagan Advisors Received Stock in Laser Concern," *New York Times,* April 28, 1983, p. A1.

34. Andrew Rosenthal, "Tower's Links to Contractors Factor in Choice for Pentagon," *New York Times*, December 4, 1988, pp. 1, 42.

35. Bob Herbert, "Spoils of War," *New York Times*, April 10, 2003, p. A27.

36. Campaign contribution information from Open Secrets, http://www.opensecrets.org/news/rebuilding_iraq/index.asp (accessed May 1, 2003).

37. Elizabeth Becker, "Details Given on Contract Halliburton Was Awarded," *New York Times,* April 11, 2003, p. B12.

38. Don Van Natta Jr., "High Payments to Hallibuton for Fuel in Iraq," *New York Times*, December 10, 2003, p. A16; Neela Banerjee, "New Information May Bolster Questions on Halliburton," *New York Times*, October 22, 2003, p. C9.

39. "In the Company of Vice Presidents, A Big Texas Contractor Prospered," *New York Times*, March 30, 2003, sec. 4, p. 5.

40. Herbert, "Spoils of War."

41. Bob Herbert, "Ultimate Insiders," *New York Times*, April 16, 2003, p. A19.

42. Elizabeth Becker and Richard A. Oppel Jr., "U.S. Gives Bechtel a Major Contract in Rebuilding Iraq," *New York Times*, April 18, 2003, pp. A1, B7; Richard A. Oppel Jr. and Diana B. Henriques, "Company Has Ties in Washington, and to Iraq," *New York Times*, April 18, 2003, p. B7; $680 million figure from Tim Shorrock, "Selling (Off) Iraq: How to 'Privatize' a Country and Make Millions," *Nation*, June 23, 2003, p. 11.

43. Simon and Eitzen, *Elite Deviance*, pp. 11–12.

44. These and further defenses can be found at http://www.bechtel.com/iraqresponse.html. Campaign contribution information from Open Secrets.

45. David R. Simon, *Elite Deviance*, 6th ed. (Boston: Allyn and Bacon, 1999), p. 170.

46. Christopher Cerf and Henry Beard, *The Pentagon Catalog* (New York: Workman, 1986), pp. 14, 16, 17; Bill Keller, "Navy Pays $660.00 Apiece for Two Ashtrays," *New York Times*, May 29, 1985; "Boeing Cuts Price of $748 Pliers but Contract Total Remains Same," *New York Times*, March 23, 1985.

47. Wayne Biddle, "5 Big Military Builders Paid No Taxes for 3 Years," *New York Times*, October 16, 1984.

48. Richard W. Stevenson, "Many Caught but Few Are Hurt for Arms Contract Fraud in U.S.," *New York Times*, November 12, 1990, pp. A1, B8.

49. Merle D. Kellerhals, "Global Arms Sales to Developing Nations Fell 43 Percent in 2001," *New York Times*, August 16, 2002. The title refers to a drop in

arms purchases compared to 2000 because of the poor economic conditions, http://www.usinfo.state.gov/topical/pol/arms/02081601.htm (accessed May 3, 2003).

50. Thad Williamson, "For Sale: Weapons or Pollution Control?" *Dollars and Sense* (May/June 1999): 42.

51. The term "imperial alibis" is from Shalom, *Imperial Alibis*; for use of the term "rogue state" see Michael Klare, *Rogue States and Nuclear Outlaws* (New York: Hill and Wang, 1995); a short version can be found in his "The New 'Rogue State' Doctrine," *Nation*, May 8, 1995, pp. 625–28. Figures from *Common Agenda Coalition*, chart 5.1, *Creating Common Agenda*, p. 58. This same source also shows that Japan spent only $39 billion and Russia $27 billion.

52. Kloby, *Inequality, Power, and Development*, 2nd ed., pp. 293–305; Elsayed M. Omran, "The U.S.'s Undeclared War against Iraq," in *Iraq: Its History, People, and Politics,* ed. Shams C. Inati (Amherst, NY: Humanity Books, 2003), p. 273.

53. James Risen, "C.I.A. Aides Feel Pressure in Preparing Iraqi Reports," *New York Times,* March 23, 2003, p. B10; Talat Rahman and Lyman Baker, "South Asia in the Wake of the Gulf War: The Pakistan Example," in *Beyond the Storm: A Gulf Crisis Reader*, ed. Phyllis Bennis and Michel Moushabeck (New York: Olive Branch Press, 1991), p. 298.

54. Amnesty International, *Rights for All: U.S. Arms and Human Rights Abuses*, http:www.amnestyusa.org/rightsforall/arms.html (accessed May 2, 2003). A useful source for current information on human rights abuses is Human Rights Watch; their Web site is http://www.hrw.org.

55. Tom Zeller, "How Americans Link Iraq and Sept. 11," *New York Times,* March 2, 2003, sec. 4, p. 3.

56. Quoted in Risen, "CIA Aides Feel Pressure in Preparing Iraqui Reports."

57. "Excerpts from Bush's News Conference on Iraq and Likelihood of War," *New York Times,* March 7, 2003, p. A12.

58. "Transcript of President Bush's Remarks on the End of Major Combat in Iraq," *New York Times,* May 2, 2003, p. A16.

59. Steve Kretzmann, "Oil, Security, War: The Geopolitics of U.S. Energy Planning," *Multinational Monitor* 24, nos. 1 and 2 (February 2003): 16.

60. "Oil the Other Iraq War," MSNBC News, http://www.msnbc.com/news/823985.asp?0cb=115114700&cpl=l (accessed November 27, 2002).

61. "Oil the Other Iraq War," MSNBC News, http://www.msnbc.com/news/824407.asp?0cb=3151147l (accessed May 3, 2003).

62. Dan Morgan and David B. Ottaway, "In Iraqi War Scenario, Oil Is Key Issue: U.S. Drillers Eye Huge Petroleum Pool," *Washington Post*, September 15, 2002, p. A1, http://www.washingtonpost.com/wp-dyn/articles/A18841-2002Sep14.html (accessed September 15, 2002).

Chapter

14

MILITARISM AND ORGANIZATIONAL VIOLENCE
Homeland Casualties

Those at the command posts of American society decide our nation's priorities. They decide whether spending will be higher for peaceful uses or for war. They decide whether conflicts with other nations will be solved peacefully or violently. These decisions touch millions of lives and cause much violence. In the previous chapter we discussed militarism's beneficiaries. Here we shall show that bureaucratic decisions connected to militarism have led, sometimes knowingly, to harm to U.S. military personnel and to American civilians.

U.S. MILITARY VICTIMS

The most direct U.S. victims of this country's war machine are those in the Armed Forces who are killed, maimed, or traumatized by what they have seen and done. Short wars and overwhelming military superiority mean the immediate physical costs for Americans and the public outrage they might lead to can be minimized. In military parlance this is a "low loss ratio."

In the 1991 war more than 100,000 Iraqi troops were killed, while the United States lost 147. In other words, U.S. forces killed 680 Iraqis for every U.S. combatant who died. Thirty-five of the American deaths resulted from "friendly fire," the oxymoronic doublespeak term for the accidental killing of American service personnel by their comrades. In the 2003 invasion and subsequent occupation of Iraq, 533 U.S. personnel died, as of mid-February 2004. At least 45 of those due to friendly fire and other accidents. In May 2003 the *Christian Science Monitor* reported, "Between 5,000 and 10,000 Iraqi civilians may have died during the recent war." The numbers of Iraqi troops killed were still not known at the time the story was filed.[1]

Inequality influences who joins the military and therefore who is at risk. When there was a draft, as during World War II and the Vietnam War, the more affluent were often able to avoid serving if they wished. Who volunteers now that there is no draft? Young men and young women need to decide their post–high school futures. Their major options include getting a job right away, going to college, or joining the military for a while. A high school graduate used to be able to get a unionized "good" job in the industrial sector. We have seen that is no longer the case. Without a college degree, job choices are very limited. But going to college is increasingly expensive even at public institutions. In 2003 tuition at four-year public colleges overall increased by 10 percent over 2002. Some systems saw much greater increases, such as the State University of New York, which raised in-state tuition by 41 percent.[2]

An increasing number of students and their families are going into debt to finance the costs of higher education. The average student debt in 2003 came to $27,600, more than triple what it was in 1993. The National Center for Education Statistics collected data indicating that in 2000, 70 percent of students had borrowed money to finance their undergraduate education compared to 46 percent in 1993.

A college education costs more than twice what it did in 1983.[3] Tuition is rising and so is enrollment, meaning there will be less financial assistance to go around unless things change. College admission offices are now giving need less consideration when granting financial aid than used to be the case. A dean of the University of Southern California described the trend, "We are experiencing a heaping on of greater privilege to wealthy and middle-class kids."[4]

To finance an education without being rich or borrowing lots of money, you can sign up for the military. Military recruiters aggressively target high schools. They promise not only a chance to serve one's country but valuable training and help with tuition. The Bush administration has intensified these recruiting efforts.

The "No Child Left Behind Act" passed in 2002 sounds like it is supposed to help young people. Among its provisions, however, is a requirement that high schools receiving federal aid have to give military recruiters student names, addresses, and phone numbers or risk losing the aid. Students can ask that the information be denied, but they or their families must know they have this right. Recruiter Staff Sergeant Andre Wilkerson feels that the law has "made a big difference. . . . We've got lists of people to call from our schools and we're calling them."[5] There is no law giving military critics the same access to students.

In some districts there is resistance to the recruiting. One reason is the military's discrimination against homosexuals. Some opponents of the recruiting policy regard it as an intrusion on students' privacy; some are opposed to militarism. The San Francisco Board of Education passed a resolution whose opening words quote soul singer Curtis Mayfield, "We got to have peace/To keep the world alive and war to cease." The board will give every student's family a card on which they can indicate whether or not they want the military to have contact information.[6]

Recruiters hand out glossy brochures promising "Up to $50,000" for college and assistance in paying off "student loans with up to $65,000 for a four-year enlistment." Besides this, the recruiting pamphlet offers "Superb health care" "while you are in the army."[7] If there were more affordable education and health care these inducements would be irrelevant.

Advocating a return to the draft during the 2003 war on Iraq, New York congressman Charles Rangel claimed, "It's not fair that the people that we ask to fight the war are people who join the military because of economic conditions."[8] One such person was Joshua M. Hotvet, who joined the National Guard because "the recruiter made it clear to me and my family that if I joined, I would get my tuition paid."[9]

The military is not a cross-section of the American people. Enlistees are more likely to be from the South and West, where there are generally lower per capita incomes than in the Northeast and Midwest. The elite order a war, but it is members of the working class, young people from small towns and rural communities without economic opportunities, who run the risks of military service.[10] Eighteen-year-old Sam Wills from a small town in Alabama hopes his service will help pay for law school and his family's health care. "My father had some medical problems, and we had medical bills to pay . . . and this was a good way to go to law school and send money back to them."[11]

Twenty-two percent of enlistees are African American, who are about 12 percent of the general population. African American women are now 46 percent of Army female personnel. One, Arlene Inniss, a single mother of two daughters, joined because, in her words, "I wanted a stable job so I could take care of my kids better."[12]

NONCOMBAT MILITARY DEATHS

Not all risks to military personnel come from enemy forces. Each year there are deaths and injuries during training and from friendly fire and accidents in combat. In addition, accidents lead to billions of dollars of damage to equipment. An investigative report in the *Boston Globe* in 1997 estimated that "since late 1979 more than 29,000 active-duty men and women in the Army, Navy, Marines, and Air Force—nearly five every day—died due to noncombat causes."[13] Here are a few recent examples:

- In March 2003 eleven soldiers died when their Blackhawk helicopter crashed. Two others were injured. They were all waiting to be sent to the Persian Gulf.[14]
- In December 2002 another Blackhawk helicopter crashed. This one was in Honduras where five military personnel were killed in a training exercise.[15]
- Four American soldiers were killed by friendly fire in Afghanistan. One was killed by shots from an Air Force gunship. One official said of the crew, "They didn't know what they were shooting at." Three others perished when a one-ton bomb hit them. Numerous Afghani civilians were also accidentally killed.[16]
- In March 2002 two separate incidents occurred. In one, five Navy personnel died when their Huey helicopter crashed into a mountain, and in the other, a mortar round unexpectedly exploded at an Army training facility in the Mohave desert, leading to three deaths. There were also several people injured.[17]
- In March 2001 a Navy fighter accidentally dropped a quarter-ton bomb on an observation spot in Kuwait, killing four U.S. soldiers along with a New Zealand army major. Two other Americans and several Kuwaitis were injured.[18]
- In April 2000 nineteen marines died when their Osprey aircraft crashed in Arizona. There had been two previous crashes of the Osprey, which combines features of a helicopter and an airplane. In 1992 another accident resulted in the death of seven people. Each Osprey costs $44 million.[19]

Service personnel are affected by combat-related illnesses. Even the short 1991 Gulf War produced problems for military personnel. "Gulf Syndrome" is the term describing the diverse health problems of those returning from the Persian Gulf. The syndrome includes chronic pain, tiredness, sleep disturbances, and memory loss. Over 100,000 Gulf veterans have reported having at least some of these symptoms.[20] It remains to be seen whether there will be long-term effects on veterans of this military episode.

From 250,000 to 300,000 military personnel received untested drugs and vaccines, including pyridostimine bromine (PB), that were supposed to protect them against potential Iraqi use of the nerve gas, soman, although there was no evidence that Iraq had this substance in its arsenal. According to journalist Steven Lee Myers, "Because of the Pentagon's acknowledged shoddy record keeping in the war it may be impossible to know how many . . . took [PB] and in what quantities." In 1999, following years of denying any responsibility for the Gulf Syndrome, the Pentagon commissioned a scientific study of PB. The researchers concluded that it could be causing Gulf War syndrome.[21]

Another health threat to U.S. service personnel and others in the Persian Gulf region comes from the effects of depleted uranium (DU), used in both wars on Iraq. Depleted uranium sounds like a harmless substance. But numerous experts take a different view. DU is a by-product of enriching uranium and is 60 percent as radioactive as ordinary uranium. Unusually dense, it is an excellent tank-piercing weapon.

Enriched uranium, from which DU is derived, is used for making nuclear weapons and reactors. After fifty years of making these, the United States has more than one billion pounds of DU. Using it in weapons systems solves the problem of storing it. After hitting its target, DU leaves behind tiny radioactive particles that float in the air to be inhaled by anyone coming in contact with it. This can lead to cancer years after the substance was first inhaled.[22]

Like their Vietnam War predecessors, veterans of the first Gulf War are experiencing marital difficulties, alcohol abuse, high rates of unemployment, and homelessness. Studies show that 10 to 15 percent of them have post–traumatic stress disorder (PTSD). Children conceived by Gulf War personnel have high rates of birth defects.[23]

The Vietnam War killed over 1,921,000 Vietnamese and 58,000 U.S. troops. One hundred and fifty-three thousand were physically wounded. According to psychiatrist Robert Jay Lifton, over a million U.S. Vietnam vets have experienced PTSD, suffering from "various psychiatric illnesses; they are five times more likely than those without the disorder to be unemployed; 70 percent have been divorced; almost half have been arrested or in jail at least once; and they are two to six times as likely to abuse alcohol or drugs." African American and Latino veterans have the highest rates of PTSD. The children of traumatized veterans are also at risk for emotional problems.[24] Seeing people killed and being in fear of death oneself leaves a mark on many.

GUINEA PIGS IN UNIFORM

Other examples of organizational violence come from the experiments conducted by the Department of Defense (DOD) during the Cold War on both armed forces personnel and on civilians. The goals were to test American weapons and see the effects of those an enemy might use. Fighting communism justified these activities. Decades after the experiments were conducted, Dr. William Winkenwerder Jr., assistant secretary of defense for health affairs, explained why they were warranted.

> We were involved in a cold war with the Soviet Union and had great concerns about what they might do. I think history has proven that these were not false concerns in terms of the offensive program that was being developed and might have been well in place at that time.[25]

Deadly nerve gases and biological weapons were tested on 5,500 servicemen between 1962 and 1973. One of these investigations was Project Shipboard Hazard and Defense (SHAD), which lasted from 1964 to 1968. Forty-three hundred sailors were sprayed with nerve and chemical agents in order to discover how these poisons work, how fast they could be detected, and how effective protective gear was against them. Sarin, one of the toxins, was released by the Japanese terrorist organization Aum Shinrikyō in five Tokyo subways in 1995.[26] The Pentagon did not do follow-up studies to see if there was harm to the subjects. It isn't clear if the subjects wore protective gear or if they had given informed consent to be tested.[27] Sarin gas was also employed in tests of rockets and artillery shells in Hawaii in 1967 in an effort to learn how the gas, if used in combat, would be affected by climate and other conditions.[28] Speaking to a Senate Armed Service subcommittee of the need for information, Georgia senator Max Cleland said, "Until that information is released and the affected veterans get the health care they need we are as guilty today as when the tests were originally conducted."[29]

In 2002 the Pentagon admitted that its testing of dangerous substances on Armed Forces personnel was more widespread than they previously acknowledged. The military is rather belatedly attempting to locate about 5,500 people who could have health problems as a result of these activities. Calling for medical assistance for the victims, Rep. Christopher Smith of New Jersey commented:

> At a time when our nation may be called up to fight a war to protect Americans from chemical and biological terrorism it is tragic to learn that four decades earlier, some of America's soldiers and sailors were unwitting participants in tests using live chemical and biological toxins.[30]

From the late 1940s the United States prepared for nuclear war against the Soviets. From 250,000 to 500,000 troops were exposed to 184 nuclear bomb tests occurring between 1946 and the ending of atmospheric testing in 1963. These "atomic veterans" were guinea pigs used by government scientists seeking information about the effects of radiation on soldiers' stress levels and the answer to the question of how ground forces would perform following a nuclear bomb.

The scientists already knew enough about radiation to wear protective clothing as they approached "ground zero." But the ordinary soldiers walked into contaminated areas shielded by little more than reassurances that "radiation from an atomic weapon when burst in the air, is all gone in a minute and a half." Years later, many are dying from cancer. Nancy Cooper, widowed by her husband's leukemia, mournfully criticized the government, "They were promised checkups. If they had looked they would have found that Paul had leukemia. . . . I feel it's just the same as if they'd shot him. They took his life."[31]

CIVILIAN RISKS: "THE BUCHENWALD TOUCH"

In 2002 California representative Mike Thompson, commenting on the Pentagon's military experiments, noted that the DOD "may have put civilians it is charged with protecting at risk."[32] "May" is the wrong word. In fact, civilians were also unknowing subjects of military experiments. Beginning in the 1940s the government began large-scale testing of nuclear devices and radioactive substances. "Downwinders" are the thousands of people who lived in the seven Western states exposed to the radioactive fallout from open-air testing, which contaminated air, food, and water. The cancer rates for downwinders are higher than for the general population.

Somewhere between ten thousand and seventy-five thousand people developed thyroid cancer as a result of the tests done in the 1950s. Many of the future victims were not even five years old when they were exposed through drinking radioactive milk. The government did not want to alarm the public and so did not tell them about the dangers of testing. They were more considerate of Eastman Kodak and other makers of photographic film, letting them know that the tests might damage their products. Sen. Tom Harkin, speaking at a Senate hearing, remarked, "It really is odd that the government would warn Kodak about its film but it wouldn't warn the general public about the milk it was drinking."[33]

Thousands of other nuclear experiments were conducted secretly between 1944 and 1974. The secrecy was partly to prevent lawsuits and public criticism. In 1993 the government released a 1950 memo warning that if knowledge of the experiments became public, the Atomic Energy Commission (AEC) would be subject to considerable criticism for having "a little of the Buchenwald touch." Buchenwald was one of the Nazi concentration camps where human experiments had been conducted. The risks of radioactivity were known at the time. Officials debated whether or not sparsely populated areas should be chosen for testing. But one scientist, Dr. Gioacchino Failla, working for the AEC, wrote in a memo, "The time has come when we should take some risks and get some information."[34]

The AEC conducted over four hundred experiments, including some on newborns who were given radioactive iodine. Scientists from Harvard and the Massachusetts Institute of Technology administered radioactive-laced cereals to retarded boys at a Massachusetts state school. The boys were told they were part of a science club and given periodic blood tests. At the University of Rochester Medical Center at least thirty-one patients were injected with plutonium and uranium in an effort to find out the possible consequences of radiation exposure should there be a nuclear war.[35]

In 1990, following years of agitation, the Radiation Exposure Compensation trust fund of $200 million was created by the federal government for persons having any of thirteen types of cancer connected to radiation exposure. The money is difficult to claim and obviously cannot make up for the loss of family and friends. Claudia Peterson of St. George, Utah, watched her six-year-old daughter and thirty-seven-year-old sister die of cancer. She grieves, "I can't close my eyes and think about my daughter without it physically tearing my heart out." Many in St. George share her experiences. Her town, she laments, is "living a nightmare, and we can't wake up."[36]

Biological weapons have also been tested on human subjects. Between 1979 and 1988 the Army sprayed bacteria at the Dugway Proving Ground in Utah. This was a repeat of 239 tests done from 1949 to 1969 at Washington National Airport, in New York City subways, and at sites in San Francisco, Minneapolis, St. Louis, Key West, and twenty-nine other communities. Political scientist Leonard Cole, who wrote a major study of the germ warfare program, estimates that "millions of citizens" were exposed to "countless trillions of bacteria and particles."[37]

Germ warfare was justified as protecting U.S. citizens against a ruthless enemy. In 1981 William M. Creasey, a retired major general involved in the programs, testified that testing in cities as opposed to an unpopulated place such as a salt mine was crucial because biological warfare is "designed to work against people, and you have to test . . . in the kind of place where people live and work." A scientist claimed with a verbal shrug that where national security is involved, "we have to do some things that are possibly not the nicest things." In 1997 a committee of the National Research Council reported that there were no health problems associated with this experiment.[38]

Class factors and racism influenced the testing. Wanting to ensure minimal interference with their experiments in St. Louis, researchers chose a "slum district" as their test site, believing that the residents in this neighborhood would be less curious and concerned about unusual activities. Should the community object, extra police were on hand "to quell any disturbances resulting from the presence of the test crew."[39]

In at least one test, African Americans were the unknowing subjects of a spraying with the bacterial agent, *Asperillus fumigatus*, which can cause potentially fatal respiratory, ear, sinus, bone, and spinal infections. Believing that African Americans might have different physiologies than whites and with a large number of blacks working as laborers, the army feared these workers might be especially vulnerable to the bacteria. The military argued they needed to see how a dispersal of this agent would spread among the blacks since if they were incapacitated this "would seriously affect the operation of the supply system." To this end, they contaminated crates at the Norfolk, Virginia, Supply Depot.[40]

The military claims the life-forms used in all tests were harmless, ignoring the dangers to infants, old people, and those with health problems. The Army did not monitor those sprayed to see if any harm had occurred; civilian medical personnel at some test sites did, however, find unusual deaths and illnesses following the sprayings. It was one of these deaths, that of Edward Nevin in San Francisco, that led to a 1977 lawsuit, finally bringing the biological warfare experiments to light. Cole concludes, "A fixation with national security," doesn't protect the public, rather "it encourages an ethos that permits suspension of safety and ethical considerations."[41]

DANGERS TO COMMUNITIES AND WORKERS

Weapons production has endangered those living in communities near the manufacturing facilities and the workers in them. Neither the people in these communities nor the workers have been warned that they might be in danger.

In the late 1980s, a *New York Times* investigation of approximately sixty-seven thousand people working in weapons plants revealed that while the workers are highly patriotic they are also afraid that they are being lied to, afraid they are in danger. At many plants workers remember colleagues who died of brain tumors or some other form of cancer. In Fernold, Ohio, one worker told a reporter, "I figure we all got the same thing. I think we all got it in our system and some day it's going to kill us." Another said, "All I can do is hope for the best, take out lots of insurance. You just keep thinking about payday. You just go home and play with the kids . . . and you don't think about the plant." Department of Energy epidemiologist Dr. Shirley A. Fry took a more complacent view: "It's understandable that people are concerned. . . . But there are many other things that affect our health other than our jobs."[42]

Unknown quantities of plutonium from the production of nuclear weapons are stored in thousands of plastic bags, metal cans, pipes, air ducts, and tanks in thirteen states, including Colorado, New Mexico, Tennessee, Texas, and California. Dr. Tara J. O'Toole, assistant secretary of energy, described the containment as "widely deficient," noting that these "containers were really only intended to hold the stuff until we got around to recycling it in the next weapons campaign." The plutonium's radiation causes leaks in the drums. The Department of Energy released a report listing 299 problems with the plutonium storage, warning that there are "significant hazards to workers, the public, and environment and little progress has been made to aggressively address the problem."[43]

Leakage of dangerous contaminants continues to be a problem. Local officials looking for ways to save money sometimes build schools on the sites of abandoned factories or landfills, including those that have been used by the Army. A coalition of community activists and parents formed a group called the Child Proofing Our Communities Campaign. They have issued a report documenting cases of schools built on contaminated sites, including ones used by the military.

In picturesque sounding River Valley, Ohio, the high school was constructed on an old Army dump in 1963. At least eleven graduates of the school developed leukemia. Admitting the site was contaminated but reluctant to close it, River Valley's school superintendent was reassuring, "Contaminated doesn't mean it's dangerous. It just means it's contaminated."[44]

Corporations run nuclear facilities. They, along with the government, bear a responsibility for what has happened to atomic workers. The government has been lax in keeping track of the risks tens of thousands of nuclear weapons workers faced from the 1940s to the late 1980s, according to a report by the independent Institute for Energy and Environmental Research. A spokesperson for the Department of Energy concurred with the Institute's findings.[45]

Nuclear weapons workers have been exposed to dangerous levels of radiation and to hazardous chemicals. For years the federal government denied this, but in the late 1990s they finally agreed with the critics who had been arguing that such work was very hazardous. President Clinton's secretary of energy, Bill Richardson, stated in early 1999, "This is the first time that the government is acknowledging that people got cancer from radiation exposure in the plants." A variety of cancers have been found in about six hundred thousand workers in the nuclear weapons industry, including cancers of the kidney, salivary glands, lungs, prostate, and Hodgkin's lymphoma.[46]

A program specifically to compensate uranium miners was begun in 1991 after the Radiation Exposure and Compensation Act of 1990 was passed. The miners, or their families if they had died, and downwinders were initially eligible for a onetime payment of $100,000. This was increased in 2000 to $150,000. However, the program ran out of money in early 2001, and some who might have been eligible do not have proper medical records to substantiate their claims. Darlene Pagel is the widow of a miner who died of pulmonary fibrosis at the age of fifty-five. She is working two jobs to pay his medical bills of nearly $27,000. Speaking of her husband, she said, "He didn't know uranium could kill him. If he'd have known he would have been dead at fifty-five, he never would have taken the job."[47]

Rockwell International operated the DOE's plant at Rocky Flats, Colorado, where the company knowingly violated environmental laws. Toxic chemicals leaked into creeks feeding the Denver water supply. Both Rockwell and the DOE lied about what was happening. In 1987 Rockwell received an $8.6 million bonus from the DOE for "excellent management." The plant has a history of accidents and is considered the most hazardous of all the nuclear weapons manufacturing sites by the DOE itself.[48]

General Electric's nuclear weapons contracts led to pollution of a huge area of Washington State, helping to make the Columbia River the most radioactive in the world. Local populations were exposed to high levels of radiation. GE's Hanford, Washington, facility was used for producing nuclear weapons components and for testing the effects of radiation on health. The federal government used Hanford to test its fallout monitoring technology. Hanford families now suffer the consequences. In one area known locally as "Death Mile," twenty-seven out of twenty-eight families have severe health problems, including cancers and deformed births. The government and GE continue to resist releasing information about the Hanford experiments. In 1997 nuclear waste was reported to be leaking out of the facility. Casey Rudd, a safety analyst for Washington State's Department of Ecology and a former whistle-blower at the DOE, described the leakage as "the worst stuff in the world."[49] Years after Rudd's observation, a million gallons of the water had leaked, and no one seemed to know what to do about it. The Department of Energy belatedly admitted it should have been prepared for such an event but explained that they did not expect any problem for at least ten thousand years.[50]

General Electric also operated a facility at the Knolls Atomic Laboratories outside Schenectady, New York. A Knolls engineer, Robert F. Coles, died of cancer that had invaded his entire body after nine exposures to radiation. In a farewell letters to his brother, he wrote: "I have been in pain for nearly a year and the thought of not being with them [his children] tears at my heart. . . . I do think it is through GE's negligent policies I was exposed to internal and external radiation of unknown quantities, and this is why I am now dying of cancer."[51] The Department of Energy has withheld data on the health impact of nuclear weapons, and the plants involved are exempt from OSHA inspections.

The production and testing of military equipment has resulted in some of the direct instances of organizational violence discussed in this chapter. Preparations for war and war itself, in more indirect ways, lead to structural and interpersonal violence. We will examine this in the next chapter.

NOTES

1. Dennis Cauchon, "Why U.S. Casualties Were Low," *USA Today*, April 20, 2003, http://www.usatoday.com.news/world.iraq/2003-04020-cover-usat_x.htm; Sara Flounders, "The Call for an Independent Inquiry," in *Metal of Dishonor: Depleted Uranium,* ed. Depleted Uranium Education Project (New York: International Action Center, 1997), p. 7, gives a higher number of U.S. troops killed in accidents in 1991; Peter Ford, "Preliminary Reports Suggest Casualties Well above the Gulf War," *Christian Science Monitor*, May 22, 2003, http://www.csmonitor.com/2003/0522/p01s02-woiq.html; see also www.Iraqibodycount.org.

2. Alan B. Krueger, "Economic Scene," *New York Times,* May 1, 2003, p. C2; Karen W. Arenson, "SUNY Trustees Vote to Raise In-State Tuition by 41 Percent," *New York Times,* January 18, 2003, pp. B1, B4.

3. Greg Winter, "College Loans Rise, Swamping Graduate Dreams," *New York Times*, January 28, 2003, pp. A1, A16. For rising college costs see National Center on Public Policy and Higher Education, *College Affordability in Jeopardy*, http://www.highereducation.org/reports/affordability-supplement. My own experience with college costs was very different and has shaped my thinking on this issue. I attended City College in New York at a time when it was tuition free, the case from 1847 to 1976. This greatly facilitated the social mobility of generations of students from New York's working-class families, many of them immigrants from southern and eastern Europe.

4. Quoted in Ethan Bronner, "College Efforts to Lure the Best Set Others Back," *New York Times*, June 21, 1998, p.1.

5. Quoted in Tamar Lewin, "Uncle Sam Wants Student Lists and Schools Fret," *New York Times*, April 29, 2003, p. B10.

6. Ibid. Several campuses, which had banned recruiters because of the military's homophobia, have let them back in order to keep federal aid. In 2002 the Department of Defense reinterpreted federal regulations on recruiting. If any part of a school denies access, such as the law or medical school, the entire institution loses federal subsidies. Harvard Law School and New York University both reversed decades-long policies in this regard. George Fisher, "Power Over Principle," *New York Times,* September 7, 2002, p. A15; Karen W. Arenson, "After 22 years, N.Y.U. Allows an Army Recruiter to Visit," *New York Times*, October 17, 2000, p. B8.

7. "Army Benefits," printed February 1999.

8. Quoted in Steven A. Holmes, "Is This Really an All-Volunteer Army?" *New York Times*, April 6, 2003, sec. 4, p. 1.

9. Quoted in Richard Pérez-Peña, "295 Students in National Guard Denied Tuition Aid," *New York Times*, April 12, 2001, p. D1. The states pay the money for National Guard members' educational assistance; the New York State legislature had more applicants than money and so denied aid. However, following protests they restored the assistance.

10. David M. Halfinger and Steve A. Holmes, "Military Mirrors a Working-Class America," *New York Times*, March 30, 2003, pp. A1, B12. Comparative per capita data for states can be found in U.S. Census Bureau, *Statistical Abstract of the United States, 2002*, table 644, p. 427.

11. Quoted in Dana Canedy, "Peacetime Recruits Getting Ready for War's Peril," *New York Times*, September 20, 2001, p. A1.

12. Halfinger and Holmes, "Military Mirrors a Working-Class America," p. B12; Holmes, "Is This Really an All-Volunteer Army?"; quote from Canedy, "Peacetime Recruits Getting Ready for War's Peril."

13. Matthew Brelis and Stephen Kurkjian, "Casualties of Peace: Deaths in the Military," *Boston Globe*, August 6, 1997, p. 5, http://www.boston.com/globe/nation/packages/military_accidents/ (accesed May 18, 2003).

14. Lydia Polgreen, "A Farewell at Fort Drum to 11 Fallen Soldiers," *New York Times*, March 14, 2003, p. B5.

15. "5 U.S. Soldiers Killed in a Crash in Honduras," *New York Times*, December 13, 2002, p. A19.

16. Eric Schmitt, "Inquiry Finds American Was Killed by Fire from U.S. Gunship, Not Enemy," *New York Times*, October 29, 2002, p. A18.

17. Nick Madigan, "5 Killed in Separate Army and Navy Training Exercises," *New York Times,* March 30, 2002, p. A8.

18. James Dao, "Bombing Accident Kills 5 Americans at Site in Kuwait," *New York Times*, March 13, 2001, pp. 1, A8.

19. Eric Schmitt, "19 Marines Die in Crash of Trouble-Plagued Craft," *New York Times*, April 10, 2000, p. A10.

20. Eric Schmitt, "The Gulf War Veteran: Victorious in War, Not Yet at Peace," *New York Times*, May 28, 1995, sec. 4, p. 4; Laura Flanders, "Mal de Guerre," *Nation*, March 7, 1994, pp. 292–93. For a skeptical view of Gulf War Syndrome, see Barry Glassner, *The Culture of Fear* (New York: Basic Books, 1999), pp. 155–61.

21. Steven Lee Myers, "Drug May Be Cause of Veterans' Illnesses," *New York Times*, October 19, 1999, p. A18.

22. Helen Caldicott, "A New Kind of Nuclear War," in Depleted Uranium Education Project, *Metal of Dishonor,* pp. 18–19: Dan Fahey, "Collateral Damage: How U.S. Troops Were Exposed to Depleted Uranium during the Persian Gulf War," in *Metal of Dishonor*, pp. 25–26.

23. Jimmie Briggs, Kenneth Miller, and Derek Hudson, "The Tiny Victims of Desert Storm," *Life,* November 1995.

24. Robert Jay Lifton, *Home from the War: Learning from Vietnam Veterans* (Boston: Beacon Press, 1992), p. ix.

25. Quoted in Thom Shanker, "Defense Dept. Offers Details of Toxic Tests Done in Secret," *New York Times*, October 10, 2002, p. A36.

26. Robert Jay Lifton, *Destroying the World to Save It* (New York: Owl Books, 2002), p. 3.

27. "Project 112," Deployment Link, http://deploymentlinkpsd.mil/current-issues/

shad/shad-intris.hmtl (accessed May 5, 2003). Deployment Link is part of the Department of Defense; Thom Shanker and William J. Broad, "Sailors Sprayed with Nerve Gas in Cold War Test, Pentagon Says," *New York Times*, May 24, 2002, p. A1.

28. Shanker, "Defense Dept. Offers Details of Toxic Tests Done in Secret."

29. Ibid.

30. Thom Shanker, "U.S. Troops Were Subjected to a Wider Toxic Testing," *New York Times*, October 9, 2002, p. A18.

31. Quotes in Harold L. Rosenberg, *Atomic Soldiers: American Victims of Nuclear Experiments* (Boston: Beacon Press, 1980), pp. 17, 165.

32. Quoted in Shanker, "Defense Dept. Offers Details of Toxic Tests Done in Secret."

33. Matthew L. Wald, "Thousands Have Thyroid Cancer from Atomic Tests," *New York Times*, August 2, 1997, p. 6; Matthew L. Wald, "U.S. Atomic Tests in '50s Exposed Millions to Risk," *New York Times*, July 29, 1997, p. A10; Matthew L. Wald, "U.S. Alerted Photo Film Makers, Not Public about Bomb Fallout," *New York Times*, September 30, 1997, p. A18.

34. Memo quoted in Keith Schneider, "1950 Note Warns about Radiation Tests," *New York Times*, December 28, 1993, p. A8; Failla quoted in Philip J. Hilts, "Fallout Risk Near Atom Tests Was Known, Documents Show," *New York Times*, March 15, 1995, p. A13.

35. Philip J. Hilts, "Radiation Test Secrecy Linked to Lawsuit Fears," *New York Times*, November 15, 1994; Philip J. Hilts, "Thousands of Human Experiments," *New York Times*, October 22, 1994; Philip J. Hilts, "Radiation Tests Used Some Healthy People," *New York Times*, January 19, 1995, p. B10; "44 Years Later, the Truth about the 'Science Club,'" *New York Times*, December 31, 1993, p. A18. Details of experiments in which plutonium was injected into eighteen people were reported in the *Albuquerque Tribune*, November 15–17, 1993.

36. Michael Janofsky, "Cold War Chill Lingers Downwind from a Nuclear Bomb-Testing Site," *New York Times*, January 11, 1994, p. A12.

37. Leonard A. Cole, *Clouds of Secrecy: The Army's Germ Warfare Tests over Populated Areas* (Totowa, NJ: Rowman & Littlefield, 1988), p. 59.

38. Quoted in ibid., pp. 156, 140; Warren E. Leary, "Secret Army Chemical Tests Did Not Harm Health, Report Says," *New York Times*, May 15, 1997, p. A24. The CIA also conducted experiments on unsuspecting subjects, including administering LSD to mental patients and to bar customers.

39. Cole, *Clouds of Secrecy*, p. 64.

40. Quoted in ibid., pp. 45–46. This use of African Americans is similar to the notorious Tuskegee syphilis experiment of 1932–1972 described in James H. Jones, *Bad Blood: The Tuskegee Syphilis Experiment: A Tragedy of Race and Medicine* (New York: Free Press, 1981).

41. Cole, *Clouds of Secrecy*, p. 155.

42. Quotes from William Glaberson, "Fear Corrodes Faith at Atomic Plants," *New York Times*, December 11, 1988, p. 36.

43. Matthew L. Wald, "Stored Plutonium Is Liable to Leak, Government Says," *New York Times*, December 7, 1994, pp. A1, D20.

44. Jacques Steinberg, "Study Cites Illness in Alumni of Schools on Industrial Sites," *New York Times*, February 19, 2001, p. A16.

45. Matthew L. Wald, "Tracking of Radiation Exposure in Bomb Work Is Questioned," *New York Times*, November 9, 1997, p. 23.

46. Quoted in Matthew L. Wald, "U.S. Acknowledges Radiation Killed Weapons Workers," *New York Times*, January 29, 2000, p. A1.

47. Michael Janofsky, "Ill Uranium Miners Left Waiting as Payments for Exposure Lapse," *New York Times*, March 27, 2001, pp. A1, A16.

48. Quoted in David Johnston, "Weapons Plant Dumped Chemicals into Drinking Water, F.B.I. Says," *New York Times*, June 10, 1989, pp. 1, 10.

49. Quoted in Matthew L. Wald, "Radiation Leaks at Hanford Threaten River, Experts Say," *New York Times*, October 11, 1997, p. A7.

50. Matthew L. Wald, "Admitting Error at a Weapons Plant," *New York Times*, March 23, 1998, p. A10.

51. H. Jack Geiger, "Generations of Poison and Lies," *New York Times*, op-ed article, August 5, 1990; quote from the film *Deadly Deception*, produced by INFACT, which has organized a boycott of GE's consumer products in an effort to pressure the company to stop making weapons. The film was broadcast on PBS, channel 13, New York City, September 27, 1992.

MILITARISM
Structural and Interpersonal Violence

In the last chapter we described organizational violence caused by militarism. In this chapter we will look at how militarism is linked to structural and interpersonal violence. Structural violence results from the economic impact of military spending. This is because unemployment is increased by heavy investments in the military rather than the civilian sector of the economy. In addition, social needs go unmet because of very high levels of military spending. We will also discuss how militarism is related to two types of interpersonal violence: domestic violence and homophobic violence.

SPENDING FOR THE MILITARY IS SPENDING FOR UNEMPLOYMENT

In earlier chapters we emphasized that prolonged unemployment affects people's health and their social relations in ways that fit our definition of violence. Very high levels of military spending contribute in several ways to joblessness rates.

Military production paradoxically creates jobs and at the same time unemployment. This is because money spent manufacturing military equipment creates fewer jobs per dollar than does civilian production. The Council on Economic Priorities estimated in the 1980s that each billion dollars spent on military equipment generated twenty-eight thousand jobs. The same amount spent for mass transit would have created thirty-two thousand jobs and if spent on education, seventy-one thousand jobs. A 1992 study by the Congressional Research Service claimed that each billion dollars transferred from the military to the civilian sector for things such as new construction of highways and streets, or health care, would produce 4,054 additional jobs. Money transferred from the military to the civilian sector would also produce usable goods and services contributing to an improvement in the quality of life rather than munitions and equipment destined for destruction.[1]

Minority groups with the highest unemployment rates benefit the least from military spending. The engineers, computer specialists, and mathematicians who work in the weapons industry are likely to be white and male. Military production has made the United States less competitive internationally. Civilian products made in the United States do not do as well as those made in Japan and Germany, which means there will be less need for workers in the consumer manufacturing sector. The United States is a premier exporter of military technology; the same is not true for our other products.

Money is spent on improving weapons but not as much goes for developing better consumer goods. About 70 percent of federal dollars for research and development goes for military purposes here, while for Germany the figures is 10 to 15 percent and for Japan it is 5 percent.[2] The siphoning of engineering talent to the aerospace industries has taken a toll on the steel, auto, consumer electronics, and machine tool industries. Experts on weapons spending Anne Markusen and Joe Yudken summarize some of the consequences:

> While American firms labor to produce a Stealth bomber, a laser gun, or a software system to demanding military specifications, their counterparts abroad are free to lavish their best brains and resources on commercial developments with far greater payoffs to the economy.[3]

The Federal Office of Technology Assessment in 1989 compared the United States to western Europe and Japan, which "construct their technology efforts with a greater emphasis on economic development over military development than does the United States."[4] They presented figures stating that while the military was receiving $23 billion for research and development from federal funds, the steel industry was given only $21 million. Military intervention itself heightens unemployment. Supporting antiunion, antiregulatory regimes, as discussed in chapter 13, encourages corporations to move jobs from the United States.

The dissolution of the Soviet Union and the end of the Cold War heralded a chance for a "peace dividend," the reallocation of monies used for the military to more useful purposes. This has not happened.

"WE DON'T HAVE ANY MONEY": WEAPONS OR SOCIAL SPENDING?

True defense spending should increase a people's security and make them safer, but in the United States we are more insecure as a result of monies expended on the military. If our high spending were truly defending us against fearsome enemies armed with the latest weapons, we would be safer, but this is not the case. We should ask which war fought since the Second World War has actually increased our security? The principle foreign threat Americans face seems to be from terrorists who may be very resourceful and motivated but who will not be stopped by aircraft carriers, unmanned drones, cluster bombs, a proposed missile shield, and new forms of nuclear weapons.

High levels of military spending are endangering our physical quality of life, which is already lower than in comparable countries. In chapter 13 we quoted former president Dwight D. Eisenhower on the military-industrial complex's influence on American life. In the same address in which he warned about the power of this coalition, he went on to say we're making the wrong choices:

> Every gun that is made, every warship launched, every rocket fired signifies in the final sense a theft from those who hunger and are not fed, those who are cold and are not clothed. We pay for a single fighter plane with a half-billion bushels of wheat. We pay for a single destroyer with new homes that could have housed more than eight thousand people. . . . Is there no other way the world can live?[5]

In addition to the "theft" described by Eisenhower, we can add that every dollar spent on war preparations is a dollar less for dealing with problems associated with structural violence: repairing our dangerously decaying infrastructure, improving health care, educating our population, providing daycare and recreation facilities, cleaning our contaminated environment, and caring for the physically and mentally ill. Social scientist

Michael Parenti argues that it is not irrational for the elite to prefer military to social spending.

> Military spending is much preferred by the business community to many other forms of government expenditure. Public monies invested in occupational safety, environmental protection, drug rehabilitation, public schools, and other human services provide for human needs and create jobs and buying power. But such programs expand the *nonprofit* public sector bringing no direct returns to business. . . . In contrast, a weapons contract injects huge amounts of public funds directly into the private corporate sector at an unusually high rate of profit.[6]

Critics of social spending like to say you can't solve a problem by throwing money at it, but they never claim this to be the case with military security. There is no guarantee that money not spent on the military would go for social spending. Campaigns for this would still be needed. However, one major argument against this spending, "we just can't afford it," could be more easily countered.

Such an argument was proffered in 1995 by then Senate majority leader Robert Dole. Explaining why the federal government would be cutting Medicare and Medicaid funding, Dole said, "We don't have any money."[7] Yet the House voted to give the Pentagon $7 billion more for 1996 and 1997 than had even been requested by the military, and the military budget continued to rise after that. Forty-six percent of the 2003 federal budget will go for military purposes.[8] If you were deciding your family's budget, would you give nearly half to a home security system, or would you choose to be sure you had decent shelter, food, health, and money for education and recreation?

The upshot is that the wealthy will sacrifice neither their bodies nor their pocketbooks for a militarism that chiefly benefits them. As was discussed in chapter 3, the tax system protects the assets of the economically privileged, and their children need not join the military because they lack other opportunities. As of mid-July 2003, the Pentagon estimated that about $48 billion had been spent on the war against Iraq. In November 2003 the president signed a bill for an additional $87 billion to pay for the costs of occupying the Persian Gulf country, with about $12 billion of that money allocated for Afghanistan. Each year, according to the Internal Revenue Service, 65 percent of that $87 billion is lost to the federal treasury because rich individuals and corporations use addresses abroad to avoid paying taxes here.[9]

Over and over the government sacrifices the real needs of the American people to defend corporate interests though military spending. Social spending cuts have lasting impacts. They adversely affect the quality of life for millions of Americans, as library hours, funding for arts and music, and parks are decreased. Some of the cuts are especially relevant to the issues we have been discussing.

After-school programs for about five hundred thousand students will end; the cost of these was $400 million. This amount is about the cost of two F/A fighter jets. The Air Force is requesting twenty-two of these at a total cost of $5.2 billion. The United States already has the strongest air force in the world, with five thousand planes and at least eight thousand helicopters. How many are needed to protect us from countries with far less air power? Since the peak hours for youth crime and drug use is between 3 P.M. and 6 P.M. the cuts to after-school programs mean there will probably be more juvenile crime.[10]

The federal government is reducing its funding to states. The National Governors Association reported in 2002 that the states are confronting "the most dire fiscal situation since World War II."[11] When the governors asked Bush for more money at a meeting with him in February 2003, he told them the federal government has its own fiscal problems and would not be able to help them.[12] States have less money to give to local governments, and at all government levels services are being slashed. The costs of public services will be raised; there may be nonfederal tax increases. States have to decide what to cut. California is planning to drop about two hundred thousand people from its Medi-Cal program. For those remaining, their physical therapy, optometry, and hospice care will not be covered.[13]

Many states are laying off workers. Connecticut laid off three thousand state employees in December 2002 and another twelve hundred the next month. Among the fired were drug counselors, mental health workers, and lab technicians. Four of the fifteen offices of the Department of Social Services were closed. This office provides food and medical assistance to the needy. Berdella White, who lives in a public housing development, predicted, "We're going to have more people out on the street and more people in jail. How are they going to survive? We're talking about people who have no public transportation."[14]

Lock-'em up and throw away the key is now too expensive, and some states are changing their sentencing policies. Eight states are considering revising their policies, and Michigan and Kentucky have already revised their mandatory minimum sentences. Some other states are also considering this cost-cutting measure. Paroling previously unparolable inmates will save the state about $28,000 per inmate.[15] Kentucky is even releasing some violent offenders. Since there are few jobs for them when they leave incarceration and they are unlikely to have received training or rehabilitation services in prison, the public is not likely to be safer after their release.

In Virginia a local prosecutor has said he can no longer afford to prosecute the more than two thousand domestic violence cases he deals with in a typical year. "I deeply regret that the victims of domestic violence will no longer have a prosecutor on their side. But something has to go. I'm two assistant attorneys short." On a more positive note, Kansas will mandate treatment for drug offenders that costs about $2,500 a year instead of sending them to prison for $21,000 a year.[16]

We have discussed in earlier chapters how inequality is increasing in the United States. There has been an upsurge in homelessness and hunger at a time when there are fewer funds for dealing with these problems. In a sense, we can say, our society is actually withholding food and shelter from those who cannot afford it. These are forms of organizational violence. The effects, particularly on children, could be lasting, producing examples of structural violence.

In 2001 the U.S. Conference of Mayors commissioned a survey of twenty-seven cities looking at hunger and homelessness. Twenty-five of the urban areas reported increases in requests for food assistance. Two-thirds of the municipalities could not provide adequate food. A majority of the cities had to decrease either the number of times a single person or family could get food or the amount they were given. Overall, about 14 percent of the requests were turned down. Between 2000 and 2001 there was an average increase of 13 percent in requests for emergency shelter.[17]

Federal housing aid to renters is likely to be cut. In Colorado the elderly were exempt from property taxes, but that is being suspended. Carol DeBoer, an older woman caring for a husband with Alzheimer's, asked, "We worked hard; we paid our taxes. If there is enough money for wars, shouldn't there be enough to help seniors?"[18]

Health care, including care for children, is becoming less affordable as governments at all levels cut back. The House Budget Committee even voted a reduction in health care benefits for veterans and cut other benefits including survivor education funds. The school week is being reduced in Oregon, and support staff such as janitors and cooks are being fired. In several states class sizes are increasing and summer schools are being canceled.[19] What will happen to the children affected by these cuts, which are on top of reductions in nonmilitary spending that have been going on for over twenty years?

Over and over the power elite tends to the desires of the military-industrial complex while neglecting the needs of the rest of the society.

At a billion dollars a day the minimal cost of the 1991 Gulf War was $49 billion. This six-and-a-half-week war cost more in dollars than the 1991 federal budget for education, job training, and employment services combined. Table 15.1 shows other choices that have been made in the past that increased interpersonal and structural violence.

In 1998 the following choice was made: building F-22 fighter planes, each costing $161 million, instead of awarding Pell grants to one hundred thousand students. Each aircraft carrier that was built cost $5.4 billion. That money could have paid for ten years of health care for five hundred thousand children.[20] Table 15.2 shows more recent military spending that has been at the expense of health, education, and nutrition.

The U.S. military relies to a large extent on very expensive, highly technological weapons systems.[21] These are unlikely to help fight terrorism and could have done nothing to prevent the attacks on September 11, 2001. Even relatively small portions of this money could fund valuable programs.

- $11 billion would pay for reducing class size for grades one to three to fifteen students a class.
- $6 billion would provide health insurance for all uninsured children.
- $1 billion would pay for public financing of federal elections.

For what the U.S. currently spends on military spending, $38 billion, eleven million lives could be saved globally fighting infectious diseases.[22]

TABLE 15.1 MILITARY VERSUS
SOCIAL SPENDING, 1980–1995

military	*received* $1,116 billion
housing	cut $390 billion
aid to cities	cut $117 billion
job training	cut $101 billion
education	cut $ 59 billion
antipoverty programs	cut $ 49 billion

Source: Common Agenda Coalition and the National Priorities Project, *Creating a Common Agenda* (Northhampton, MA: National Priorities Project, n.d.), p. 8.

TABLE 15.2 MILITARY VERSUS SOCIAL SPENDING

military spending	cost	social spending alternative
1 year of nuclear weapons program	$16 billion	health care coverage for 7 million children
1 bunker-buster guided bomb	$145,600	associate degree training for 29 RNs
1 minute of war on Iraq	$763,000	annual salary/benefits for 15 RNs
Amphibious Warfare Landing Ship Program	$413 million	child care for 68,000 needy children
1 hour of war on Iraq	$46 million	repair and modernize 20 schools
1 Stealth bomber	$2.1 billion	annual salary/benefits for 38,000 elementary school teachers
7 unmanned Predator drone aircraft	$130 million	federal nutrition program for 200,000 families

Source: Adapted from "Which Path to a Safer World?" Dollars and Sense (May/June 2003): 9.

If this military spending were truly defending us against fearsome enemies armed with the latest weapons, then perhaps the military spending would be justifiable. But this is not the case.

Ironically, the U.S. government's past support for anti-Communist fundamentalist forces is itself leading to American deaths. In 1979 the Soviet Union sent troops to Afghanistan to battle fundamentalist forces seeking to overthrow the Soviet-supported government. The United States backed the fundamentalists, providing them with funds and weapons. The Soviet-backed government was defeated, and then these groups began fighting among themselves. The Taliban won this battle and then provided their own support for al Qaeda, the anti-American terrorist organization who organized the September 11 attacks.[23]

There were earlier fundamentalist terrorist strikes in the United Sates and at U.S. targets abroad. The first terrorist attack on the World Trade Center occurred in 1993. An explosive-filled van blew up in an underground garage killing six people and injuring over a thousand. In May 2003 suicide bombers killed twenty people, including seven Americans, in a Western enclave in Riyadh, Saudi Arabia. At this date it is not known who was responsible. Earlier suicide bombers had been part of the U.S.-supported forces that overthrew the pro-Soviet regime in Afghanistan. In June 1996 an explosion in Saudi Arabia killed nineteen American soldiers.[24]

Providing the technology that will supposedly protect the United States against foreign terrorists will be a boon to military contractors. They, along with politicians, will have a vested interest in raising people's fears about this threat. In 2002 the Department of Homeland Security was established. It is currently headed by Tom Ridge who as governor of Pennsylvania presided over a Philadelphia police force accused of numerous infractions of people's rights. Congress approved the establishment of this department in spite of the fact that it is allowed to contract with American companies that have offshore operations to avoid paying U.S. taxes. Heightened "security" measures are a bonanza to business. The military contracting firms are making plans to cash in on what is likely to be a lucrative market. Daniel P. Burnham, CEO of Raytheon, optimistically remarked, "It could be a substantial market and we're proceeding as if it is."[25]

The new department has a large budget, about $40 billion in 2003, and lobbyists from companies that manufacture security equipment are competing for contracts. John J. Pavlick, whose law firm lobbies for military contractors such as Lockheed Martin, explained, "We're trying to help our clients avoid the land mines and find the gold mines in homeland security. The major defense contractors want to move into the homeland security area in a big way." [26]

Some of the lobbyists used to work for Ridge when he was Pennsylvania's governor. One refused to answer questions asked by a *New York Times* reporter on a possible conflict of interest, hanging up the phone with the comment, "This conversation is over." Some former aides who will be working with Ridge in the new department come from a law firm, Blank Rome, whose customers are in the domestic security business.[27]

"A WARRIOR NATION": TRAINED FOR VIOLENCE

On April 4, 1967, exactly one year before his assassination, Martin Luther King Jr. eloquently expressed his opposition to the Vietnam War. Speaking at the Riverside Church in New York City, he outlined how the war took away "skills and money like some demonic, destructive suction tube" and told how he had come "to see the war as an enemy of the poor." King believed that the war had more than a material effect on the United States. It taught lessons of malice and violence to the troops, "injecting poisonous drugs of hate into the veins of people normally humane." King asked how he could preach against violence at home when young men would ask him, "What about Vietnam?" Isn't the United States using massive doses of violence to solve its problems, to bring about the changes it wanted? Their questions hit home, and I knew that I could never again raise my voice against the violence of the oppressed in the ghettos without having first spoken clearly to the greatest purveyor of violence in the world today—my own government.[28]

Since King's speech, U.S military interventions have occurred in Laos and Cambodia, Grenada, Panama, Nicaragua, El Salvador, Bosnia, Afghanistan, Somalia, and Iraq.[29] People are still being taught that force is the way to achieve goals. As Sen. Daniel Moynihan explained to Arab leaders in September 1990, "You must understand that Americans are a warrior nation."[30]

Recent presidents provide warrior role models for dealing with crises. They have done this by attacking other countries with little provocation but with increases in their approval ratings. Pollsters refer to such attacks as "rally events." Political opponents mute their criticisms of the commander in chief when the nation is at war, fearful of being labeled "unpatriotic." Reagan's popularity increased after the 1983 invasion of Grenada, which followed the bombing of a U.S. Marine installation in Lebanon. That humiliation could be forgotten because of the success in Grenada. After the 1989 invasion of Panama, George H. W. Bush proudly described himself as a "macho man," and Lee Atwater, then chair of the Republican National Committee, declared that now Bush had "knocked the question about being timid and a wimp out of the stadium."[31]

On June 26, 1993, President Clinton ordered a U.S. missile attack on intelligence headquarters in the Iraqi capital of Baghdad. The president claimed that there was, in his words, "compelling evidence that there was in fact a plot to assassinate former president Bush," as retaliation for the Gulf War in 1991. Twenty-three cruise missiles were launched; seven of these struck a civilian neighborhood killing eight people and wounding many more. It is highly doubtful the plot to kill Bush existed. Clinton's action is not so different from that of Colin Ferguson, mentioned in chapter 12, who believed he had a right to kill Long Island Railroad passengers because whites and "Uncle Toms had mistreated him." Clinton's attack on Iraqi civilians won him a boost in the polls. In September 1996, with the election campaign in full swing, Clinton again ordered Cruise missile strikes at Iraq.[32]

WARRIOR MEN = PROBABLE HOMOPHOBES AND SEX OFFENDERS

The military's influence is pervasive, seen in popular movies, video games, toys, and in the rise of paramilitary organizations. The military has helped shape U.S. conceptions of masculinity, promising for years to make men out of boys. A real man is aggressive, a protector, and assertively heterosexual. This is one reason homosexuality was so anathema to the military, and why women have had a difficult time gaining equality in the armed forces. Terry Spahr Nelson, a psychotherapist who has done extensive research on sexual assault in the military, describes the misogynistic aspect of military training:

> References are frequently made, especially in basic training, to a man's masculinity and ability to perform. Those who do not meet the standards are often referred to as a "wimp, pussy, or girl." Drill instructors have been known to call their troops "ladies" as a form of degradation and humiliation. The male persona is one that is strong, powerful, and in control, whereas the female stereotype is considered weaker, powerless, and physically unequal to their male counterparts. This particular aspect of military culture serves only to complicate the problems of integrating women as equal partners in the military.[33]

In 1993, with President Clinton's approval, the military established what is called the "Don't Ask, Don't Tell" policy, an implicit condemnation of homosexuality. The policy was supposed to protect gays and lesbians. As long as their sexual preferences were unknown, they could continue to serve. Journalist and economist Doug Ireland reports, however, that discharges of alleged gays and lesbians increased "from 617 in 1994 to 1,034 in 1999."[34]

The gay rights organization Servicemembers Legal Defense Fund claimed that from the time the policy was enacted until December 2003 close to ten thousand military personnel have been forced to leave the military because of homosexuality This not only costs some people their careers, but it costs the taxpayer millions since these trained personnel have to be replaced. The policy can also make Americans more vulnerable to terrorist attacks from Islamic fundamentalists. Between 2001 and 2003, with Arabic-speaking staff in short supply, the Army discharged thirty-seven gay, Arabic-fluent linguists working at the army's Defense Language Institute in Monterey, California.[35]

Harassment is common and homophobic assaults, discussed in chapter 11, occur in the military. A survey released by the Department of Defense in early 2000 indicated that 10 percent of the 71,750 respondents had seen physical assaults while 80 percent had heard homophobic comments. Of those who said a senior officer was present during an incident, nearly three-quarters reported that the authority did nothing to intervene. Some women feel pressured to have sex with military men out of fear they will otherwise be labeled lesbians.[36]

The consequences of these attitudes and policies are demonstrated by what Doug Ireland calls the "grisly antigay murder" of twenty-one-year-old private Barry Winchell at Fort Campbell in Kentucky. The soldier reported that he was being harassed but was not protected by his superior officers. Finally, one night while he slept, another soldier beat him to death with a baseball bat. Army investigators came to the contradictory conclusion that there was no antigay atmosphere on the base although there were homophobic attitudes in some members of Winchell's unit. A spokesperson for the Servicemembers Legal Defense Network disagreed and recommended that "superior officers deal with [the] problem head-on and stop the harassment." In December 2003 the commanding general at the Fort Campbell was promoted.[37]

Allen R. Schindler was a twenty-two-year-old navy radio operator who was tired of hiding his sexual identity. In 1992, shortly before his ship reached Japan, he came out to his commanding officer. A month later two fellow sailors beat him to death in a public restroom. His face was so disfigured by the battering that his mother had to use his tattooed arms to identify him.[38]

We noted earlier that sexual assaults can provide an affirmation of masculinity for some men. The view of masculinity encouraged by the military has been associated with sexual violence and a predatory attitude toward women. In basic training men used to chant

This is my rifle.
This is my gun. [Pointing to their crotch]
One is for fighting.
The other's for fun.

The military even helps to arrange the "fun." Prostitution is tolerated around U.S. bases, and rapes of foreign women are rarely punished.[39]

Training for war reinforces traditional beliefs concerning maleness for some in the Armed Forces. There are few punishments for engaging in sexually aggressive behavior or for domestic violence. The women have few supports, whether they are serving themselves or living on a military base. A 1994 congressionally sponsored study of the Naval and Air Force Academies and West Point found from 36 to 42 percent of female respondents claiming they had experienced some form of sexual harassment. In 1995 a thoroughly researched series of articles published in the *Dayton Daily News* described a pattern of very lenient treatment given to hundreds of sex offenders by military courts.[40]

Terry Spahr Nelson's survey of over forty-seven thousand military personnel found 78 percent of women "experiencing behavior consistent with a form of sexual harassment or sexual assault." These numbers should be assumed to be underestimates for the same reasons that exist in collecting civilian sexual assault statistics. The victim may be reluctant to come forth out of embarrassment or fear of retribution. She, or less frequently he, may fear being stigmatized or blamed for inciting the attack. In addition, commanding officers may deal with the accusation themselves. The attack never becomes part of official records.[41]

At least thirty-three 1991 Gulf War servicewomen claimed they were raped by their own military colleagues. One twenty-nine-year-old Army mechanic, Jacqueline Ortiz, was among them. A year later she was suffering from insomnia, headaches, and nausea. She told Senate investigators, "It's very difficult to deal with. I was very proud to serve my country but not to be a sex slave to someone who had a problem with power." Specialist Ortiz and other women testified that their superiors were unresponsive to their complaints.[42]

In 2003 a scandal broke out at the Air Force Academy in Colorado Springs when female cadets began to tell stories of being raped or sexually assaulted. They charged that their accusations were met by inaction and even retaliation by their superior officers. One victim, identified by the journalist reporting her story only as Ruth, left the academy as a result of sexual attacks, as did several other victims. She claimed a health counselor told several female cadets that she herself had been raped and warned the young women, "It will probably happen to you." The counselor further advised the women not to report assaults because if they asked for an investigation, "your entire life at the academy is over, and you'll probably get kicked out."[43] A survey conducted in May 2003 indicated that 70 percent of the women at the academy had experienced some form of sexual harassment, with 19 percent reporting some type of physical assault, including rape. Eighty percent of the victims never reported the attacks.[44]

Women who came forth were blamed for the incidents. Brig. Gen. Taco Gilbert said of one incident where the woman had played strip poker, "When you put yourself in situations with increased risk, you have to take increased precautions to mitigate those risks." As more and more women spoke up, several of the Air Force Academy's highest administrators were replaced. The Air Force is also planning to replace the large metal letters on an academy wall that read "Bring Me Men."[45]

The tough-guy attitude toward women is also illustrated by the Tailhook scandal. At the annual naval aviators' convention in Las Vegas in 1991, ninety women were sexually assaulted by at least 117 young officers. Some of the men wore T-shirts with the words "Women Are Property." The officers protected one another, and since the women could not identify individual attackers, none of the pilots were punished. In the Naval Inspector General's report on the incident, Rear Adm. George W. Davis noted the nonchalance of the men involved: "A common thread running through the overwhelming majority of interviews was 'What's the big deal?' There is still little understanding of the nature, severity, and number of assaults which occurred."[46]

Domestic violence is a problem in military families, sometimes with fatal results. In the summer of 2002, Fort Bragg, North Carolina, was the scene of four murders of soldiers' wives. In addition, one woman killed her husband. Three of the men had returned from serving in Special Operations units in Afghanistan. One wife was stabbed seventy times, another was strangled, and the other two shot. Two of the husbands committed suicide with their guns after killing their wives. In keeping with the tough, self-reliant image of soldiers, none of the people in the troubled marriages had requested help with their problems.

An Army psychiatrist who has recommended adding mental health workers to combat the problem admitted, "There was a prevalent attitude that seeking behavioral health care was not career-safe."[47] The four women killed had been threatening to leave their husbands. Women working in support services for victims of domestic violence claim that some Special Force veterans threaten their wives with techniques of killing they had learned in the service. Women are afraid that if they complain they jeopardize not only their own safety but their husband's careers, the household's incomes, and health care.[48]

Military families are geographically mobile. This gives them less opportunity to develop close ties with others on the bases where they are housed. Consequently, they may have few peers they can turn to for advice and support, peers who could also be aware of potential danger and might act to prevent it. This social isolation that some military personnel and their dependents experience can itself be a source of stress.[49]

In 1998 the Army funded a study that revealed that "severe aggression" in marriages was three times higher in Army families compared to civilian ones, and the rates were increasing. When we consider that violence is explicitly taught and approved of in the military, this is perhaps not so surprising. It is the conclusion of David Grossman, a former military psychologist. He helped train recruits to develop what he terms "disengagement," the breaking down of the reluctance to kill. He describes disengagement as "the ability to watch a human being's head explode and to do it again and again—that takes a kind of desensitization to human suffering that has to be learned." A former Special Forces veteran with experience in Haiti and Vietnam, Stan Goff, explains, "Go to Afghanistan, where you are insulated from outside scrutiny, and all the taboos you learned as a child are suspended. You take life more and more with impunity . . . that's a real sense of power."[50]

It is not only training for masculinity that helps explain sexual violence in the armed forces. The culture and structure of the military is relevant here as in other cases where violence is committed in a bureaucratic context. Soldiers, sailors, Marines, and those in the Air Force learn to be loyal to their fellows. What happens when individuals in the military know a peer has committed an offense? Should they be loyal to their buddy or to their own values, which may tell them to support the victim. There is also a strict hierarchy, and the higher officers set the tone for those beneath them. Commanding officers' own attitudes and reactions have been found to be associated with the amount of sexual misconduct in their units, as mentioned above in the case of Barry Winchell. However, the Army's inspector general claimed there was no homophobic atmosphere at the base, and in October 2003 the Senate Armed Services Committee approved the commanding general of the base's promotion.[51]

WARRIOR MEN = PARAMILITARY ACTIVISTS

Right-wing militia members see the federal government as threatening their freedom. They have accepted the idea that the way to correct a problem is to identify those responsible and kill them, the military response to a troublesome situation.

Keystones in the paramilitary subculture are *Soldier of Fortune* (*SOF*) magazine and the National Rifle Association (NRA). Since 1981, *SOF* has hosted an annual four-day convention in Las Vegas, described by participant sociologist James William Gibson as "a celebration of violence." Conventioneers can attend seminars, some of which feature foreign military officers, and lectures such as the one with an *SOF* editor on "Submachine Guns: Their History and Use." They can buy T-shirts trivializing killing, for example, one showing snipers with sophisticated weapons and the words, "Reach Out and Touch Someone." Given the association between militarism and male sexuality, it is not surprising that posters of barely clad women decorate the convention site. Similarly scantily dressed women are part of the exhibits and events.[52]

The federal government supports the *SOF* convention by sending agents from law enforcement agencies, such as the Drug Enforcement Agency, to give speeches. Local, state, and federal police also send personnel to gun schools run by those with close ties to paramilitary groups such as the NRA. Jeff Cooper, formerly on the NRA board of directors, runs a training camp in Arizona, the Gunsite Ranch, known more formally as the American Pistol Institute. Cooper believes that patriotic Americans must defend themselves against the CLAMS, an acronym standing for "Congressional Left, Academics, and Media."[53] The Marine Corps, the Department of Energy, and the Los Angles Police Department are among those using the facilities at this ranch. Some police agents spend their vacation time teaching at Cooper's Arizona school.

Little boys have long played war games. Now adult males and a very few females play them, too, in the form of paintball. James William Gibson estimates that between 1988 and 1994 over two million men had put on camouflage uniforms and picked up their toy weapons at one of over a thousand sites all over the country. It is easy to buy a real gun at a store or through the pages of magazines. Since the end of the Vietnam War, according to Gibson, "millions of American men [have] purchased combat rifles, pistols, and shotguns and begun training to fight their own personal wars."[54]

Some individuals have formed citizen militias who plan to fight the "enemy" on U.S. soil. The enemy can include African Americans, gays, Jews, or federal employees. Radical or progressive groups may be targeted as well, labeled as Communists, the justification the U.S. government used for killing people around the world for two decades.

In Greensboro, North Carolina, in 1979, the paramilitary racist and anti-Communist tendencies came together in a joint neo-Nazi, Ku Klux

Klan shooting of an anti-Klan march organized by a group called the Communist Workers Party. Five marchers were killed, and twelve of the perpetrators were arrested. One was a former U.S. Army Special Forces sergeant who proudly declared that the shootings were "the only armed victory over communism in this country."[55] The April 1995 bombing in Oklahoma City by combat veteran Timothy McVeigh and associates also demonstrates the violent threat posed by these groups.

ANOTHER VICTIM: DEMOCRATIC INSTITUTIONS

At different times, different rationales are offered for the military spending that supposedly protects us and preserves our freedoms. We have discussed above how our physical well-being is actually lessened by the huge military budget and by military activities. Freedom and democracy have been jeopardized as well as part of the costs of militarism.

Transforming our society to become more egalitarian and less violent is more difficult if we cannot exercise our democratic rights. The government has used the argument of protecting "national security" to weaken progressive dissent. Wars fought to supposedly protect our rights usually involve limiting them. During World War II, 110,000 Japanese, two-thirds of them U.S. citizens, were thrown into internment camps without any proof that they had committed crimes or were a danger.

The Cold War saw the antiprogressive repression identified with but not caused by Sen. Joseph McCarthy. Anti-Communism was successfully used in the United States to weaken movements for social change. Progressives of all political persuasions were labeled "Communists" and purged from the entertainment industry, the media, schools, the labor movement, and government positions.[56]

The Vietnam era was accompanied by the FBI's COINTELPRO (Counterintelligence Program), established in 1967 to disrupt and destroy progressive groups. U.S. intervention in Central America during the Reagan-Bush administrations was accompanied by new rules giving the CIA the right to spy on domestic dissenters.

Military strategies and technologies have been applied to domestic rebellions. Between 1964 and 1969 the National Guard was called on to quell 196 racial disturbances and about 20 campus protests, during which time there were the infamous shootings at Kent and Jackson state universities. When the 1992 uprising in Los Angeles took place, Gen. Marvin L.

Covault was put in charge of twelve thousand troops to be brought to the scene if his superiors thought it necessary. Covault developed the Army's "light infantry," units that can be rapidly deployed but have a great deal of firepower.[57]

In New York City in 1995 the police came in tanks to forcibly eject squatters from the building they had spent ten years renovating. Watching these roll down the city streets, an observer exclaimed, "It's like we're at war with ourselves."[58] The Pentagon is equipping special units of urban police forces with grenade launchers, M-16s, and tanks. These are likely to be used against those protesting injustice, as has happened already with antiglobalization and antiwar demonstrations.

When the Department of Justice (DOJ) asked police departments in cities and counties to identify potential threats, they included groups whose motivations could be "political, religious, racial, [or] environmental." A DOJ-sponsored training program in Wichita, Kansas, wants the police to conduct surveillance on "enemies in our backyard." These include "the green movement," which is described as "environmental activism that is aimed at political and social reform."[59]

Following the attacks on the World Trade Center (1993) and the Federal Building in Oklahoma City (1995), Congress passed the Antiterrorism and Effective Death Penalty Act in 1996. Among the provisions of the bill was giving the secretary of state the authority to establish a list of organizations he or she considers terrorists. Support for these organizations, including helping to fund schools and hospitals, is now punishable by up to ten years in prison.

In the years before this bill was passed, organizations fighting for more just societies were labeled as "terrorist" by our government. The African National Congress (ANC) that led the struggle against apartheid in South Africa and the FMLN in El Salvador are examples. In the future, individuals in this country who support various foreign liberation movements could find themselves charged with aiding terrorists. Almost all organizations fighting for the rights of Palestinian people are currently on the list.

In October 2001 Congress passed and the president signed the USA Patriot Act. Barbara McKenna, writing for the American Federation of Teachers publication *On Campus*, summarizes the act's provisions:

> The Patriot Act gives the Justice Department broad information-gathering and surveillance capabilities. It can collect sensitive private data on individuals, eavesdrop on telephone conversations, monitor computer use, and detain suspects without probable cause—all with reduced judicial

oversight. These powers are not limited to terrorism investigations but can be extended to all federal investigations.

If federal investigators visit a site such as a campus or library to collect information, the people being asked to provide it are forbidden to speak of the request to anyone.[60]

Patriotism seems to mean giving up accustomed and previously protected rights. The act defines "domestic terrorism" as actions that "appear to be intended to influence the policy of a government by intimidation or coercion." We need to ask "appear" to whom, and how are "intimidation" and "coercion" defined? Will rallies, nonviolent demonstrations, sit-ins, and strikes be considered instances of these?

The FBI's powers to investigate citizens are expanded, and the federal death penalty can be applied to some terrorist acts. The latter is a problem not only if you are against capital punishment but because it can inhibit the fight against terrorism. European countries that have abolished capital punishment may refuse to extradite suspects to the United States if they think the person's execution could result.

The Patriot Act allows the government to deny a visa to a foreigner who is an alleged member of a terrorist organization whether or not he has actually done anything. It also facilitates deportation.[61] These may seem like reasonable steps, but keep in mind that the definition of a terrorist is subject to political manipulation. If the government doesn't agree with an organization's goals, the organization could wind up with the label, and supporters of it here could be prosecuted.

Worried about the implications of these measures, New York representative Jose E. Serrano, a Democrat, confronted Attorney General John Ashcroft during a congressional hearing: "I fear some officials are so intent on fighting against terror that they forget what we are fighting for. People across the spectrum fear for our civil liberties." Corroborating this view, former congressman, Republican Dick Armey accused the attorney general and his Justice Department of being "out of being control."[62]

Male noncitizens over sixteen from eighteen Arab and Islamic countries are being ordered to register with the Immigration and Naturalization Service. The very act of doing this to tens of thousands of people, many of them with student or work visas, sends a message that we face terrible dangers and these are people we need to be afraid of. Secret tribunals are being used against noncitizens who can be arrested, charged, and deported without having a lawyer and without knowing what the evidence against them is. Some people have already been deported. Maybe they did have ties to terrorist organizations, or maybe they did not.[63] Colleges and universities are being ordered to provide information on foreign students to federal law enforcement agencies.

Among the provisions of the act is the right of the FBI to demand that librarians provide records of their patrons' use of library materials. Some librarians are shredding records rather than comply. This is the case in Santa Cruz, California, where the library director said, "I am more terrified of having my First Amendment rights to information and free speech infringed than I am of the . . . terrorist acts that have come down so far."[64]

Under the guise of protecting national security, the rights of people to information that could make their lives safer from corporate malfeasance are being limited. For example, while President Clinton had proposed giving the public more access to materials on the possible consequence of chemical plant accidents, the EPA has rescinded the order because the information might supposedly help terrorists. In addition, the EPA is using its relatively small staff of 220 investigators to work more on counterterrorism and less on corporate attacks on the environment. Other agencies are also restricting the public's ability to gain knowledge. Television commentator Bill Moyers summarizes this trend, "In the name of fighting terrorists, the government is pulling a veil of secrecy around itself."[65]

The atmosphere of intimidation is spreading beyond the government itself. Students are being punished at some schools for expressing antiwar views. In West Virginia, Katie Sierra, from Panama, was suspended for three days after she wore a T-Shirt with the words, "When I saw the dead and dying Afghani children on TV, I felt a newly recovered sense of national security, God bless America." School administrators charged her with disrupting student learning. A circuit court agreed. The state supreme court refused to hear her case. At school she was physically and verbally abused. Another student was not punished for wearing a T-shirt signed by fellow classmates with words directed at Sierra, "Go back where you come from." Sierra dropped out of school to study at home.[66]

The fight against Communism and now against "terrorism" and "terrorist nations" has wasted resources and chipped away at our hard-won rights. The alleged battle to protect democracy has made us less democratic. We still have rights and freedoms that can be used to fight for a more egalitarian and less violent society, as will be discussed in the next, concluding chapter.

NOTES

1. Elliot Currie and Jerome Skolnick, *America's Problems: Social Issues and Public Policy*, 2nd ed. (Glenview, IL: Scott, Foresman and Company, 1988), p. 394; Martin Tolchin, "Shift of Spending Seen as a Benefit," *New York Times*, January 26, 1993, p. A17; Anne Markuson and Joel Yudken, *Dismantling the Cold War Economy* (New York: Basic Books, 1992), p. 134.

2. Currie and Skolnick, *America's Problems*, pp. 400–402.

3. Markuson and Yudken, *Dismantling the Cold War Economy*, p. 2. See also Seymour Melman, *The Permanent War Economy: American Capitalism in Decline* (New York: Simon and Schuster, 1985), pp.74–104.

4. Markusen and Yudken, *Dismantling the Cold War Economy*, p. 64.

5. Quoted in Felix Green, *The Enemy: What Every American Should Know about Imperialism* (New York: Random House, 1970), p. 228.

6. Michael Parenti, *Democracy for the Few*, 7th ed. (Boston: Bedord/St. Martin's, 2002), pp. 83–84.

7. Seymour Melman, *The Demilitarized Society: Disarmament and Conversion* (Montreal: Harvest House, 1988), pp. 62–63; Dole quoted in Adam Clymer, "An Accidental Overhaul," *New York Times*, June 26, 1995, p. A1.

8. Eric Schmitt, "House Votes Big Increase in Military Budget for '96," *New York Times*, June 16, 1995, p. A20. The percentage being spent on the military is from the War Resisters League (WRL), who each year put out a chart, "Where Your Income Tax Money Really Goes." Their figure is higher than the government's own, 17 percent for 2003, because the government includes trust funds such as Social Security in its total revenues. These can only be spent on the purpose for which they were collected. The War Resisters League's budget is based on tax revenues alone and includes monies going for both present wars and to pay continuing costs of past ones. The WRL Web site is www.warresisters.org.

9. Cost of war from Associated Press, "Pentagon: Iraq War Cost Now $48 Billion," reported July 16, 2003, Fox News, http://www.foxnews.com/printer _friendly_story/0,3566,92029,00.html (accessed December 8, 2003); CBC (Canadian Broadcasting Corporation), "Bush Signs Bill Approving $87 Billion for Iraq," November 6, 2003, http://www.cbc.ca/cgibin/templates/print.cgi?/2003/11/06/ usiraqo3110c (accessed December 8, 2003); Robert L. Borosage, "Sacrifice Is for Suckers," *Nation*, April 28, 2003, p. 4. To find out what the war costs your state, see the National Priorities Project chart "The Cost of War for States and Selected Cities," http://www.nationalpriorites.org/issues/Military/iraq/CostOFWar.html (accessed December 8, 2003).

10. Fox Butterfield, "Lifeline for Troubled Oregon Teenagers Is Imperiled by Planned U.S. Cuts," *New York Times*, March 9, 2003, p. 26; cost of F/A fighter jets, David E. Rosenbaum, "How Would You Cut the Federal Budget?" *New York Times*, February 9, 2003, p. 3; numbers of planes and helicopters, John Isaacs, "Superpower Stats," op-ed article, *New York Times,* October 29, 1997, p. A27.

11. Bob Herbert, "States of Alarm," *New York Times*, December 26, 2002, p. 9.

12. Marta Russell, "Billions to Turkey, Screw the Govs and the Poor Too," *Znet Commentary*, March 5, 2003.

13. John M. Broder, "Californians Hear Grim News on Budget," *New York Times*, January 11, 2003, p. A11.

14. David M. Herszenhorn, "3,000 Workers Get Pink Slips in Connecticut," *New York Times*, December 7, 2002, pp. B1, B2; Paul von Zeilbauer, "Budget Crisis in Connecticut Forces Layoffs," *New York Times,* January 18, 2003, pp. B1, B6.

15. "Michigan to Drop Minimum Sentence Rules for Drug Crimes," *New York Times,* December 26, 2002, p. A26.

16. Fox Butterfield, "Inmates Go Free to Reduce Deficits," *New York Times*, December 19, 2002, pp. A1, A30.

17. "Hunger and Homelessness Up Sharply in Major U.S, Cities," press release, December 12, 2001, http://usmayours.org/uscm/news/press_releases/documents/hunger_121101.asp (accessed September 12, 2002).

18. Timothy Egan, "States, Facing Budget Shortfalls, Cut the Major and the Mundane," *New York Times*, April 21, 2003, pp. A1, A20.

19. Sam Dillon, "School Year Ending Early among Efforts to Cut Costs," *New York Times*, January 12, 2003, p. 16.

20. Based on data from the National Priorities Project, *Are You Winning or Losing: How Federal Choices Affect You and Your Community,* 1998, pp. 28–29.

21. Michael Renner, "Military Expenditures on the Rise,"in *Vital Signs 2003*, ed. Linda Stark for Worldwatch Institute (New York: W. W. Norton, 2003).

22. "Which Path to a Safer World?" *Dollars and Sense* (May/June 2003): 9.

23. Tariq Ali, *The Clash of Fundamentalisms* (New York: Verso, 2002) pp. 206–13.

24. C. Philip Shenon, "Holy War Is Home to Haunt the Saudis," *New York Times*, July 14, 1996, sec. 4, p. 3; Michael Parenti, *The Terrorism Trap: September 11 and Beyond* (San Francisco: City Lights, 2002), pp. 62–64.

25. David Firestone, "House Approves Domestic Security Bill," *New York Times,* November 14, 2002, p. A32; quote from James Dao, "Internal Security Is Attracting a Crowd of Arms Contractors," *New York Times*, March 20, 2002, p. C1.

26. Philip Shenon, "Former Domestic Security Aides Make a Quick Switch to Lobbying," *New York Times*, April 29, 2003, pp. A1, A20.

27. Quoted in ibid., p. A20.

28. Quotes from "Declaration of Independence from the War in Vietnam," *Essay Series* (New York: A. J. Muste Memorial Institute, n.d), pp. 37, 38. In November 1993 President Bill Clinton addressed a group of black ministers and imagined what King would say to violent ghetto youths were he still alive. The president fantasized that King would say he "did not fight for the right of black people to murder other black people." Clinton did not choose to quote what King actually said. See H. Bruce Franklin, "What King Really Would Have Said," *Philadelphia Inquirer*, December 7, 1993.

29. Not all of these wars were fought for the same reason. The point here is that war was the strategy for dealing with conflict rather than seeking nonviolent solutions.

30. Quoted in Barbara Ehrenreich, "The Warrior Culture," in *Beyond the Storm: A Gulf Crisis Reader*, ed. Phyllis Bennis and Michael Moushabeck (New York: Olive Branch Press, 1991), p. 129.

31. Richard L. Berke, "Poll Shows Raid on Iraq Buoyed Clinton's Popularity," *New York Times*, June 29, 1993, p. A7; Bush quoted in Ehrenreich, "The Warrior Culture," p. 130; Atwater quoted in James William Gibson, *Warrior Dreams: Violence and Manhood in Post-Vietnam America* (New York: Hill and Wang, 1994), p. 291.

32. "Action Update," *International Action Center* 1, no. 1 (Summer 1993). The FBI had reported that there was a plan to kill George Bush during his visit to Kuwait (April 1993) with a car bomb. A car bomb was discovered in Kuwait, but there was no evidence that it had been manufactured in Iraq or was in any way connected with Iraqi intelligence. Tim Weiner, "Plot by Baghdad to Assassinate Bush Is Questioned," *New York Times*, October 25, 1993; "Clinton Cites L.I.R.R. Shootings," *New York Times*, December 12, 1993, p. 57. For a critique of the 1996 attack, see editorial, "The Iraq Lesson," *Nation*, September 23, 1996, p. 3.

33. T. S. Nelson, *For Love of Country: Confronting Rape and Sexual Harassment in the U.S. Military* (New York: Haworth Maltreatment and Trauma Press, 2002), p. 67.

34. Doug Ireland, "Search and Destroy: Gay-Baiting in the Military under 'Don't Ask, Don't Tell,'" *Nation*, July 10, 2000, p. 11.

35. John Files, "Gay Ex-Officers Say 'Don't Ask' Doesn't Work," *New York Times*, December 10, 2003, p. 18; "Despite Increased Post-9/11 Need, Military Fires 37 Arabic Translators for Being Gay," "Democracy Now" transcript (WBAI 99.5 FM New York), http://www.democracynow.org/article.pl?sid=03/12/05/160238 (accessed December 6, 2003); "Gay Linguists Say They Were Ousted," *New York Times*, November 15, 2003, p. A20. For a personal account by a gay linguist, see the op-ed article by Alastair Gamble, "A Military at War Needs Its Gay Soldiers, *New York Times*, November 29, 2002, p. A39.

36. Ireland, "Search and Destroy," pp. 11–12.

37. Ibid., p. 12; quote from Elaine Scolino, "Army Exonerates Officers in Slaying of Gay Private," *New York Times*, July 19, 2003, p. A9; John Files, "Committee Approves Promoting General in Gay-Bashing Case," *New York Times*, October 24, 2003, p. A16.

38. James Sterngold, "Death of a Gay Sailor: A Lethal Beating Overseas Brings Questions and Fear," *New York Times*, January 31, 1993, p. 22.

39. For an account of prostitution, see Sandra Pollock Sturdevant and Brenda Stoltzfus, *Let the Good Times Roll: Prostitution and the U.S. Military in Asia* (New York: New Press, 1992).

40. Eric Schmitt, "Study Says Sexual Harassment Persists at Military

Academy," *New York Times*, April 5, 1995, p. B8; Russell Carollo, "Military Secrets," *Dayton Daily News*, October 1–5, 1995.

41. Nelson, *For Love of Country*, pp. 18–19. She also has data on males who are sexually harassed. Females in countries where the United States has a military presence are also subject to assault by military personnel, see pp. 27–31.

42. Ortiz quoted in Anne Marie Connell, "Boys Will Be Boys: The Tailhook Scandal," *On Guard* 13, no. 9 (1992): 12.

43. Quoted in Michael Janofsky, "Air Force Begins an Inquiry of Ex-Cadets Rape Charges," *New York Times*, February 20, 2003, p. A18.

44. Diana Jean Shemo, "Rate of Rape at Academy Is Put at 12% in Survey," *New York Times*, August 29, 2003, p. A12.

45. Quote from Robert Weller, "Cadets Say Criticized for Reporting Rapes," *Seattletime.com*, February 17, 2003, http://seattletimes.nwsource.com/text/134635739_academy17.html (accessed February 19, 2003); Diana Jean Schemo, "4 Top Officers at Air Force Academy Are Replaced in Wake of Rape Scandal," *New York Times,* March 26, 2003, p. A10.

46. T-shirts described by Michael R. Gordon, "Pentagon Report Tells of Aviators' 'Debauchery,'" April 24, 1993; "Excerpts from the Pentagon Report," *New York Times*, April 24, 1993, p. 9; quote in Eric Schmitt, "Navy Says Dozens of Women Were Harassed at Pilots Convention," *New York Times*, May 1, 1992.

47. Quote in "Mental Health Workers Must Go to Combat Units, Report Says," *New York Times*, November 9, 2002, p. A13.

48. Catherine Lutz and Jon Elliston, "Domestic Terror," *Nation*, October 14, 2002, pp. 28–30.

49. Mary Stewart, *Ordinary Violence: Everyday Assaults against Women* (Westport, CT: Bergin & Garvey, 2002), p. 101.

50. Quotes in Alexander Cockburn, "Blowback: From Unruh to Muhammad," *Nation*, November 18, 2000, p. 8; Goff quoted in Lutz and Elliston, "Domestic Terror," p. 28.

51. Ireland, "Search and Destroy"; Files, "Gay Ex-Officers Say 'Don't Ask' Doesn't Work."

52. Gibson, *Warrior Dreams*, pp. 148–69.

53. Ibid., p. 172.

54. Ibid., p. 8.

55. Quoted in ibid., p. 215.

56. A good discussion of this can be found in Marty Jezer, *The Dark Ages: Life in the United States, 1945–1960* (Boston: South End Press, 1982).

57. Jason DeParle, "General and Troops Have Domestic Mission," *New York Times*, April 3, 1992.

58. Vivian S. Toy, "Differing Viewpoints on Squatters Next Door," *New York Times*, May 31, 1995, p. B2.

59. Silja J. A. Talvi, "The Public Is the Enemy," *Nation*, May 12, 2003, pp.

30–31; Robert Dreyfuss, "The Cops Are Watching You," *Nation*, June 3, 2002, p. 16.

60. Barbara McKenna, "A Question of Balance," *On Campus* (May/June 2003): 10–11. "USA PATRIOT" act is an acronym for the bill's full name, "The Uniting and Strengthening of America by Providing Appropriate Tools Required to Intercept and Obstruct Terrorism Act."

61. Pamela L. Griset and Sue Mahan, *Terrorism in Perspective* (Thousand Oaks, CA: Sage, 2003), pp. 282–83. In appendix B they list the organizations the State Department defines as terrorist as of 2001.

62. Quoted in Eric Lichtblau and Adam Liptak, "On Terror, Spying, and Guns, Ashcroft Expands Reach," *New York Times*, March 15, 2003, p. A1.

63. John M. Broder and Susan Sachs, "Facing Registry Deadline Men from Muslim Nations Swamp Immigration Office," *New York Times*, December 17, 2002, p. A20.

64. Dean E. Murphy, "Some Librarians Use Shredder to Show Opposition to New F.B.I. Powers," *New York Times*, April 7, 2003, p. A12; McKenna, "A Question of Balance," p. 10.

65. Carl Hulse, "A Reversal on Public Access to Chemical Data," *New York Times*, March 27, 2001, p. A18; Jennifer Lee, "E.P.A. Is Said to Be Concentrating on Terror," *New York Times*, April 29, 2001, p. A27. Nelson, *For Love of Country*, pp. 6, 149–50, 266–80.

66. Reported in *Dollars and Sense* (January/February 2002): 4.

Chapter
16
REDUCING THE CASUALTIES

Beginning his reelection campaign in 1998, New York's Republican governor George Pataki attacked the idea that sociology can help explain crime and violence. He explained, "As servants of the people we are not charged with carrying out a sociological study. We are charged with maintaining public order and saving lives." Republican presidential hopeful Robert Dole, speaking in Ohio in May 1996, said we live in an "age of violence" but, he added, "the debate [is] not about root causes. . . . It [is] about right and wrong."[1] Pataki and Dole are mistaken: violence can only be lessened if its root causes are understood and addressed. Much of the violence in the United States, we have argued, stems from decisions made by a very small group of wealthy and powerful people protecting their class interests. Their decisions ripple into the lives of the rest of us, sometimes with devastating results.

Too much of the public discussion on violence focuses on street crime, attributing this to a lamentable decline of values. We agree that people should not deal dangerous illegal drugs nor use violence to solve their emotional or financial problems. By the same standards, capitalists should put the health and safety of workers and consumers before profits and take care not to degrade the environment. Politicians should put the public welfare before their own narrow career goals. They should be educating the public about the "root causes" of our problems.

We have tried to show that crime and many examples of violence are

370 INEQUALITY AND VIOLENCE IN THE UNITED STATES

caused by economic and political inequalities. These inequalities lead to a lack of opportunities, and they also produce unhealthy working conditions, environmental degradation, unsafe products, and militarism. Even if interpersonal violence, the focus of most media and political discussion, were drastically reduced, organizational and structural violence could still continue at high levels. However, the three types are linked, all rooted in the unequal distribution of power and wealth in our society.

Debates as to how best to deal with violent behavior should be trying to bring us to a better understanding of how to create social environments where violence is minimized. Without large-scale changes, efforts to reduce violence will have a limited impact at best. Violence will lessen when inequality lessens. This will happen when we bring about progressive social change, which means working with others to build movements that can successfully challenge corporate power and government priorities. Michael Parenti, in his discussion of the need for popular action, points out, "It is often frustrating and sometimes dangerous to challenge those who own and control the land, capital, and technology of society. But in the long run it is even more dangerous not to do so."[2]

American capitalism has created many casualties. Although some suffer more than others, an awareness of our common problems is a first step toward seeking common solutions. In 1976 William Ryan wrote in *Blaming the Victim*:

> Everyone who depends for the sustenance of [themselves] and their family on salary and wages, and who does not have a separate source of income through some substantial ownership of wealth is a potential victim in America. [They] are vulnerable to the disaster of catastrophic illness in a private-enterprise medical-care system; . . . vulnerable to the deliberate manipulation of inflation and unemployment; . . . vulnerable to the burden of grossly unfair taxes; . . . vulnerable to the endemic pollution of air and food and to the unattended hazards of the factory and the highway that will likely kill [them] before [their] time; . . . vulnerable to the greed of the great oil companies and food corporations.[3]

All the threats to well-being listed by Ryan are still with us, the result of an inequitable distribution of power that must be challenged. Thoughtful critics of American society—some cited in this book—have produced useful suggestions of what needs changing, how street and corporate crime can be reduced, how corporations can be made more accountable to workers and communities, how public health can be improved, the environment protected, and how government can be made more responsive to the will of the people.[4]

We have tried to show that the search for profits by the few does not benefit the many. As long as capitalism exists, we will have to find ways to lessen its harmful impact. Violence will not appreciably lessen in this country until we, the public, have more power over the economic and political institutions that most affect our lives. Communities and workers need to find ways to increase their own political power and exercise more control over capitalist enterprises.

The Preamble to the U.S. Constitution says that government is created to "promote the general welfare" and "domestic tranquility," not to promote corporate welfare and general anxiety. The links that bind politicians to corporations need to be broken. This means changes in campaign financing and meaningful restrictions on corporate lobbying and office holding by former CEOs. The "general welfare" cannot be achieved without a truly progressive tax system that redistributes from the wealthy to the rest of the society in the form of social services that will lessen structural violence. We still have a war economy even though we have no powerful enemies. Our taxes should be meeting human needs not those of the military industries and their allies.

Government commitment to full employment will address some of the problems we have discussed, if the employment is reasonably paid and healthy. In addition, public ownership and control of vital services is necessary. If present trends continue, environmental rehabilitation and protection are not going to be high priorities.

Analysts of criminal violence have useful suggestions, especially for lessening street crime.[5] Instead of more punishment, more repression, and more revenge, they emphasize the need for more prevention and more rehabilitation. There may be people whose rehabilitation is so difficult that long-term incarceration of some kind is the only way to protect the public, but their numbers will be small. For many current inmates, prisons could provide socially valuable skills instead of honing their abilities to commit crimes while increasing their anger and bitterness.

NO STRUGGLE, NO PROGRESS

No strategies for change will be effective unless we organize and fight for their implementation. Frederick Douglass's 1853 admonition remains true today: "If there is no struggle there is no progress. . . . Power concedes nothing without a demand, it never did and it never will."[6] We have democratic rights to speak, to protest, to organize, and to vote. These rights are the result of struggles by past generations, and we can use them to reduce the casualties of the present system. Past injustices and suffering that seemed entrenched were overcome by the determined efforts of ordinary people motivated by visions of a more just society. Learning about these efforts teaches us how progressive changes are brought about, gives us respect for ordinary people, and provides inspiration and models for dealing with present problems. We can learn from our own history and the history of other countries as well.[7]

Making major social changes is always likely to seem an unrealistic goal. Looking only at the last hundred years, it must have seemed that legal segregation would never be abolished; women would never have reproductive choices, be able to vote, or have independent lives; gays and lesbians would always be treated as pariahs; child labor would not be abolished; the working day would never shorten, work never become safer, nor unions be recognized. In addition to making specific gains, movements past and present have deepened our knowledge of how our system works, knowledge that is vital to future struggles.

In the midst of the Great Depression of the 1930s, organized movements, many led by the Communist Party, built industrial unions, organized the unemployed, and helped bring about social programs that enriched the arts and attacked poverty and unemployment. The activism of the Depression was cut short by World War II, and, following that war, by the corporate- and government-sponsored purge of activists in the 1950s, often called McCarthyism, mentioned in chapter 15.

In the 1960s a new generation of activists emerged—first in the South, then in northern ghettos, fighting racism. Then came struggles against the war in Vietnam and against poverty, sexism, and homophobia. There were victories, some of which we have discussed in earlier chapters. But government repression, internal weaknesses, and political disagreements seriously weakened these movements.

Nonetheless, activism has continued. In the recent past anti-intervention movements critical of U.S. policy toward Central America likely forestalled U.S. military invasions in that region, while solidarity movements have provided useful support to progressive forces abroad. New groups have emerged, for example, fighting to protect affirmative action, immigrant rights, and public services like education and health care. In the 1990s the antiglobalization movement targeting the consequences of corporate activity has attracted many thousands of people here and abroad.

In 2002 millions of people in the United States, part of an unprecedented global antiwar movement, tried to stop the invasion of Iraq. High school and college students joined older veterans of earlier antiwar movements. As we know, the war occurred. Still, new organizations were created, ties were built, and knowledge was gained. Many who became involved in trying to prevent the war are still politically engaged in fighting budget cuts, militarism, and attacks on civil liberties. This latter is especially important for ensuring that future struggles will not be confronted with heightened repression.

Once change does occur, a collective amnesia is encouraged; we are not taught how our gains were won. When social reforms are described, they are "explained" as the result of alleged individual achievements instead of collective efforts. In describing the past, U.S. popular culture and most education emphasizes the role of individuals rather than showing the importance of collective action. Given this emphasis, it is easy to believe a benevolent leadership or extraordinary individuals almost single-handedly created new social programs and policies.

Media neglect of current protests and grassroots actions encourages pessimism. There is little news coverage of progressive political activities, and even nationally organized large demonstrations are usually covered in misleading ways. The numbers attending are underestimated, and equal media attention is given to small numbers of dissenters, diluting the impact of the protesters' message. We rarely learn of the accomplishments of people in other countries.

FEW ILLUSIONS

Even if most people are not protesting the system, many are aware that things are not working very well. We can be told over and over this is the greatest and most democratic country in the world. We hear repeatedly that "you can be anything you want to be," but personal experiences and knowledge of at least some of the injustices have raised public awareness. It took years before there were huge protests against the war in Vietnam. Many could not believe their country would so betray its ideals or that the government would lie to the people. When the war against Iraq loomed, however, there was a very quick recognition by numerous people that the public was being lied to and that a war was not justified.

In spite of the great influence of the corporate-owned media, there is skepticism and questioning about the real intentions of those in positions of power. The public does not have much confidence in business or in government. A 2001 survey asked people to state their level of confidence in major American institutions. They could choose a lot, some, or none. Fifty percent said they had no confidence in Congress, and 59 percent had no confidence in political organizations and political parties. Forty-two percent had no confidence in major corporations. There was no institution in which there was a lot of confidence.[8]

Without faith in government, there is little certainty of how to change things. Even exercising the most basic of democratic rights, the right to vote, does not interest many citizens. The United States has the lowest voter turnout of any advanced capitalist country.[9] Registering and voting are more difficult in the United States than in other countries, but widespread pessimism and alienation regarding the candidates lowers turnout as well.[10]

In the 1994 congressional elections, in a *New York Times*/CBS poll 68 percent of the respondents answered, "not much" to the question, "How much say do you think people like yourself have about what the government does?" In 2003 about the same percentage, 69, told a Louis Harris poll that public opinion "has too little power." Eighty percent thought "big companies" had "too much power."[11]

In the 2000 presidential elections only 55 percent of those eligible to cast a ballot did so. In contrast, Israeli turnout for their 2003 national elections was the lowest ever, with 69 percent of those eligible voting.[12] The winner in an American election is actually elected by a minority of voters, if we add up all those who don't vote but could and those voting for other candidates. Of course, in the 2000 presidential election the winner did not even have a majority of the votes that were actually cast, a fact that might make people even more cynical about the electoral process.

Voter turnout is even lower in nonpresidential election years. The 2002 congressional elections brought out only 39 percent of the eligible voters.[13] With neither major party in the United States committed to their interests, lower-income people are especially unlikely to vote, even though they could drastically affect the outcome of many elections. This association between class and nonvoting is not found in other industrial democracies.[14] An expert in voting patterns, Walter Dean Burnham, refers to this lower electoral participation as "selective demobilization." Commenting on the fact that those most in need of change are least likely vote, S. M. Miller comments, "The disparities in voting rates by socioeconomic groups form one of the most biting indictments of the practice of American democracy."[15] Even the lesser of two evils means less harm will be done in the short run. Furthermore, when large numbers do not even go to the polls, the major parties can justifiably feel they can continue with business as usual without electoral reprisals. If neither a Democrat nor a Republican candidate appeals to you, you can vote for a third party or write in a name.

FIGHTING BACK: SOME EXAMPLES

There is evidence that people want to protest the status quo, take a collective stand, and build a better society. The political system does respond to pressures from below. Organizations throughout the country are fighting against some of the problems discussed in this book. The antiwar demonstrations across the United States in 2003 cumulatively involved a few million people. In October 1995 the Million Man March brought virtually a million, mostly African American men, to Washington, DC, while in June 1996 about a quarter of a million people rallied at the nation's capital for the Stand for Children Rally. One participant, Kathy Simons, a day care worker from Massachusetts, described why she had made the long trip:

> We're excited to come down here and have the opportunity to scream a little. There is such an overwhelming frustration in the compromises you have to make every day in quality and availability of child care.[16]

Other examples will illustrate the more sustained ways in which concerned groups are trying to make their communities safer, healthier, and more humane, some fighting around single issues and some with broader concerns. In May 2003 the people of Vieques, Puerto Rico, celebrated their victory over the U.S. military. For sixty years the Navy had bombarded the island to test weapons and for target practice, and in May 2003, after years of protests, they agreed to stop. The government even agreed to clean up the contamination the Navy's activities had caused. One protestor, Ardelle Ferrer, described the islanders' feelings, "People are very jubilant. Everyone is so happy seeing something that seemed so impossible."[17]

In Boston's Roxbury section in 1995, an organization called the Dudley Street Neighborhood Initiative (DSNI) grew out of the despair of local residents trying to find a way to rebuild their blighted community. The conditions in Dudley were a result of the processes described in chapter 9. Decisions of government agencies, banks, and realtors had led to a downward spiral where Dudley ended up looking "like Beirut," according to Nelson Merced, a community activist.[18]

The ethnic makeup of Dudley includes African Americans, Latinos from a number of areas, whites, and Portuguese-speaking immigrants from the Cape Verde Islands. A formal but democratic governing structure was created with representatives of all the community's ethnic groups, businesses, social service agencies, and religious organizations. It was difficult at first to convince people that they could make a difference. Knocking on doors, organizer Andrea Nagel found that "at times the negativity was really alarming."[19]

The group came up with the slogan "Don't Dump on Us" to emphasize residents' disgust with their neighborhood being used literally as a garbage dump. The often illegally dumped trash was not only an eyesore but also a breeding ground for insects, rats, and disease. The slogan had another meaning as well: "Stop trashing the community" in other ways.

DSNI did more, however, than deal with specific problems such as sanitation. They created a vision of a multiuse urban village. One of the key elements in this was a concern for safety. The people of Dudley wanted stores, housing, and public spaces designed to encourage "eyes on the street." The development plan DSNI drew up provided not only for this but also for improving employment opportunities, child care, recreation, and for protecting cultural diversity. This was an ambitious agenda for a neighborhood group and required outside support and advice. Nonetheless, the initiative and energy came from a community many of whose residents were stereotyped by the larger society as criminals, lazy, and so forth. Eventually the DSNI got a $2 million loan from the Ford Foundation, and power of eminent domain gave it some authority over land use.

With their resources DSNI has been able to support a number of services, some especially relevant to the issues raised in this book, including community centers providing drug treatment, counseling to reduce substance abuse and child abuse, pre- and postnatal advice, employment counseling, a rape crisis center, and the establishment of a local health care center. DSNI has also targeted environmental racism and lead poisoning. The neighborhood association has even engaged in a home building project.

The DSNI has intervened in cases of racist police actions, has challenged racist stereotypes in the media, involved young people in the organization's activities, and created an inspiring document, a declaration of community rights. If this declaration could be put into practice throughout communities in the United States, much of the violence we have discussed could very likely be reduced. In this neighborhood, demoralization, indifference, and despair have been replaced with optimism and a sense of community growing out of the experiences of people working together to realize a common vision.

Another inspiring example comes from Los Angeles. Concerned with that city's severe air pollution, mentioned in chapter 6, veteran activist Eric Mann joined with others to create the Labor/Community WATCHDOG Organizing Committee in 1989. The committee describes itself as "multiracial and anticorporate" with an emphasis on "rebuilding the labor movement, fighting for environmental justice, . . . mass transit, and immigrant rights" while "actively opposing the growing criminalization, racialization, and feminization of poverty."[20] It has established a center for research, publications, and outreach.

As with the DSNI, support from other groups, including unions, has helped build the Labor/Community WATCHDOG Organizing Committee, which takes the position that corporations "along with the finest politicians their money can buy, are largely responsible for . . . toxic air." The organization also believes that since the corporate decision-making process excludes the affected public, creating a healthy environment means creating a more democratic one as well.[21]

The WATCHDOG's Labor/Community Strategy Center maintains that affordable local transportation is an important issue. Working people need to be able to get to their jobs; those without jobs need transportation to look for employment. In 1995, as part of a coalition that included the NAACP, the Korean Immigrant Workers' Advocates, and the Southern Christian Leadership Conference, they were able to mount court challenges to the Los Angeles County Metropolitan Transit Authority. As a result, bus fares in Los Angeles were kept more affordable.[22]

WATCHDOG also organized a Boycott Texaco campaign with the slogan "Communities and Workers Demand Public Health Before Corporate Profits." Texaco (now Chevron/Texaco) is a leading producer of carcinogens and other toxic products; it spends millions to lobby against air pollution regulations and engages in numerous unsafe practices in the United States and abroad. Even if WATCHDOG's demands are not all met, this organization, in conjunction with the Sierra Club, Greenpeace, Acción Ecológica, and the Rainforest Action Network, is doing more than protesting a problem. It is suggesting democratic solutions and demanding corporate responsibility, helping to create a vision of a more egalitarian community.

Community groups can work against interpersonal violence. An impressive example of fighting racist violence comes from Billings, Montana, a town of 84,000, whose residents, in the words of a documentary filmmaker, decided "the only way to really be safe is to take a stand." Racist groups threatened Billings's residents. They sent death threats to an African American resident and tried to intimidate the congregation of an African American church by going to their services and standing in intimidating poses. They threw a cinder block through the window of a Jewish family's home, where six-year-old Isaac Schnitzer had put a cardboard menorah in celebration of Chanukah. In addition, they desecrated a Jewish cemetery and painted racist slogans on Native American Dawn Fast-Horse's home.

One of the organizers of antiracist activity was Randy Siemenes, president of the local laborers' union. He went to the labor council, which passed a strong resolution against hate groups. Union members worked with police to provide security at antihate meetings, and after their day's work, thirty members of the painters' union, along with one hundred other people, painted over the graffiti on the home of Dawn Fast-Horse. Gary Modie, one of the painters, said, "So many of the times when there's a cause, you end up standing on the sidelines too much. . . . I never really did a lot to do anything about anything and I was really glad to help paint the home, more so to help convey a message to these guys that the community will not stand for that."[23]

Many are involved in Billings's continued antiracist efforts including unions, local human rights activists, religious leaders, journalists, the editor of the *Billings Gazette*, and the Billings police chief, Wayne Inman. He had been a member of the Portland, Oregon, police department when Ethiopian student Mulugeta Seraw, mentioned in chapter 12, was killed, and he didn't want to see racist violence in his Montana hometown.

Using the model of the Danes who, during the Nazi invasion, put on yellow stars in support of their Jewish countrymen, in response to the attack on the Schnitzer's home, ten thousand families and businesses placed paper menorahs in their windows. One business put up a sign reading "Not in Our Town. No Hate, No Violence." In support of the African American congregation, members of other churches went and attended services, conveying the message, in the words of the Rev. Bob Freeman, "If you bite one of us you bite us all. And that was a very good feeling we had."[24] Instead of having to face threats in isolation, perhaps arming themselves in desperation, those threatened in Billings got support and solidarity, and community ties were strengthened. Numerous other communities have followed Billings's example, organizing their own antihate crime activities.[25]

Groups can overcome their past antagonisms and build alliances when they realize they are in the same badly leaking boat. An example of this comes from northern Wisconsin, where white sports fishermen had mounted an ugly campaign against Ojibwa Indians who had treaty rights to exclusively spearfish. Using slogans such as "Save A Walleye—Spear an Indian," whites engaged in shootings, arson, and beatings. Now, both Ojibwas and the sportsmen have formed an alliance against EXXON, whose proposed mining operations would include the creation of an enormous toxic waste site the size of three hundred football fields, endangering the whole northern Wisconsin watershed.[26]

An example of youth activism comes from Massachusetts. Project HIP-HOP was started there in 1993 by the state chapter of the American Civil Liberties Union. An ethnically diverse group of high school students travel to the South on a "civil rights tour" where they speak to activists and learn that there is "unfinished business" that they have a role in completing. They not only learn about the past, but meet members of current grassroots movements and become inspired. One youngster, Marco Garrida, described the transformation of his feelings:

> I have felt the spirit that fueled the movement. . . . HIP-HOP has stirred me to social consciousness. . . . I have also seen and heard and felt the injustice the movement sought to end. This injustice, which before had overwhelmed me, now angers me. Stronger, I accept my responsibility to continue what the Movement began, to finish the unfinished business.

The students share their experiences at schools and community centers, addressing more than ten thousand other students, encouraging them "to learn not to give in to that sense of helplessness."[27]

In San Francisco, ¡PODER!, Spanish for power, organizes for alternatives to crime and gangs, demanding jobs and recreation instead of repression. In the city's 1995 election, the group helped create a coalition to fight a ballot referendum establishing a curfew for those under eighteen. ¡PODER! member fifteen-year-old Raquel Moreno saw the curfew as a form of scapegoating and as "part of a war going on between the police department and the community."¡PODER! won the referendum.[28]

In addition to bringing about positive change, joining in social movements can enhance a participant's own psychological well-being. A recent study in England found that people who became involved in protests, demonstrations, and strikes developed "feelings of encouragement and confidence" from being part of a "collective action." Even when the political activity ended, these feelings were sustained for some time. John Drury, one of the researchers, described the interviews he had:

> Empowering events were almost without exception described as joyous occasions. Participants experience a deep sense of happiness and even euphoria in being involved in protest events. Simply recounting the events in the interview brought a smile to the face of the interviewees.[29]

"WE CAN BUILD A NEW WORLD"

As the examples above show, activism in the interests of social betterment continues.[30] But reducing violence, extending and protecting our rights, and creating a more egalitarian society will take national movements and a political party that truly represents the majority of the population in this country. A revitalized labor movement is a crucial part of any strategy for progressive change. We need a labor movement that can fight effectively for working people's interests, that will have the resources and the collective strength to fight corporate power, and that can effectively pressure elected officials to act in the interests of the majority. The immense wealth the working people of this country produce needs to be used for social programs that benefit all of us, not just a small group of investors.

The labor organizations' leadership is now more diverse, with a greater representation of women and people of color than was the case in the past. There is discussion of how to be connected to grassroots movements. Trade unionists have joined environmentalists and others in protesting corporate-dominated globalization. One example of this occurred in Seattle in 1999 when participants proudly pointed to a coalition between "teamsters and turtles."[31] The latter reference was to some environmentalists who had worn green turtle costumes. Links between workers and students are being forged, using the model of Freedom Summer. During the Civil Rights Movement, students from many campuses went to the South to help local activists register voters. The AFL-CIO has organized "Union Summer," which gives students a chance "to participate in and develop skills useful for union organizing drives and other campaigns for workers' rights and social justice."[32]

There are many groups throughout the country fighting inequality and seeking greater voice for ordinary people in their communities and the larger society. They struggle against militarism, racism, sexism, and the exploitation of workers here and abroad. Their members work for economic justice, civil rights, peace, environmental protection, and decent health care.[33]

Successful movements require visions of a better future. Is it absurd to imagine a society in which everyone can have health care, a decent home, quality education, satisfying work, leisure, and a healthy environment? Is it unreasonable to expect to live in a country where everyone can walk the streets without fear, and where racism, sexism, homophobia, and violence are subjects only for the history books? The people united have won important victories in the past; we can organize to win them in the present and create that healthier, happier future.

There is no guarantee that a particular battle will end in victory, but even if we fail to reach a specific goal, the knowledge we gain, the skills we learn, the friendships we develop, and the cultures of resistance that we create remain. Our lives are enriched, and we are better able to succeed in future struggles.

NOTES

1. Pataki quoted in Adam Nagourney, "Pataki Says Root of Crime Is Criminals, Not Society," *New York Times*, November 24, 1998, p. 4; Dole quoted in Katherine Q. Seeyle, "Revisiting the Issue of Crime, Dole Offers List of Remedies," *New York Times*, May 29, 1996, pp. A1, B7.

2. Michael Parenti, *Land of Idols: Political Mythology in America* (New York: St. Martin's Press, 1994), p. 5.

3. William Ryan, *Blaming the Victim* (New York: Vintage Publications, 1976), p. xiii. Where Ryan used "he," I have substituted a more general pronoun.

4. Useful ideas can be found in David R. Simon, *Elite Deviance*, 6th ed. (Boston: Allyn and Bacon, 1999), pp. 329–56; Holly Sklar, *Chaos Or Community? Seeking Solutions, Not Scapegoats for Bad Economics* (Boston: South End Press, 1995), pp. 161–77.

5. These include Albert J. Reiss and Jeffery A. Roth, eds., *Understanding and Preventing Violence* (Washington, DC: National Research Council, 1993); Felice J. Levine and Katherine J. Rosich, *Social Causes of Violence: Crafting a Science Agenda* (Washington, DC: American Sociological Association, 1996); American Psychological Association, *Violence and Youth: Psychology's Response, Volume I: Summary Report of the American Psychological Association on Violence and Youth* (Washington, DC: American Psychological Association, 1993); Steven R. Donziger, ed., *The Real War on Crime: The Report of the National Criminal Justice Commission* (New York: HarperPerennial, 1996), pp. 195–253; Elliot Currie, *Reckoning: Drugs, the Cities, and the American Future* (New York: Hill and Wang, 1993), pp. 280–332.

6. Quoted in Lerone Bennett Jr., *Before the Mayflower* (New York: Penguin Books, 1984), pp. 160–61.

7. This book concentrates on the United States, but we can learn from, for example, the antiapartheid struggle in South Africa, the achievements in Cuba and of the Sandinista regime in Nicaragua, and even from what was successfully achieved by eastern European socialism. Through their mass struggles the people of Kerala State, India, have made impressive gains as well, Richard W. Franke and Barbara H. Chasin, *Kerala: Radical Reform as Development in an Indian State,* 2nd ed. (Oakland, CA: Institute for Food and Development Policy, 1994).

8. U.S. Census Bureau, *Statistical Abstract of the United States—2002,* table 390, p. 251.

9. Harold Kerbo, *Social Stratification and Inequality: Class Conflict in Historical, Comparative, and Global Perspective,* 5th ed. (New York: McGraw-Hill, 2003), p. 238.

10. Michael Parenti, *Democracy for the Few*, 7th ed. (New York: Bedford/St. Martin's, 2002), pp. 211–14.

11. Harris data from the Harris Poll, no. 16, March 17, 2003, http://www .harrisinteractive.com/harris_poll/index.asp/?PID=364; Katherine Q. Seelye, "Voters Disgusted with Politicians as Election Nears," *New York Times*, November 3, 1994, pp. A1, A28.

12. James Bennet, "Israeli Voters Hand Sharon Strong Victory," *New York Times*, November 29, 2003, p. A8.

13. Center for Voting and Democracy, http://www.fairvote.org/turnout/csae 2002.htm (accessed May 23, 2003).

14. Kerbo, *Social Stratification and Inequality*, pp. 238–40.

15. S. M. Miller, "Equality, Morality, and the Health of Democracy," in *Myths about the Powerless*, ed. M. Brinton et al. (Philadelphia: Temple University Press, 1996), p. 29.

16. Quoted in Tim Weiner, "A Capital Rally Attracts Groups from across the Nation to Focus on Children's Needs," *New York Times*, June 2, 1996, p. 30.

17. Dana Canedy, "Navy Leaves a Battered Island, and Puerto Ricans Cheer," *New York Times,* May 2, 2003, p. A22.

18. Peter Medoff and Holly Sklar, *Streets of Hope: The Fall and Rise of an Urban Neighborhood* (Boston: South End Press, 1994), p. 42.

19. Quoted in ibid., p. 69.

20. From their Web site, http://www.igc.apc.org/lctr/ (accessed May 31, 1996).

21. Eric Mann, *L.A.'s Lethal Air: New Strategies for Policy, Organizing, and Action* (Los Angeles: Labor/Community Strategy Center, 1991), p. 6.

22. Robin G. Kelley, "Freedom Riders (the Sequel)," *Nation*, February 5 1996, p. 19.

23. Quoted in video *Not in Our Town* (Oakland, CA: Working Group, 1995).

24. Ibid.

25. Information about these can be found by going to http://www.pbs.org/niot, and by a Google search under Not in Our Town.

26. The Institute for Natural Progress, "In Usual and Accustomed Places: Contemporary American Indian Fishing Rights Struggles," in *The State of Native America*, ed. M. Annette Jaimes (Boston: South End Press, 1992), pp. 231–35; news broadcast, WBAI-FM, New York, April 15, 1996.

27. Quoted in Nancy Murray, "Rolling through History: Project HIP-HOP Teaches Lessons of Activism," *Resist Newsletter* (May 1996): 2–3.

28. Quoted in Lisa Pagan, "Being Young Is Not a Crime: Youth Organizing in San Francisco," *Resist Newsletter* (May 1996): 4.

29. "Protesting May Be Good for Your Health," Reuters, December 23, 2002.

30. This section's heading is part of the line from the old union song, "Solidarity Forever." The whole line is "We can build a new world from the ashes of the old, for the union makes us strong."

31. "The Meaning of Seattle," editorial, *Multinational Monitor* (December 1999): 5.

32. Quote is from http://www.aflcio.rog/aboutunions/unionsummer/, which gives information on how to participate.

33. The best way to support these groups is to join one or several. You can also obtain a socially responsible credit card and/or long distance calling card. Working Assets provides both of these. Each time the holder uses her/his card, Working Assets puts aside a portion of what is spent to go to progressive organizations. Annually, the cardholders vote on how they want their portion allocated. Each year the amount Working Assets donates has risen. In 1996 it was $3 million; in 2001 it was $6 million. Information can be obtained from its Web site, http://www.workingassets.com.

BIBLIOGRAPHY

Abraham, Laurie Kay. *Mama Might Be Better Off Dead: The Failure of Health Care in Urban America*. Chicago: University of Chicago Press, 1993.

Aldridge, Robert C. *First Strike: The Pentagon's Strategy for Nuclear War*. Boston: South End Press, 1983.

Alford, C. Fred. *Whistleblowers: Broken Lives and Organizational Power*. Ithaca, NY: Cornell University Press, 2001.

Allen, Laura. "Women Workers at Perdue: A Chicken in Every Pot, Health Hazards in Every Shop." *Resist Newsletter* (October 1988): 3–6.

American Psychological Association. *Violence and Youth: Psychology's Response*. Washington, DC: American Psychological Association, 1993.

American Public Health Association. Position Paper 9211, "Domestic Violence." Washington, DC: APHA, n.d.

Amnesty International. *United States of America: Rights for All*. New York: Amnesty International, 1998.

———. *United States of America: Police Brutality and Excessive Force in the New York City Police Department*. New York: Amnesty International, June 1996.

Amott, Theresa. *Caught in the Crisis: Women and the U.S. Economy Today*. New York: Monthly Review Press, 1993.

Anderson, David C. "Assault Rifles Dirt Cheap and Legal." *New York Times Magazine*, May 24, 1998, pp. 36–38.

———. "The Crime Funnel." *New York Times Magazine*, June 12, 1994, pp. 56–58.

Anderson, Elijah. *Code of the Street: Decency, Violence, and the Moral Life of the Inner City*. NewYork: W. W. Norton, 1999.

Anderson, Sarah, John Cavanagh, and Thea Lee. *Field Guide to the Global Economy*. New York: New Press, 2000.

Aponte, Robert. "Urban Employment and the Mismatch Dilemma: Accounting for the Immigration Exception." *Social Problems* 43 (1996): 268–83.

Arditti, Rita, and Tatiana Schreiber. "Breast Cancer: The Environmental Connection." *Resist Newsletter* (May/June 1992): 1–8.

Austin, Regina, and Michael Schill. "Black, Brown, Red, and Poisoned." In *Unequal Protection: Environmental Justice and Communities of Color*, edited by Robert D. Bullard, 53–74. San Francisco: Sierra Club Books, 1994.

Bacon, David. "Screened Out: How 'Fighting Terrorism' Became a Bludgeon in Bush's Assault on Labor." *Nation*, May 12, 2003, pp. 19–22.

Baldwin, James. "Report from Occupied Territory." *Nation*, July 11, 1966, pp. 39–43.

Balkan, Sheila, Ronald J. Berger, and Janet Schmidt. *Crime and Deviance in America: A Critical Approach*. Belmont, CA: Wadsworth, 1980.

Ballinger, Jeffrey. "The New Free-Trade Heel." In *Annual Editions: Global Issues, 93/94*, edited by Robert M. Jackson, 130–31. Guilford, CN: Dushkin Publishing Group, 1993.

Barclay, Gordon, Cynthia Tavares, and Arsalaan Siddique. "International Comparisons of Criminal Justice Statistics, 1999," issue 6/01, May 2001. http://www.homeoffice.gov.uk./rds/pdfs/hosb601.pdf.

Baron, Larry, and Murray A. Straus. *Four Theories of Rape in American Society: A State-Level Analysis*. New Haven, CT: Yale University Press, 1989.

Barry, David. "Screen Violence: It's Killing Us." *Harvard Magazine* (November–December 1983): 38–43.

Bastian, Lisa. *Criminal Victimization, 1993*. Washington, DC: Bureau of Justice Statistics, May 1995.

Beck, Allen J. *Prison and Jail Inmates at Midyear, 1999*. Washington, DC: Bureau of Justice Statistics, April 2000.

Beers, David. "Just Say Whoa!" In *Solutions to Social Problems, Lessons from Other Societies*, edited by D. Stanley Eitzen and Craig S. Leedham, 226–38. Boston: Allyn & Bacon, 1998.

Bellant, Russ. *The Coors Connection: How Coors Family Philanthropy Undermines Democratic Pluralism*. Boston: South End Press, 1991.

Benedict, Jeff. *Public Heroes, Private Felons: Athletes and Crimes against Women*. Boston: Northeastern University Press, 1997.

Bergman, Jack, and Julia Reynolds. "The Guns of Opa-Locka: How U.S. Dealers Arm the World." *Nation*, December 2, 2002, pp. 29–34.

Berman, Daniel. *Death on the Job: Occupational Health and Safety Struggles in the United States*. New York: Monthly Review Press, 1978.

Berrill, Kevin T. "Anti-Gay Violence and Victimization in the United States: An Overview." In *Hate Crimes: Confronting Violence against Lesbians and Gay Men*, edited by Gregory M. Herek and Kevin T. Berril, 19–45. Newbury Park, CA: Sage, 1992.

Bingham, Eula, and William V. Meader. "Governmental Regulation of Environmental Hazards in the 1990s." *Annual Review of Public Health* 11 (1990): 419–34.

Birnbaum, Jeffrey R. *The Lobbyists: How Influence Peddlers Work Their Way in Washington*. New York: Times Books, 1993.

Blackburn, McKinley L., David E. Bloom, and Richard B. Freeman. "The Declining Economic Position of Less Skilled Men." In *A Future of Lousy Jobs: The Changing Structure of U.S. Wages*, edited by Gary Burtless, 31–76. Washington, DC: Brookings Institution, 1990.

Blackwell, James E. *The Black Community: Diversity and Unity*. New York: HarperCollins, 1991.

Blank, Rebecca M. "Are Part-Time Jobs Bad Jobs?" In *A Future of Lousy Jobs: The Changing Structure of U.S. Wages,* edited by Gary Burtless, 123–64. Washington, DC: Brookings Institution, 1990.

Bluestone, Barry, and Bennett Harrison. *The Deindustrialization of America: Plant Closings, Community Abandonment, and the Dismantling of Basic Industry*. New York: Basic Books, 1982.

Blumberg, Paul. *The Predatory Society: Deception in the American Marketplace*. New York: Oxford University Press, 1989.

Blumstein, Alfred. "Violence by Young People: Why the Deadly Nexus." *National Institute of Justice Journal* (August 1995): 2–9.

Boisjoly, Russell, Ellen Foster Curtis, and Eugene Mellican. "Ethical Dimensions of the *Challenger* Disaster." In *Corporate and Governmental Deviance,* 5th ed., edited by M. David Ermann and Richard J. Lundman, 207–31. New York: Oxford University Press, 1996.

Bok, Derek. *The Cost of Talent: How Executives and Professionals Are Paid and How It Affects America*. New York: Free Press, 1993.

Bonaich, Edna, and David W. Waller. "Mapping a Global Industry: Apparel Production in the Pacific Rim Triangle." In *Global Production: The Apparel Industry in the Pacific Rim*, edited by Edna Bonaich, Lucie Cheng, Norma Chinchilla, Nora Hamilton, and Paul Ong, 21–41. Philadelphia: Temple University Press, 1994.

Bourgeois, Roy. "Human Rights Watch: School of Assassins," *Z* (September 1994): 14–16.

Bourgois, Philippe. "Just Another Night on Crack Street." *New York Times Magazine*, November 12, 1989, p. 52.

Boyer, Richard O., and Herbert M. Morais. *Labor's Untold Story*. New York: UE, 1955.

Bradsher, Keith. *High and Mighty: SUVs—The World's Most Dangerous Vehicles and How They Got That Way*. New York: PublicAffairs, 2003.

Braverman, Harry. *Labor and Monopoly Capital: The Degradation of Work in the Twentieth Century*. New York: Monthly Review Press, 1974.

Brecher, Jeremy, and Tim Costello. "A New Labor Movement in the Shell of the Old: New Voice in Labor Organizing." *Z* (April 1996): 45–49.

Brenner, Claudia. "Survivor's Story." In *Hate Crimes: Confronting Violence against Lesbians and Gay Men,* edited by Gregory M. Herek and Kevin T. Berrill, 11–15. Newbury Park, CA: Sage, 1992.

Brenner, M. Harvey. *Economy, Society, and Health.* Washington, DC: Economic Policy Institute, 1992.

Broman, Clifford L., V. Lee Hamilton, and William S. Hoffman. *Stress and Distress among the Unemployed: Hard Times and Vulnerable People.* New York: Kluwer Academic/Plenum Publishers, 2001.

Bronfenbrenner, Kate. "Uneasy Terrain: The Impact of Capital Mobility on Workers, Wages, and Union Organizing." Paper submitted to the U.S. Trade Deficit Review Commission, September 6, 2000.

Brown, Jonathan. "Opening the Book on Lending Discrimination." *Multinational Monitor* 13, no. 11 (November 1992): 8–14.

Bruno, Kenny, and Jim Valette. "Cheney and Halliburton: Go Where the Oil Is." *Multinational Monitor* 22, no. 5 (May 2001): 22–25.

Bullard, Robert D. "Environmental Justice for All." In *Unequal Protection: Environmental Justice and Communities of Color,* edited by Robert D. Bullard, 3–22. San Francisco: Sierra Club Books, 1994.

Burghardt, Tom. "Neo-Nazis Salute the Anti-Abortion Zealots." *CAQ: CovertAction Quarterly* (Spring 1995): 26–33.

Burrason, Bert. "Infant Mortality in the United States: Racial Differences and Social Stratification." Paper presented at the annual meeting of the Pacific Sociological Association, San Diego, CA, April 1994.

Burris, Val. "The Myth of Old Money Liberalism." *Social Problems* 47 (2000): 360–78.

Burtless, Gary. Introduction and Summary to *A Future of Lousy Jobs: The Changing Structure of U.S. Wages,* edited by Gary Burtless, 1–30. Washington, DC: Brookings Institution, 1990.

Carey, James. "Benton Harlow: Distributor of Unsafe Drugs." In *Corporate Violence: Injury and Death for Profit,* edited by Stuart Hill, 163–69. Totowa, NJ: Rowman & Littlefield, 1987.

Casten, Liane Clorfene. "Toxic Burn: Agent Orange's Forgotten Victims." *Nation,* November 4, 1991, pp. 550–54.

Chambliss, William J. "Policing the Ghetto Underclass: The Politics of Law and Law Enforcement." *Social Problems* 41 (1994): 177–94.

Chiricos, Ted, Sarah Escholz, and Marc Gertz. "Crime, News, and Fear of Crime: Toward an Identification of Audience Effect." *Social Problems* 44 (1997): 342–57.

Chomsky, Noam, and Edward S. Herman. *The Washington Connection and Third World Fascism: The Political Economy of Human Rights, Volume I.* Boston: South End Press, 1979.

Clawson, Dan, Alan Neustadtl, and Denise Scott. *Money Talks: Corporate PACS and Political Influence.* New York: Basic Books, 1992.

Claybrook, Joan. *Retreat from Safety: Reagan's Attack on America's Health.* New York: Pantheon, 1984.

Clinard, Marshall. *Corporate Corruption: The Abuse of Power.* New York: Praeger, 1990.

Clinard, Marshall, and Peter Yeager. *Corporate Crime.* New York: Free Press, 1980.

Cockburn, Alexander. "Beat the Devil." *Nation,* December 11, 1995, pp. 736–37.

Colapinto, John. "Armies of the Right: What Campus Conservatives Learned from the '60s Generation." *New York Times Magazine,* May 25, 2003, p. 30.

Cole, Leonard A. *Clouds of Secrecy: The Army's Germ Warfare Tests over Populated Areas.* Totowa, NJ: Rowman & Littlefield, 1988.

Coleman, James W. *The Criminal Elite: The Sociology of White-Collar Crime.* 3rd ed. New York: St. Martin's, 1994.

Coleman, Wanda. "Remembering Latasha: Blacks, Immigrants, and America." *Nation,* February 15, 1993, pp. 187–91.

Common Agenda Coalition and the National Priorities Project. *Creating a Common Agenda.* Northhampton, MA: National Priorities Project, n.d.

Commoner, Barry. *The Closing Circle: Man, Nature, and Technology.* New York: Bantam, 1971.

Comstock, George, and Erica Scharrer. "Public Opinion on Television Violence." In *Violence in Film and Television,* edited by James Torr, 70–74. San Diego: Greenhaven Press, 2002.

Cook, Philip J., and Jens Ludwig. *Guns in America: National Survey on Private Ownership and Use of Firearms.* Washington, DC: U.S. Department of Justice, Office of Justice Programs, 1997.

Cookson, Peter W., Jr., and Caroline Hodges Persell. *Preparing for Power: America's Elite Boarding Schools.* New York: Basic Books, 1985.

Cooper, Marc. "Sickness on Evelina Street." *Village Voice,* September 7, 1993, pp. 33–37.

Corea, Gena. *The Invisible Epidemic: The Story of Women and AIDS.* New York: HarperCollins, 1992.

Cottle, Thomas. *Hardest Times: The Trauma of Long-Term Unemployment.* Westport, CT: Praeger, 2001.

———. "When You Stop, You Die: The Human Toll of Unemployment." In *Crisis in American Institutions,* 9th ed., edited by Jerome Skolnick and Elliot Currie, 75–81. New York: HarperCollins, 1994.

Covington, Sally. "Right Thinking, Big Grants, and Long-Term Strategy: How Conservative Philanthropies and Think Tanks Transform U.S. Policy." *CAQ: Covert Action Quarterly* (Winter 1998): 6–16.

Cray, Charlie. "Chartering a New Course: Revoking Corporations' Right to Exist." *Multinational Monitor* 23, no. 11 (October/November 2002): 8–11.

———. "Lord of the Fries." *Multinational Monitor,* 22, no. 12 (December 2001): 7.

Critser, Greg. *Fat Land: How Americans Became the Fattest People in the World*. New York: Houghton Mifflin, 2003.

Currie, Elliot. *Reckoning: Drugs, the Cities, and the American Future*. New York: Hill & Wang, 1993.

———. *Confronting Crime*. New York: Pantheon, 1985.

Currie, Elliot, and Jerome Skolnick. *America's Problems: Social Issues and Public Policy*. 2nd ed. Glenview, IL: Scott, Foresman, 1988.

Cusac, Anne-Marie. "Open to Attack: Bush Gives In to Chemical Companies, Leaving the Nation Vulnerable." http://www/progressive.org/nov03/cusac1103.html.

Davis, Mike. *Ecology of Fear: Los Angeles and the Imagination of Disaster*. New York: Vintage, 1998.

———. *City of Quartz: Excavating the Future in Los Angeles*. New York: Vintage, 1990.

Davis, Robert. "Racial Differences in Mortality: Current Trends and Perspectives." In *Race and Ethnicity in America: Meeting the Challenge in the 21st Century*, edited by Gail Thomas, 115–28. Washington, DC: Taylor & Francis, 1995.

"Declining Unionization, Rising Inequality: An Interview with Kate Bronfenbrenner." *Multinational Monitor* (May 2003): 21–24.

Derber, Charles. *Corporation Nation*. New York: St. Martin's Griffin, 1998.

———. *The Wilding of America: How Greed and Violence Are Eroding Our Nation's Character*. New York: St. Martin's, 1996.

di Leonardo, Michaela. "Murder by Public Policy." *Nation,* September 2/9, 2002, pp. 31–35.

Domhoff, G. William. *Who Rules America? Power and Politics*. 4th ed. New York: McGraw-Hill, 2002.

———. *The Powers That Be: Processes of Ruling Class Domination in America*. New York: Vintage, 1979.

———. *The Bohemian Grove and Other Retreats: A Study in Ruling-Class Cohesiveness*. New York: Harper & Row, 1974.

Donziger, Steve R., ed. *The Real War on Crime: The Report of the National Criminal Justice Commission*. New York: HarperPerennial, 1996.

Doress-Worters, Paula B. "Choices and Chances." In *Myths about the Powerless,* edited by M. Brinton Lykes, Ali Banuazizi, Ramey Liem, and Michael Morris, 201–18. Philadelphia: Temple University Press, 1996.

Dowie, Mark. "Pinto Madness." In *The Best of Mother Jones*, edited by Richard Jones, 56–59. San Francisco: Foundation for National Progress, 1985.

Downs, Alan. *Corporate Executions: The Ugly Truth about Layoffs—How Corporate Greed Is Shattering Lives, Companies, and Communities*. New York: AMACOM, 1995.

Dreyfus, Robert "The NRA Wants You." *Nation*, March 29, 2000, pp. 11–18.

Dunn, Seth, and Christopher Flavin. "Moving the Climate Change Agenda Forward." In *State of the World, 2002,* edited by Linda Starke, 24–50. New York: W. W. Norton, 2002.

Dye, Thomas R. *Who's Running America? The Conservative Years.* 4th ed. Englewood Cliffs, NJ: Prentice-Hall, 1986.

Ebert, Allan. "Un-sporting Multinationals: Baseball Manufacturers Taking a Walk on Workers Rights." *Multinational Monitor* 6, no. 18 (December 1985): 11–12.

Ebner, Johnna. "Sociologist Takes 'Supporting' Role in Columbine Documentary." *Footnotes* (January 2003).

Ehrenreich, Barbara. "The Warrior Culture." In *Beyond the Storm: A Gulf Crisis Reader,* edited by Phyllis Bennis and Michel Moushabeck, 129–31. New York: Olive Branch Press, 1991.

Ehrlich, Howard J. "Reporting Ethnoviolence." *Z* (June 1994): 53–58.

Elliot, Delbert. "Serious Violent Offenders: Onset, Developmental Course, and Termination." *Criminology* 32 (1994): 5–14.

Epstein, Samuel S. *The Politics of Cancer.* San Francisco: Sierra Club Books, 1978.

Erickson, Brad, ed. *Call to Action: Handbook for Ecology, Peace, and Justice.* San Francisco: Sierra Club Books, 1990.

Ermann, M. David, and Richard J. Lundmann. Overview to *Corporate and Governmental Deviance: Problems of Organizational Behavior in Contemporary Society,* 7th ed., edited by M. David Ermann and Richard J. Lundmann, 3–49. New York: Oxford University Press, 2002.

Escholz, Sarah, Ted Chiricos, and Marc Gertz. "Television and Fear of Crime: Program Types, Audience Traits, and the Mediating Effect of Perceived Neighborhood Racial Composition." *Social Problems* 50 (2003): 395–415.

Fagan, Jeffrey. "Interactions among Drugs, Alcohol, and Violence." *Health Affairs* 12 (1993): 65–79.

––––––––. "Drug Selling and Licit Income in Distressed Neighborhoods: The Economic Lives of Street-Level Drug Users and Dealers." In *Drugs, Crime, and Social Isolation: Barriers to Urban Opportunity,* edited by Adele V. Harrell and George E. Peterson, 99–146. Washington, DC: Urban Institute Press, 1992.

Fee, Elizabeth, and Nancy Krieger. "Health, Politics, and Power." *Women's Review of Books* 11 (1994): 4–5.

Ferraro, Kathleen J. "Cops, Courts, and Woman Battering." In *Violence against Women: The Bloody Footprints,* edited by Pauline B. Bart and Eileen Geil Morgan, 165–76. Newbury Park, CA: Sage, 1993.

Flanders, Laura. "Is It Real . . . Or Is It Astroturf? PR Firm Finds 'Grassroots' Support for Breast Implants." *Extra!* (July/August 1996): 6.

––––––. "Mal de Guerre." *Nation,* March 7, 1994, pp. 292–93.

Floegel, Mark. "The Dirt on Factory Farms: Environmental and Consumer Impacts of Confined Animal Feeding Operations." *Multinational Monitor* 21, nos. 7/8 (July/August 2000) 24–28.

Fontanarosa, P. B. "The Unrelenting Epidemic of Violence in America." *Journal of the American Medical Association* 273, no. 22 (June 14, 1995): 1792–93.

Fox, Robin. *The Challenge of Anthropology: Old Encounters and New Excursions.* New Brunswick, NJ: Transaction Publishers, 1994.

Franke, Richard W., and Barbara H. Chasin. *Kerala: Radical Reform as Development in an Indian State.* 2nd ed. San Francisco: Institute for Food and Development Policy, 1994.

Fraser, Jill Andresky. *White Collar Sweatshop.* New York: W. W. Norton, 2001.

Freedman, Jonathon. *Media Violence and Its Effect on Aggression: Assessing the Scientific Evidence.* Toronto: University of Toronto Press, 2002.

Freeman, Richard B. "How Much Has De-unionization Contributed to the Rise in Male Earnings Inequality?" In *Uneven Tides: Rising Inequality in America*, edited by Sheldon Danziger and Peter Gottschalk, 133–63. New York: Russell Sage Foundation, 1993.

———. "Crime and the Employment of Disadvantaged Youths." In *Urban Labor Markets and Job Opportunity*, edited by George Peterson and Wayne Vroman, 202–37. Washington, DC: Urban Institute Press, 1992.

Freund, Peter, Meredith B. McGuire, and Linda Podhurst. *Health, Illness, and the Social Body: A Critical Sociology.* 4th ed. Upper Saddle River, NJ: Prentice-Hall, 2003.

Freund, Peter, and Meredith B. McGuire. *Health, Illness, and the Social Body: A Critical Sociology.* Englewood Cliffs, NJ: Prentice-Hall, 1991.

Fried, Albert. *The Rise and Fall of the Jewish Gangster in America.* New York: Holt Rinehart and Winston, 1980.

Fried, Marlene Gerber. "Reproductive Wrongs." *Women's Review of Books* (July 1994): 6–7.

Friedman, Michael S., et al. "Impact of Changes in Transportation and Commuting Behaviors during the 1996 Summer Olympic Games in Atlanta on Air Quality and Childhood Asthma." *Journal of the American Medical Association* 285, no. 7 (February 21, 2001): 903.

Fuchs, Ester R. "The Permanent Urban Fiscal Crisis." In *Big Cities in the Welfare Transition*, edited by Alfred J. Kahn and Shelia B. Kammerman, 43–73. New York: Columbia University School of Social Work, 1998.

Gans, Herbert. "Deconstructing the Underclass." In *Race, Class, and Gender in the United States*, 3rd ed., edited by Paula S. Rothenberg, 51–57. New York: St. Martin's, 1995.

Gelles, Richard J., and Murray A. Straus. *Intimate Violence: The Causes and Consequences of Abuse in the American Family.* New York: Simon & Schuster, 1988.

Gettleman, Marvin E., Jane Franklin, Marilyn Young, and Bruce Franklin, eds. *Vietnam and America: A Documented History.* New York: Grove, 1985.

Gibbs, Nancy. "Till Death Do Us Part." In *Crisis in American Institutions*, 9th ed., edited by Jerome H. Skolnick and Elliott Currie, 231–42. New York: HarperCollins, 1994.

Gibson, James William. *Warrior Dreams: Violence and Manhood in Post-Vietnam America.* New York: Hill and Wang, 1994.

Gilbert, Dennis. *The American Class Structure in an Age of Growing Inequality.* 6th ed. Belmont, CA: Wadsworth/Thompson Learning, 2003.

Glassner, Barry. *The Culture of Fear: Why Americans Are Afraid of the Wrong Things.* New York: Basic Books, 1999.

Glazer, Myron Peretz, and Penina Migdal Glazer. *The Whistleblowers: Exposing Corruption in Government and Industry.* New York: Basic Books, 1989.

Glazer, Nathan, and Daniel Patrick Moynihan. *Beyond the Melting Pot: The Negroes, Puerto Ricans, Jews, Italians, and Irish of New York City.* Cambridge: MIT Press, 1970.

Gold, David, and Stephen Rose. *A Primer on the Arms Race.* Baltimore, MD: Social Graphics, 1983.

Goldsmith, William W., and Edward J. Blakely. *Separate Societies: Poverty and Inequality in U.S. Cities.* Philadelphia: Temple University Press, 1992.

Goldstein, Jeffrey, ed. *Why We Watch: The Attractions of Violent Entertainment.* New York: Oxford University Press, 1998.

Goldstein, Richard. "The New Anti-Semitism: A *Geshrei.*" In *Blacks and Jews: Alliances and Arguments*, edited by Paul Berman, 204–16. New York: Delta, 1994.

Goldstein, Robert Justin. *Political Repression in Modern America.* Cambridge, MA: Schenkman, 1978.

Goode, Judith. "Polishing the Rustbelt: Immigrants Enter a Restructuring Philadelphia." In *Newcomers in the Workplace*, edited by Louise Lamphere, Alex Stepick, and Guillermo Grenier, 199–230. Philadelphia: Temple University Press, 1994.

Graber, Lena. "The Value of Life." *Dollars and Sense* (September/October 2002): 4.

Greenstein, Robert, and Isaac Shapiro. "The New, Definitive CBO Data on Income and Tax Trends." Center on Budget and Policy Priorities, September 23, 2003, 16 pages.

Greider, William. *Who Will Tell the People? The Betrayal of American Democracy.* New York: Simon & Schuster, 1992.

Grofman, Bernard, and Chandler Davidson, eds. *Controversies in Minority Voting: The Voting Rights Act in Perspective.* Washington, DC: Brookings Institution, 1992.

Groger, Jeff. "An Economic Model of Recent Trends in Crime." In *The Crime Drop in America*, edited by Alfred Blumstein and Joel Wallman, 266–87. New York: Cambridge University Press, 2000.

Hall, Bob. "Perdue Farms: Poultry and Profits." *Multinational Monitor* 10, no. 9 (September 1989): 18–20.

Hardert, Ronald A. "Environmental Whistle-Blowers, Anger, and the Power Elite." Working paper presented to the annual meetings of the Pacific Sociological Association, San Diego, CA, April 1994.

Hardisty, Jean V., and Ellen Leopold. "Cancer and Poverty: Double Jeopardy for Women." In *Myths about the Powerless*, edited by M. Brinton Lykes, Ali Banuazizi, Ramey Liem, and Michael Morris, 219–36. Philadelphia: Temple University Press, 1996.

Harrell, Adele V., and George E. Peterson, eds. *Drugs, Crime, and Social Isolation: Barriers to Urban Opportunity*. Washington, DC: Urban Institute Press, 1992.

Harris, David A. *Profiles in Injustice: Why Racial Profiling Cannot Work*. New York: New York University Press, 2002.

Harris, Marvin. *America Now: The Anthropology of a Changing Culture*. New York: Simon & Schuster, 1981.

Hawkins, Howie. "Progressive Politics: Independent Progressive Politics Network," *Z* (June 1999): 17–21.

Heiss, Jerold. "Effects of African American Family Structure on School Attitudes and Performance." *Social Problems* 43 (1996): 246–67.

Helvarg, David. "The War on Greens." *Nation*, November 28, 1994, pp. 646–51.

Herman, Edward S. "The Natural Rate of Unemployment." *Z* (November 1994): 62–65.

———. *The Real Terror Network*. Boston: South End Press, 1982.

Herman, Edward S., and Noam Chomsky. *Manufacturing Consent: The Political Economy of the Mass Media*. New York: Pantheon, 1988.

Herrnstein, Richard, and Charles Murray. *The Bell Curve: Intelligence and Class Structure in American Life*. New York: Free Press, 1994.

Higham, Jon. *Strangers in the Land: Patterns of American Nativism, 1860–1925*. New Brunswick, NJ: Rutgers University Press, 1966.

Hill, Richard C., and Cynthia Negry. "Deindustrialization and Racial Minorities in the Great Lakes Region, USA." In *The Reshaping of America: Social Consequences of the Changing Economy*, edited by D. Stanley Eitzen and Maxine Baca Zinn, 168–78. Englewood Cliffs, NJ: Prentice-Hall, 1989.

Hills, Stuart L. Epilogue to *Corporate Violence: Injury and Death for Profit,* edited by Stuart L. Hills, 187–206. Totowa, NJ: Rowman & Littlefield, 1987.

Hogan, Bill. "Pulling Strings from Afar." *AARP Bulletin* (February 2002): 3–4.

Holmes, Ronald M., and Stephen T. Holmes. *Murder in America*. Thousand Oaks, CA: Sage, 1994.

Horn, Patricia. "Beating Back the Revolution." *Dollars and Sense* (December 1992): 12.

Human Rights Watch. "Unfair Advantage: Worker's Freedom of Association in the United States under International Human Rights Standards, 2000." http://www.hrw.org/reports/2000uslabor/.

Iadicola, Peter, and Anson Shupe. *Violence, Inequality, and Human Freedom*. Dix Hills, NY: General Hall, 1998.

Institute for Natural Progress. "In Usual and Accustomed Places: Contemporary American Indian Fishing Rights Struggles." In *The State of Native America*, edited by M. Annette Jaimes, 217–39. Boston: South End Press, 1992.

Institute of Medicine. *Care without Coverage: Too Little, Too Late*. Washington, DC: National Academy Press, 2002.

Isaac, Katherine. "Losing Jobs to 936." *Multinational Monitor* 14, no. 7 (July/August 1993): 6–7.

Jackall, Robert. *Moral Mazes: The World of Corporate Managers*. New York: Oxford University Press, 1989.

Jackson, Janine, and Peter Hart. "Fear and Favor 2000: How Power Shapes the News." *Extra!* (June 2001): 15–22.

Jackson, Janine, and Jim Naureckas. "U.S. News Illustrates Flaws in Crime Coverage." *Extra!* (May/June 1994): 10–13.

Jacoby, Russell, and Naomi Glauberman, eds. *The Bell Curve Debate*. New York: Times Books, 1995.

Jaffe, Frederick S., Barbara L. Lindheim, and Philip R. Lee. "Legal Abortion Improves Public Health." In *Abortion: Opposing Viewpoints*, edited by Bonnie Szumski, 147–51. St. Paul: Greenhaven Press, 1986.

James, David, and Michael Soref. "Managerial Theory: Unmaking of the Corporation President." *American Sociological Review* 46 (1981): 1–18.

Jennings, James. *Understanding the Nature of Poverty in America*. Westport, CN: Praeger, 1994.

Jezer, Marty. *The Dark Ages: Life in the United States, 1945–1960*. Boston: South End Press, 1982.

Johnson, Michael P. "Patriarchal Terrorism and Common Couple Violence: Two Forms of Violence against Women." *Journal of Marriage and the Family* 57 (1995): 283–94.

Jones, Jacqueline. *The Dispossessed: America's Underclasses from the Civil War to the Present*. New York: Basic Books, 1992.

Jones, James. *Bad Blood: The Tuskegee Syphilis Experiment: A Tragedy of Race and Medicine*. New York: Free Press, 1981.

Kahn, Alfred J. Kahn, and Shelia B. Kammerman. *Big Cities in the Welfare Transition*. New York: Columbia University School of Social Work, 1998.

Kaiser Health Reform Project. *Uninsured in America*. Henry J. Kaiser Family Foundation, 1994.

Kaplan, Janice. "Are Talk Shows Out of Control?" *TV Guide*, April 1, 1995, pp. 8–10.

Karliner, Joshua. "Earth Predators." *Dollars and Sense* (July/August 1998): 7.

Kasarda, John D. "The Severely Distressed in Economically Transforming Cities." In *Drugs, Crime, and Social Isolation: Barriers to Urban Opportunity*, edited by Adele V. Harrel and George E. Peterson, 45–98. Washington, DC: Urban Institute Press, 1992.

Katz, Michael B., ed. *The 'Underclass' Debate: The View from History*. Princeton, NJ: Princeton University Press, 1993.

Kay, Jane. "California's Endangered Communities of Color." In *Unequal Protection: Environmental Justice and Communities of Color*, edited by Robert D. Bullard, 155–88. San Francisco: Sierra Club Books, 1994.

Kay, Jane Holtz. *Asphalt Nation: How the Automobile Took Over America and How We Can Take It Back*. New York: Crown Publishers, 1997.

Kelley, Robin G. "Freedom Riders (the Sequel)." *Nation*, February 5, 1996, pp. 18–22.

Kenney, Catherine T., and Karen R. Brown. *Report from the Front Lines: The Impact of Violence on Poor Women*. New York: NOW Legal Defense and Education Fund, 1996.

Kerbo, Harold R. *Social Stratification and Inequality: Class Conflict in Historical and Comparative Perspective*. 5th ed. New York: McGraw-Hill, 2003.

King, Martin Luther, Jr. "Declaration of Independence from the War in Vietnam." In *Essay Series*, 35–50. New York: A.J. Muste Memorial Institute, n.d.

Klare, Michael. *Rogue States and Nuclear Outlaws*. New York: Hill and Wang, 1995.

———. "Making Enemies for the '90s: The New 'Rogue State' Doctrine." *Nation*, May 8, 1995, pp. 625–28.

Klinenberg, Eric. *Heat Wave: A Social Autopsy of Disaster in Chicago*. Chicago: University of Chicago Press, 2002.

Kloby, Jerry. *Inequality, Power, and Development*. 2nd ed. Amherst, NY: Humanity Books, 2004.

———. "Increasing Class Polarization in the United States: The Growth of Wealth and Income Inequality." In *Critical Perspectives in Sociology,* edited by Berch Berberoglu, 39–53. Dubuque, IA: Kendell/Hunt, 1991.

Konner, Melvin. *Dear America: A Concerned Doctor Wants You to Know the Truth about Health Reform*. Reading, MA: Addison-Wesley, 1993.

Korten, David. *When Corporations Rule the World*. 2nd ed. Bloomfield, CN: Kumarian, 2001.

Kozol, Jonathan. *Savage Inequalities: Children in America's Schools*. New York: HarperCollins, 1991.

Kurz, Demie. "Battering and the Criminal Justice System: A Feminist View." In *Domestic Violence: The Changing Criminal Justice Response*, edited by Eve S. Buzawa and Carl G. Buzawa, 21–38. Westport, CN: Auburn House, 1992.

Kwik, Phil. "Pittston Power." *Nation*, October 16, 1989, pp. 409.

Langer, Elinor. "The American Neo-Nazi Movement Today." *Nation*, July 16/23, 1990, pp. 82–107.

Larson, Erik. *Lethal Passage: How the Travels of a Single Handgun Expose the Roots of America's Gun Crisis*. New York: Crown Publishers, 1994.

Lawson, Bill E., ed. *The Underclass Question*. Philadelphia: Temple University Press, 1992.

Leach, William. *Land of Desire: Merchants, Power, and the Rise of a New American Culture*. New York: Vintage, 1993.

Lemann, Nicholas. *The Promised Land: The Great Black Migration and How It Changed America*. New York: Vintage, 1991.

Lerman, Lisa G. "Prosecution of Wife Beaters: Institutional Obstacles and Innovations." In *Violence in the Home: Interdisciplinary Perspectives*, edited by Mary Lystad, 262–65. New York: Brunner/Mazel, 1986.

Levin, Jack, and Jack McDevitt. *Hate Crimes: The Rising Tide of Bigotry and Backlash*. New York: Plenum, 1993.

Levine, Felice J., and Katherine J. Rosich. *Social Causes of Violence: Crafting a Science Agenda*. Washington, DC: American Sociological Association, 1996.

Liebman, Bonnie. "For Women Only." *Nutrition Action Health Letter* 22 (March 1995): 4–7.

Liem, Ramsey, and Paula Rayman. "Health and Social Costs of Unemployment." *American Psychologist* 37 (1982): 1116–23.

Lifton, Robert Jay. *Home from the War: Learning from Vietnam Veterans*. Boston: Beacon Press, 1992.

Lipsman, Dr. Joshua. "White Man's Medicine." *Nation*, March 26, 1988, p. 401.

Livingston, Jay. *Crime and Criminology*. Englewood Cliffs, NJ: Prentice-Hall, 1992. 2nd ed., 1996.

Lunneborg, Patricia. *Abortion: A Positive Decision*. New York: Bergin & Garvey, 1992.

Lusane, Clarence. *Pipe Dream Blues: Racism and the War on Drugs*. Boston: South End Press, 1991.

Lutz, William. *The New Doublespeak: Why No One Knows What Anyone's Saying Anymore*. New York: HarperPerennial, 1996.

———. *Doublespeak: From 'Revenue Enhancement to Terminal Living': How Government, Business Advertisers, and Others Use Language to Deceive You*. New York: HarperPerennial, 1989.

Malcolm X. *By Any Means Necessary*. New York: Pathfinder Press, 1970.

Mann, Eric. *L.A.'s Lethal Air: New Strategies for Policy, Organizing, and Action*. Los Angeles: Labor/Community Strategy Center, 1991.

Markuson, Anne, and Joel Yudken. *Dismantling the Cold War Economy*. New York: Basic Books, 1992.

Marx, Karl. *Capital*. Vol. 1. Moscow: Foreign Languages Publishing House, n.d. Originally published 1887.

Massey, Douglas, and Nancy A. Denton. *American Apartheid: Segregation and the Making of the Underclass*. Cambridge: Harvard University Press, 1993.

Mauer, Marc. "Race to Incarcerate." In *Understanding Prejudice and Discrimination*, edited by Scott Plous, 178–81. New York: McGraw-Hill, 2003.

———. "A Generation behind Bars: Black Males and the Criminal Justice System." In *The American Black Male: His Present Status and His Future*, edited by Richard G. Majors and Jacob U. Gordon, 81–93. Chicago: Nelson-Hall, 1994.

Mauer, Marc, and Meda Chesney-Lind, eds. *Invisible Punishment: The Collateral Consequences of Mass Imprisonment*. New York: New Press, 2002.

McClure, Laura. "Union Organizing: AFL-CIO Changes." *Z* (January 1996): 18–21.

McCord, Colin, and Harold P. Freeman. "Excess Mortality in Harlem." In *Crisis in American Institution,* 9th ed., edited by Jerome Skolnick and Elliot Currie, 426–32. New York: HarperCollins, 1991.

McCoy, Alfred W. *The Politics of Heroin: CIA Complicity in the Global Drug Trade.* New York: Lawrence Hill, 1991.

McGehee, Ralph. *Deadly Deceits: My 25 Years in the CIA.* New York: Sheridan Square Press, 1983.

Medoff, Peter, and Holly Sklar. *Streets of Hope: The Fall and Rise of an Urban Neighborhood.* Boston: South End Press, 1994.

Melman, Seymour. *The Demilitarized Society: Disarmament and Conversion.* Montreal: Harvest House, 1988.

Merva, Mary, and Richard Fowles. *Effects of Diminished Economic Opportunities on Social Stress: Heart Attacks, Strokes, and Crime.* Washington, DC: Economic Policy Institute, n.d.

Milgram, Stanley. *Obedience to Authority.* New York: Harper & Row, 1974.

Miller, S. M. "Equality, Morality, and the Health of Democracy." In *Myths about the Powerless,* edited by M. Brinton Lykes, Ali Banuazizi, Ramey Liem, and Michael Morris, 17–33. Philadelphia: Temple University Press, 1996.

Mills, C. Wright. "The Cultural Apparatus." In *Power, Politics, and People: The Collected Essays of C. Wright Mills,* edited by Irving L. Horowitz, 405–22. New York: Ballantine, 1963.

———. *The Power Elite.* New York: Oxford University Press, 1959.

Mintz Morton, "No Shame: Corporate Immorality Elicits Little Press Comment." *Extra!* (July/August 2000): 24–25.

Misch, Ann. "Assessing Environmental Health Risks." In *State of the World, 1994,* edited by Linda Starke, 117–36. New York: W. W. Norton, 1994.

Mishel, Lawrence, Jared Bernstein, and Heather Boushey. *The State of Working America, 2002/2003.* Ithaca, NY: ILR Press, an imprint of Cornell University Press, 2003.

———. *The State of Working America, 1992–1993.* Armonk, NY: M.E. Sharpe, 1993.

Mokhiber, Russell. "The 10 Worst Corporations of 1993." *Multinational Monitor* 14, no. 12 (December 1993): 9–16.

———. *Corporate Crime and Violence: Big Business Power and the Abuse of Public Trust.* San Francisco: Sierra Club Books, 1988.

Mokhiber, Russell, Julie Gozan, and Holley Knaus. "The Corporate Rap Sheet: The 10 Worst Corporations of 1992." *Multinational Monitor* 13, no. 12 (December 1992): 7–16.

Mokhiber, Russell, and Robert Weissman, "Rotten Apples in a Rotten System: The Ten Worst Corporations of 2002." *Multinational Monitor* 23, no. 12 (December 2002): 8–19.

Moore, Joan. "Gangs, Drugs, and Violence." In *Gangs: The Origins and Impact of*

Contemporary Youth Gangs in the United States, edited by Scott Cummings and Daniel J. Monti, 27–46. Albany: State University of New York Press, 1993.

Moore, Richard, and Louis Head. "Building a Net That Works: SWOP." In *Unequal Protection: Environmental Justice and Communities of Color*, edited by Robert D. Bullard, 191–206. San Francisco: Sierra Club Books, 1994.

Morris, Michael "Culture, Structure, and the Underclass." In *Myths about the Powerless,* edited by M. Brinton Lykes, Ali Banuazizi, Ramsey Liem, and Michael Morris, 34–49. Philadelphia: Temple University Press, 1996.

Moses, Marion. "Farmworkers and Pesticides." In *Confronting Environmental Racism*, edited by Robert Bullard, 161–78. Boston: South End Press, 1993.

Murray, Nancy. "Rolling through History: Project HIP-HOP Teaches Lessons of Activism." *Resist Newsletter* (May1996).

Nader, Ralph, and William Taylor. *The Big Boys: Power and Position in American Business*. New York: Pantheon, 1986.

National Issues Forum. *Crime: What We Fear, What Can Be Done*. Dayton, OH: National Issues Forums, 1987.

National Television Violence Study. "The Effects of Media Violence." In *Violence in Film and Television*, edited by James Torr, 105–109. San Diego: Greenhaven Press, 2002.

Nelson, T. S. *For Love of Country: Confronting Rape and Sexual Harassment in the U.S. Military*. New York: Haworth Maltreatment & Trauma Press, 2002.

Nersesian, William S. "Infant Mortality in Socially Vulnerable Populations." *Annual Review of Public Health* 9 (1988): 361–77.

New Jersey Council of Churches. *The Reshaping of New Jersey: The Growing Separation*. East Orange, NJ: New Jersey Council of Churches, 1988.

Newman, Kathleen. *No Shame in My Game: The Working Poor in the Inner City*. New York: Vintage, 1999.

Noble, Charles. *Liberalism at Work: The Rise and Fall of OSHA*. Philadelphia: Temple University Press, 1986.

OECD. *International Road Traffic and Accident Database*, May 2002. http://www.bast.de/htdocs/fachtemen/irtad/english/we2.html.

Ortiz, Solomon P. "America's Third World: Colonias." In *Annual Editions: Race and Ethnic Relations, 91/*92, edited by John A. Kromkowski, 80–82. Guilford, CT: Dushkin Publishing Group, 1991.

Osborn, Barbara Bliss. "If It Bleeds It Leads—If It Votes It Don't: A Survey of L.A.'s Local News Shows." *Extra!* (September/October 1994): 15.

O'Toole, Laura, and Jessica Schiffman. Preface to *Gender Violence: Interdisciplinary Perspectives*, edited by Laura O'Toole and Jesscia Schiffman, xi–xiv. New York: New York University Press, 1997.

———. "The Roots of Male Violence." In *Gender Violence: Interdisciplinary Perspectives*, edited by Laura O'Toole and Jessica Schiffman, 3–8. New York: New York University Press, 1997.

Pagan, Lisa. "Being Young Is Not a Crime: Youth Organizing in San Francisco." *Resist Newsletter* (May 1996): 4–5.

Palast, Greg. *The Best Democracy Money Can Buy: An Investigative Reporter Exposes the Truth about Corporate Cons, Globalization, and High-Finance Fraudsters.* New York: Plume, 2003.

Parenti, Michael. *The Terrorism Trap: September 11 and Beyond.* San Francisco: City Lights Books, 2002.

———. *Democracy for the Few.* 7th ed. Boston: St. Martin's, 2002

———. *Democracy for the Few.* 6th ed. New York: St. Martin's, 1995.

———. *Land of Idols: Political Mythology in America.* New York: St. Martin's, 1994.

———. *Inventing Reality: The Politics of News Media.* 2nd ed. New York: St. Martin's, 1993.

Perry, Susan, and Jim Dawson. "Nightmare: Women and the Dalkon Shield." In *Corporate and Governmental Deviance: Problems of Organizational Behavior in Contemporary Society*, 3rd ed., edited by M. David Ermann and Richard J. Lundman, 145–62. New York: Oxford University Press, 1987.

Phillips, Kevin. *The Politics of Rich and Poor: Wealth and the American Electorate in the Reagan Aftermath.* New York: HarperPerennial, 1990.

Pinderhughes, Howard. "The Anatomy of Racially Motivated Violence in New York City: A Case Study of Youth in Southern Brooklyn." *Social Problems* 40 (1993): 478–91.

———. "Down with the Program: Racial Attitudes and Group Violence among Youth in Bensonhurst and Gravesend." In *Gangs: The Origin and Impact of Contemporary Youth Gangs in the United States*, edited by Scott Cummings and Daniel J. Monti, 75–94. Albany: State University of New York Press, 1993.

Piven, Frances Fox, and Richard A. Cloward. *Regulating the Poor: The Functions of Public Welfare.* Upd. ed. New York: Vintage, 1993.

———. "The Historical Sources of the Contemporary Welfare Debate." In *The Mean Season: The Attack on the Welfare State*, edited by Fred Block, Richard A. Cloward, Barbara Ehrenreich, and Frances Fox Piven, 3–43. New York: Pantheon, 1987.

President's National Bipartisan Commission on Central America. *The Report of the President's National Bipartisan Commission on Central America.* New York: Macmillan, 1983.

Prince, Stephen. "A Brief History of Film Violence: Public Opinion in Television Violence." In *Violence in Film and Television*, edited by James Torr, 21–32. San Diego: Greenhaven Press, 2002.

Rabin, Yale. "Highways as a Barrier to Equal Access." In *Majority and Minority: The Dynamics of Racial and Ethnic Relations*, 2nd ed., edited by Norman R. Yetman and C. Hoy Steele, 463–75. Boston: Allyn & Bacon, 1975.

Reiman, Jeffrey. *The Rich Get Richer and the Poor Get Prison.* 7th ed. Boston: Allyn & Bacon, 2004.

————. *The Rich Get Richer and the Poor Get Prison.* 6th ed. Boston: Allyn & Bacon, 2001.

————. *The Rich Get Richer and the Poor Get Prison.* 3rd ed. New York: Macmillan, 1990.

Reisine, Susan T. "The Impact of Dental Conditions on Social Functioning and the Quality of Life." *Annual Review of Public Health* 9 (1988): 1–19.

Reiss, Albert J., and Jeffrey A. Roth. *Understanding and Preventing Violence.* Washington, DC: National Academy Press, 1993.

Renner, Michael. "Military Expenditures on the Rise." In *Vital Signs, 2003*, edited by Linda Starke for Worldwatch Institute, 118–19. New York: W. W. Norton, 2003.

Ridgeway, James. "The Posse Goes to Washington: How the Militias and Far Right Got a Foothold on Capitol Hill." *Village Voice*, May 23, 1995.

Rome, Dennis M. "Murderers, Rapists, and Drug Addicts." In *Images of Color, Images of Crime,* 2nd ed., edited by Coramae Richey Mann and Marjorie S. Zatz, 71–81. Los Angeles: Roxbury, 2002.

Rosenberg, Howard L. *Atomic Soldiers: American Victims of Nuclear Experiments.* Boston: Beacon Press, 1980.

Rosenberg, Mark L. "Violence Is a Public Health Problem." In *Unnatural Causes: The Three Leading Killer Diseases in America*, edited by Russell C. Maulitz, 147–68. New Brunswick, NJ: Rutgers University Press, 1988.

Rosenfeld, Richard. "Patterns in Adult Homicide, 1980–1995." In *The Crime Drop in America*, edited by Alfred Blumstein and Joel Wallman, 130–63. New York: Cambridge University Press, 2000.

Rubenstein, Richard L. *The Age of Triage: Fear and Hope in an Overcrowded World.* Boston: Beacon Press, 1983.

Ruby-Sachs, Emma, and Timothy Waligore. "Alternative Voice on Campus." *Nation*, February 17, 2003, pp. 27–29.

Ruel, Susan. "Body Bag Journalism: Crime Coverage by the U.S. Media." Paper presented at International Conference on Violence in the Media, St. John's University. New York, NY, October 3, 1994.

Russell, George. "Corporate Restructuring." In *The Reshaping of America: Social Consequences of the Changing Economy*, edited by D. Stanley Eitzen and Maxine Baca Zinn, 33–36. Englewood Cliffs, NJ: Prentice-Hall, 1989.

Ryan, William. *Blaming the Victim.* New York: Vintage, 1976.

Sampson, Robert J., and W. Byron Groves. "Community Structure and Crime: Testing Social-Disorganization Theory." *American Journal of Sociology* 94 (1989): 774–802.

Schaefer, Richard T. *Racial and Ethnic Groups.* 8th ed. Upper Saddle River, NJ: Prentice-Hall, 2000.

————. *Racial and Ethnic Groups.* 7th ed. New York: Longman, 1997.

————. *Racial and Ethnic Groups.* 5th ed. New York: HarperCollins, 1993.

Schmitt, Christopher H., and Edward T. Pound. "Keeping Secrets." *U.S. News &*

World Report, December 22, 2003. http://www.usnews/issue/03/22/usnews/22secrecy.htm.

Schulman, Kevin A., et al. "The Effect of Race and Sex on Physicians' Recommendations for Cardiac Catheterization." *New England Journal of Medicine* (February 25, 1999): 618–26.

Scully, Diane. *Understanding Sexual Violence: A Study of Convicted Rapists.* Boston: Unwin-Hyman, 1992.

Serrin, William. "The Wages of Work." *Nation*, January 28, 1994, pp. 80–81.

Shalom, Stephen Rosskamm. *Which Side Are You On? An Introduction to Politics.* New York: Addison Wesley Longman, 2002.

———. *Imperial Alibis: Rationalizing U.S. Intervention after the Cold War.* Boston: South End Press, 1993.

———. "Drug Policy and Program." *Z Papers* (January 1992): 9–17.

Sheahen, Allen. "Poverty in America Is a Serious Problem." In *Poverty: Opposing Viewpoints*, edited by William Dudley, 17–24. St. Paul: Greenhaven Press, 1988.

Sherman, Lawrence W., and Richard A. Berk. "The Specific Deterrent Effects of Arrest for Domestic Assault." *American Sociological Review* 49 (1984): 261–72.

Shernoff, David. "Workers at Risk." *Multinational Monitor* 9, no. 10 (October 1988): 21–22.

Shipler, David K. "Robert McNamara and the Ghosts of Vietnam." *New York Times Magazine,* August 10, 1997, pp. 30–35, 42, 50, 56–57.

Shorrock, Tim. "Selling (Off) Iraq: How to 'Privatize' a Country and Make Millions." *Nation*, June 23, 2003, pp. 11–16.

Simon, David R. *Elite Deviance.* 6th ed. Boston: Allyn & Bacon, 1999.

———. *Elite Deviance.* 5th ed. Boston: Allyn & Bacon, 1996.

Simon, David R., and D. Stanley Eitzen, *Elite Deviance.* 4th ed. Boston: Allyn & Bacon, 1993.

Simpson, Sally S. *Corporate Crime, Law, and Social Control.* New York: Cambridge University Press, 2002.

Sklar, Holly. *Chaos or Community: Seeking Solutions, Not Scapegoats for Bad Economics.* Boston: South End Press, 1995.

Skolnick, Jerome H., and James J. Fyfe. *Above the Law: Police and the Excessive Use of Force.* New York: Free Press, 1993.

Soll, David. "Corporate Taxes." *Z* (June 2002): 8–9.

Solomon, Norman. "The Media's Favorite Think Tank: How the Heritage Foundation Turns Money into Media." *Extra!* (July/August 1996): 9–12.

———. *The Power of Babble: The Politician's Dictionary of Buzzwords and Double-Talk for Every Occasion.* New York: Laurel, an imprint of Dell Publishing Co., 1992.

Sontag, Debra. "The Power of the Fourth: How One Appellate Court Is Quietly Moving American Ever Rightward." *New York Times Magazine*, March 2, 2003, pp. 38–40, 54, 56, 77, 80.

Southern Poverty Law Center. *Intelligence Report* (March 1994).

Sponsel, Leslie E. "The Mutual Relevance of Anthropology and Peace Studies." In *The Anthropology of Peace and Nonviolence*, edited by Leslie E. Sponsel and Thomas Gregor, 1–36. Boulder, CO: Lynne Rienner, 1994.

Squires, Gregory D. "Runaway Factories Are Also a Civil Rights Issue." In *The Reshaping of America: Social Consequences of the Changing Economy*, edited by D. Stanley Eitzen and Maxine Baca Zinn, 179–81. Englewood Cliffs, NJ: Prentice-Hall, 1989.

Stark, Evans, and Anne H. Flitcraft. "Women and Children at Risk: A Feminist Perspective on Child Abuse." In *Women's Health, Politics, and Power: Essays on Sex/Gender, Medicine, and Public Health*, edited by Elizabeth Fee and Nancy Krieger, 307–31. Amityville, NY: Baywood, 1994.

Stefanic, Jean, and Richard Delgado. *No Mercy: How Conservative Think Tanks and Foundations Changed America's Social Agenda*. Philadelphia: Temple University Press, 1996.

Steinberg, Stephen. *The Ethnic Myth: Race, Ethnicity, and Class in America*. Boston: Beacon Press, 1989.

Sturdevant, Sandra Pollock, and Brenda Stoltzfus. *Let the Good Times Roll: Prostitution and the U.S. Military in Asia*. New York: New Press, 1992.

Sutherland, Edwin H. "White Collar Criminality." In *Crime and Delinquency: A Reader*, edited by Carl Bersani, 25–34. Toronto: MacMillan, 1970.

Swasy, Alecia. *Soap Opera: The Inside Story of Procter & Gamble*. New York: Times Books, 1993.

Sweezy, Paul. *The Theory of Capitalist Development*. New York: Monthly Review Press, 1942.

Szymanski, Albert. *The Logic of Imperialism*. New York, Praeger, 1981.

Tabor, Michael. "The Plague: Capitalism + Dope = Genocide." In *The Triple Revolution Emerging: Social Problems in Depth*, edited by Robert Perrucci and Mark Pilisuk, 241–49. Boston: Little Brown, 1971.

Taft, Philip, and Philip Ross. "American Labor Violence: Its Causes, Character, and Outcome." In *The History of Violence in America,* edited by Hugh Davis Graham and Ted Robert Gurr, 281–395. New York: Bantam, 1969.

Thompson, E. P. *The Making of the English Working Class*. New York: Vintage, 1963.

Tiger, Lionel, and Robin Fox. *The Imperial Animal*. New York: Delta, 1971.

Tonry, Michael. *Malign Neglect*. New York: Oxford University Press, 1995.

———. "Sentencing Guidelines, Disadvantaged Offenders, and Racial Disparities." *Report from the Institute for Philosophy and Public Policy* (Summer/Fall 1994): 7–13.

Torr, James D. Introduction to *Is Media Violence A Problem*, edited by James D. Torr, 6–9. San Diego: Greenhaven Press, 2002.

———. *Violence in Film and Television: Examining Pop Culture*. San Diego: Greenhaven Press, 2002.

Truax, Hawley. "Minorities at Risk." *Environmental Action* (January/February 1990): 21.

United Nations Development Program. *Human Development Report, 2002.* New York: Oxford University Press, 2002.

United Nations Development Program. *Human Development Report, 2000.* New York: Oxford University Press, 2000.

U.S. Census Bureau. *Statistical Abstract of the United States, 2002* (also 2001, 1995, 1994, 1993, 1987, 1983, 1980). Washington, DC: Government Printing Office.

U.S. Commission on Civil Rights. *Civil Rights Issues Facing Asian Americans in the 1990s.* Washington, DC: Government Printing Office, February 1992.

U.S. Congress. House of Representatives. Committee on Education and Labor. *Hearings on H.R. 1280, Comprehensive Occupational Safety and Health Reform Act.* April 28–July 29, 1993.

U.S. Congress. Office of Technology Assessment. *Indian Health Care.* Washington, DC: U.S. Government Printing Office, 1986.

U.S. Department of Justice. *Sourcebook of Criminal Justice Statistics, 2000.* Washington, DC: Bureau of Justice Statistics, 2001.

———. *Prisoners in 1994.* Washington, DC: Bureau of Justice Statistics, August 1995.

———. *Violence between Intimates.* Washington, DC: Bureau of Justice Statistics, November 1994.

———. *Crime and Neighborhoods.* Washington, DC: Bureau of Justice Statistics, June 1994.

———. *Criminal Victimization in the United States, 1973–1992, Trends.* Washington, DC: Bureau of Justice Statistics, July 1994.

———. *Drugs and Crime Facts, 1994.* Washington, DC: Bureau of Justice Statistics, 1994.

———. *Drugs and Crime Facts, 1993.* Washington, DC: Bureau of Justice Statistics, 1993.

———. *Comparing Federal and State Prison Inmates, 1991.* Washington, DC: Bureau of Justice Statistics, 1992.

U.S. Government. "Drugs, Law Enforcement, and Foreign Policy." *Congressional Record* 135, no. 62 (May 16, 1989).

U.S. Riot Commission. *Report of the National Advisory Commission on Civil Disorders.* New York: Bantam, 1968.

U.S. Senate. Committee on the Judiciary. *Hearings before the Subcommittee on Antitrust and Monopoly, Part 4A,* "American Ground Transport." Washington, DC: U.S. Government Printing Office, 1974.

Useem, Michael. *Executive Defense: Shareholder Power and Corporate Reorganization.* Cambridge: Harvard University Press, 1993.

Vaughn, Dianne. "The *Challenger* Space Shuttle Disaster: Conventional Wisdom and a Revisionist Account." In *Corporate and Governmental Deviance: Prob-*

lems of Organizational Behavior in Contemporary Society, 7th ed., edited by M. David Ermann and Richard J. Lundmann, 306–33. New York: Oxford University Press, 2002.

Voorst, Bruce Van. "Toxic Dumps: The Lawyers' Money Pit." *Time*, September 13, 1993, pp. 63–64.

Wallace, Deborah. "Roots of Increased Health Care Inequality in New York." *Social Science and Medicine* 31 (1990): 1219–27.

Wallace, Roderick. "Urban Desertification, Public Health, and Public Order: 'Planned Shrinkage,' Violent Death, Substance Abuse, and AIDS in The Bronx." *Social Science and Medicine* 31 (1990): 801–13.

Weiner, Tim. "The Pentagon's Post–Cold War Black Budget Is Alive and Prospering." In *Censored: The News That Didn't Make the News—And Why,* edited by Carl Jensen, 52–53. Chapel Hill, NC: Shelburne Press, 1993.

Weinstein, Deena. *Bureaucratic Opposition: Challenging Abuses of the Workplace.* New York: Pergamon, 1979.

Weir, David, and Mark Schapiro. *Circle of Poison: Pesticides and People in a Hungry World.* San Francisco: Institute for Food and Development Policy, 1981.

Weissman, Robert. "The Money Trail, Corporate Investments in U.S. Elections Since 1990." *Multinational Monitor* 21, no. 10 (October 2000): 25–29.

Weitz, Rose. "Sex, Class, Race: Health and Illness in the United States." *Race, Sex, and Class* 2 (1994): 127–43.

Whitman, Steve. "The Crime of Black Imprisonment." *Z* (May/June 1992): 69–72.

Widon, Cathy Spatz. *The Cycle of Violence.* Washington, DC: U.S. Department of Justice, 1992.

Wilson, Edward O. *Sociobiology: The New Synthesis.* Cambridge: Harvard University Press, 1971.

Wilson, William J. "Work." *New York Times Magazine*, August 18, 1996, p. 26.

———, ed. "The Ghetto Underclass: Social Science Perspectives." *Annals of the American Academy of Political and Social Science* 501 (1989).

———. *The Truly Disadvantaged: The Inner City, the Underclass, and Public Policy.* Chicago: University of Chicago Press, 1987.

Wolf, Edward N. *Top Heavy: A Study of the Increasing Inequality of Wealth in America.* New York: Twentieth Century Fund, 1995.

World Bank. *World Development Report, 2003: Sustainable Development in a Dynamic World, Transforming Institutions, Growth, and Quality of Life.* New York: World Bank and Oxford University Press, 2003.

World Health Organization (WHO). *World Report on Violence and Health.* Geneva, Switz.: World Health Organization, 2002.

Yeoman, Barry. "Unhappy Meals." *Mother Jones* (January/February 2003): 41–45, 81.

Zawitz, Marianne W. *Guns Used in Crime.* U.S. Department of Justice, Bureau of Justice Statistics, 1995.

Zimring, Franklin E., and Gordon Hawkins. *Crime Is Not The Problem: Lethal Violence in America.* New York: Oxford University Press, 1997.

Zinn, Howard. *A People's History of The United States.* New York: HarperCollins, 1995.

Zweigenhaft, Richard L., and G. William Domhoff. *Diversity in the Power Elite.* New Haven, CT: Yale University Press, 1998.

VIDEOS

Hidden in Plain Sight. Ravens Call Productions. http://www.HIDDENINPLAINSIGHT .ORG. Running time, 71 minutes.

The Killing Screens: Media and the Culture of Violence. Media Education Foundation, 26 Center St. Northampton, MA 01060. http://www.mediaed.org. Running time, 37 minutes.

The New Patriots. SOA Watch, P.O. Box 4566, 202-243-3440. http://www.soa.org. Running time, 18 minutes.

Pockets of Hate. 1988. Films for the Humanities, Inc., P.O. Box 2053, 743 Alexander Rd., Princeton, NJ 08540. Running time, 26 minutes.

School of Assassins. Maryknoll World Productions, P.O. Box 308, Maryknoll, NY 10545-0308, 1-800-227-8523. Running time, 18 minutes.

Taken for a Ride. New Day Films, 22D Hollywood Avenue, Hohokus, NJ 07423. http://www.newday.com.

The Wrath of Grapes. United Farm Workers of America, P.O. Box 62, Keene, CA 93531. Running time, 15 minutes.

INDEX